Kintyre Places and Place-Names

Previous books by Angus Martin

History

The Ring-Net Fishermen
Kintyre: The Hidden Past
Kintyre Country Life
Fishing and Whaling
Sixteen Walks in South Kintyre
The North Herring Fishing
Herring Fishermen of Kintyre and Ayrshire
Fish and Fisherfolk
Memories of the Inans, Largybaan and Craigaig, 1980-85
An Historical and Genealogical Tour of Kilkerran Graveyard
Kintyre Birds
The Place-Names of the Parish of Campbeltown (with Duncan Colville)
The Place-Names of the Parish of Southend (with Duncan Colville)
Kilkerran Graveyard Revisited
Kintyre Families
Kintyre Instructions: The 5th Duke of Argyll's Instructions
     to his Kintyre Chamberlain, 1785-1805 (with Eric R. Cregeen)
By Hill and Shore in South Kintyre

Poetry

The Larch Plantation
The Song of the Quern
The Silent Hollow
Rosemary Clooney Crossing the Minch
Laggan Days: In Memory of George Campbell Hay
Haunted Landscapes
Paper Archipelagos
Always Boats and Men (with Mark I'Anson)
One Time in a Tale of Herring (with Will Maclean)

Kintyre Places and Place-Names

Angus Martin

The Grimsay Press

Published by:

The Grimsay Press
An imprint of Zeticula Ltd
The Roan
Kilkerran
KA19 8LS
Scotland
http://www.thegrimsaypress.co.uk

ISBN 978-1-84530-134-7

Front cover illustration. A peaty pool at the back of Ben Gullion to which the author gave the name 'Dragonfly Lochan', from golden-ringed dragonflies he watched there on 24/8/1997. The view is to the west, with Cnoc Moy the highest point in the distance. Photograph by the author, 4/9/2011.

Back cover illustration. The same lochan, but looking north-east towards the Arran mountains. Photograph by the author, 8/8/2012.

The Sanda map is a reproduction of a sketch which was made (probably by Duncan Colville) from a map in the office of C. & D. Mactaggart, solicitors, Campbeltown, and bound with the 'Schedules' of *The Place-Names of the Parish of Southend.*

This is the core of our condition, that we do not know why nor at what point we squandered our heritage; we only know, too late always, that it cannot be recovered or restored.

Gavin Maxwell

Landscape was the paper on which everything was written, and afterwards it gets torn and nobody looks at the paper.

S. Yizhar

If there is any substitute for love, it's memory.

Josef Brodsky

It was a dream; its people were images in a dream, never seen before or to be seen again.

Norman Macleod D.D.

Contents

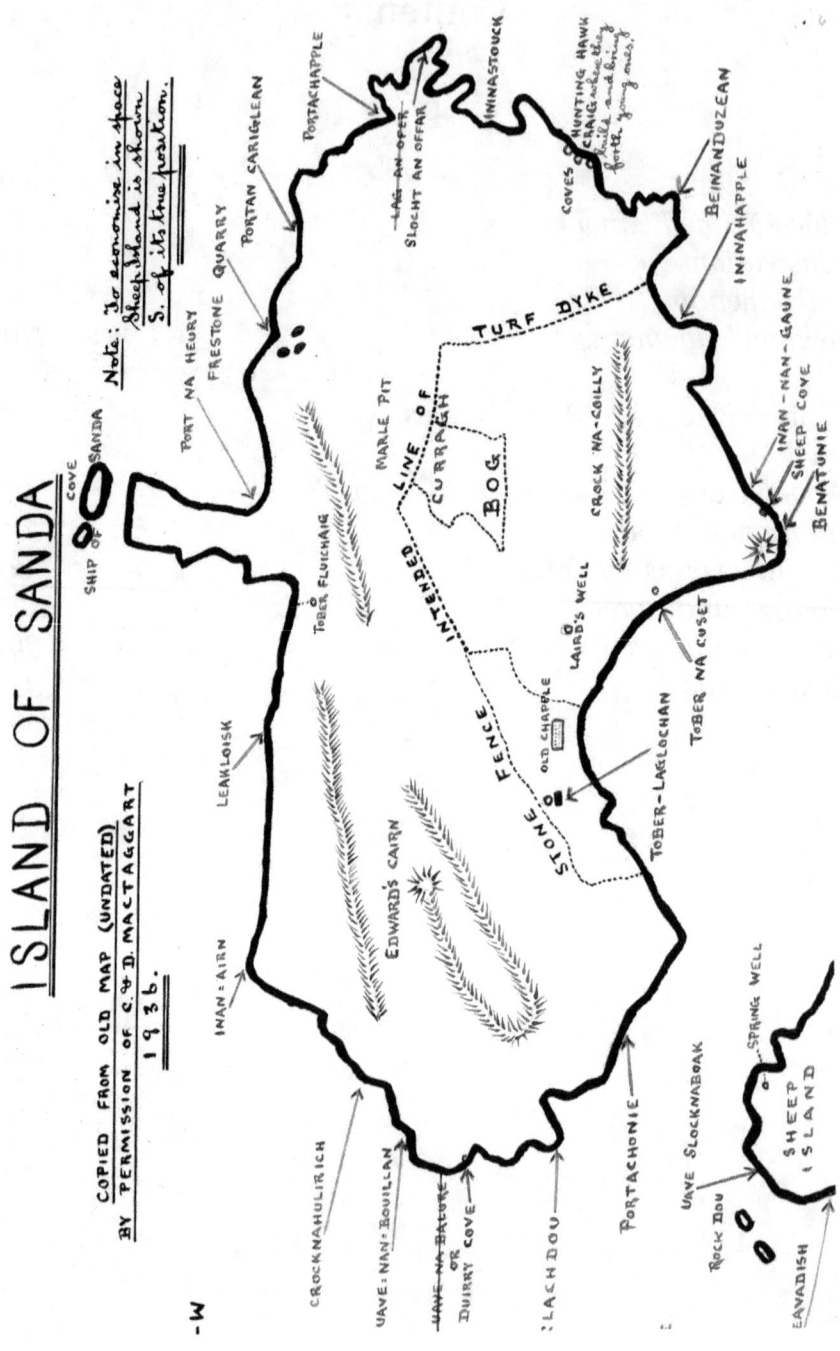

ISLAND OF SANDA

COPIED FROM OLD MAP (UNDATED)
BY PERMISSION OF C. & D. MACTAGGART
1936.

Note: To economize in space
Sheep Island is shown
S. of its true position.

SHIP OF SANDA
COVE

PORT NA HEURY
FRESTONE QUARRY

PORTACHAPPLE

PORTAN CARIGLEAN

TAG AN OFER
SLOCHT AN OFFAR

ININASTOUCK

COVES OF HUNTING HAWK
CRAIG where the
kittie and osprey
forth, young ones.

BEINANDUZEAN

ININAHAPPLE

TURF DYKE

MARLE PIT

LINE OF CURRAGH

BOG

INTENDED

CROCK NA-COILLY

INAN-NAN-GAUNE
SHEEP COVE
BENATUNIE

TOBER FLUICHAIG

LAIRD'S WELL

LEAKLOISK

FENCE

OLD CHAPPLE

TOBER-LAGLOCHAN

TOBER NA CYSET

STONE

INAN=AIRN

EDWARD'S CAIRN

CROCKNAHULIRICH

UAVE-NAN=BOUILLAN

UAVE-NA-BATURE
or
DURKY COVE

'LACHDOU

PORTACHONIE

UAVE SLOCKNABOAK

SPRING WELL

ROCK DOU

SHEEP ISLAND

EAVADISH

-W

Place-Name Elements

(Interpretations in some cases simplified or incomplete)

abhainn – river, stream
achadh – field
àirigh – shieling, summer
    pasturage
allt – stream
aodann – face, hill-face
aoireann – foreland, headland
àrd – high, lofty
àros – house
àth – kiln, ford
bàgh – bay
baile – township, farm-town, farm
bàn – white, fair, pale
bàrr – hilltop
bealach – pass, gap
beinn   hill
béist – beast, wild cat
beith – birch tree
binnein – hillock
blàr – field, battle
bodach – old man
bodha/bogha – sunken rock
bog – wet, marshy
bòrd – table
bràghad – upper
breac – speckled, spotted
buaile – cattle-fold
buidhe – yellow
bun – foot, bottom
caibeal – chapel
cailleach – old woman, witch, nun
caisteal – castle
calltuinn – the hazel
calman – dove, pigeon
camas/camus – bay
caora – a sheep
caorunn – the rowan
capull – mare
carragh – standing stone
carraig – rock
càrn – cairn, hill

cat – cat
ceann – head, end
cèardach – smithy
ceathramh – quarter (division of
    land)
cill – church
clach – stone, boulder
clachan – village with a church
cladh – graveyard
clèireach – clerk, beadle
cleit – sea-rock
cnoc, cnocan – hill, hillock
coille – a wood
coirce – corn, oats
coire – corrie
corr – hill
corran – promontory, sickle-shaped
    land-feature
craobh – tree
creag – rock, crag
creamh – wild garlic
crìoch – boundary
crois – cross
croit – croft
croman – the raptor red kite
cruach – stack-shaped hill
crùban – the edible or red crab
cùil – nook, corner
cuilionn – holly
cùl – back
currach – bog, marsh
dail – valley, field, water-meadow
damh – ox, stag
dàpheighinn – a two-penny land
darach – the oak
dearc – berry
dearg – red
dìg – ditch
dòid – croft
doire – oak-grove
doirlinn/doirling – tidal isthmus

donn – brown
drochaid – bridge
druim – ridge
dubh – black
dùn – fort or round-topped coastal hillock
each – horse
eas – waterfall
eilean – island
eileirg – deer-trap
eirbhe – fence, wall
eun – bird
fad/fada – long
faire – watching, of a look-out hill
famhair/fomhair – a giant
faochag – a winkle
feannag – a crow
feòirlin – farthing-land
feur – grass
fionn – white, fair, the legendary hero Fionn mac Cumhaill
fitheach – raven
fliuch – wet
fraoch – heather
fuar – cold
gamhain – stirk
gaoth – wind
gàradh – garden, wall
garbh – rough
gèadh – goose
geal – white, bright
glac – a hollow
glas – grey, green
gleann – valley
gob – beak or small promontory
gobha/gobhainn – blacksmith
gobhar/gabhar – goat
gort, goirtean – enclosure, little enclosure
grianan – a sunny spot
guala/gualann – a shoulder
innean – cove
innis – river-meadow, island
iolaire – eagle
lag, lagan – a hollow, little hollow

laogh – calf
làrach – a ruin or foundations of a ruin
leac – flat rock
leacann – hillside
lèan(a) – meadow
leannan-sìth – fairy lover
learg – a slope
leathan – broad
leth – half
leth-pheighinn – half-penny land
leum – a jump, leap
liath – grey, hoary
lìon – lint, flax, a net
loch – lake
lodan – little pool
loisgte – burnt
lòn – meadow or marsh
longphort – ship-port, fort
losaid – kneading-trough
losgann – toad, frog
luachair – rushes
lùb – bay
lurgann – ridge
machair – a plain, usually coastal and sandy-soiled
madadh – dog, wolf
magh – a plain
maol – bald hill
marbh – dead
meadhonach – middle
meall – a lump of a hill
mòine – peat, peat-bog
molach – rough, hairy, overgrown with vegetation
mór – big
muc – pig
muileann – a mill
nathair – a snake
odhar – dun-coloured
oitir – tidal rock-shelf
pairc – field
peighinn – a penny land
ploc – a lump
poll – pool, hole

port – harbour, inlet, bay
pubull – tent, booth
raineach – fern, bracken
reamhar – fat, plump
riabhach – brindled
roc – rock
ros – promontory
ruadh – red
rubha – promontory, point of land
ruighe – a slope, sloping field
sabhal – barn
sagart – priest
saidhean – saithe
samh – common sorrel
sean – old
seasgan – marsh
seileach – the willow
sgadan – herring
sgarbh – cormorant or shag
sgeir – rock, reef
sgrìodan – landslip or scree
sionnach – fox
sìthich – 'fairy'
slabhraidh – pot-chain
sliabh – moor-slope
sloc – pit, gully
socach – a snout of land
srath – valley, often broad-
    bottomed and wet
sròn – the nose, a point of land
sruth – stream
stac – a columnar isolated rock
suidhe – seat, resting-place
tarsuinn – transverse, across
teanga – tongue
teine – fire
tigh – house
tìr – land
tobar – a well
tom – hummock or knoll
tòn – the backside
torc – wild boar
tòrr – a heap of a hill
tràigh – strand, shore
uachdar – top or summit

uaigh – a grave
uamh(a) – cave
uchd – the breast, side of a hill
uinnseann – the ash tree
ulaidh – buried treasure
ùruisg – a solitary supernatural
    creature of lonely places

Illustrations

Introduction

I can put a year to the awakening of my interest in place-names: 1973. I was working that summer on a Carradale ring-netter, the *Maid of Honour*, and was travelling by bus to Carradale one Monday with two other Campbeltown fishermen, John Short and John Lang, who were also crewing Carradale boats. As the bus descended Peninver brae, one of them pointed to a rocky inlet and asked me if I knew its name. I didn't and was duly given it, 'The Geelut' (a local form of English 'gullet'). A year later, when I began researching my first book, *The Ring-Net Fishermen*, the place-names of the Kintyre fishermen would flood into my awareness.

I quickly realised that there was more to place-names than maps and road signs revealed. Little places as well as big had names, and some of them had more than one name. Some names were Gaelic and had clearly been around for many generations; others – particularly on the coast around Campbeltown – were Scots, and, from certain obsolete elements they contained, had also been around for generations; still others – such as 'The Sewage Pipe' and 'The Telephone Box' – were English and clearly of no great age.

Fishermen had their own names for the smallest of features, such as rocks and trees, as well as for bays and headlands. These place-names, for the most part, were exclusive to the fishing community. Many of them will be encountered in this work and the rest will be found in my books on fishing history, particularly *The Ring-Net Fishermen*. When I began tape-recording elderly farmers and shepherds in Kintyre in 1977, I found that they too were repositories of place-names which had no existence outwith their own communities.

'Places' in the title of this book precedes 'Place-Names', and the order is deliberate. I am not a linguist and was well aware of the dangers of tackling the frequently difficult subject of place-names. By and large, I have tried to confine this study within the bounds of existing scholarship, but I have also sought advice.

Human attachments to place need not be examined at length here. Most people have favourite places. I have no love of cities and avoid them if I can, but I realise that city-dwellers too have favourite places. These might even be pubs or night clubs, but they are just as valid as my seashore bay or hilltop crag. Nothing in my life, family and friends aside, means more to me than the places in Kintyre which I have grown to love. In these places, whether an hour away on Ben

Gullion or many hours away in remoter parts, I can reconnect with my inner self and with the natural world around me. In these places, too, I can be reunited with my children and my friends of old, living or dead, human or otherwise, by no more sophisticated means than the power of memory.

Some of these people, or events connected with them, are commemorated in place-names which I, or they, have coined. None of these names will enjoy wide circulation and none will endure, but I mention them to demonstrate that the naming of places is not a process which is fixed on maps at its end-point. Place-names are still needed, and if a particular place has no name it can be given one by walkers or climbers who visit it frequently and have to refer to it. Ben Gullion alone has scores of place-names known only to my walking companion George McSporran and me, and through these names our shared past endures. With some minor place-names – streams, knolls and rocks – recorded by the Ordnance Survey and other collectors in the 19th and early 20th century, familiarity and use may have been similarly restricted, to just a few families in farms or smallholdings.

Such minor place-names are understandably more likely to fall out of use and into oblivion. The poet Alasdair Maclean gave eloquent expression to that loss. As a boy in the township of Sanna, Ardnamurchan, he roamed all over the neighbourhood, sometimes accompanied by his grandfather, who had a name for 'every least hillock, every creek and gully'. Maclean felt that such knowledge set his grandfather apart, invested him with a 'form of spiritual privilege', so that he 'lived in a different landscape from me, seeing it in a different way and – I came to feel – being seen differently by it'. Maclean lived to see the disappearance of scores of these names, and with them 'a host of associations and meanings and attitudes'.[1]

To the 'Places' and 'Place-Names' of the title, I might also have added 'People', because part of my object in writing this book was to repopulate the landscape and so, in some small degree, revive it. I have, therefore, mentioned individuals and families in connection with many of the places examined in the work. These might be local writers or visitors or the families who occupied the land, and the idea was to enable readers to visit at least some of the places and to understand a little of their history and see them as others saw them.

The first dedicated place-names collector in Kintyre was the Rev D. J. Macdonald, who was active in the 1890s and about whom I shall have more to say; but folklore-collectors had already been at work.

The first was the Rev Donald Kelly (1791-1843), son of a Campbeltown merchant, and the minister of Southend and afterwards of the Lowland Church, Campbeltown. Parts of his manuscript collection were published by his son, Neil Munro Kelly (1823-1906), who later took his mother's surname Robertson, but the collection itself seems to have been lost. Many of the Kelly tales contain local place-names which, however, tend to be idiosyncratically spelled and interpreted.

Another significant source of folklore and place-names is the *History of Kintyre*, first published in 1857. It was written by Peter MacIntosh, who was born at Ardnacross and died in Campbeltown in 1876 in his ninetieth year. The work is coloured by MacIntosh's religious zeal, but contains many interesting tales and a substantial crop of place-names.

Gaelic scholarship was elevated to proper respectability and given greater impetus in 1882 with the foundation of the first Chair in Celtic Studies at the University of Edinburgh. Its first occupant was Professor Donald MacKinnon (1839-1914), a native of Colonsay, whose series of 17 articles on 'Place Names and Personal Names in Argyll', published in *The Scotsman* in 1887-8, demonstrated 'the sound, sane scholarship and literary expositive power that ever since has marked his work'.[2]

The Chair itself was founded and endowed by John Stuart Blackie (1809-95), 'a fervent nationalist and promoter of Gaelic culture'.[3] Professor Blackie came to Campbeltown in 1876 to lecture the Parish Church Young Men's Literary Association on 'The Language and Literature of the Highlands of Scotland', and was welcomed as a celebrity. Charles Mactaggart, chairman, remarked that although this was Professor Blackie's first visit to Campbeltown, 'he was no stranger to them, as his enthusiastic exertions to establish a Celtic Chair in the University of Edinburgh had given him a name and fame which reached far beyond the Highlands of Scotland'.

Blackie delivered a lively, if rather eccentric, lecture. He believed that anyone could learn Gaelic and that 'all those who did not study their language, being born in the atmosphere, and having obvious opportunities, were great fools or cowards, or both'. He was sure that from Kintyre place-names alone, two or three hundred Gaelic words could be learned. An 'historical sketch of the Gaelic language' followed, which opened with an explanation that Gaelic belonged to 'the western branch of the Aryan family', which did not include the languages of Hungary or Lapland, which were 'out of the world places'; nor did the European family of languages include that of the

Turks, 'and the sooner they were out of the world the better'. He concluded with the exhortation: 'We ought to be proud that we are Scotchmen – stand up for the pladdie, stand up for a mac before your name. We would never have made the discoveries in Africa had it not been for a Livingstone, and he was a Scotchman.'[4] To what extent the eminent Professor's rhetoric encouraged an awakening of Gaelic consciousness in Kintyre is impossible to evaluate, but it no doubt played a part.

Blackie had his local detractors, one of whom, Commander Duncan Stewart R.N., laid into him six years later in a lecture on 'The Agriculture of Kintyre' delivered to the same association Blackie had addressed.

> There were people going about the country, such as Professor Blackie, talking nonsense. He was a man who spoke of the management of land who could not manage his Greek class. He laid down the law, and told the landlords exactly what they should do. Unhappily Professor Blackie had discovered that 'glen' and 'ben' rhymed to 'men', so he wrote something like the following: –
> 'Men of the glen, and the birk and the ben,
>   Gather together!
> And fight for your bonny brown heather.'
> He might have added:
> 'Perish like rats in a pen.'
> He talked of deep glens having cottages; but the sun never shone in these glens, and it was almost impossible to grow oats in them ... In these old days, which he would have them return to, they gathered the corn before it was ripe, because they were starving, just like the other animals. In spring they had to bleed their cattle to drink the blood, and it would be the same tomorrow if they had a great population in the glens and on the bens. There was so much nonsense talked that it made him quite angry to think of it.

Stewart, a local landowner, was a grandson of Captain Duncan Stewart of Glenbuckie, the Argyll Estate factor in Kintyre from 1790 to 1829, whose father, John Glas Stewart of Benmore, had been killed at Culloden in 1746, fighting on the Jacobite side,[5] which renders the following remarks of Stewart's all the more perverse: 'After speaking generally of the supremacy of race, the lecturer said he looked upon the Irishman as the Maori of Great Britain. (Laughter and applause.) Just as the Highlander of Kintyre had "gone west" before the Lowlander, the Irishman would require to go also before a superior race. (Applause.)'[6]

The founding of local branches of An Comunn Gàidhealach, the national society for the promotion of the Gaelic language and culture, undoubtedly conferred on Gaelic a greater degree of social respectability. By the end of 1913, Largieside, Carradale, Clachan and Skipness had branches, all headed by the local minister. In March of that year, the Taobh na Leargaidh branch held a ceilidh in Killean schoolhouse. Rev D. J. Macdonald was in the chair and the main item on the programme was an *òraid*, or speech, by the Rev. D. McFarlane, who explained the objects of An Comunn 'in a most inspiring and enthusiastic manner'.[7]

An Comunn Gàidhealach Ceannloch, however, was almost stillborn. At the inaugural meeting in Campbeltown in 1921, only 22 persons turned up. Many of them 'doubted the wisdom of proceeding further', but were persuaded by the society's president, Rev P. W. Mackay, and organising secretary, Neil Shaw. By the annual general meeting of the following year, the branch had almost 200 members. Branch activities included concerts, lectures and Gaelic classes, and, in June 1922, a picnic at Tangy House, courtesy of Miss Hall, an 'enthusiastic member of the branch'. There were speeches by Latimer MacInnes and Sheriff J. Macmaster Campbell, field sports, dancing, piping and fiddling, a 'generous repast' served by the ladies of the executive committee, and, at the end of the day, tea served on the lawn while a sunset of 'rare beauty and charm' flared out, after which the party 'formed into fours and, headed by the pipers, marched down the glen to the main road, where the buses awaited them for the return journey'.[8]

I have examined the decline of Gaelic in *Kintyre: The Hidden Past* (pp. 26-47), and will here remark only that, as a spoken language, Gaelic remained robust in the northern half of the peninsula into the 20th century. The collapse, when it came, was rapid and complete, and the last remaining native speakers died out in the 1980s. The following vignette came to my notice recently, and I record it without comment. During the trial in Campbeltown of a man accused of assault at Achnacarnan, Kilcalmonell Parish, in 1880, one of the witnesses, Margaret Blair, wife of James Smith, 'desired to give her evidence in Gaelic, but the court considered she could speak English well enough and she gave it in the latter language'. At one stage in the proceedings, however, 'The witness here began amid laughter to volubly describe in Gaelic the scene, but was stopped'.[9]

John Macmaster Campbell's attitude to Gaelic was entirely different. He was sheriff at Campbeltown from 1910 until his death in 1939, and would intervene in court cases to help out Gaelic speakers who were struggling to understand legal issues. Macmaster Campbell, who was born in Inverness, was one of the remarkable group of local historians which came to prominence after the Kintyre Antiquarian Society was formed in 1921. He was a founder-member of the K.A S. and also of An Comunn Gàidhealach, established in Oban in 1891. Angus Robertson, in 1923, in what was clearly intended as a compliment, asserted that: 'Everyone knows that he is the founder of An Comunn Gàidhealach and that his word is law at all its Council meetings.' The same writer described Macmaster Campbell as 'one of the first lawyers to take an interest in the Highland question, social and linguistic', and attributed to Sheriff David Brand, chairman of the first Crofters Commission, the remark that Macmaster Campbell 'knew more about land legislation than any other living person'.[10]

My sources for this book have been wide-ranging. The foundation has been the work done by the Kintyre Antiquarian Society, which, in the year of its inception, set up a committee to collect and interpret Kintyre place-names, at the suggestion of its first president, J. R. Moreton Macdonald of Largie, who died later that year. Three booklets were subsequently published – on the parishes of Southend (1938), Campbeltown (1943) and Gigha and Cara (1945) – but work on the remaining three parishes, Killean and Kilchenzie, Kilcalmonell, and Saddell and Skipness, unaccountably stalled. I have, however, taken on the task myself, using as a foundation such notebooks and papers as survived in the collection of Duncan Colville, and these booklets should follow this book.

Since Duncan Colville's time, however, many other sources of information on local place-names have become available, and I have used these to great advantage, particularly the national censuses, 1841-1901, which are available on microfilm in Campbeltown Public Library, along with the Old Parish Registers and local newspapers dating to the mid-19th century, which also proved most useful. The censuses have been of particular value, since they preserve place-names in the forms which the enumerators – all local men – heard them spoken in their own localities, and also contain place-names which are otherwise unknown. Finally, gravestone inscriptions have been sources of place-name spellings as well as of people.

For the understanding of place-names and their etymology, I have relied heavily on a few outstanding scholars of the past, most notably Professor Donald MacKinnon, Professor William J. Watson, Dr Alexander Macbain and Edward Dwelly, whose accomplishments need not be recounted in a local work such as this.

Dr H. Cameron Gillies is not in the above company, but although his *The Place-Names of Argyll* has been discredited, I have found in it, despite his lazy methodology, elements to admire. Linguistic considerations aside, one must know the ground, and Dr Gillies, as will be seen, was not familiar with Kintyre, and, rather than visit places and consult local people on topography and pronunciation, was content to rely on maps and correspondence. Indifference to proper methods of investigation was his undoing. Gillies was a native of Sunart, Argyll, and graduated M.B., M.Ch. from the University of Glasgow in 1882. He was the author of several other books on Gaelic subjects, including *The Gaelic Names of Disease and Diseased States* (1899).

I have benefited greatly from Nils M. Holmer's *The Dialect of Kintyre*, particularly the folk tales it contains. The book, a linguistic study, was published in 1962, but the work had been done in the late 1930s when Holmer, a Swede, was visiting Kintyre and recording native Gaelic speakers for the Norwegian Linguistic Survey. He based himself for a month in Campbeltown towards the end of 1937 and in the following year made Tayinloan his base. One old woman in the Largieside advised him: 'Don't bother with the Gaelic – there's no money in it!'[11]

In addition to these, and to the individuals listed in the Acknowledgements, the following local sources have to be recognised, and I have compiled a biographical paragraph on each. Among these, D. J. Macdonald was an outstanding source of place-names and the lore attached to them, yet he covered only his own parish, Killean and Kilchenzie. Had there been a collector of Macdonald's calibre in each of the other four Kintyre parishes at the end of the 19th century, the harvest of Kintyre place-names would have been a far heavier one. I have drawn extensively on his paper 'West Kintyre Field Names', which is a testimony to his fascination with minor names, and have reproduced, in its entirety, as an Appendix, his introduction to that paper. Field-names, as he himself eloquently argued, tended to be overlooked in the collection and study of place-names, yet they have much to tell us about the land and the people who worked the land. At a time when many cultural projects depend on public funding for their very existence, it is perhaps worth pointing out that none of the following individuals received so much as a penny for their efforts.

John Cameron was the principal Gaelic adviser on the Kintyre Antiquarian Society's place-names committee, a service which he performed with admirable scholarship and commonsense. He was a native Gaelic speaker, born in Tiree in 1903. After primary schooling on the island, he was educated at Oban High School and Glasgow University. He gained his M.A., which included 'a double credit in Celtic', before the age of 21.[12] His first teaching post was at Bowmore, Islay, followed by headship of Ardbeg. He married Mary Fraser in 1932, and in 1934 was appointed head of Southend Primary School, where he remained until his untimely death on 18/2/1951 at the age of 47. He was buried in the new section of Kilcolmkill. He wrote Gaelic poetry, short stories and critical essays, none of it published and most of it lost at the time of his death.[13] Mary Fraser Cameron died in 1984 at the age of 78.

Duncan Colville was convenor of the Kintyre Antiquarian Society's place-names committee and unquestionably its driving force, but he worked quietly, methodically and anonymously in the background, leaving a vast resource, from meticulously compiled bound volumes to bundles and packages containing letters, extracts from diverse publications and scraps of paper bearing his scribbled notes. Without his commitment and industry, this book would not have been contemplated and I owe him a great debt. He was born into a prosperous Campbeltown whisky-distilling family in 1883 and lived until 1981. An authority on a diverse range of other local subjects – archaeology, history and natural history among them – he was a founder-member of the Kintyre Antiquarian Society, its first Secretary (1921-25), its President (1947-66) and, finally, its Honorary President.[14]

'**Mrs Higginson**' was a daughter of John Campbell, shepherd in Skipness, and married a shoemaker named Higginson. The story of her arrival in Skipness is a curious one. Her father, in Arran to help a farmer with lambing, had sexual relations with an islander, who left the resulting baby – the future Mrs Higginson – on Campbell's doorstep.[15] Her remarkable collection of folk tales and anecdotes is now in the School of Scottish Studies archive, but so little is known about her that she seems almost as mythical as some of the characters in her tales. I have to thank Madeleine Slater for the following notes, which help towards an understanding. Census

1881 has an unmarried shepherd, John Campbell, aged 50, living with his daughter Isabella, aged 27, in Skipness Village, but there is no sign of her in C1891. Isabella, if that's our Mrs Higginson, was supposed to have married the tailor and lived for years in Greenock, but Madeleine has been unable to find them there. John Campbell died in 1908, aged 78; the informant wasn't Mrs Higginson, but his nephew, Malcolm Campbell.[16]

John McCallum was one of Duncan Colville's outstanding informants, particularly for unmapped place-names around Cnoc Moy. An ideal informant, of a class which has since died out in Kintyre, he was brought up within a Gaelic-speaking family and spent his entire life shepherding. His parents, Donald and Christina, were both born in Killean Parish, shared the surname McCallum and were second cousins. They married in 1843 and had nine children, of whom John was the second youngest. His wife, Jessie Stewart McDougall, whom he married in 1888, was also from Killean. In 1933, John was awarded a gold medal from the Highland and Agricultural Society for his long service in the employ of Argyll Estate. He walked the hills of South Kintyre for 56 years in all, ending his service at Dalbuie.[17]

Donald John Macdonald became minister of Killean in 1880 and died in 1930. He was born at Nunton, Benbecula, of Skye extraction, and Gaelic was his first language. He was also literate in the language, which remained in everyday use in the Largieside throughout his time there. Indeed, he was active in preserving Gaelic through his bi-lingual services and his classes in the language. His wife Margaret, who died in 1936, was a daughter of Robert Colvill of Muasdale, a Campbeltown whisky-distiller. During his 50 years in the Largieside, Macdonald amassed a store of local tradition. The best of it was published in two papers which he contributed to the *Transactions of the Gaelic Society of Inverness* (specified in Sources), and in his *Annals of Killean* and *Antiquities of Killean and Kilkenzie*, published posthumously as a single booklet by the Kintyre Antiquarian Society. I have also drawn on a field notebook of his, dateable to 1897 and copied for me by Mr Murdo MacDonald. Place-names, and especially – and unusually, for the time – field-names, were his special interest. In March 1922, his paper, 'The Place Names of the Landward Parish of Campbeltown', was read to a meeting of the Kintyre Antiquarian Society. A copy, annotated by J. Macmaster Campbell, is preserved in Duncan Colville's papers. In Macdonald's obituary, it was remarked of him that, 'He loved the

Largieside, knew the name of every field and hill in the district [and] every legend and historical association connected with them'. He left his library, containing some 500 books, to Campbeltown Public Library, 'subject to one condition – that they be kept together as one collection',[18] a condition which has certainly lapsed.

Ian MacDonald remains the foremost authority on the genealogy and social history of North Kintyre, and for most of his life has given freely of his knowledge to researchers from all over the world. I am indebted to him for his assistance with the places and place-names of Killean and Kilchenzie and Kilcalmonell parishes. He was born in 1919 on the Largieside farm of Beachmenach, a son of Malcolm MacDonald, one of Nils M. Holmer's informants for *The Gaelic of Kintyre*. He worked on the farm until 'called up' on 6/9/1939. He joined the army and attained the rank of Captain in 1945, after a 'special mission overseas'. He married in 1952 and he and his wife, Ina Park, lived at Portachoillan, Clachan. In 1955, he joined Unilever and in 1971 was seconded to Kintyre Farmers as a sales representative. He retired in 1982 and now lives in Lochgilphead.[19]

Archie McEachran was the main living source of Southend place-names. Most of these were from oral tradition, but he was also an inveterate forager in books and manuscripts. He was the fourth generation of McEachrans in Kilblaan. Hugh, the first, who died in 1855, was followed by his son, Angus,[20] who was the oldest tenant of the Duke of Argyll's in Southend when he died in 1907, and an 'excellent Gaelic scholar'.[21] Archie's uncle, Hugh McEachran, with whom he lived, was a fund of local lore, and much of Archie's knowledge came from him. He died in 1945 at the age of 82. Archie himself was found dead in bed on 9/12/1956. When Duncan Colville last saw him, he was 'still feeling some of the effects of the attack his bull made on him, but he was carrying on with his work as usual'. 'His loss,' Duncan added, in a letter to Norman Conley, 'will be greatly felt in Southend for nobody knew more about the district and its people than he did, and he would go to no end of trouble to get information for anyone seeking it ...'[22] In his reply, Conley confessed: 'I had no idea that he would die so soon when I said "Goodbye" at the end of my visit in September ... To me he was the soul and spirit of Southend, the beautiful landscape of fields, hills, burns, leafy trees and wildflowers personified ... He always remembered to put the care of his animals and the daily jobs of his farm first and never let his enthusiasm for his correspondence and local researches get the better of his love for his home ... He lived apart from the vanities and follies of the modern world but he was not old-fashioned, rather he was more sensible and more at peace with the world.'[23] Duncan Colville attended his funeral. There was a gale and heavy rain that day, 'nevertheless there was a large turnout of farmers, with their cars stretching a long distance on the road, as Archie was so well known and liked by everyone down there'.[24] His manuscripts and notebooks are preserved in the Kintyre Antiquarian and Natural History Society's archive, at present lodged in Argyll and Bute Council Archive, Lochgilphead.

Latimer MacInnes was a Gaelic learner and a founder-member of the Campbeltown branch of An Comunn Gàidhealach in 1921,[25] the same year the Kintyre Antiquarian Society came into existence. He was prominent in that organisation, too, and a member of its place-names committee, with a particular interest in Carradale and the Largieside. MacInnes, like Duncan Colville, was a man of many parts. He gained local expertise in botany, ornithology and dialect – his unsurpassed *Dialect of South Kintyre* was published in 1934 – and was also a writer of merit, best known for his lovely song, 'Nostalgia'. Though born in England, the son of a Dalintober seaman, Duncan MacInnes, he was brought up in Kintyre.[26]

'**Mr McQuilkan**' is the sole identification of one of Latimer MacInnes's informants in Carradale. It is a pity MacInnes didn't take the trouble to record his forename, because the old man drew a sketch map of Carradale Estate which is covered in interesting names, some of them recorded by the Ordnance Survey and others not. I can only assume that he was a son – presumably either Angus, aged 13, or Robert, aged nine, who appear in C1871 – of Duncan McQuilkan, a native of Saddell Parish, who was tenant in 'Duchrau' (Deucheran) until 1888.[27]

Charles Reppke was born in Lossiemouth in 1888 and died at 9 Glebe Street, Campbeltown, in 1957. He learned Gaelic, was an active member of the Campbeltown branch of An Comunn Gàidhealach and was heavily involved in the organisation of the Kintyre Mòd. He married Catherine McMillan and settled in Kintyre as a fish-curer and kipperer. In 1921, he established a business in Carradale, specialising in mail order. His 'Gannet' kippers were despatched to hotels and clubs all over Britain, particularly London.[28] In 1942 and '43, he was living at Airds, Carradale, and sending Latimer MacInnes lists of place-names which he had collected in the Carradale district. These names are of real interest, but unfortunately most of them are impossible to transfer to a map. Reppke was a prolific composer of

poems and songs, the best known of which is 'Carradale'.[29] Willie
Mitchell paid tribute to him in the following verse: 'And one Charlie
Reppke we cannot forget,/ The whole Irish sweep wouldn't pay him
our debt,/ A Mod organiser, a grand Fear-an-tighe,/ And a far better
poet than Pursell or I.'[30]

'**Siol Chuinn**' was the author of the colourful and evocative article
'Beyond Cnoc Moy: A Few Days' Wandering on the Moil Hills', which
was published in 1921 in the *Campbeltown Courier* and from which
I have drawn extensively for this book. He was brought up in the
Laggan, and remarks that, as a boy, he had often wondered what lay
beyond the hills to the south, 'over whose summits rolled the ever-
changing cloud'. In the summer of 1921, in middle-age, he at last
explored that 'far-off fairyland'. I cannot even guess at his identity,
but his pen-name, which is Gaelic for 'Seed of Conn', is associated
with Clan Donald. Whoever he was, he could write.

I should explain how the material in this book has been selected.
First, the islands of Gigha and Cara have not been included, except
for a few place-names mentioned comparatively. I have taken certain
place-name elements and worked around them. Most of these
generics are predictable – *allt, àirigh, baile, beinn, gleann, loch,
rubha*, and so on – but others are more obscure. All are Gaelic, since
the great majority of Kintyre place-names are in that language, but
Norse, Scots and English place-names are interspersed throughout.
Since I am no linguist, my approach to difficult place-names has
been to present the evidence for others more competent to interpret.
My approach, I should stress, is not always comprehensive. In many
cases, examples are selective, and some place-name elements are
excluded, but these may be found in the place-names booklets for
the Kintyre parishes, published, or to be published, by the Kintyre
Antiquarian and Natural History Society. Where possible, I have
given – usually in square brackets – the location of the name in six-
figure Ordnance Survey grid-references, all NR. A word of caution
is necessary in relation to settlement-names. Grid-references for
modern steadings do not necessarily represent the sites of earlier
steadings. Additionally, many farms were subdivided, and the one
reference by which I represent a present-day farmhouse might mark
the site of only one among several habitations with the name, or
might, indeed, have had no settlement there prior to the 19th century.
Concerning accents on vowels, I resolved, after much indecision, to
stick with past convention, despite the recent abolition of the acute.

In a densely factual work of this kind, there are bound to be errors, despite my best efforts to eradicate them. If you find any, let me know and I shall correct them in any future edition which might appear. I give the final word on the matter to Dr Samuel Johnson, who, when a lady charged him with having included a wrong definition in his Dictionary, excused himself with the answer: 'Ignorance, madam, pure ignorance.'

Angus Martin,
13 Saddell Street,
Campbeltown,
Argyll
PA28 6DN.
30/10/2012.

Acknowledgements

I am grateful to many friends and acquaintances for assistance with this book and I shall try to mention them all. To: my wife Judy for scanning and putting in order the illustrations, for help with computer matters, company on hikes, and general advice; Ian A. Fraser, School of Scottish Studies, University of Edinburgh, for advice over the past 30 years and for having read the penultimate draft and given me the benefit of his onomastic expertise; Gilbert Márkus, Department of Celtic and Gaelic, University of Glasgow, for his scrutiny of the penultimate draft, which added much to my understanding and spared me a few blushes; Eleanor MacDougall, Fionnphort, Mull, for assistance with Gaelic spellings; Moira Burgess, Glasgow, for her valuable contributions and critical scrutiny of the penultimate draft; Agnes Stewart, Campbeltown, for her advice on matters of history, botany and topography; Murdo MacDonald, Balliemore, for his valued contributions over the years; Duncan McLean, Winslow, for having proof-read the penultimate draft and for suggestions as well as corrections; the staff of Campbeltown Public Library for their unfailing assistance with research; likewise the staff of the RCAHMS, Edinburgh; Donald McKerral, Campbeltown, for his photographs and tunes on melodeon; George McSporran, Campbeltown, for his companionship, photographs and other contributions; Lachie Paterson, Carradale; Bob Smith, Linlithgow; Jimmy MacDonald, Campbeltown; Archie K. Smith, Perth; Donald and Jean C. MacLeod, Stornoway; Iain Henderson, Machrihanish; Denis Rixson, Glasgow; Norman Newton, Culloden; Ian MacDonald, Lochgilphead; Iain McAlister, Campbeltown; Anne P. Landin, Siler City, U.S.A.; Elizabeth Marrison, Campbeltown; and to all the dead fishermen, farmers and shepherds, whose names will be found in the text, for sharing their knowledge during the past 40 years.

Kintyre Places and Place-Names

ABHAINN is generally defined as 'river', but none of the Kintyre instances matches that definition except for **Abhainn Breacàirigh** [656 108], which has lately replaced 'Breackerie Water' on Ordnance Survey maps. **Dubh Abhainn** was 'black' and ran on the farm of West Darlochan, but is so insignificant that its course is unknown and it may not now even exist.[31] **An Abhainn** [791 338], 'The River', was Graham McKinlay's name for the Ordnance Survey's 'Whitestone Burn'.[32] In Killean and Kilchenzie Parish, **Abhainn Beag** [701 445], 'Little River', and **Abhainn a' Chnocain** [724 367], 'River of the Hillock'. In Kilcalmonell Parish, two streams named after farms, **Abhainn Achachoish** [857 663] and **Abhainn Bardaravine** [850 649], and in Saddell and Skipness Parish **Abhainn Laoigh** for which see under LAOGH. For **Bun na h-Abhainn** see under BUN.

ACHADH, with its 'primary reference to fields rather than buildings', is considered to post-date BAILE,[33] 'township' or 'farmstead'. Surviving *achadh* names are attached to habitations, mostly farms or former farms or crofts, and the fields from which the place-names sprang centuries ago are forgotten. The map devoted to the distribution of place-names containing *achadh* in W. F. H. Nicolaisen's *Scottish Place-Names* (p. 140) records about 25 in Kintyre. That figure is no doubt based on the evidence of a small-scale map, but the true figure is double that, including farms and crofts which, through abandonment, disappeared into obscurity.

John MacQueen had this (and more) to say on *achadh*: 'The word originally referred, not to fields in the modern sense, for the most part situated at some distance from the farm buildings, but to the central area of the actual fermtoun, the cultivated parts of which were arranged in "rigs", assigned by lot to individual tenants, in the middle of which stood the houses and other buildings of the little community. The settlement, in other words, was an essential constituent of the *achadh* ...'[34] The antiquity of Kintyre *achadh* names is a matter of conjecture, but theoretically some might rank among the earliest Gaelic settlement-names. Some, demonstrably, were formed in medieval times, and appear at the end of that period, when records began to multiply. These examples are from Saddell and Skipness Parish: **Auchanandunan** [c. 897 576], in 1511 'Auchydownwall'; **Auchenbreck** [783 440], in 1500 'Auchinbrek'; **Auchenrioch** [787 424], in 1500 'Auchinreauch'; **Auchnasavil** [790 394], in 1500 'Auchinsaull'.

But there were many, many *achadh* names which remained fixed to the fields they described. The number will never be known because these names, with few exceptions, have been forgotten, but it would probably have reached triple figures in the 19th century. Duncan Colville in Campbeltown Parish and Archie McEachran in Southend collected *achadh* and other field-names, which are scattered through the parish place-names booklets, but I shall turn to D. J. Macdonald, with his love of fields and their names, for examples. He collected 17 *achadh* names in Killean and Kilchenzie Parish, and here they are, exactly as he presented them in his paper 'West Kintyre Field Names', delivered in 1908 (for Ardach see also under ÀRD):

Ardach: 'High Field' (Largie);
Acha' leth-ròid: 'Half-road field (Glenacardoch);
Ach' a phuill: 'Mud or pool field' (Kilmaluag);
Ach' nan tighean: 'Housefield' (Barr-uchdarach);
Ach' nan aorgnuinn: [no interpretation] (Glenacardoch);
Ach' na cloich: 'Stone field' (N. Muasdale and Skerrinish);
Ach' ruadh: 'Red field' (Barrmains);
Ach' nan cladhannan: 'Burial place field' (Kilmory);
Achadacheallair: 'Does this mean the cellarer's field?' (Achadaduie);
Ach' na saorach: 'The wright's field, we take it' (Beacharra);
Ach a bheumhais: 'Pronounced so. We understand it to mean Ach' a Sheumais' (Crubesdale);
Ach' fada: 'Long field' (Tangy);
Acha' beithe: 'Birch field' (Kilmory);
Acha' na curradh: 'Heron field' (Skerrinish);
Ach' a fhraoich: 'Heather field' (Rosshill);
Achadh cruaidh: 'Hard field' (Tangy);
Achadachonachar: [no interpretation] (Achadaduie).[35]

These, then, were all minor names, their ages unknown and most of them since deceased, though I once heard an acquaintance refer to the 'Ach' na cloich' on North Muasdale: he was brought up on the farm and remembered the name of the field, but not where it lay. In the case of the little farm of **Achaglen** [724 117] in Southend, its genesis is on record. Described as 'new' in 1807, when a lease was drawn up, it was formed out of part of the 'Common Muir cut off the farms of Kildavies', and its boundaries 'marked on the ground by Pitts'. The name is clear in meaning, even as anglicised, *Achadh a' ghlinne*, 'Field of the glen', and may have been adopted from a nearby field. The farm was leased in two parts, one going to Malcolm MacTaggart and the other to Malcolm Dryan (O'Drain), 'workman in Machririoch', at an annual combined rent of £20 Sterling and 10s for each goat kept. When the lease of 'Achagleen' came up for renewal in 1826, both divisions went to Malcolm MacTaggart's son, Edward, at a rent of £34. Edward had assured the Argyll Estate factor that he had three sons and two daughters who were all able and willing to work the farm.[36] The steading is now a ruin.

Auchalochy, like Achaglen, has for its specific a major topographical feature. There were actually two farms of that name in South Kintyre, both in ruins now. The one [728 224] north of Knock Scalbert gave its name to Campbeltown's reservoir, Auchalochy, which was earlier known as **Drumore Loch**.[37] But it was from the loch that the farm took its name *Achadh locha*, 'Field of the loch', in the first place, and the same with the other [698 281], which lies to the north-east of Tangy Loch and was variously spelt 'Achalocha', 'Achilochy' and 'Achalochy' in the late 18th and early 19th centuries, during which period the farm was tenanted by a Ballantine family.[38]

Auchaleek [706 225], to the west of Campbeltown, and still a working farm, takes its name from a far smaller landscape feature, a flat rock: *Achadh-lice*, 'Field of the flagstone'. The 1507 spelling, 'Auchleik', in the Exchequer Rolls, is close to the modern form. A wool-mill established at Auchaleek in the early 19th century was later converted into a farina-mill, for the manufacture of potato flour, an enterprise which failed after a year's trial. In 1866 the O.S. reported a 'starch mill' in ruins there.[39]

Achnaslisaig [645 135], at the head of Glenbreackerie, has been interpreted *Achadh na sliseige*, 'Field of the little slice or shaving',[40] but cf. *Allt Achadh nan Sliseag*, 'Burn of the Field of the Wood-shavings', on Arran.[41] Achnaslisaig was of 1 merkland in value and grouped with Uigle in early charters. The earliest spellings are: 1481 'Auchnaslesok'; 1502 'Achnansleshog'; 1507 'Achenachlesage'; 1562 'Auchnaslisseg'.[42] Cameron Gillies sparred with D. J. Macdonald in 1900 on the derivation of this name, dismissing Macdonald's suggestion of *slios*, 'side or flank of a hill', in favour of *sliseag*, 'a shaving': 'First, the last element, whatever it means, is clearly feminine, with the feminine article. *Slios* is masculine, and would give *Achadh-an-t-slios*. Then again the diminutive of *slios* would be *sliosan*, and could not possibly be *sliosaig*'.[43] I dare say Duncan Mcintailzor, Duncan Mcosenog, Duncan Mcilvorrie and Gilchreist Mcarthur could have come up with a credible answer; they all lived at 'Auchinslissaig' around 1636.[44]

Achinhoan [760 167] was the name of a farm and was later attached to a headland. The standard spelling perfectly represents the present spoken form, but the derivation is troublesome.

Professor MacKinnon in 1888 confidently referred to *Achadh-nan-tonn*, 'field of waves',[45] which he almost certainly copied from the *Second Statistical Account* of Campbeltown (p 455). Had he seen the place, he might have questioned the derivation; however, one of the suggestions for **Ballinatunie** [762 160], a neighbouring farm, is *Baile na tuinne*, 'The farm of the wave'.[46] The only suggestion offered in *The Place-Names of the Parish of Campbeltown* (p 5) was *Achadh na h-uamhain*, 'Field of the cave', which certainly has in its favour the fact that Saint Kieran's Cave, or **Covie Kieran** as it was known in the 19th century, is on Achinhoan Head, along with lesser caves. Ian A. Fraser considers 'Field of the cave' more likely and remarks that he has 'never heard of "wave" being used in place-names, especially habitative names'.[47] Early forms include: 1502 'Auchaquhone'; 1507 'Achaquhone'; 1562 'Achaquhona'; 1629 'Achachonzie' and 'Achachoan'.

Acharua [705 086], Southend, is *Achadh ruadh*, 'Red field'. **Achinsavil**, near Carskey, but ruined, is *Achadh an t-sabhail*, 'Field of the barn',[48] of which there is another, already mentioned, near Carradale. **Achachoirk** is *Ach' a' choirce*, 'Field of the oats'. **Oatfield** [684 176], near Campbeltown, once an estate, was originally so named,[49] and there was also a farm Achachoirk [709 417] near Muasdale, in 1507 'Auchaquhork'. The O.S. in 1867 described it as a ruin, 'now blended with ... High Crubisdale'. Ann McCallum, from her 'comeliness' in youth, was known as 'The Star of Achadh a' Choirce', which doesn't quite have the same ring as 'The Blazing Star o' Drum', the title of a local folk-song about a girl at Drum farm who was courted by a blacksmith. Ann married Neil McFater and spent 40 years at Kilmory, where she died at the age of 81 in 1918. Neil was one of D. J. Macdonald's sources of field-names.[50] **Achaglass** [709 414], a small farm also near Muasdale, is simply *Achadh glas*, 'Grey field', and **Achapharick** [690 422], again in the same area, is *Achadh Phàdhruig*, 'Patrick's Field'. **Auchenbreck**, Carradale Glen [783 440] and Campbeltown [735 209], represents 'Speckled Field', but see BREAC.

ÀIRIGH. You are walking across a moor and come to a burn with unnaturally green banks. You follow the meandering water for a little way, listening to its song, then you notice an unnatural mound ahead of you. When you step on to it, you see that it is circular and hollow. It's a fallen-in shieling-hut, last lived in two hundred years ago or more; and along the burnside you will find one mound after another. This was where the women and children of the townships came in spring, taking the cattle, sheep and goats with them to the new grass. At the shieling, the animals were milked and butter and cheese made, but the shieling was also a kind of summer holiday camp, which Professor MacKinnon described as 'the most delightful time in the Highlander's life ... which has furnished the finest Gaelic lyrics and innumerable place-names'.[51]

The academic term for the custom is transhumance, 'the movement of cattle to summer pastures on higher ground, allowing crops on the lower arable to ripen undisturbed'.[52] Despite Kintyre's rich legacy of history and folklore, there is not a single first-hand account of shieling life that I can find, and the answer must be that since agricultural improvements came early to Kintyre, the shieling system disappeared early, and by the mid-19th century had become a vague tradition.

These shielings once dotted the Kintyre interior, before the sheep invasion, before 'sportsmen' came in droves with their guns and dogs, and, of course, before the Forestry Commission began its coniferous assault on the landscape and its heritage. A 'shieling' is a summer pasture. It is a Scots word (which has gone over to English) and can also apply to a herd's hut;[53] but the relevant word here is *àirigh*, its Kintyre Gaelic equivalent.

Àirigh is from Old Irish *áirge*, 'a place for milking cows', but in Ireland the usual word for a shieling is not *áirí* – the modern Irish form – but *buaile*, which is generally anglicised in place-names as 'booley'. In central and eastern Scotland, the usual term was *ruighe*.[54] In the west of Scotland, *àirigh* place-names are widespread, but Norse *setr/saetr*, for 'shieling', intrudes in the Outer Isles, on Skye and – minimally – on Islay.[55]

That each and every *àirigh* in Kintyre once had a name attached to it is a certainty, but as the shielings were abandoned in the wake of agrarian change, their names, for the most part, were also abandoned and then forgotten. The names that do survive are mostly attached to farms which came into existence on or near shieling ground and were given the name of the shieling, or else are preserved within the names of landscape features such as streams and glens. One such survives in a legal document of 1788 which discusses 'the spot called Glendragheat between Loch Croman and the burn called **Arisheloch**',[56] which is *Àirigh sheilich*, 'Shieling of the willow'. This appears to be Drochaid Burn at 755 445 on O.S. maps, and there is, indeed, in Glen Drochaid, a string of shieling huts.

1. ÀIRIGH. Christina Macaulay seated inside a shieling-hut on the moors above Glenramskill, 25/5/1983. Photograph by the author.

There are in Kintyre, by my calculations, no more than 17 straightforward place-names which survive with the *àirigh* generic, and seven are in Campbeltown Parish; but there are others which incorporate *àirigh*.   The following two are from Campbeltown Parish. **Allt Àirighe Corraiche** [616 154], 'Steep shieling stream', runs to the immediate west of Gleneadardacrock ruins, while immediately to the east there is a prominent cluster of big turf huts. **Glenairiecreggan**, on Glenramskill farm, appeared on a Langlands plan of 1818. It is *Gleann àirigh chreagain*, 'Glen of the shieling of the rocky place', and is almost certainly the glen at 729 164, later known as **Meal Kist Glen**, and containing a string of shielings-huts along its length.[57] This is a favourite spot of mine, which I celebrated in *By Hill and Shore in South Kintyre*, pp. 261 and 263, and in the poem 'Winter Memories' (*Paper Archipelagos*, p 7).

Five of the seven *àirigh* names in Campbeltown Parish were collected from oral tradition. John McCallum gave **Arivicar**, *Àirigh a' Bhiocair*, 'The vicar's shieling', and **Ariholish**, with its 'fine view looking towards Killellan', which he suggested was *Àirigh sholuis*, 'Shieling of the light'. In 1929, Daniel Sillars and Agnes Buchanan, Skeroblingarry, together contributed **Ariscreeboch**

– Àirigh sgrìobach, 'Scarred land shieling' – and Miss Buchanan, alone, **Arivore** – Àirigh mhór, 'Big shieling' – both sites close to each other and close to the road above East Skeroblin steading. **Arichlarie** has been interpreted as Àirigh a' chlèirich, 'Shieling of the church officer', and came from Archibald Stewart, farmer in High Ugadale, on whose land it lay. **Arinarach** [724 150], a ruined farm, is Àirigh nathrach, 'Serpent shieling', and is discussed under NATHAIR. Nearby **Arinascavach** [721 137] was also a farm and therefore well documented. The K.A.S. place-names committee considered the name too difficult to interpret with confidence, but Cameron Gillies ventured Àirigh na Sgabhach, 'Shieling of the sawdust'.[58] The earliest-known spellings are: 1481 'Areskeauch'; 1562 'Arenaskawcha'; 1505 'Arnaskwauch'; 1596 'Arnaskeoch'; 1605 'Arnaskauch' and 1629 'Arinscavach',[59] and Ian A. Fraser suggests that the forms '-skeauch', '-skeoch', etc, may point to sgitheach, 'hawthorn',[60] perhaps not a tree one would expect to find there now, but possibly present when the name was coined.

Arinanuan [733 390], close to the head of Barr Glen, is Àirigh nan Uan, 'The Lambs' Shieling'. Iver, son of John McLarty, was baptised there on 13/1/1796, and Jean Keith, widow of Duncan McCallum, Arinanuan, died at High Glenramskill aged 84 on 8/7/1921.[61] **Arivore** [824 606], a farm near Whitehouse, once again represents Àirigh Mhór, 'Big Shieling'. It is on record as far back as 1481 as 'Arymore', and in 1511 appeared as 'Airmore'. There was a substantial house there, which in 1867 the Ordnance Survey noted, along with a small burial enclosure containing a stone inscribed: 'Archibald Campbell 1777.'[62] William S. Campbell, Lagavullin, Whitehouse, a retired naval carpenter, stated in 1939 that 'old residents' called the house 'The Old Castle' and that it was last occupied by the Sheriff Depute of Argyll, Archibald Campbell of Stonefield, 'having been purchased by him from the ancestors of the Campbells of Blythswood'.[63]

The only group of Kintyre shielings so far archaeologically surveyed is that [778 528] south-east of Talatoll. There are some 43 huts there,[64] but no name for that summer milking-place survived. **Àirigh nan Cuilean**, 'Shieling of the Pups', was in an O.S. name-book,[65] but not on any map I have seen. The stream **Allt Àirigh nan Cuilean** [893 647], however, preserves its general location. Sheiling names do survive in that way. Three more in the very north of Kintyre will serve as examples: **Stuagh Àirigh Alasdair** [c. 861 641], 'Pinnacle of Alasdair's Shieling', **Allt Àirigh nan Eun** [864 662], 'Stream of the Birds' Shieling', and **Allt Àirigh Hyman**, for which see under ALLT. For **Àirigh Fhuair**, 'Cold Shieling', refer to FUAR, and for **Glenbreackerie** see BREAC.

Several untraceable *àirigh* places appear on old maps which are topographically unreliable. '**Ariskeoch**', on the mid-17th century Gordon map roughly east of 'Bal na heglis' (Clachan), is probably the hawthorn (*sgitheach*) shieling. The specific in '**Arinabail**', on the same map at Glenreasdell, Skipness, may be *baile*, 'township'. '**Arinloan**', on the 1801 Langlands map located west of what appears to be Loch Romain, may be 'Marshy shieling', but see LÒN. The specific in '**Arrinhinnich**' (Glen), on an 1827 map of Carradale Estate, is *aonaich*, genitive of *aonach*, which has many meanings, of which 'hill', 'steep height' and 'moor' are just three which might fit.[66]

With **Crochrie** [735 219], if the Kintyre Antiquarian Society's interpretation *Cròch àirigh*, 'Yellow shieling', is correct, the adjective precedes the noun, but there must be doubt about the interpretation. *Àirigh* may be safe, but *cròch* seems less so: its primary sense is 'saffron' and it is a loan-word from Latin *crocus*.[67] There is also an alternative form, 'Crachrie', to consider. The ruin stands in what is now marshland to the east of Knockscalbert, with no stream nearby, and seems an unlikely spot for a shieling; but, of course, the nature of land may undergo drastic change. It has been described as a 'hill farm',[68] but there is no record of it as such, and it is missing from both Langlands maps, of 1793 and 1801. It is also missing from C1841, but appears in 1851 as 'Crockery', a shepherd's house occupied by John Blackstock. My guess is that it was built post-1841. According to tradition, 'a desperate fight ... took place among a band of tinkers on the braes of Crachrie ... when some of these lawless wanderers and outcasts of society met their death, and where the graves in which they were interred are still to be seen'.[69]

Until the 19th century, when land-surveyors were able to produce accurate maps and efficient fencing was introduced, trespass disputes were frequent (and occasionally bloody). One such, involving John Macdonald of Largie and the 2nd Duke of Argyll, provides an insight into pasturing customs and the tensions surrounding them. John Macilchattan, Bellochgerran, alleged in 1736 that in the first year (c. 1690) that the people of Kilmory, which was the Duke's, built 'Sheal-Houses' on the grazings of Lecknacrounie, the tenants of Bellochgerran complained to their laird, Largie, but he told them to 'forbear at that Time' and build their own huts elsewhere, for he had given liberty to John Dow, son of Archibald Oig Campbell, his cousin, to have the disputed huts built 'for the Use of poor people in

Kilmory, who could not conveniently go further off', having 'some weak Cows'. But John Dow prolonged the favour over several years, and after his father Archibald's death, Largie ordered the huts on Lecknacrounie to be destroyed and then went looking for Campbell. Failing to find him in his house at Kilmory, he continued to Killean and found him in the house of Duncan MacVicar, where, 'in a great Anger', he reproached him. Alexander MacAlaster in Bellochgerran, in his evidence, stated that Campbell's cattle would be 'poinded' when found trespassing on Lecknacrounie and elsewhere. A woman's coat or plaid, or some other article of clothing, or 'Gripes' (forks) or spades, would be given in pledge by the Kilmory tenants, which the women of Bellochgerran would return, seeking financial compensation, which they never received.[70]

ALLT in Kintyre is taken to mean a 'stream' or 'burn', but there is more to it than that. In his study of the place-names of North-East Antrim and Rathlin, Fiachra Mac Gabhann preferred to leave the definition open, between 'stream' and 'steep glen', and cited Colm O Baoill (1978) who indicated that *allt* usually means 'stream' or 'burn' in Scotland, but 'where it occurs in Ireland ... generally retains an older meaning, "wooded valley" or "deep glen"'.[71] Alexander Macbain defined *allt* as 'a stream', derived from 'Irish *alt*, height, (topographically) glen-side or cliff, Old Irish *alt*, shore, cliff'.[72]

In **Allt Domhain** [732 365 and 851 545], *domhain* means 'deep', but what does the depth relate to: water or its conduit, i.e. the ravine? The great majority of Kintyre burns are features of hill and moorland, and, as one who has crossed, or failed to cross, many burns in such terrain, I can testify that the obstacle to crossing is invariably the steepness of the gully through which the stream runs and not the stream itself, which, the occasional pool aside, will be anything but 'deep'. I offer this slight observation as an example of how an assumed interpretation might not fit specific cases, and might, indeed, belie an earlier naming intention. In the story of how **Allt na Béiste** got its name, in *Argyll's Highlands* – see under CAT – Cuthbert Bede, or his editor John Mackay, translated the name as 'Glen of the Wild Beast', not a startling piece of evidence, but I mention it anyway.

Linguistic considerations aside, a burn, for me, consists of unoccupied as well as occupied space. In times of drought, when the water-course dries out, what then is the 'burn'? It is the gully, the geological creation of ice and water. **Allt Dubh** [604 160], which flows off Cnoc Moy into the Inneans Bay, is 'Black Burn', and I suggest that the name relates not to water-colouration – from its journey through peat – but to the shade which progressively fills the gorge as afternoon draws towards evening.

Allt, by a long way, is the most common place-name element in Kintyre. From my records, there are 170 place-names with that generic, to which may be added others in which the element is otherwise incorporated. Very few of these names attach to habitations. The two main ones are on the coast between Tarbert and Skipness, **Allt Beithe** [885 668], 'Birch Burn' – see under BEITH – and **Altagalvash** [917 609], for which no interpretation can be confidently offered. Like Allt Beithe, Altagalvish is an old name: 1495 'Le Altgallereas'; 1549 'Altgalwesrych'; 1631 'Altezawais'; 1632 'Altezalvois'; 1642 'Allechalvois'; 1655 'Allezalwois'.

Norman Conley, who worked at the Mitchell Library, Glasgow, and was a son of the Rev Neil Conley, studied this name in depth and described it as 'one of the most intriguing of the Kintyre place-names'. His suggestion, in a letter (29/9/1953) to Duncan Colville, was *Allt a' Ghailbhis*, 'Burn of fury', while Ian A. Fraser, in a letter to the author (18/1/1980), ventured a 'speculative' derivation from *galbha*, 'hard, vigorous'. In the 1970s, I asked some of the oldest of the Tarbert fishermen if they had ever heard a meaning. Only Hugh MacFarlane had an answer, 'The Wolf Burn', because 'they wir supposed tae have got a wolf there at wan time'.[73] The inquisitive mind cannot abide a mystery, and I have little doubt that fishermen and others would have chewed the name over from generation to generation until something finally got spat out, mixed in perhaps with a scrap of an old story. 'Wolf Burn' sounds good, but I'd be surprised if anyone could link it etymologically with 'Altagalvish'.

Archibald McTavish, 'farmer in Altghalbhais', who died in 1790 aged 55, is buried in Kilbrannan, Skipness, with his wife Catherine Taylor, who outlived him by almost 42 years. Of Gilbert McVourich and his wife Mary McIlverichan, in 'Altagalvish' in 1762,[74] I know nothing, but unfortunate people lived there in the latter part of the 19th century. Mary and Margaret MacFarlane, daughters of Robert MacFarlane, shepherd at 'Altogalvich', and both 'wholly disabled', went on to the poor roll in 1870, and their brother Robert, on grounds of 'deformity and general weakness', followed in 1877, by which time the family was in Laggan. Mary Lindsay, an 18-year-old domestic servant at 'Altagalvais', whose parents were both dead, was declared insane and 'removed to Asylum at Lochgilphead' on

18/6/1877. On 14/6/1880, her 'wholly disabled' brother John, aged 14, in 'Altagolvais', was also removed to the Asylum.[75]

A third *allt* habitation-name on that coast, **Allt Romain**, also presents difficulties in its interpretation. The settlement [842 530] – in C1891 'Altdroman', comprising three houses, occupied by a shepherd and two crofters – took its name from the burn which runs from **Loch Romain** [823 535], on Roy's mid-18th century map 'L. Romin'. *Allt an Dromain*, 'Burn of the Ridge', may have been the original form, later shortened.[76]

2. ALLT. The two bridges over Allt na Dunach, erroneously described, on this postcard, published by Raphael Tuck & Sons, as 'Old Roman Bridges'. Author's collection.

The name **Allt na Dunach** [662 312], which is spanned by two derelict bridges close together, was explained by D. J. Macdonald as follows: 'Between Killocraw and Putechan there is a stream spanned by a narrow bridge with a high arch. Here two funeral processions met. Both parties had been entertained on too liberal a scale. Neither would yield precedence to the other. They came to blows and several fell on both sides. A memorial to the disaster is preserved in the name of the stream – Allt-na-Dunach – the stream of misfortune.'[77]

This is oral tradition, but there was no known historical record of the event until the transcript of a legal document turned up after Rev Macdonald's account was published. In Duncan Colville's papers there is a note dated 29/10/1936 which states that the transcript appeared in a letter to 'some newspaper'. Duncan was shown a copy by Latimer MacInnes, who got it from Mrs Macalister Hall of Killean. The authenticity of the transcript is not in doubt, but its contents do not validate the tradition.

In 1718, the Bailie of Kintyre, Donald Campbell, dealt with a 'disturbance', and a legal agreement was entered into after his judgement. The case papers do not appear to have survived, except for the agreement itself, which was dated 20/8/1718 at Campbeltown, and witnessed by Captain Dugald Campbell of Kilberry, Hector McNeill of Lossit, James Forrester of Knockrioch, Duncan Campbell of Kildaloig and Archibald Stewart in Ballergy.

Torquil McNeil in Kiligruir, Neil McNeil, son of Donald McNeil in Kilmaluaig, and Neil McInroich in Killocra were each fined £50 Scots for their 'doings of disturbance at, and stopping of the bier and burial of the deceased Maurice MacMoran, sometime in Skeroblinraid, who perished in the water of Altindunach on the fourth of August current ...' The guilty parties were also ordered to build 'Ane good and sufficient Stone Bridge upon the said water of Altindunach', design and materials detailed. I offer a few remarks on the legal document.

1. The burn in 1718 was already 'Altindunach', so the 'misfortune' must already have been in the past.

2. There is no reference to fatalities.

3. The place where MacMoran's funeral procession was stopped isn't mentioned. If, as tradition avers, a clash of mourning parties did take place on a bridge across Allt na Dunach, it is an odd coincidence that MacMoran also drowned in that burn. Might not the bridge that was ordered to be built, 'within four or five yards below the common fford', have spanned the spot where MacMoran drowned? It was to

be 'six feet of common measure in breadth', and archaeologists of the Royal Commission on the Ancient and Historical Monuments of Scotland, who surveyed the bridges in 1965, measured the older one at 2.2 m, or about 6 ft. 7 ins., whereas the 'roadway' of the newer bridge was 5.3 m, or over 16 ft. broad. The Commission ascribed the older, or lower, bridge to the 18th century and the newer one to 'about the middle of the 19th century'. The latter estimate was influenced by Archibald Munro's *The Story of Burns and Highland Mary* (1896), in which he stated that 'The modern one was erected in my boyhood'.

Munro was born in 1827, more than a century after the second bridge was traditionally supposed to have been built. His reason for mentioning the bridges at all was a romantic tradition associated with 'Highland Mary' Campbell, Robert Burns's tragic fiancée, who was brought up in Dalintober. She was supposed to have rested at the old bridge with her mother in 1778 on their way to Bellochantuy to stay with Macdonald relatives. Munro alludes to 'the peaceful termination of a controversy in which, among others, representatives of the Campbell clan were prominently concerned', and refers to 'an interesting stone tablet set in one of the parapets of the bridge, in which was engraved a brief statement of the circumstances that led to its erection'. The commemorative plaque was on the older bridge, which was therefore the one erected around 1718. The newer bridge, therefore, was built as a replacement for a structure 'too narrow for the passage of any wheeled vehicles of the present day', as Munro put it.[78]

Archibald Munro was born near Bellochantuy, graduated M.A. from the University of Edinburgh and operated private schools.[79] It is indicative of the strength of the Marianist cult of the time that he could recommend (p 36) the old bridge as a shrine to Mary Campbell: 'The circumstance that a world-renowned damsel once paced and crossed that now moss and broom-covered bridge should, when combined with the romance of its origin, form, and situation, make it, in the estimation of Scottish antiquaries at least, one of the attractive monuments in the kingdom.' Munro certainly padded out the Highland Mary traditions he heard in Kintyre, but concerning the old bridge at Allt na Dunach he had a point – it deserved to be better known, and still does.

Allt na Togsaide [733 190] is 'Stream of the Hogshead', the earlier Gaelic name for the **Rocky Burn** on the south shore of Campbeltown Loch. Boats visiting the loch would water there,[80] and the name probably alludes to the big casks – a 'hogshead' usually holds 50 gallons – into which the water would be filled; or else the water itself ran into a cask, lodged in the shore.

Allt Àiridh Hyman [865 642], in Kilcalmonell Parish, is the 'Stream of Hyman's Shieling'. 'Hyman' represents the surname Hyndman, which occurs in Kintyre, with variants, from the 17th century on, particularly in and around Skipness. The origin of this family, which was Gaelic-speaking right into the 20th century, has not, so far, been established,[81] but G. F. Black, in *The Surnames of Scotland* (p 372), records the name in Renfrewshire in the 16th century, and in the 17th century in Bute, where in 1662 Annie Heyman was 'at a meeting of witches'.

Three stream-names constitute interesting natural history records. **Allt na Pioghaid**, 'between Drumavulline and Low Cattadale', Southend, was preserved by Archie McEachran. It means 'Stream of the Magpie', and is the only place-names record of *Pica pica*, which has been extinct as a breeding species in Kintyre since the 19th century, though individual birds have been seen from time to time in recent decades.[82] Malcolm MacNeill of Carskey's 'brownie' was said to have predicted to him that a battle would be fought in Kintyre and that a Magpie would 'drink human blood off a standing-stone near Campbeltown'.[83] **Allt Giubhais** [851 678], which flows into the head of West Loch Tarbert, was interpreted by the O.S. as 'Scots fir tree burn'.[84] **Allt Gràinig** [773 345], which runs into Saddell Glen near Ifferdale, was recorded as 'Hedgehog's Burn' by the O.S., but the Hedgehog (*Erinaceus europaeus*) is a relatively recent arrival in Kintyre. It goes unmentioned in both the *First* and *Second Statistical Accounts*, and Gibson and Colville postulate an arrival 'during the last quarter of the 19th century, apparently by direct spread from Knapdale down the peninsula'.[85] A Hedgehog captured near Campbeltown in 1882 was exhibited in the town and attracted much attention as a rarity.[86] Since the place-name was recorded in 1867, it must be considered an enigma.

AODANN is 'face', which in place-names is 'hill-face'. The Southend farm **Eden** [710 102] is so derived. Cameron Gillies blamed the Ordnance Survey for the spelling, which he condemned as 'pure ignorance',[87] but 'Eden' appeared before the O.S. appeared, along with many other forms, including 'Edyn' in 1481 and 'Edwin' in 1584. Robert Hall and Alexander and James Ralstone were in 'Eden' in 1694,[88] and when Neill Olynachan erected a stone in Kilcolmkill to his wife Catherine Milloy, who died in 1810, he was 'tenant in Eden'. I fancy that 'Eddan' in C1861 was representative of local pronunciation, which now conforms to the sound of the Biblical garden. Belle Robertson, who was Scottish and British women's golf champion, belongs to the MacCorkindale family in Eden.[89] **Aodann nan gallan-greannchair**, from an old map in Lossit House, is 'Hill-face of the coltsfoot', and is now known as the **Galdrans** [624 197]. Agnes Stewart assures me that *Tussilago farfara* is still a plant of the Galdrans and that often she sees her first of the season there.[90] The Ordnance Survey's **Eudan** (or **Iunan**) **nan gallan** [625 203], 'a small creek or bay', is to the north. Peter MacIntosh, who was recommended to the officers as a 'Gaelic scholar' by Captain Macneal of Lossit, said that 'iunan' – which clearly represents INNEAN – was a 'rocky face' and 'gallan' 'an herb'.[91] John Cameron noted that *eudan* was 'the Kintyre form' of *aodan* and that *gallan* could be 'a large pillar stone (natural)'.[92]

AOIREANN is unrecognised in any Gaelic dictionary with which I am familiar, but may mean 'foreland', 'headland' or '(raised) beach', though Professor Donald MacKinnon, as quoted in George Henderson's *The Norse Influence on Celtic Scotland* (p 140), maintained that 'The *aoireanns* of South Argyll are, or have been, "ferries"', and included *Rubha na h-aoireann* among his examples, with the note, 'the ferry to Gigha is adjacent' (see **Rhunahaorine** under RUBHA).

As a generic, the term survives in Kintyre in only one place-name, which is now pronounced 'Erinvore' or 'Aranvore' for **Aoireann Mhór**. There is no raised beach there and the place [799 349] was almost certainly never a ferrying point, notwithstanding the 'port' – a rocky creek – associated with it. It is not easily accessible and, in any case, there are two far more serviceable harbours nearby, **Port Sgadain** and **Port Bàn**. The most persuasive definition appears to be 'Big Headland' or 'Big Foreland', as in the Arran interpretation in the final paragraph, and the name appears to equate with the **High Rocks**, which covers the whole cliffy headland. In 1980 Donald McIntosh very precisely gave Erinvore's location as 'fifty yards north of the High Rocks'; but it is possible that the High Rocks was a later name for Erinvore, and that Donald, by 'Erinvore', was referring to the ring-net haul later discussed.

Maps don't quite represent the physical presence of Erinvore, which has to be seen from sea or shore for the headland to emerge. On 29 October 2012, the day before this book was sent to the publisher, Lachie Paterson took me out in his boat, the *Rolling Wave*, to view the tree-clad headland from seaward, which reinforced the conclusions my wife Judy and I reached when we examined the coast by foot on 3 July.

Like certain other fishermen's place-names, Erinvore led a double life. As I probed the Carradale fishermen's understanding of both place and place-name, it became clear that for most the name referred only to a ring-net 'haul': the headland itself had, as it were, disappeared underwater.

Archie Paterson remembered Erinvore as 'a fine wee haul', a patch of clean seabed where a 'chancer' – a speculative set of the net, without signs of fish having been noticed – might yield a score or so baskets of herring in spring.[93]

3. AOIREANN. Looking south towards Erinvore. Photograph by the author, 3/7/2012.

Another retired skipper, John McConnachie, associated the name with a particular rock-face on the headland, which Lachie Paterson knows as **The Ivy Face**. See my *Herring Fishermen of Kintyre and Ayrshire* (pp. 47-48) for John's account of a memorable catch of herring there in November 1959, involving his family's *Florentine* and Jamie Campbell's *Bairn's Pride*. When he last passed the spot, he was dredging for scallops – the ring-net fishing by then had ended – and saw that his old ring-net mark was overgrown with ivy.

Yet another retired Carradale skipper, Jim Campbell, named his house, built at South Dippen in 2009, after the headland, so the name now has an 'official' existence. He had considered several names, but his brother Peter finally suggested 'Erinvore' and Jim agreed. He remembered, as a boy in Waterfoot, his father Jamie going off in a punt with an outboard motor in the spring to inspect the ring-net hauls through the seasonally clear water. He'd go as far south as the Pluck, and Erinvore was one of the spots he'd check – it was 'pure sand'. Jim also remembered a 'white stone' on the headland, which, when picked out by searchlight, was a mark for dropping the end of the net.[94]

Erinvore may not have been coined by fishermen – Graham McKinlay, who farmed Whitestone, gave me the name in 1977, and added **Port na h-Aoireann Mhór**, which, he said, 'split' the headland at full tide[95] – but it was certainly kept alive by Carradale fishermen. The Kintyre fishing communities as a whole had a fund of place-names common to them – generally the most significant of the coastal features – but each of them also had a stock of localised names for its own use, and Erinvore was one such.

I wish I had asked Graham McKinlay for his interpretation of *aoireann*, but I didn't, so the chance was lost to secure a local understanding of that place-name element; but in his estimation *mór* denoted extent, area, rather than height. He was also of the opinion that **Erines**, near Tarbert, likewise derived from *aoireann*.[96] Whitefarland, on the opposite coast of Arran, appears on Blaeu's 17th century map as 'Row na Heren' and was locally known as *An Aorinn*, 'the foreland' or 'headland',[97] hence 'Erins Bank' [842 424], the name which the Admiralty put on the notorious underwater pinnacle which Kintyre fishermen knew starkly as **The Rock**.

ÀRD, which represents 'high', sometimes takes the form *àird*, which is also 'point', 'promontory', 'headland', but there is little risk of confusing the two in Kintyre since there appear to be no points so named.

Aird(s) [814 384] is the historical nucleus of the present scattered community known as **Carradale**. The O.S. in 1867 described Low Airds as a 'small village' (opposite Carradale Hotel), Mid Airds as '3 rows of small thatched cottages' (to the north-west) and High Airds as a 'small cot house' (further north, on the hillside above Port na Cùile).[98] Airds Castle [820 383] is a ruinous medieval fortification south of Carradale harbour.[99] In 1754, 'the inhabitants of the lands of Aird, Ronadil, and Duppin in Glencaradill, in place of the usual Work on the high roads', were to 'work three days this Season in making a Key at the Ferry of Aird ...'[100] 'The Aird at Carradale' was said in 1852 to have been 'the resort of a band of witches, headed by Jean Gorach, or "Jean the wicked"'.[101] Poor Jean, however, was misrepresented: *gòrach* is 'silly', 'foolish' or 'mad', but hardly 'wicked'. When Neil S. Stalker, as a Campbeltown schoolboy, visited Carradale by steamer in the summer of 1902 with two friends, as they walked through the 'village of Airds', they were 'greeted at every turn by the guttural sound of the Gaelic'.[102]

Àird Bhàn [856 545] was translated 'Fair head' by the O.S.,[103] but is more likely to refer to height, particularly since the 'head' is covered by **Rubha na h-Àirde Bàine** [860 545]. 'Airdvaan' was marked as a settlement on the 1801 Langlands map, but on the first O.S. map, surveyed in 1867, appears as 'Airdbhan (Ruins)'. **Ardnacross** [767 262], north of Peninver, is *Àrd na croise*, 'Height of the cross' (see CROIS). **Sgeiràrd**, a submerged rock north-east of Skerryvore, at the south end of Machrihanish Bay, is 'High rock'.[104] **Àrdach**', on Largie Home Farm, appears as 'Ardochy field' in a report in 1870 of a ploughing match organised there by Killean and Kilcalmonell Ploughing Association. The field having been under pasture for about 25 years, the soil was 'exceedingly stiff' and only 15 competitors came forward, far fewer than usual.[105] D. J. Macdonald interpreted the name as 'High field',[106] *Àrd achadh*, but *àrd* + the suffix *ach* = 'high place' is a possible alternative.[107]

ÀROS [681 212] in the Laggan – spelt 'Arrows' in a 1709 lease[108] – is a singular occurrence in Kintyre, though in 1995 a retired shepherd, Dugald McKendrick, mentioned to me a 'hollow' west of Killypole steading [641 177] which he called 'The Ariss'; but, since nothing more has emerged about the place, the name has to be set aside as a curiosity. According to Macbain, in 'Place-Names of the Hebrides', *áróss* in Norse is a 'river mouth',[109] but that sense is inapplicable here, not least on grounds of topography. Aros is always spoken of locally as 'The Aros', and Gaelic *àros*, 'house', may be taken to signify a dwelling of some importance, perhaps a chief's house. Yet, the name is absent from old charters and first appears as late as 1685, when spelt 'Arrass'. The name **Arrassett**, however, which does appear in old charters, is almost certainly its earlier form. Arrassett was an old estate of the MacNeills of Gigha, comprising Machrihanish, Trodigal, Clochkeil and Lochsanish, which they sold in 1554 to the Macdonalds, and which passed in 1632 to Lord Lorne and was leased in 1669 to 'Hellebeeth', who was John Cuninghame of Hill of Beith, a cadet of the Earl of Glencairn.[110]

Of that chiefly residence, if it existed, there are no known remains. The present farmstead of Aros is on improved land, and on such land there tend to be few traces of early settlement. The artist William McTaggart was born in 1835 at Aros, where his father Dugald was a cottar and peat-cutter. Aros sat in bogland, and it is likely that the McTaggart house was built of peat and turf. Its site is now unknown, which disappoints disciples of McTaggart's art who come to Kintyre in the hope of visiting his birthplace. Eleanor MacDougall, however, when researching McTaggart and his Gaelic background, heard of a woman whose grandfather mentioned a field on Aros with different-coloured soil in a part of it. 'He would point it out when ploughing and say it was where McTaggart was born.' The internationally acclaimed Scottish sculptor, George Ralston Wyllie (1921-2012), was, in early manhood, an occasional visitor to Aros, which was farmed by a Mitchell family with whom he shared a common ancestor in Kintyre, Patrick/Peter Ralston (1712-95).[111]

ÀTH is 'kiln', but can also represent 'ford' in place-names. As Cameron Gillies remarked, only 'local knowledge' can separate the two usages,[112] and in Kintyre 'kiln' is generally the interpretation. A kiln is a furnace or oven, and the oldest remaining kilns in Kintyre are the corn-kilns for the drying of grain for milling. These were built in or near the township, and some that survive intact, like the one at Craigaig, are admirable structures. Gaelic *cutag* was used in Kintyre for the corn-kiln, but does not appear in place-names. Corn-kilns are sometimes wrongly identified as lime-kilns on O.S. maps, but the lime-kiln is altogether different in appearance, of upright construction and with its chamber to the front, whereas the circular corn-kiln's chamber is in the top. Finally, there were the seashore kelp-kilns for burning wrack, but these were crude structures – pits edged with stones – most of them of 19th century origin, and few have survived the ravages of storm. All evidence considered, the kilns referred to in Kintyre place-names are likely to have been for the firing of limestone to produce fertiliser or building-mortar. Early lime-kilns tended to be temporary turf structures raised in the fields where the lime was to be spread, but by the end of the 18th century more substantial structures were being built of stone, to utilise limestone outcrops. At Fort Argyll, Campbeltown, where two large kilns may still be seen, limestone-burning was a commercial enterprise, but most lime-kilns were for the use of tenant-farmers, and the limestone was imported, much of it from Ireland.[113]

Achnaha [674 383] at Muasdale is *Achadh na h-àtha*, 'Field of the kiln', also known as **North Belloch**. In 1847 Alexander McMillan, tenant in 'Auchnaha', wrote to John Fleming Esq of Muasdale to state that he found it 'impossible to pay the rent you have put on it'.[114] **Altnaha**, Southend, 'a tributary of Strone Water, slightly north of Garvallt', has been interpreted as *Allt na h-àtha*, 'Stream of the kiln', though this name might suggest 'ford'. It appears only in Malcolm MacNeill of Carskey's rental book: 'Ane fencible ditch betwixt the foot of Altnaha and Garvalt was made by Donald McIlheanie and Mall. McGibbon between Nov. 1720 and May 1721.'[115] **Knocknaha** [688 179] has been interpreted *Cnoc na h-àtha*, 'Hillock of the kiln', though Duncan Colville had doubts and thought that 'ford' might apply in this case: 'A much older road than the present one to Southend, crossed the stream by a ford close above the Mill at Knocknaha and proceeded past the present Laggs cottage, a branch road leading to Uigle.' 'Knocknaha' is absent from early charters, and Colville speculated that it might be a later name for **Octoran** (see UACHDAR), a place-name the location of which is unknown.[116] D. J. Macdonald recorded four minor *àth* names: **Cùl na h-àth**, 'Kiln back' (Low Clachaig), **Druim na h-àth**, 'Kiln ridge' (Achadaduie and Tangy), and **Leac na h-àth**, 'Kiln face' (Phairc Mhòir).[117]

BÀGH is a bay, but whether it derives from English 'bay', or Norse *vágr*, is debatable, though both of these Germanic terms have a common root.[118] In either case, the generic is rare in Kintyre, which is hardly surprising given the available alternatives, CAMUS, LÙB and PORT. The only South Kintyre example of this place-name element, of which I am aware, is the obscure **Bàgh Inbhir** [626 207], 'River mouth bay', near Uisaed, which owes its survival to Duncan Colville, who copied it from an old estate map in Lossit House.[119] **Bàgh na Còmhraig**, 'The Battle Bay', is south of Eilean a' Chòmhraig, on the Tarbert West Shore, but see under EILEAN. Further south, **Croit Bàgh** [918 615] represents 'Croft Bay', from a ruin marked 'Croit' on the earliest O.S. maps (see CROIT).

BAILE. The use of *baile* in Scottish place-names appears to represent 'a revolution in land-management, taxation, and administration, which took place in the twelfth and thirteenth centuries, and probably reflects the use of the Latin *villa*, referring to new kinds of farming establishment'.[120] The simplest definition of *baile* is 'settlement'. Its standard meanings range in dimension from 'farm' to 'town'. Here, we are dealing with farms, and in Kintyre none of these farms expanded into villages or towns. They remain farms and their names remain relatively obscure. In Ireland the story is different. In County Antrim alone, no great distance from southern Kintyre, Ballycastle, Ballymoney and Ballymena come to mind at once, and, on Islay, Ballygrant. *Baile*, as is clear from the examples above, is commonly anglicised as 'Bally-', but it also occurs as 'Ball-' and 'Ballie-', and in one instance in Kintyre as 'Bale-', which is noteworthy only because the pronunciation (which rhymes with 'pale') is unique and, I have to tentatively conclude, has been contrived to distinguish the two identically named farms in Campbeltown Parish, **Balegreggan** [718 214] and **Ballygreggan** [668 191], both representing *Baile a' chreagain*, 'Farm of the little rocky place'.[121]

Historically, however, *baile* translated as 'farm' is a gross over-simplification. As I have elsewhere remarked, until the concept of the farm as an independent agricultural unit, worked by a single tenant, was forced into the frame of Gaelic society, the *baile* was a communal tenancy land-holding in which farming was only one of many occupational pursuits, albeit the pivotal one. 'The farm, as now understood, was a 19th century creation, the full-grown child of the Improvements. By then, farmers did little else but farm – it was their settled occupation, not least when dairying, with its heavy commitments in time and labour, was adopted in mid-century – whereas their grandfathers and great-grandfathers might turn their hands to almost anything: labouring, house-building, boat-building, cobbling, herring-fishing, whisky-distilling, cattle-raiding, and, a bit further back, by choice or by coercion, the dark arts of battle.'[122]

That the concentration of people into pockets of settlement had a defensive value is often overlooked. In 18th century Kintyre – with its civilising Lowland planter-stock firmly in place, the power of the tacksmen broken, and their big land-holdings split into smaller units – cattle-raiding, clan feuding and other extremes of lawlessness were already receding into history, and the prospect of living and working in a remote spot, with only one's family and servants at hand, no longer held the apprehensions of old.

In Kintyre, *baile* has tended to be interpreted as 'township', and in general I'll stick with that, despite its limitations. In Ireland, the preferred interpretation is 'townland',[123] the elements of which better express the function of the *baile*: a settlement with land attached to it. Scots 'ferm-toun' (farm-town) seems to me to be the most incisive of them all, and that was how Peter MacIntosh chose to describe the *baile* in 1857: 'The farm towns were little villages, in which a great many lived.'[124]

In W. F. H. Nicolaisen's map of names containing *baile*, in *Scottish Place-Names* (p 137), there are 11 locations shown in Kintyre. I appreciate that the map was not intended to be comprehensive, but the true figure is closer to 36. Kintyre was evidently notable for the abundance of its *baile* names, if one may judge by a Gaelic proverb: '*Ceithir "busa" fichead an Ìle; Ceithir "tire" fichead am Muile; 'S ceithir "bailte" fichead an Cinn-tìre.*' Translated, this reads: 'Twenty-four "busses" in Islay; Twenty-four "lands" in Mull; And twenty-four "ballys" in Kintyre.'[125]

Almost two-thirds of *baile* place-names are in the parishes of Southend and Campbeltown, and I shall focus initially on those on the coast between Machrihanish and Carskey. The most northerly is **Ballygroggan** [622 191], *Baile a' ghroigein*, 'Township of the stunted one' – referring to a person or a natural feature[126] – which has incorporated Craigaig since the 19th century and is still a hill farm. Close to Ballygroggan there are two other *baile* names for which there is no known evidence of settlement.

The first, **Ballykelly**, is now a field [626 196] above the south end of the Galdrans. Duncan Colville took the name 'Baile Kelly' from an estate map and also found it, as 'Ballykily', in a 'letter book' dated 1856/57. In any case, the name was in no danger of disappearing – it is still known to a few elderly villagers in Machrihanish. In *The Place Names of the Parish of Campbeltown* (p 9), the derivation given is *Baile Mhic Ealaidh*, 'Kelly's township', which seems odd. The surname Kelly in Kintyre goes back to the 17th century in its many anglicised forms, and these, e.g. 'O Kaldie' and 'O Kelly', do not hint at a *Mac-* prefix;[127] cf. Ballykelly in County Derry, *Baile Uí Cheallaigh*, 'Ó Ceallaigh's homestead'.[128]

About **Ballygevrie** nothing is known except that it pertained to a field on High Lossit farm and was noted from Hugh Mitchell, High Lossit, in 1938. Unless the generic is corrupt, the name represents *baile geamhraidh* and means 'winter town'.[129] As with Ballykelly, no steading has been identified, but some of these *baile* names could be a thousand years old, and perhaps the settlement had ceased to exist before leases and other records began to proliferate in the post-medieval period. The same name was earlier recorded, as a field-name on Glenacardoch, by D. J. Macdonald.[130] This is an interesting name, more interesting than is suggested by Professor Watson's gloss, 'a good wintering place'.[131] In Highland districts, Albert Bil states, the term 'wintertown' (*baile-geamhraidh*) referred to 'the permanently occupied farms', whereas 'summertown' (*baile-samhraidh*) described the shieling settlements 'beyond daily travelling distance from the farm'.[132] The shieling in Kintyre is ÀIRIGH, and if *baile-samhraidh* was ever used in Kintyre, there is no trace of it in place-names. But the distinction is clear – the grazing on high ground was utilised in summer, and in winter people and livestock withdrew to lower ground, the better to endure the rigours of weather in permanent settlements. The same principle applies in shepherding – sheep are taken off high ground and wintered on low, formerly at great distances when necessary. In 1866, almost 30,000 Argyll sheep were transported to other counties, including Perthshire, Stirlingshire and Ayrshire.[133] In the winter months, Bil remarks, the deserted summertowns might become 'the haunts of fugitives and vagrants'.[134]

South of Ballygroggan and Craigaig, a belt of six townships all with INNEAN as their generic ends at **Balmacvicar** [593 097], north of the Mull Lighthouse. It represents *Baile Mhic a' Bhiocair*, 'MacVicar's township', and is noteworthy for the survival there of a ruined 'horizontal' water-mill. In 1541, Gilquhane McVicar was joint tenant of the Mull with Hector MacNeill of Carskey, and Balmacvicar itself was occupied by MacVicars from at least the early 17th century until 1776, when Archibald McVicar lost the lease to sheep-graziers.[135]

The next one, close to the Lighthouse, was **Balimacilchonalie** [c. 590 079], for *Baile Mhic Ille Chonalaich*, 'Conley's son's township'. In 1684, the holding was let to Donald McIlchonalie, and in 1720 Neill McIlchonaly was there. That family later assumed the surname Conley, which is still found in Campbeltown, whence the family removed and became largely involved in the fishing industry.[136] Balimacilchonalie appears to have been deserted after the Mull was stocked with sheep, and **Ballinamoil** [591 082] – *Baile na maoile*, 'The Mull farm' – took its place nearby. 'Ballymule' appears on Roy's mid-18th century map, though 'Balimaconolly' is later (1780) named as the holding in a lease signed by graziers Colin Campbell, Colin McEachran and Petter Brolochan.[137] The two names appear to be effectively interchangeable.

Further round the coast, heading east, is **Balmagomery** [606 064], *Baile Mhicumra*, 'Montgomery's township'. In MacNeill of

Carskey's accounts for 1725, Donald McComra in 'Balimacomra' was owing 15 shillings, 'being the remainder of the price of aquavitie he got from me to his wifes funerall'.[138] This name, whatever its Gaelic origin, was anglicised as Montgomery. The family has died out locally, but the ancestry of Canadian novelist Lucy Maud Montgomery (1874-1942), whose 'best-seller' *Anne of Green Gables* was published in 1908, has been traced to Hugh Montgomery and Mary McShannon, Southend, who sailed in 1771 in the *Edinburgh* from Campbeltown to Prince Edward Island.[139]

According to Southend tradition, there were five holdings at the Mull named after their tenants. If correct, then two are missing from this list, but only one other can be offered, **Balimacmurchie** – *Baile Mhic Mhurchaidh*, 'MacMurchy's township' – on Carskey Estate into the 18th century, but location unknown.[140] *Mac Mhurchaidh* probably represents a form of *Mac Mhuirich*, the name of the celebrated hereditary bardic family to Clan Donald which was associated with Kintyre from at least the early 16th century. A prominent fishing rock on the south side of Davaar Island, **MacVoorie's Rock** [755 198], probably derives from the *Mac Mhuirich* surname.[141]

Another bardic family in Kintyre, *Mac Mharcuis*, gave its name to a land-holding in Glen Lussa, probably post-1506, when John McMarkish, tenant in 'Kyram Mor' (Kerranmore), also acquired 'Lagane'. This he held at a reduced rent until 1528, when payment appears to have been entirely waived, 'by the grace of the lord king' (James IV), in virtue of his office – he was designated *carminista*, 'singer' or 'versifier'.[142] The Laggan land-holding is represented on two 17th century maps as 'Balamak marquis' and 'Balamackmarkish': **Baile mhic Mharcuis**, 'Township of MacMarcus'. From one of these maps, Timothy Pont's of 1610, Duncan Colville reckoned that the MacMarcus house would have lain on the opposite side of the river from Gartgreillan.[143] For the later history of the family, refer to my *Kintyre: The Hidden Past*, pp. 10-12.

Balinakill [771 560] is *Baile na cille*, 'Township of the church'. On Pont's map it appears as **Balnaheglish**, from *Baile na h-eaglaise*, which may also be translated as 'Township of the church', from Latin *ecclesia*. (See under DAIL for **Dalnaheccleis**, which shares the specific.) Campbeltown-born Sir William Mackinnon (1823-93), 1st Baronet of Strathaird and Loup, purchased the estates of Balinakill and Loup in 1867. The house was completed in 1893 and is now an hotel.

Jean C. MacLeod, Stornoway, informs me that **Baile Chill Chiarain**, 'Town of Ciaran's Church', was an alternative Gaelic name for **Ceann Loch Chille Chiarain**, 'Head of the Loch of Ciaran's Church', often shortened to **Ceann Locha** (see CEANN). The *baile* form was taught as the Gaelic name for Campbeltown by Alex Urquhart and Zena Nicoll at the Nicolson Institute, Stornoway. 'Baile Chill Chiarain' appears in the 5th (1965) edition of MacEachen's Gaelic-English Dictionary. The editors of that edition, Mrs MacLeod notes, acknowledged the assistance of Alex Urquhart, Gaelic Master at the Nicolson.[144]

BÀN has an etymological spoor which shines brightly across millenia,[145] but in place-names English 'white' can seldom be got to fit. Dwelly, as ever, has ample alternatives, of which 'pale', 'light in colour' and 'wan'[146] are eminently serviceable; and Gilbert Márkus points out that *bàn* 'can be used of land in the sense of "vacant, waste, untilled"'.[147]

For **Largiebaan**, the interpretation *Leargaidh bàn*, 'The light-coloured slopes', was offered in *The Place-Names of the Parish of Southend* (p 24), and it seems to me to be a judicious one, but questions naturally follow: where are the slopes and why should they have been so perceived? On 21/3/2012, I visited the cliffs at Largiebaan with Murdo MacDonald, Dr Sandy McMillan and my daughter Amelia, and I was looking that day, more intently than ever before, for clues as to the origin of the name. On the south-facing slope of the glen, as one approaches the cliffs, we were walking over ground covered with pale, dead winter grasses. No certainty is possible, of course, because the name is centuries old and landscapes change, but the effect was immediate and persuasive. Whether or not correct in this case, I believe that the effects of light on certain vegetation – grasses in particular – account for some of the place-names described by *bàn*.

Largiebaan was a township in its origins and became, in the 19th century, a shepherds' place. I remember three shepherds there at one time. Archie Ronald was the last, and, since he left, the remaining house [614 143] is only occasionally occupied by representatives of the Scottish Wildlife Trust, which was gifted the farm as a nature reserve by Marion Campbell in 1993.[148] In 1921, a walker on 'the Moil hills' spent a night at Largiebaan and claimed 'the privilege of sleeping in the highest bed in Kintyre for it is the case that Largiebaan is the most highly-situated house in the district'.[149]

Largiebaan is now a Site of Special Scientific Interest, a status which its botany alone – yellow oxytropis, mountain avens, purple

4. BÀN. *The cliff-face on the south side of Rubha Dùin Bhàin. At the foot of the cliff, barely perceptible, stand Donald and Malcolm Docherty Snr., at the entrance to a cave occupied nocturnally by wild goats.   Photograph by the author, 10/4/1984.*

saxifrage, yellow saxifrage and mossy saxifrage – more than justifies; but the rest of that wild and spectacular Atlantic coast, between Machrihanish and the Mull, has no such legal protection, however nominal, an anomaly which should be addressed, and quickly, particularly in the current climate of wind-farm proliferation. The three caves at Largiebaan have attracted visitors since the mid-19th century, and many names can still be seen cut into or pencilled on to the limy walls, but the stalactites and stalagmites which were once the principal wonders of the caves have all been removed by souvenir-hunters.[150] In June 1884, for 1s or 6d steerage, the RMS *Kinloch* conveyed day-trippers to Largiebaan Caves. Publicity for the excursion referred to a visitor who had taken to the caves 'chemicals for purposes of illumination'; when he viewed the stalactites thus revealed, he enthused that 'the result rivalled visions of fairyland'.[151] When John McMath and Helen McShenoig erected a gravestone in Kilcolmkill to their daughter Flora, who died on 12/3/1818, aged 31, her place of death was inscribed 'Leargybaan'.

Rubha Dùn Bhàin [590 144] further south – 'White Pt.' on Admiralty charts – has been interpreted 'The headland of the fair hill', with a note: 'There is no fort in the vicinity.' **Dùn Bàn** [594 140], still further south, is 'light-coloured hillock', again with a note: 'No evidence of a fort observed there.'[152] There is no evidence of a hillock there either! There is, however, the fortified rock of **Greanan Dheardruin** to the north – see under GRIANAN – which would certainly qualify as a *dùn*. If that isn't the *dùn* of Dùn Bàn, then I suggest that the summit of the promontory is. I had hoped that the Ordnance Survey record would clarify the issue, but it only serves to complicate it. Dùn Bàn is described as 'A very prominent rocky feature, or large precipice, signifying the white barrier'. Here, the word popularly understood to mean 'castle' or 'fort' is being made to describe a cliff and defined as a 'barrier'. The main informants for this name were Archibald Mathieson, Glenahanty, and John Campbell, Remuil,[153] both of them natives of Southend and certainly Gaelic-speaking. That the name continued in speech is certain because shepherds in the 20th century referred to it as 'Largiebaan Dun Ban' and another to the north as 'Ballygroggan Dun Ban', to distinguish them.

The latter [612 191] is a classic Kintyre dun, with its rounded head, modest cliffs and grassy top. Duncan Colville recorded the name from John McCallum, Dalbuie, whose pronunciation was 'Toon Vaan';[154] but I have always heard 'Ton Vaan', or even 'Tin Van', and

5. *BÀN.   Rubha Dùin Bhàin from the south, with Jimmy MacDonald
lounging in foreground. Photograph by the author, 3/6/2012.*

wondered sometimes if the generic might be TÒN – a massive rump
thrust seaward. I didn't find out until 2012 that Agnes Stewart also
knew the name as 'Ton bhan' (her spelling).[155] Since this is a name
which has survived only in oral tradition, along with its alternative,
The Falcon Cliff, there are no maps or written records to turn to for
assistance with interpretation. Iain Henderson, however, points out
that, in his native Ardnamurchan, Dùn Bàn, at Plocaig, was spoken
as 'An Tun Ban', which was 'much easier to say and probably sounds
to the English ear as Ton Van'.[156]   William McTaggart painted the
northern Dùn Bàn into two of his major works, 'The Coming of St.
Columba' (1895) and 'The Preaching of St. Columba' (1897). In the
former, Dùn Bàn is included far left, and McTaggart has added two
towering structures at the back of it. These have no basis in reality,
and, since he ordinarily painted landscapes as he saw them, are quite
inexplicable.

   Càrnbàn [854 681] was interpreted 'White cairn' by the O.S. in
1867 and described as a 'Range of dwelling houses on County road
half a mile W. of Tarbert'.[157] In C1851 it was described as the 'Village
of Carnbane', though merely six occupied houses were recorded, and
by Dugald Mitchell in 1908 as 'the hamlet of Carnban'.[158] **A' Gheata**

Bhàn [862 684], 'The White Gate', is the area of Tarbert village in which the graveyard is situated. Hugh MacFarlane remarked that, before his time, it was a bay, with 'the sand comin in' and 'cuddies' (little saithe) 'comin up at high water'.[159] For **Strabane** see under SRATH and for **Mealbaan** under MEALL.

Sac Bàn, literally, is 'white sack', which scarcely begins to define a very peculiar supernatural phenomenon. The *Sac Bàn* was a pig-shaped thing which would follow people who were out and about at night, and grip and bite their heels,[160] but I would have had no excuse to mention the tradition here had D. J. Macdonald not recorded a very minor place-name, **Glac an t' saic bhàin**, which he translated as 'The Hollow of the Sac Ban' and described as 'a small valley behind Dun Ach-na-h-àth' [673 386] at Muasdale. In the following tale, the *sac bàn* is no dog-like mischief-maker, but a 'spirit', and a malevolent one at that.

There were sixteen old men in Muasdale. One of them had a servant girl, and the son of the old man was courting her. His mother took a great spite to the girl. She did not know how she might do away with her. They sold drink over at the Creggan. No one dared to cross the hollow of the White Sac once the sun had set. The way that his mother took was that she should send her to the Creggan to fetch drink. When she was going she found the shaggy covering [*luman*] that was on the White Sac, and she swept away with her the shaggy covering. She knew that he could not do anything without it. When she got the drink at the Creggan, she gave the shaggy covering to the change-house wife. She said to her to keep the shaggy covering until she thought that she would be at the house. Then came the White Sac, and every blow that he would give to the door, they would think that he would break through the house. The wife was waiting (making patience) to see if the girl would be at the house ere she gave back the shaggy covering. But with the awe she felt, she threw the shaggy covering at him. The lad understood how matters were, and he was at the door to catch her. The White Sac was at the door as soon as she, but he was able to pull her from him. Then the White Sac got a hold of the plaid which was about her, and with the fright that the girl got she died. The woman was very sorry that she did the like, and she got no rest after that.[161]

Moira Burgess remarks that 'The shaggy covering without which the White Sac is powerless links this story to the widespread tales of swan maidens and selkies, where a man gains power over a supernatural creature by stealing the swan feathers or seal skin'.[162]

BÀRR, 'hill' or 'pointed hillock', is 'almost exclusive to Argyll' as a hill term.[163] The best known place in Kintyre with this name is the village of **Glenbarr** [670 364] at the foot of **Barr Glen**, which extends seaward from Arinanuan. Cuthbert Bede in 1861 described it, under 'Barr Village', as 'one short, wide street', with low, thatched, whitewashed houses and an inn, post office, shop, smithy and 'a shoemaker's'.[164] That one street appears to have become two by 1875, when to 'Vulcan Street' was added the equally mysteriously-named 'Tread Street'. In fact, in the *Campbeltown Courier* of 1/12/1875 the two names appear together: Mrs Neil Paterson gave birth to a son at Tread Street and Sarah McMillan, relict of D. McCorkindale, Killegruar, died at Vulcan Street. Glenbarr Abbey nearby was built by Colonel Matthew Macalister, 1st laird of Glenbarr and Rosehill, and remains the seat of that family, which is an offshoot of the Macalisters of Loup. It is now a visitor centre. In 1780, Matthew suffered multiple wounds and was left for dead on the battlefield of Pollilur in India, but recovered and was imprisoned in chains for nearly four years by Hyder Ali (1728-82), *de facto* ruler of the Kingdom of Mysore.

For artificial place-names, Glenbarr Estate was unsurpassed in all Kintyre. **Skernish** [679 370] was from a farm in the parish of Snizort, Skye, and replaced the name (Lower) **Bàrr Uachdarach** (see UACHDAR). Colonel Macalister's father, Ranald, was factor on the Macdonald estate of Trotternish and tenant of Skernish there. **Charlottan** [677 367], for 'Charlotte town', commemorates Charlotte Brodie of Brodie, who was Colonel Matthew's second wife, as also probably does **Brodie**, which was on Dalkeith farm and appears on record in 1808 when Angus McKinlay and Janet McStockair had a child baptised at 'Brody'.[165] **Duff**, north of Glenbarr village, was named after Lady Margaret Duff, mother of Charlotte Brodie. **Dalkeith** [660 359] was earlier known as **Port a' Bhorrain** and probably commemorates the 2nd laird of Glenbarr, Keith Macalister. **Barrmains** [669 349] was earlier **Rome**. Since in Protestant Kintyre the name is unlikely to have been a respectful nod to the holy city, another explanation must be sought. Gilbert Márkus ventured, as a 'shot in the dark', Old Gaelic *ruam*, from

Latin *Roma*, 'Rome', which could mean 'cemetery', as attested in Watson (1926).[166] Cladh nam Paitean cemetery is certainly on the foreshore below the farm. In Duncan Colville's papers, he postulates a link with Romsdal Valley and River, near Skernish, Skye, but the name predates the Macalister influence, since it appears in the Kintyre Presbytery Records, in the period 1687-1707, as 'Rome alias Trainapathion ...' (see under TRÀIGH). I have never heard the name alluded to by anyone. It is almost as though it never existed, yet it was later recorded without comment by the O.S. in 1867,[167] and in the *Argyllshire Herald* of 1869: Mrs John Stalker gave birth to a daughter on 14 July at 'Room Farm, Glenbarr', and on 21 October, at Ballochantee, Robert Stewart, Sunnyside Cottage, Glenbarr, married Grace, daughter of Charles Stalker, 'Rome'.[168] **Rosehill** [669 376] was evidently another contrived name, replacing **A' Ghrodaidh**, 'The putrid place', which was supposedly 'changed to Rosehill in deference to the wishes of the minister's wife' – the minister of Killean lived there until about 1803, when Muasdale Manse was built. D. J. Macdonald, however, interpreted the name as *A' Chrotach*, presumably with the sense of 'humped', 'uneven', which may be preferred.[169] See **Rosshill** under EILEAN. (**Paisley**, near Lagalgarve, further south, is another peculiar name, which is presumably a borrowing from the Renfrewshire town. Angus McKeich, 'Paisley', and his wife Margaret McPhail erected a stone in Cladh nam Paitean in 1858 to their children.)

6. BÀRR. *Glenbarr Village, c. 1910. Postcard published by Martin Stationers, Campbeltown, in author's collection.*

The name of the now-deserted farm **Margmonagach** [Low 671 355, High 676 355] was interpreted by Macdonald as *Barragmònachach*, 'The little peaty hill top'.[170] In early records the generic is predominantly 'mar-/mer-', which may represent *marg*, 'merkland': 1502 'Margmonich'; 1507 'Markmonagach'; 1545 'Barmonagach'; 1596 'Mermonogath'; 1605 'Mergmonogach' and 'Margmonanache'; 1653 'Barmonagach'. In the latter part of the 19th century, High and Low Margmonagach were on Glenbarr Estate and, with Upper and Lower Rome, comprised Glenbarr Mains farm,[171] now Barrmains.

Baraskomill [741 210], a farm near Campbeltown, is generally 'Barasky' in local speech, and as such it also appears in C1841. The generic is *bàrr*, but the specific is not so clear. Two other land-holdings also contained the specific, **Askamillmore**, the big one (*mór*), and **Askamillbeg**, the little one (*beag*). The earliest forms are: 1502/7 'Baraskynell', 'Baraskemyle' and 'Barraskymmyl'. Norse *Askar-muli*, 'Ship or ash tree point', or Gaelic *Aiseag maoil*, 'Monk's ferry', have been proposed.[172] Ian A. Fraser considers the Norse derivation 'more sensible' than the rather 'speculative' Gaelic one.[173]

Barrmore [715 273], a hill near Drumgarve, is *Bàrr mór*, 'Big height'.[174] **Bàrr nan Cnoc** [863 671] is 'The uppermost hills', and **Bàrr Reamhar** [868 674] 'Fat hill', but see under REAMHAR, and for **Barmollach** under MOLACH. For **Blarphern**, with its intrusive 'l', see under BLÀR.

BEALACH is popularly translated in Kintyre as 'gap' or 'opening', but 'pass' – which is the only definition Macbain gives – is better. As to etymology, he cites Irish *bealach*, 'pass, road', and tellingly offers a comparison with Sanskrit *bíla*, 'gap, mouth', which connects *bealach* with Gaelic *beul*, 'mouth'. In Ireland, according to the Flanagans, *bealach* means both 'road' and 'pass', with 'the common concept of "passage"'.[175]

The best known of the *bealach* names is **Bellochantuy** [662 323], to use the now-standard anglicisation. It is a notorious challenge to visitors, and, while I understand the sound that the '-tuy' ending represents, it is no longer heard, and 'Ballochantee' would better represent contemporary pronunciation. The meaning has long been debated, but *Bealach an t-suidhe*, 'Pass of the sitting', now appears to be accepted. In 1897, John Smith, tenant in High Bellochantuy, told D. J. Macdonald that 'people sat on the edge of the hill, where there is an old graveyard, on occasions when there were burials'; but there is no record of a graveyard there, and Macdonald suggested this explanation: 'The old road [re-routed by the coast in 1777] wound up the steep ascent in front of the village of Ballochantee, and kept the higher ground until within a few miles of Campbeltown. It was natural that the weary pedestrian should, on gaining the upper level, halt in order to draw breath. Hence the name Bealach-an-t-suidhe – the sitting pass.'[176] In 1775, the 'one merk land of Bellochantuy' was let on condition that the new lessee, Charles McNeill, should occupy the change house, or inn, and 'keep the same and stables ... in sufficient repair and properly filled up and provided for the entertainment and accommodation of Travelers – with at least three good furnished rooms and a kitchen besides suitable cellars and keeping places'.[177] In 1867, the 'small hamlet' comprised a few thatched cottages, a school, a public house, and a church, in which the parish minister officiated 'Sunday about' with the church at Cleit.[178] A selection of the oldest spellings: 1764 'Beallochantuigh'; 1775 'Bellochantuy'; 1789 'Beallochntugh'; 1800 'Ballochantugh'; 1813 'Bealachantuy'; 1832 'Ballochantuye'; 1848 'Ballachantie'. See also SUIDHE.

Bealach a' Chaochain [672 385] is no less of a challenge to pronounce, but the later among the old spellings may offer guidance: 1545 'Ballochtogreichane'; 1751 'Bellochichichan'; 1753 'Beallochgoachan'; 1769 'Ballochageachan'; 1772 'Bellochgoichan'; 1810 'Bealachgoichan'. In a legal document of 1830, the place was referred to as ' ... the pass of Ballachgoichan'. In 1977, Neil Thomson interpreted it as 'windy gap' and Donald Watson as 'windy opening', from *caochan*, 'eddy of air', but Ian A. Fraser considers *caochan* here to be literally 'little blind one', applied to 'a bog-stream which is overgrown by moss, but continues to flow a short distance underground'. The Ordnance Survey in 1867 also fixed on *caochan*, but in the sense of 'spirit or whisky' – Dwelly specifies 'whisky in its first process of distillation', Scots 'wash' – and linked it to 'smuggling' operations conducted in **Uamh Bealach-a-Chaochain**[179] (see also under UAMH). The reason so many early forms survive is that a three-merkland farm – also known as 'Belloch', 'Balloch' and 'Bulloch' – took its name from the pass. In 1779, there were 11 families there, 6 of them of 'tacksmen', or leaseholders, and 5 of them of cottars, or sub-tenants.[180] The present **Belloch** is at 672 378, and North Belloch, also known as **Achnaha**, was at 674 383.

When I visited Mrs Margaret Littleson at Killegruer farm on 5/3/1977, she was about 94 years old (she was born Margaret Black at Portavorrain in 1881). She soon asked me if I had heard about 'the

man and the boy that was lost in a snowstorm at Bealachagaichan'
– I hadn't. They were found 'dead wi' starvation' down on the shore,
but their horses were the wonder of the story. She was told they were
found the next morning eating thatch from the houses at Portavorrain.
This is clearly the same tragedy recorded in the *Argyllshire Herald* in
1866 and dated to 1826. Only one of the names was known, Donald
MacDonald, who was a son of Roderick/Roger MacDonald, a native
of Skye who died in Campbeltown at the age of 103 in 1865.[181] The
snowstorm broke about noon, and before nightfall had drifted 12
feet deep in places. The men worked on a Glenbarr farm and had
been to Largie for timber to repair a house. They decided to unyoke
the horses and continue on foot, but they strayed off the road within
half-a-mile of the village and next morning their corpses were found
in the shelter of a rock. In the mouth of the younger man was found
a bit of oat-cake, 'which he wanted sufficient strength to enable him
to chew'.[182]

Ballochgerran [703 463] is *Bealach a' Ghearrain*, 'Pass of the
Garron', which is Gaelic *gearran*, 'a gelding'.[183] The word entered
Scots as 'garron', defined in that language as 'a small sturdy type of
horse, used especially for rough hill work',[184] which corresponds to
the understanding in Kintyre. Duncan McNicol in Strathmollach,
whose peat-bank lay in a hollow, kept a garron for hauling the cut
peats by 'slipe' (sledge) to the higher drying ground.[185] The place-
name is of some antiquity – 'Ballochgorrane', 'Ballachgerran' and
'Ballochgarrane' are recorded in the 16th century – and may be
equated with 'Largie'; after the Macdonalds abandoned the castle at
Rhunahaorine, their new seat, with its 'hoary appearance of antiquity',
was built at Ballochgerran in 1857-9, only to be demolished in
1958.[186] The O.S. in 1867 described a 'fine mansion of the castellated
style' with a 'large garden and an ornamental demesne attached'.[187]
See also **Largie** under LEARG. The 'pass' or 'road' itself, wherever
located, was doubtless used by pack-horses in the transportation of
goods.

Ballochroy [727 521] represents *Bealach ruadh*, 'Red pass'. In
1857 Peter MacIntosh remarked of 'Bealachruadh Glen' that a 'good
many inhabitants resided in it fifty years back, but at present it is
almost depopulated, in order to leave space enough for the sheep
and heather fowl'.[188] This is an allusion to a 'clearance' of the glen
which ran through oral tradition in Kintyre but of which no firm
documentary evidence has so far emerged. An anonymous emigrant
from Kintyre referred in 1864 to the same event, but in even more

guarded terms: 'It will be well remembered when the deluge swept through Bellochroy and other estates it swept off corners in its course. Many a sore heart they had as they bundled and packed trying to save enough to take them to Canada.'[189]   What factors deterred these writers from supplying details, if details were known to them?   Mary MacIntyre, for one, would have known the story. She was 'possessed of a retentive memory, and being an interesting conversationalist both in Gaelic and English, she could recall many of the important happenings of her earlier days and relate these with a vividness that was remarkable'.   When she died on 25/3/1917 at Kilmory Place, Dalintober, she was in her ninetieth year.   Her father was John Campbell, 'schoolmaster, Ballochroy Glen', who emigrated to Canada when she was about 20 years old.[190]

The farm **Ballochgair** [775 274], for *Bealach geàrr*, 'Short pass', is on record back to 1502.[191] For **Bealach na Gaoith** see under GAOTH and for **Bealach a' Ghille Dhuibh** under GRIANAN.

BEINN.   Watson says that in 'old Gaelic' *benn* meant 'a horn' and then 'a peak' and that 'with reference to hills, strictly speaking it should be applied only to such as are peaked, and as a rule it is so applied'.[192]   Gillies, a lesser authority, describes *beinn* in similar terms: ' ... always a distinct mountain, rising sharp and definite to a top or point, like Ben Dorain, Ben More, etc.'[193]   In Ireland, *beann/binn* is 'peak' or 'mountain peak'.[194]   These definitions don't quite apply in Kintyre.   I can visualise plenty of peaked knolls in Kintyre landscapes, but no actual hills.   *Beinn* in Kintyre certainly relates to magnitude.   With two exceptions, all eight in mainland Kintyre are over 1000 ft. They are, south to north:

Beinn a' Theine	[601 073]	1263 ft.
Beinn na Lice	[602 085]	1405 ft.
Beinn Bhreac	[614 089]	1293 ft.
Beinn na Faire	[603 171]	923 ft.
Ben Gullion	[726 176]	1154 ft.
Beinn an Tuirc	[752 361]	1491 ft.
Beinn Bhreac	[752 386]	1398 ft.
Beinn Bhreac	[791 477]	791 ft.

On Sanda, two more O.S. names occur with the generic, **Beinn a' Theine** [722 046] and **Beinn na Béiste** [730 046], interpreted respectively as 'Hill of the firebrand' (*aithinne*) and 'Hill of the beast',[195] but these are comparatively minor features on an island whose highest point is 405 ft., and do not meet the criteria of the mainland bens. Another hill on Sanda has an interesting, if questionable, legend attached to it. **Prince Edward's Hill** or **Edward's Cairn**, as it appears on a 19th century estate map, traditionally commemorates Robert the Bruce's brother Edward, who was 'placed there to give timely notice to the king of the approach of danger',[196] presumably in 1306 (see Dunaverty under DÙN). From the old map, it would appear that the hill was the highest point of Sanda [730 043], unnamed on O.S. maps, which would make sense as a watch hill. The O.S. recorded an offshore **Prince Edward's Rock** [724 037], which was also assumed to be connected with Edward Bruce.[197] Bruce, whether on Sanda or not in 1306, became in 1316 the last *de facto* High King of Ireland and was killed in 1318 at the Battle of Faughart.[198]

For the first name on the list, **Beinn a' Theine**, see under TEINE. **Beinn na Lice**, nearby, is 'hill of the flat stone' – see LEAC. The third name at the Mull, **Beinn Bhreac**, is 'speckled hill' – see BREAC. Then comes **Beinn na Faire**, 'Hill of the Watching', a look-out point – see FAIRE. **Ben Gullion**, 'Hill of Shoulders', is discussed under GUALANN.

7. *BEINN. Ben Gullion, showing the 'shoulders' at top of picture, looking south across reservoir from Crosshill, summer of 1975, before the hill was planted with trees. Photograph by George McSporran.*

8. *BINNEIN. Jimmy MacDonald and dog Kosi atop Binnein Fithich, 15/5/2012. Photograph by the author.*

In mid-Kintyre there are three *beinn* names. **Beinn an Tuirc**, the highest hill in Kintyre, has an Ossianic legend attached to it, discussed at length under TORC. The two most northerly bens are both **Beinn Bhreac**, one of them just north of Beinn an Tuirc and the other near Cour. The latter gave its name to a small farm marked on the 1801 Langlands map as 'Benvreak', which the O.S. described in 1867 as the 'ruins of a shepherd's house at foot of Beinn Bhreac'.[199] When Duncan Colville visited the area c. 1950, he found 'a ruined cottage at the base of Beinn Bhreac ... converted into a sheep fank' [788 468]. See also under BREAC. *Beinn*, while admittedly not common in Kintyre, is entirely absent in the north of the peninsula.

BÉIST – see CAT.

BEITH is the Birch, a short-lived but common tree. As a place-name element, it is probably best known from the trio of neighbouring Largieside farms, **Beachar**, **Beachmenach** and **Beachmore**, except that 'beach' – as *beitheach* = 'birchwood' was anglicised – generally proved difficult to those who had never heard these names spoken. This wouldn't have mattered much but for the fact that when North Beachmore was a restaurant, and a very popular one at that, the pronunciation became a matter of debate. The uninitiated generally plumped for a pronunciation identical with English 'beach', as in shore, but 'bay-ach' is correct. The generic is also found in Ireland, and, closer to home, the town of Beith in Ayrshire is '(place of) birches'.[200]

Beachar [693 432] is *Beitheach charra*, 'Birchwood of the standing stone', Beachmenach [688 427] is *Beitheach meadhonach*, 'Middle birchwood' – which geographically it is – and finally Beachmore is *Beitheach mhór*, 'Big birchwood'. South Beachmore is at 685 414 and North at 689 419, but the latter was also known as **Gaigan** from at least the late 18th century.[201]

Beachar takes its name from the standing stone, or *carragh* – the tallest in Kintyre – on its land. The round-bottomed pottery vessels excavated in 1892 from the Neolithic cairn there, embedded this place-name in archaeological nomenclature as 'Beacharra ware', which describes 'the most important pottery series ... characteristic of the *Clyde cairns* as a whole'.[202] The O.S. interpretation of 'Beachair', incidentally, was 'beehive',[203] from *beach*, 'bee, bee-hive', etc.[204]

Prehistoric remains on the landscape were seen as the creations of giants and heroes. Standing stones, of which 34 were identified in Kintyre by 1971, were raised in the Bronze Age,[205] the archaeological period roughly between 2000 and 500 B.C. These monoliths, some grouped, but most of them standing in isolation, tended in legend to have got where they are as missiles hurled by feuding giants. The Beachar monolith may well have had such a legend attached to it, but, if so, it was replaced by a story which featured the Cara Broonie, that helpmate of the Macdonald family of Largie. That he was a little person, or at least a spirit manifest in miniature, renders his feat all the more remarkable. He emerged from sleep one day over on Cara Island and said to himself, 'There's a stone in my boot', so he took off his boot and heaved the annoying stone through the air and it 'landed over in Beachar hill – that's the standing stone'.[206]

Early forms include: 1502/7 'Beachcar', 'Beythacarra', and 'Beauchaquharrar'; 1545 'Baiauchter'; 1675 'Beachar'; 1751 'Beacher'. In 1937, John Macdougall in Beachar was moved to write to Sheriff Macmaster Campbell on aspects of the name which vexed him: 'Some make out that it should be spelled with a "d" added, making it "Beachard" but this does not appeal to me, in the first place because the proper name of the farm is "High Beachar". It would be strange to call it "High Beachard" and in the second place there is another "Beachard" within a mile of this. To me a more probable origin of the word is that there is on the farm a standing stone, 17 feet high, called in Gaelic "an Cara". On account of this some make out that the name ought to be "Beach-a-Cara" or given shortly "Beachara". In my young days all the old people pronounced the name "Bay-a-Cara".[207] The location of 'Beachard' mentioned by John Macdougall has so far eluded me.

In 1502, 'Beachmanach' was recorded for Beachmenach, and 'Beauch' and 'Beauchewir' for Beachmore. In a plan of 'Beachmor Hill' by James Robertson in 1832, an elongated area of 153.977 Scots acres – 'Common to High and North Farms' – contains in the north-west corner 'Shepherds house', in the north-east corner 'Creag an daurain', in the south-east 'Cnoc Ach na teang' and in the south-west 'Nactachall scoill'.[208]

South of Tarbert lie the ruins of **Allt Beithe** [885 668], beside the 'Birch Burn' from which the settlement took its name. That this was formerly a place of some importance is clear from its appearance in early records: 1481 'Altbeith'; 1642 'Altbeoch' and 1669 'Altbea'. Some of its inhabitants are known by name: in 1683 Malcolm McIlcher, 'Aldbc'; in 1786 John macPhaiden, 'Altbea'; in 1799 Donald McVicar, 'Altbeatha',[209] and in C1841 John Leitch, fisherman, 'Altbea'.

That Allt Beithe remains well known is attributable to the attention paid to it by writers, chief among these the Tarbert poet George Campbell Hay, who was drawn there in his youthful wanderings. In his Gaelic poem *Luinneag*, he evokes Allt Beithe as a loved place recalled to memory in England: '*Gu'n tig fuaim an Uillt Bheithe / eadar mise s mo chadal*' ('The sound of the Birch Burn / comes between me and my sleep.') It was from George in 1979 that I heard the tale of a MacFarlane wizard who arrived at Allt Beithe in a day of blistering heat and asked the women there for a drink of milk, and, when they refused him and told him to take a drink from the burn, produced a hazel twig from a pouch under his arm and began jabbing it into the thatch of the house, causing the women to perform a supernatural dance until they collapsed in exhaustion, a punishment which he considered salutary.[210]

To Allt Beithe is also attached the tradition of a visitation by plague, to which the settlement's desertion is attributed. The family, by name Leitch – enumerated there in the 1841 census, above – was almost decimated, but one of the surviving children, Archibald, became a ship's carpenter and established a boat-yard which he ran with his sons Dugald and Calum. Archibald, who died in 1930 at the age of 87, was a great-grandfather of John Smith (1938-94), leader of the Labour Party and a future prime minister of Great Britain had death not intervened.[211]

Allt nam Beithe [792 378], 'Stream of the Birches', flows near Bridgend, Carradale. There are two of **Achadh Beithe**, 'Birch Field', one a ruined cottage at the side of the road up to Lussa Loch [712 261], and another on Kilmory farm, Largieside.[212] For **Innean Beithe** see under INNEAN.

BINNEIN, diminutive of BEINN, is 'pinnacle',[213] and is 'often applied to hills that taper to a sharp point'.[214] In Kintyre, however, just as *beinn* does not carry a sense of 'peaked', neither does *binnein* from what I can judge from the few surviving examples. Graham McKinlay's interpretation of **Am Binnein Buidhe** was 'The small yellow ben', which he described as the top of **Creag a' Chreamha**,[215] to which refer under CREAMH. The name was also, by transference as a landmark, a submerged rock and ring-net 'fast', or snag, off **Greenhill** [794 345].[216] For **Binnein dà Néill** [650 072], Carskey, the O.S. in 1866 was given 'Hillock of the two Neills'.[217] It is something of a linguistic curiosity. The K.A.S. place-names committee tried 'The pinnacle of the two Neils', but considered it 'very doubtful' and moved into more creative space, finally agreeing that there might be 'some connection with *neul*: cloud'.[218] 'Pinnacle/hillock of the two clouds' hardly seems likely unless some now-forgotten legend lies behind it; but, in any case, one of the derivations of the forename Neil (Gaelic *Niall*) is *neul*, 'cloud', from Old Irish *nél*.[219] I went looking for that *binnein* on 3/8/2012. The feature isn't at all clearly marked on maps and I decided that it must be a stac. I climbed the slope above the likeliest rock to have a clearer look at it, and was actually on Binnein dà Néill without realising it. It was after I left my resting-place and began ascending towards the Mull road that I looked back over the fence I'd crossed and saw the perfectly rounded hillock. Like certain other knolls I know, the defining shape is visible only from certain angles, and I had found the right one by accident. While I was on the hillock, smoking and watching little groups of gannets streaming westward at eye-level, a 'cloud' of noisy gulls suddenly appeared. Their unexpected flurry was explained seconds later when a screeching peregrine falcon passed over me. **Binnein Fithich,** despite its appearance in Illustration 8, viewed from directly beneath, is not characteristically peaked. See under FITHEACH.

BLÀR in place-names has a range of meanings, of which 'field', 'plain', 'peat-moss' and 'battle' are perhaps the most relevant here;

but the primary sense is *blàr*, 'spot'.[220] **Blary** [696 373] in Barr Glen is not a straightforward construction, but is most likely to be *blàraidh*, 'Place of many level fields'. D. J. Macdonald suggested *blàr*, 'field', and – with question mark – *ì*, 'island'. By way of explanation he notes, 'probably so called because enclosed on two sides by Barr river and stream',[221] but this, while true, may be a case of seeing too much. Blary was originally a one-merkland holding, the early forms of which are: 1502 'Blaar'; 1507 'Blaeir'; 1545 'Blaarie'; 1596 'Blair'; 1605 'Blarie'. **Allt a' Bhlàir** [733 373] rises north of the wind farm near Beinn an Tuirc. For **Sgeir a' Bhlàir** see under SGEIR.

Blarphern on the Learside appears to belong here, but has been interpreted *Bàrr fèarna*, 'Alder height', on the strength of early spellings, which demonstrate that the 'l' is intrusive. The first record, in 1481, is 'Barfarnay', and the 'bar-' generic continues through the 16th century until, in 1596, 'Blairfairne' appears. This form recurs in 1605, after which the name dies, being preserved only as part of an amalgam with Glenmurrell, Clachavulline and Caorphin (in a lease of 1776, it was described as a 'Pendicle of Corphine'). The location of this holding has been the subject of speculation, with the nameless ruin [767 156] at the foot of Corphin Glen being suggested, but the early disappearance of Blarphern as an independent holding would appear to rule out that 18th/19th century building.[222]

BODACH is basically 'old man', the partner word of CAILLEACH. I remember hearing some of the old folk in Kintyre, with Gaelic or a smattering of it, call the little cod that spend their youth among the offshore rocks and tangles, 'bodach ruadhs' (*bodaich-ruaidh*), 'red old men', from the tinge on their skin, which served as camouflage. **Cruach a' Bhodaidh** [731 448], well inland from Tayinloan, translates as 'Hill of the Old Man' (but see also CRUACH). Named topographical features, as distinct from settlements, are relatively rare in Kintyre records before the Ordnance Survey's arrival in the mid-1860s, but this one appeared in 1736 as 'Cruachvoddy' in the statements of witnesses in a boundary dispute. **Gortean a bhodaich**, 'Old man's little corn field', was on Barruchdarach farm.[223] For **Bodach nan Gabhar**, 'Old Man of the Goats', see under GOBHAR.

Drumore na bodach [674 329] is popularly interpreted 'Big ridge of the old man', one of the quirkiest of Kintyre place-names. The form is also quirky and should probably be either plural *Druim mór nam bodaich* or singular *a' bhodaich*. There is no tradition of who the old man was, but the name is an old one – 'Drummoirnabodach' in 1545. The holding was of two merklands and was one of the Lands of Saint Ninian, which belonged to the Priory of Whithorn in Galloway until 1584, when acquired by Archibald Campbell, 'Lord of the fief of Argyll'.[224] In the 19th century there was a 'changehouse' attached to the farm. In 1854, when Donald McKendrick was tenant, it was one of three inns where the mail-car horses were changed, the others being at Clachan and Tayinloan. The contractor for the service was Donald MacDonald, flesher in Campbeltown, who operated with 'Dog Carts or Cars seated to carry three passengers and a Driver'. The car generally left Tarbert at about 3 p.m. and arrived in Campbeltown at about 8.30.[225] The name appears in records shortened to **Drumore**, now the house [665 326] at the north end of Bellochantuy village.

Robert Fraser, innkeeper at Drumorenabodach in the early 1870s, was no stranger to the courts in Campbeltown. He belonged to Stirlingshire and appears to have had a violent temper, which can't have encouraged business. His most controversial court appearance was in January 1875, when he was tried for a serious assault on James McDermaid, shepherd at Arnicle. Against the advice of the presiding sheriff, Fraser chose to conduct his own defence. He was found not guilty, a verdict which drew upon the jury much public ridicule. Here, in admirable prose, is the *Argyllshire Herald* reporter's description of mine host himself: 'The accused being rather a famous man in his way, on entering the court, we naturally turned our attention to the dock, to have a good look at him. There he leaned back in the far-off corner, his right arm resting on the dock, his hand tightly closed, and his eyes half shut, with the air of one fully conscious that he would astonish the whole assemblage. His hair appeared to have been innocent of comb or scissors for at least six months, and his whole appearance betokened that a liberal supply of soap and water might be beneficially bestowed upon him.'[226]

BODHA/BOGHA. Malcolm Maclennan is expansive in his definition of *bodha*: 'a rock over which the sea breaks; a rock visible only at low tide, and often not visible at all; the wave called a heaver.' Like SGEIR, also a sea rock, *bodha* comes from a Norse word, *bodi*, 'a breaker, boding a sunken rock or bank'.[227] Considering the seafaring history of the Vikings, it is hardly surprising that their language left such a mark on the nomenclature of the western seaboard. But what is this wave, which Dwelly, under *bogha*, also calls a 'heaver'?[228] It is one which, as in the Norse definition, is thrown up by the unseen rock it encounters, and it may be assumed that the word for the revelatory wave passed to the rock itself. In maritime history, before reliable charts were created, such phenomena were crucial in the navigation of unfamiliar waters, and the senses of all experienced seamen would be attuned to the reception and interpretation of danger signs.

There are perhaps six Kintyre *bodha* names, none recorded by the Ordnance Survey, all applying to offshore rocks, and four of them concentrated around Uisaed Point at Machrihanish. In fact, the short stretch of coast on either side of old Pans village is thick with place-names. The explanation isn't hard to find. Not only was there a settled community there – Gaelic-speaking in the 19th century – but fishing families made up a big part of that community, and wherever fishermen operate, names will proliferate: for little harbours, for line-fishing banks, for reefs and rocks which may be hazardous in certain conditions and productive in others, and so on.

'So on' includes the practice of snatching edible crabs from their rock lairs, and **Bogha a' Chrùbain**, 'Crab Rock', was one which could be visited in the near-certainty of catching a few crabs for the pot or for bait; but see CRÙBAN. The name **Bogha Néill Bhàin** appears to have covered two rocks off Clachaig a' Bhorran, both submerged at high tide, and only the inner one showing at low tide. This is 'Fair Neil's Rock', but no tradition survives as to why it was given the name. W. F. H. Nicolaisen records a similar name near the Butt of Lewis, Bodha Dhomhnuill Bhàin, 'the (submerged) rock of Fair Donald'.[229] **Bogha Fad**, near the old lifeboat house, is the 'Long Rock', and the last has been rendered **Boghas an Duine** [629 209], with the suggestions *Bogha an duine*, 'Rock of the man', or *Bogha sean duine*, 'Rock of the old man'. John Cameron questioned these derivations and suggested that 'bois' might be a corruption of either *bodhaig*, 'figure or person', or *bathais*, 'forehead or front'.[230] Perhaps, after all, there are only three rocks named *bodha* at Machrihanish.

BOG is 'wet', 'marshy', just what it means in English, which borrowed the word from Irish and Gaelic. The curious place-name **Bogwilly**, which appears on the Langlands 1793 map east of Gobagrennan and south of Clachfin, has been interpreted as a corruption of *Beag-bhail*, 'Little farm', but cf. 'Bog Willie' on Arran, which has been interpreted as *boglach*, 'marshy or wet ground'.[231] **The Boggrie**, Southend, which was evidently a piece of land for which MacNeill of Carskey was paid rent in 1729, has been interpreted as *Bogaraidh*, 'a marshy place',[232] but Gilbert Márkus suggests that the specific might represent *àirigh*, 'sheiling'.²³³ **Bog Beag**, 'Little Bog', was merely a bit of a field on the Laggan farm of Darlochan.²³⁴

BÒRD, 'table', is from English 'board'. Of **Bordadubh** steading [725 314] only a bit of wall is left standing to mark its location. John Cameron questioned the interpretation *Bòrd Dubh*, 'Black Table', noting that in native pronunciation he heard the plural *dubha*. 'Borddadow' is the spelling in a charter of 1633.²³⁵ After its abandonment as a shepherd's house, Bordadubh became an outdoor centre for youth groups. **Bòrd Mór** [752 339], which stands at 1338 ft. two miles north-east of Bordadubh, was interpreted weakly as 'Big hill' by the O.S. ²³⁶

BRÀGHAD originally meant 'neck' or 'throat',²³⁷ but in place-names denotes 'upper', and there are several of them, variously anglicised. The location of the settlement shown as **Brade** on the 1801 Langlands map is unknown, but **Braid Hill** [737 340] must indicate roughly where it was. The hill is in Killean Parish, but the settlement was in Saddell. It appears to have been the upper part of Iffernan (Ifferdale), as indicated in the earliest of the old spellings: 1556, 1626, 1634 'Bradiffernan'. The *bràghad* generic was attached to three Killean Parish settlements, Kilmory, Auchaluskin, and Drumnamucklach, which appear in a row on the 1793 Langlands map. In 1797, Archibald McConnachy, 'alias Campbell', stated that the sub-tenants in 'Braid Auchaloisken' and 'Braid Drumnamucklach' had been 'in runrig possession with the tackswoman in Drumnamucklach',²³⁸ by then, in Kintyre, a rare reference to the traditional system of rotational land-distribution. The only reference to a 'Braid' in the work horse tax lists of 1797-8 appears between 'Achaluskin' and 'Drumnamucklach': Duncan McDougal had five horses there.²³⁹ On North Corputechan farm there is **Auchabrad** [677 333] for *Achadh a' bhràghaid*, in 1867 'a house with some ruins and a sheepfold attached'.²⁴⁰ There are two of the same name in Kilcalmonell Parish, **Achavraid** [785 578] near Clachan, and **Auchabrad** [756 521], the name of which was changed to **Minen**. The O.S. interpreted the former as *Achadh a' bhràghaid*, 'The field of the gully'.²⁴¹ For the Learside holding **Balnabraid** [753 158], alternative interpretations have been offered, *Baile a' bhràghaid*, 'The gully farm', and *Baile a' bhràghad*, 'The upland farm'.²⁴² Finally, **Braid Buie**, a 'slope' on Langholm, Southend, interpreted as *Bràghad Buidhe*, 'Yellow gully or upland',

and described as a 100-acre farm in C1861, and **Leth-bhràgadh,**[243] to which refer under LETH. I can find no dictionary justification for the interpretation 'gully', unless as an extension of *bràghad*, 'throat' = gullet.

BREAC is Gaelic 'speckled' or 'spotted' and is a common descriptor in place-names. **Auchenbreck** [783 440] in Carradale Glen, is *Achadh Breac*, 'Speckled Field'; **Breckachy** [670 268] has the same meaning, but in reverse, *Breac achaidh*. **Beinn Bhreac** is 'Speckled Hill', and there are two in Saddell parish, at 791 477 – also the name of a nearby settlement – and at 752 386, a Kintyre giant at 1398 ft.

Breac is one of those Gaelic adjectives, like RIABHACH, which requires some effort to 'see' on the landscape what those who gave the names were seeing. For a 'speckled hill' one can imagine a surface strewn with light-catching stones; and for a 'speckled field' perhaps stones again, or flowers, in profusion and variety long since a faded memory in these times of routine chemical intervention.

Breac is also, aptly, the Gaelic name for the trout (*Salmo trutta*), in which sense it appears in **Loch nam Breac** [794 482], 'Loch of the Trout', a little moorland loch inland from Cour, described in 1843 as containing fish of 'exquisite quality', from two to four pounds in weight.[244]

In **Breaclaraich**, the adjective precedes the noun it qualifies. There are two places named 'speckled ruin' in Kintyre. One, a farm – and now, indeed, a ruin – is in upper Carradale Glen, at c. 778 450. In 1758, Duncan, son of Archd McOlchallum, 'Brecklarrach', was baptised there.[245] It disappeared into coniferous forest, but was restored to view in the mid-1990s after clear-felling. Iain McAlister explored the ruin and its environs in 1995 and photographed a corn-kiln, a knockin-stane — a stone with a cup hollowed out of it in which barley was pounded; see *By Hill and Shore in South Kintyre*, pp. 255-56, for description of method and discussion of the knockin-stane at Innean Dùnain ruins — and a chimney-head of peculiar construction.[246] The other, at 875 687, was described in 1867 as a 'Small ruin a little S. of pier at mouth of E. Loch Tarbert',[247] but the name was subsequently revived, and the poet George Campbell Hay rented a flat in the house of that name when he returned to Tarbert, briefly and for the last time, in 1983.[248]

I notice that on recent O.S. maps **Glenbreackrie** has been given a Gaelic form, *Gleann Breacàirigh*, 'Valley of the speckled sheiling', and rightly so. This is a wide, deep-reaching glen, once heavily populated. A walker, in August 1921, described a charming sight at the head of the glen: 'At Achnaslishag we turn off the road and make for Glenahanty. Beneath us lie Dalsmirran and Amod nestling among trees by the waters of the Brekerie. In a sunlit field by the riverside are lads and lassies ricking hay – a beautiful study of light and shade being completed by the dark background of the hill of Remuil.'[249]

In *The Place-Names of the Parish of Southend*, **Brecklate** [690 120] was interpreted as Norse *Breidha-klett*, 'The broad eminence or brow', in preference to Cameron Gillies's *Breac-leathad*, 'Speckled slope',[250] but Ian A. Fraser considers Gillies's interpretation 'the more likely in this case'.[251]

Pollan Breac [794 502], in North Kintyre, is 'Little speckled pool', and was described by the O.S. in 1867 as a 'very small loch at head of Gleann Cailliche Beag'.[252] On the 1793 Langlands map it appeared as 'Polinbreck'. On the farm of Killegruer, a field named **Creagan breac**, 'Speckled crags', and on Glenacardoch one named **Barr a' bhreac**, 'Speckled top'.[253] See also **Cruach Bhreac** under CRUACH.

BUAILE is essentially a cattle-fold, though in Ireland the 'booley' equated more with summer pasturing of cattle (see under ÀIRIGH). Before the fencing of land became prevalent, cattle had to be watched constantly to prevent their raiding crops and straying on to neighbouring grazings or dangerous terrain. **Cnocan a' Bhuachaill** [793 329] at Whitestone is 'The Herd's Knoll', from which was afforded a 'commanding view of the whole area', as Graham McKinlay recalled in 1977. The herds were often children who stayed with the cattle all day, then brought them home to be milked and folded for the night. (In winter, the livestock lived indoors with the people.) These cattle-enclosures may still be seen on unimproved landscapes, for example on the coast between Machrihanish and the Mull. They are commonly circular and low-walled, but the cattle were apparently content to stay put, as long as there was ample grazing for them inside.

I know of just two *buaile* place-names in Kintyre, near Cour, **Cnoc na Buaile Salaich** [811 494] and **Allt na Buaile Salaich** [825 492], a hill just over 700 ft., and a burn to the east of it. They are close together and no doubt relate to the same feature, which is itself now obscure. The O.S. interpreted *buaile salaich* as 'foul shealing'[254]

– *salach* is 'dirt' – but 'dirty enclosure' might be preferable. Gaelic for a sheep-enclosure is *fang*, from Scots 'fank', but I am aware of only one place-name in Kintyre incorporating the word, **Allt na Faing** [625 138], 'Stream of the sheep-pen', near Glenahanty; the O.S. map-form might be better as *Allt an Fhaing*.[255]

BUIDHE is 'yellow', and, as Cameron Gillies put it poetically, its applications run 'all the way from clay to gold'.[256] It is a very common adjective in Kintyre place-names, partly, I suppose, because there are no competing terms for 'yellow'. In landscape names the colour may have a botanical origin – gorse on hills and buttercups in fields, for example. Coastal names – notably the reefs called **Sgeir Bhuidhe** (see under SGEIR) – generally describe dense barnacle and limpet encrustations, which in certain light conditions have a pale-yellow appearance.

Cnoc Buidhe [695 307], 'Yellow Hill', stands at 1023 ft. west of Lussa reservoir. **Knockbay** [724 192], the farm at Kilkerran, also represents *Cnoc buidhe*,[257] though the sound of the colour is lost in the anglicisation. The feature after which the farm was named was in doubt until I checked the O.S. record of 1866, which described it as 'a small prominent eminence' north-east of the farmhouse,clearly the quarried hill [726 194] opposite the cemetery. On 'the hill called Knockbae' in 1605, the King's Lieutenant Lord Scone held a court and received the submission of Angus MacDonald of Dunyveg and his Kintyre vassals. [258] **Dalbuy** [691 138] in Southend Parish is *Dail buidhe*, 'Yellow field'. During a thunderstorm in May 1864, a 'ball of fire' appeared inside the steading there. A big mirror was shattered, the mantel-piece split and its ornaments scattered about the room along with plaster from above the fire-place.[259]

Leac Bhuidhe, south of Machrihanish, is the 'Flat yellow rock', but see under LEAC. **Carnbuie**, close to the head of West Loch Tarbert, is 'Yellow Cairn', but see under CÀRN. **Glenbuie** [886 573], near Skipness, is *Gleann Buidhe*, 'Yellow Glen'. In the 19th century it was a small farm, and Duncan Campbell was there when C1841 was taken. This list could continue, but I conclude with two examples from D. J. Macdonald's 'West Kintyre Field Names' (p 37): **Druimbuidhe**, 'Yellow ridge' (one on Beacharra and another on Auchadaduie) and **Àiridh bhuidhe**, 'Yellow shieling' (Portavorrain).

BUN is 'foot' or 'bottom', a sense which is clear in **Bun na h-Abhainn**, 'Foot of the River', the original Gaelic name for the little village of **Waterfoot** [801 372].[260] **Bun an Uisge** [623 197] has the same meaning – *uisge* is 'water' – and applies to the mouth of the little stream at the south end of the Galdrans.[261] For **Bunlarie** see under LÀRACH.

CAIBEAL is 'chapel', from Latin *capella*.[262] The chapel and burial-ground in Glenadale, Southend, appears on O.S. maps as **Caibeal Cairine** [643 113], but **Caibeal Caitrìona**, 'Catherine's Chapel', was the local name. The dedication is evidently to Saint Catherine,[263] who is commemorated also in nearby **Saint Catherine's Well** (see under TOBAR). Cameron Gillies ascribed the name, along with **Carrine** – two farms at the lower end of Glenbreackerie – to Saint Ciaran,[264] mere guesswork on his part. **Caepil Iunan co-Caillach**, south of Largiebaan, is an enigma on which few words need be expended, but see under INNEAN. **The Caibeal** [794 361] at Torrisdale appears to be a relatively modern name. T. Harvey Thomson speculates on the existence of a chapel in the wood at Torrisdale Castle known as the **Caibeal Wood**,[265] but archaeologists in 1962 found no trace of such a structure, only a private cemetery in which the earliest legible inscription was early 19th century.[266]

CAILLEACH is basically 'old woman', but has a range of meanings, including 'witch' and 'nun'. The word comes from Old Irish *caillech*, 'veiled one',[267] i.e. a nun. In Kintyre, as elsewhere, the last sheaf of corn to be cut was prized by the harvester who secured it, and a bunch from it – the *cailleach* – would be crossed or plaited, dressed in ribbons and hung on the kitchen wall until New Year, when it would be fed to the oldest cow or horse.[268]

Innean Coig Cailleiche, the ruined township near Largiebaan, was traditionally associated with five nuns who sought refuge there during the travails of the Reformation. The story is almost certainly fictitious – see under INNEAN – but the 'five old women' of the place-name remain inexplicable, unless the reference is to a group of natural features, such as rocks or mounds. **Cailleach Uchd an Tùir**, 'The Old Woman of Uchd an tùir' (see under UCHD), was a small, detached rock on Tangy shore, below the gamekeeper's house. It was 'exceedingly like an old woman in a sitting posture', until, some time in the 19th century, 'Baldy' McSporran, who was 'subject to fits of insanity', hurled a rock at it and damaged its appearance. He was said to have shouted (in Gaelic) as he hurled the missile, 'I've been long enough looking at you, Old Woman of Uchd an Tùir, your mouth spouting rubbish.'[269] The O.S. defined **Allt Caillich** [683 355], near High Margmonagach, as 'Old Wife's Stream'.[270] **Allt na Cailliche** [811 387] flows past the west end of Carradale village. Charles Reppke recorded a tradition that a 'vagrant woman was drowned in the burn and that her spirit haunts the locality. Some local people,' he added, 'have an aversion to passing over the bridge after dark'. **Loch Caillich** [795 514], 'Old Woman's Loch',[271] is west of Crossaig, close to the boundary between Skipness and Kilcalmonell parishes.

CAISTEAL is 'castle', from Latin *castellum*.[272] In surviving Gaelic place-names in Kintyre, *caisteal* is usually attached to a natural feature, but that wasn't always the case. '**Macharie-castell**' in Southend, first recorded in 1562, represents *Machair a' chaisteil*, 'Machair of the castle' (see MACHAIR), the field on Machribeg farm [686 080] – now a caravan site – which extends to the headland on which the castle of Dunaverty once stood.[273]

Castle Moil [c. 742 209] was the fortified house on High Askomil which Sir James MacDonald infamously set alight in 1598, in a feud involving the Macalisters of Loup. His parents were inside the house at the time, and his badly burned father, Angus MacDonald of Dunyveg, was taken in chains to Smerby Castle and imprisoned there.[274] This house is recorded in various guises – as 'Caisteal Maoil', 'Moil Castle', 'Askomel House' and 'Moyle House' – and appears on the Langlands draft map of 1793, squeezed in as 'Castle Moil'. The Gaelic form, *Caisteal Maoil*, was interpreted by Donald McKinlay, librarian in Campbeltown, as 'Bald Castle', from its roofless state after the fire, but J. Macmaster Campbell offered a derivation from *mal*, 'rent', suggesting that it was there 'the local rents of the Macdonalds used to be paid or collected'.[275] The meaning is obscure, just as the precise location of the site is unknown; I have looked for it, without success, as have others before me.

Port a' Chaisteil [654 272], north of Westport, is 'Castle Port', from a nearby dun [654 273] on a prominent rock, which, according to tradition in 1867, was 'used for a beacon fire when Kintyre was subject to invasion'.[276] **An Caisteal** is simply 'The Castle', and the name occurs thrice in Kintyre. In Barr Glen [702 376] it was given to an oval dun on a rocky knoll;[277] it was a field-name on High Dunashery farm, but the feature referred to is unknown;[278] and it was attached to a 'bold rocky crag'[279] [772 453] in Carradale Glen, now rather obscured by afforestation. **Cnoc a' Chaisteil** [841

666], 'The Castle Hill', on West Loch Tarbert, took its name 'from a large portion of slate rock forming a somewhat rude resemblance to a tower'.[280] The name also occurs in English relating to natural features, e.g. **The Castles** [746 101], three rock pinnacles on the shore at Polliwilline.[281] For **Roc a' Chaisteil** see under ROC.

CALLTUINN is the Hazel (*Corylus avellana*), which provides autumnal nuts and whose coppiced wood had many traditional uses: as hurdles (for fencing or bridging: see under GORT), in basket-making, and as crooks and walking-sticks.

In *The Place-Names of the Parish of Campbeltown* (p 14), the interpretation 'Hazel Stream' for **Calliburn** [720 255] is offered as a probability, but behind that unsubstantiated one-line summation lay much vexation. D. J. Macdonald had suggested, and I quote exactly: 'From "Cal", water (Root "cal", sound) and "bùrn", water.' He added in the margin: 'A case of re-duplication (*sic*) – common.'[282] Duncan Colville clearly brought up this place-name during his meeting with Professor Watson (p 214), and remarks in the 'Schedules' that Watson 'was emphatic in saying that Rev. D. J. M. was wrong'. Watson instead proposed *callach* (genitive *callaigh*), 'hazel place', in support of which Colville cites footnote 39 on page *xxxv* of Watson's *Place-Names of Ross and Cromarty* (1904). John Cameron at first accepted Watson's suggestion, but had second thoughts: 'Possibly Lowland, but may be translation of *Allt na Caile* = Girl's Burn.'

Interpretation of 'Calliburn' is complicated, indeed quite possibly negated, by its earlier form **Killypole** and variants: 1545 'Callebull'; 1629 'Cailzieboll'; 1650 'Kellipull'; 1751 'Kylipol'.[283] The earliest form of 'Calliburn' which I have been able to find is a lease of 1775 which refers to 'Callyburn'; and in 1809, Donald Blue, 'tenant at Taycroman and son of Donald Blue, Miller at Killean', signed the lease for 'The Miln of Callyburn or Kylipoll and Croft Lands'.[284] The compilers of *The Place-Names of the Parish of Campbeltown* (p 30), treating Killypole distinctly, offered a Norse derivation, *Kolli-bol*, 'The summit steading', while Cameron Gillies, treating the two names as one, plumped for a derivation from *coille*, 'wood', remarking that although both forms were corrupt, 'the one explains the other in a very interesting way';[285] but he doesn't explain the explanation.

There is another Killypole [640 177] on Lossit Estate, with a loch next to it which also carries the name, for which the alternative suggested derivation was *coille*, 'wood' + *poll*, 'pool'.[286] It is ruinous now, but was occupied in 1940 by a shepherd, Jamie McShannon, with whom Hamish Henderson, quite by chance, enjoyed a night of song.[287] Jamie's repertoire that night included 'Boys of Calliburn', the moving Kintyre emigration song, which takes us back to where we started. (In *Tocher* 25, p 40, one of two versions published was recorded in 1958 from Jamie's brother, Alec, but under the title 'Machrihanish'. Willie Mitchell and his family knew the song as 'Boys of Calliburn'.[288])

Denis Rixson (2010) has suggested for these 'Killypole' names a derivation from Old Norse *ból*, 'farm', citing 'Killepoll' (1502-5) for the first and 'Calybole' (1485, 1481) for the second.[289] See also PUBULL.

'Calton' in **Calton Hill** [713 211], Campbeltown, is clearly *calltuinn*, 'hazel'. The hill was ringed with council houses after the Second World War and one of the streets was named Calton Avenue. In Killean and Kilchenzie Parish **Allt Calltuinn**, 'Hazel Stream', occurs twice [736 451 and 755 462], and in a charter of 1502 'Altcaltyn', the same, is linked with 'Gorttenafale' (Gortnafal) north of Tayinloan. A field on Largie was called simply **A' Challtuinn**.[290] For **Glac Challtuinn**, 'Hazel Hollow', see under GLAC.

CALMAN in place-names would have been the Rock Dove (*Columba livia*), which roosts and nests in coastal caves and fissures. As a consequence of interbreeding with the Feral Pigeon, which shares its scientific name, its genetic purity is now suspect, and numbers in Kintyre are decreasing.[291] These pigeons can still be seen, in small numbers, from the cliffs at Dùn Bàn and the Aignish. The Gaelic name has several guises – *calaman, calman, colman* and *columan* – all of which stem from Latin *columbus, columba*,[292] which latter is the generic of the scientific name. **Uamh nan Calman** [839 521], 'The Pigeons' Cave', on the coast north of Crossaig, was described by the O.S. as a 'large chasm in rock situated about 10 chains S. of Port Alasdair Ruadh'.[293] **Allt Calmain** [762 273], 'Pigeon Stream', is on Ardnacross farm, and **Cnoc nan Calaman**, 'Pigeon hillock', on Amod farm, Barr Glen.[294]

CAMAS/CAMUS. *Cam* in Gaelic is 'crooked' or 'bent', and the word is all around us: the surnames Campbell (*Caimbeul*, 'crooked mouth') and Cameron (*Camshron*, 'crooked nose') have it, as well as place-names; and I used to hear it from old Dalintober fishermen, who would talk of a 'cam', or bend, in a mast or bowsprit. *Camus* in place-names is a bay with a well-defined bend in it, and there are only three on the Kintyre coast, all of them between Tarbert and Skipness.

The most northerly is **Camus na Ban-tighearna** [896 659], 'The Lady's Bay'. 'Lady' here is 'gentlewoman', an expression not much encountered now. Archie Smith has a tradition, from his father Malcolm, that the lady in question was Anna Campbell, daughter of a laird of Skipness. When she and Charles MacAlister, laird of Tarbert (died 1741), were courting, they would meet at the bay, which was roughly half-way between their homes. As a trysting-place, it isn't exactly an easy spot to reach, but it's probably as close as we'll get now to an explanation of the name. Both Charles and Anna are buried together in Cill Aindreis, the cemetery in Tarbert. Camus na Ban-tighearna is the boundary between Kilcalmonell and Skipness parishes, and was also known to fishermen as **Colla's Bight**, from the forename *Coll*.[295]

Camus na Cèardaich [914 625] is 'Bay of the Smithy'. Given the remoteness of the spot, it is unlikely that there was ever a smithy there, so a connection with itinerant tin-smiths seems more likely; and that is how Tarbert fishermen understood the name. According to Willie McDougall in 1980, when Queen Victoria sailed the 'Royal Route' in 1847, she remarked when passing Camus na Cèardaich that 'it was the best bit of scenery she had seen'. I have failed to find where Willie got the anecdote.

Camus an Tobair [920 602] does not appear on O.S. maps and was almost certainly named by fishermen. It translates as 'Bay of the Well', though some fishermen, such as John Weir in Tarbert,[296] interpreted it more literally as 'Bend of the Well'. It was one of the coastal springs which skiff fishermen would visit to refill their water-casks.[297] There is, indeed, in that bay, a well marked **Tobar a' Ghaill** [919 602], which the O.S. translated as 'The Lowlander's Well',[298] though *gall* can also mean 'rock, stone, pillar-stone'.

CAORA is a sheep. Before the advent of intensive sheep-stocking in the 18th century, the small native breed was reared almost exclusively for domestic use: wool for clothing and milk for consumption and for cheese- and butter-making. The breed was mainly white-faced, but many individuals were black or grey in the fleece, which 'saved the trouble of dyeing the wool'. Compared with the black-faced breed which largely replaced them, they were less hardy and required to be 'housed in winter and spring'.[299] Whether the following place-names refer to primitive sheep or to the commercial breeds which replaced them is a matter of uncertainty. The steading of **Gartnagerach** [747 107] was sited where Glenahervie, one of the few remaining Learside farms, now stands. The name represents *Gart nan caorach*, 'Field of the sheep', which is on record as far back as 1481 as 'Gartanagarauch'.[300] In Kilcalmonell Parish: **Easan nan Caorach** [846 639], 'Little Waterfall of the Sheep', **Cnoc nan Caorach**, 'Hill of the Sheep', twice [873 670 and 845 647], and **Rubha nan Caorach** [907 645], 'Sheep Point'. For **Eilean nan Caorach**, 'Sheep Island', see under EILEAN.

CAORUNN is the Rowan (*Sorbus aucuparia*), from *caor*, which is its berry, and, Macbain suggested, 'the same word as *caoir*, blaze, the idea arising probably from the *red* rowan berries'.[301] For anyone who has seen a Rowan laden with berries in a good fruiting season, the connection is absolute. The effect is indeed fire-like, not least in an otherwise drab moor or mountain setting, for the Rowan will grow at altitudes of up to 2000 feet, where other native trees cannot thrive. Rowans spread through dispersal of their seeds in bird-droppings, and, since the coniferous plantation of large tracts of Kintyre and the consequent exclusion of grazing livestock, have proliferated on uplands. They will grow in acidic soil just as readily as in the rich soil of gardens, and while they seldom reach more than a few feet high in windswept places, they are natural survivors, even when lodged in a mere crack of rock. The Rowan is also a tree around which a large body of superstition has accumulated. Close to the door of many ruined steadings, an old, gnarled Rowan will be found, as protection against witchcraft, and there are still country folk who will not cut so much as a branch from a rowan, let alone cut one down, for fear of incurring some supernatural penalty.[302]

Glen Kerran [716 133], Southend, has been interpreted *Gleann Chaorunn*, 'Rowan Glen', but its meaning remains uncertain. In *The Place-Names of Argyll* (p 24), Gillies included 'Kerran' among the 'very interesting ... land-names ... all which are explained in their place', but Duncan Colville failed to find his explanation and so have I. The two farms in the glen are recorded far back. The 'little' one, 'Keranbeg', appears in 1481, and the 'big' one in 1505 as 'Keranemore', 'Kiramoir' and 'Kyranmoir'. Hugh McEachran, Kilblaan, believed that the name came from *caoran*, 'small peat', and cited a tradition that 'small black peats were dug there, and were famous for their lasting and lighting qualities'; but the word strictly applies to a fragment of peat.[303] Ian A. Fraser was tempted to suggest CEATHRAMH, 'quarter-land', as the generic of these farms, but considered the intrusive 'n' a problem.[304]   In C1841, Duncan 'McShenaug' is shepherd at 'Caoranbeg'; in 1851 he is the more genteel Duncan 'McShannon' and is at 'Coaren'.

Allt a' Chaoruinn [641 107], which flows into Glenadale, is 'Stream of the Rowan', and the same name appears in Carradale Glen [782 422]. **Cruach Chaoruinn** [849 565], 'Hill of the Rowan', is at Oragaig, Skipness, and gave its name to a stream [851 561]. **Loch a' Chaoruinn** [804 503], 'The Rowan Loch', appears on the 1793 Langlands map as 'Lochkearanmore', for 'The Big Rowan Loch'; the smaller unnamed loch to the south of it, which is also unnamed on O.S. maps, was presumably the little one (*beag*).

CAPULL is a horse, but more commonly a mare. The place-names, of course, go back to times when workhorses were numerous the length and breadth of Kintyre. **Port a' Chapuill** [762 201] is on Davaar Island. The only record was in 1977, from a retired Dalintober fisherman, Duncan McSporran, whose interpretation was 'The Mare's Port'. I wondered naively at the time what connection there might be between a mare and a shore which is almost totally devoid of grazing, and considered *Port a' Chaibeil*, 'Port of the Chapel', as an alternative, but there is no record of any ecclesiastical building on the island. Teddy Lafferty later (1981) told me that he had heard the place called **The Horse Bay**, from a dead horse which washed ashore there. Whether that is the truth behind the name, and 'The Horse Bay' is an anglicisation of the older Gaelic form, is impossible to ascertain. Another Port a' Chapuill [633 207] was marked at Machrihanish on an old estate map.[305] **Allt a' Chapuill** [611 116], which flows off the Currach Mór, Southend, is 'The Mare's Stream', and there is another [785 375] at Torrisdale, which gave its name to a 19th century settlement in the upper glen, 'Altacapil' and 'High Altacapil' in C1841. **Allt nan Capull** [875 581] is 'Stream of the Mares', **Coire nan Capull** [c. 858 607] is 'Corrie of the Mares', and **Capull Cruaidh** [c. 845 552] is 'Hard Mare', a boulder on the southern slope of Cruach Oragaig, all three in Skipness Parish. See also EACH, 'horse'.

CÀRN is a heap of stones, which gives us English 'cairn'. It can also mean 'rock'[306] and 'a rocky hill or mountain',[307] with the sense 'cairn-shaped' inferred.[308] There is no scarcity of stone in Kintyre, as the earliest farmers knew when they laboured at clearing fields for cultivation. In unimproved landscapes, the stones they collected into heaps can still be seen, lichen-clad monuments to their labours, lying here and there around the little fields which have reverted to nature. When needed, these 'clearance cairns' would have been used for house- or dyke-building, but many remain untouched. In the defining of land-boundaries, cairns, along with ditches and walls, were important man-made markers which supplemented such natural features as boulders and streams. The following evidence from a boundary dispute in 1736, involving Kilmory and Bellochgerran, demonstrates this: to the cairn atop a rock at 'Brailochgleinbeg', thence to a cairn at the north end of 'Lochfinglein', thence to 'Fedanbraifinglein', thence upon a steep rock at 'Braifinglein', thence to a hill with two cairns on it, one on the west side and the other on the east, called 'Cnockvraichraigdaveallan'.[309]

9. *CÀRN. Amelia Martin at the cairn atop Cruach an Eich, 12/4/2012. Photograph by the author.*

When human remains were being carried a long distance for interment, at every resting-place the coffin-bearers would establish a cairn, and later travellers 'were expected of their charity to put a stone on it, and pray for the soul of the deceased'. Wherever a person was found dead, a few stones would be immediately placed on the spot,[310] a custom which survives, except that almost anything other than stones might now be left as markers. See also SUIDHE.

All *càrn* place-names are in North Kintyre. **Carnmore** [733 524, North; 732 523, South], near Ballochroy, represents *Càrn Mór*, 'Big Cairn.' Duncan Colville connected this name with a large cairn which covered the stone cist at Ballochroy [730 553] and was subsequently robbed by drystone dyke-builders. Its neighbour **Carnbeg** [739 538] is *Càrn beag*, 'Little cairn', and Colville related this name to a roadside cairn at 738 540.[311] The name 'Carnbeg' appears to have been replaced by 'Corriecravie'. **Carnbuie** [842 658], near Escairt on West Loch Tarbert, is *Càrn buidhe*, 'Yellow cairn', but has mutated on O.S. maps into 'Corranbuie', which has an entirely different meaning – see CORRAN. For **Càrnbàn**, near Tarbert, see under BÀN. **Càrn Chaluim** [892 625] is 'Calum's Hill'. **Càrn na Lòinidheach**, 'The Rheumatic Stone', was at the head of Rhonadale Glen, but its location is unknown to me. Willie McGougan in Largie described it as a 'big rock' on a steep hillside, and said that he had often sat on it when returning from Carradale to Largieside. He was told of a man named Smith who was 'very bad wi' rheumatism' and was somehow conveyed to the stone, which he sat on in the hope of being cured, but 'it didn't do him any good'.[312] **Càrnliath**, 'Grey cairn', was on Low Clachaig farm, and **Càrnabàn**, 'White cairn', on High Bellochantuy. **Càrnan Fionn**, 'Little white cairn', is a hillock on Rosehill.[313]

CARRAGH has the same deep root as CARRAIG, which is 'hard'. Macbain's sole definition, 'a pillar stone',[314] describes all Kintyre examples. **Carragh an Tàlaidh** [793 418] in Brackley burial-ground, Carradale, was also known as 'The Charm Stone', which is a neat enough translation. The Ordnance Survey's local 'authorities' in 1867 – Keith Campbell, farmer in Brackley, W. Steel, Carradale, and John McArthur, Bridgend, a native of Skipness – supposed that the stone covered 'the remains of a prominent Highland Chief', but it is actually the portal stone of a Neolithic chambered cairn. The O.S. notes continue: 'It was at one time said to have been a Sanctuary. It was also believed to be a charm for the toothache and the sufferer being cured if he could succeed in driving a nail into the Standing

Stone. At the present time many of these nails are to be found in it.'[315] It is now generally known as **The Toothache Stone**. Duncan Colville, in his Chalmers-Jervise Prize-winning essay, 'Notes on the Standing Stones of Kintyre', refers to the tradition of a sanctuary which lay between **Slighe-Aoraidh** ('The Way to Worship') and **Dail Sleuchdaidh** ('Field of Prostration').[316] Duncan Reid, writing earlier (1889), is more expansive on the sanctuary tradition, which he ascribes to an 'Arch Druid' who was buried under the *carragh*, and 'left a law that any one guilty of a crime would be pardoned, if the guilty person were fortunate enough to reach a consecrated space near his grave before being overtaken'. Reid explains the place-name **Carradale** in terms of the cairn, *carragh + dail*, hence 'the field of monumental erections',[317] a definition which, one suspects, he would have phrased differently had he been writing a bit later. The usual derivation of Carradale is Norse *kjarr-dalr*, 'brushwood glen'.[318] There was a 'toothache stone', *Clach an Déididh*, below the road between Portnahaven and Coultoon, Islay, which the late Gilbert Clark pointed out to Ian A. Fraser. 'You hammered a nail into the stone and recited a verse to cure the toothache.'[319] **Carragh Muasdale** [679 391], on South Muasdale farm, is a standing stone which has been incorporated into a dyke.[320] **Achadh na Carragh**, 'Field of the Standing Stone', was the name of a field – later **The Triangle** – immediately to the north of that standing stone.[321] **Beacharra**, 'Birchwood of the standing stone', is discussed at length under BEITH.

10. CARRAGH. *Carragh an Tàlaigh chambered cairn at Brackley, 6/8/2012. Photograph by the author.*

CARRAIG, like *sgeir*, *bodha* and *cleit*, is 'rock', and usually coastal. Professor MacKinnon in 1887 remarked that 'In some of the southern isles, the form *carraig* designates a rock to fish off ...'[322] These fishing stations were often provided with cups, hollowed out of the solid rock, in which limpets would be pulverised for ground-bait, to draw in fish.[323]

By my calculations, there are nine recorded *carraig* names in Kintyre. The one near West Loch Tarbert, **A' Charraig** [844 670], is simply 'The Rock'. A newspaper report in 1960 referred to 'the road now under construction over the Carrick';[324] and the nearby burial-ground was given the name 'Carrick' from the rock. I was at a ceilidh in Tarbert close on 40 years ago, and the *fear-an-tighe*, Dan Johnson, had a great stock of humorous local anecdotes, one of which stuck in my memory. It must date to around the time Carrick cemetery was created to replace Cill Aindreis, the burial-ground in Tarbert. When one old fellow heard about the new cemetery, he was quite adamant that he wouldn't be going there. 'I'm no' yollach oot there,' was his indignant response – he wasn't familiar (*eòlach*) with the place and would have nothing to do with it, alive or dead.

Three *carraig* names are close together at Pans, mixed in with the *bodha* names and with a big *sgeir* offshore for good measure. The Pans names are all in *The Place-Names of the Parish of Campbeltown* and I shall expand on only one here. It has a very beautiful name, **Carraig na h-Oidhche** [634 209], 'The Night Rock', but a name which would also have been very obscure without James McNeill's account in *Meanders in South Kintyre*. It is a tidal rock a little to the north-east of the promontory **Sgonn Mór**, 'Big Lump', now known as the 'Big Scone'. As James McNeill explained, 'It was customary to "make a scrape" here at nightfall with a large net, and drag in a cartful or more of saith, lythe [pollack], flounders, etc'.[325] A cartful indeed! One would be fortunate nowadays to take a bucketful of fish. His expression, 'make a scrape', clearly identifies the fishing method. The men were using a beach seine-net, *lìon-sgrìobaidh*, 'scrape-net', in Gaelic, and 'screenge' in Scots,[326] of the type from which the ring-net evolved at Tarbert – see CREAG for 'MacQuilkan's Rock'. These Tarbert men were fishing for a living, but at Pans, and other coastal communities, the 'scrape' combined recreation with subsistence, in other words a 'ploy' which might put food on the table.

Carskey, a major place-name in local history as the seat of the MacNeills of Carskey from at least the early 17th century, represents *Carraig Sgeithe*, 'Wing Rock', from its supposed 'resemblance to a bird's wing'.[327] The part-submerged rock [656 071] is below the site of successive Carskey mansions, and the estate is believed to have taken its name from the rock. Early spellings for the land-holding are many and varied: 1545 'Karschaych'; 1565 'Carrig na skaith'; 1505 'Carskae', 'Carskeich' and 'Carskeitht'; 1596 'Carska' and 1605 'Carskay'.[328] I had a good view of Carraig Sgeithe from the top of Binnein dà Néill on 3/8/2012, and its significance quite eluded me. It is, as maps show, a small offshore rock of no apparent distinction, suggesting a maritime origin for the name, its shape perhaps suggestive only from close up in a boat. Or is 'wing' the sole remnant of some forgotten event or myth?

On the east coast of Kintyre, **Carrick Point** [775 263] is at Ardnacross. The spelling is, of course, *carraig* in an anglicised form, as in the ancient regality in Ayrshire and in such Irish place-names as Carrickfergus. **Carraig an Leim** [816 366] translates as 'The Leap Rock', which is precisely the name by which it was latterly known to Carradale fishermen. The fishermen, at certain stages of the tide, when landing from their ferry-boats or punts, could leap ashore from the rock, this being necessary, I understood, when the wind was strong easterly and the fishing fleet required a lee for mooring. Donald McIntosh, one of the retired Carradale fishermen I consulted on place-names in 1980, remarked that 'It was supposed to be a place old women could jump across', but when I later asked him, in the hope of hearing a snippet of witch lore, why the old women would be jumping from the rock, his reply, disappointingly, was: 'I don't know.' The O.S. location of the rock has been locally disputed and an alternative on the west side of Carradale Point proposed. **Carraig a' Chàbaill** [901 650], on the Tarbert West Shore between Lùb Dhubh and Fionn Phort, translates as 'The Cable Rock', from a vein of quartz resembling a cable or rope.[329] For **Carraig an Daimh**, near Kilchamaig, see under MUC. The simple translation is 'The Ox's or Stag's Rock', but whatever the name signifies, I have been unable to find it on any map.

CAT is Gaelic for 'cat', the animal, in Early Irish *catt* and in Latin *catta*, but the word may be of Celtic origin.[330] In topographic names, a Wild Cat is usually the species denoted.[331] There are relatively few *cat* names in Kintyre. The main one, **Cattadale** in Southend [High 678 104 and Low 676 100], is not Gaelic, but represents Norse *Kattardalr*, 'Cat dale', the earliest record of which is 1481 'Catadill'. **Allt a' Chait** [644 107], 'The Cat's Burn', is also in Southend.[332]

Cat's Burn [809 419], north of Carradale, is an English form, recorded in 1867 by the O.S., and may represent an earlier Gaelic form. In '**Geo Chaytch**', between Port Crannaig and Port Rìgh, the generic represents *geòdha*, 'gullet, inlet', which Nils M. Holmer in *Studies on Argyllshire Gaelic* remarks on as being 'common in place-names'.[333] As a place-name element in Kintyre, however, it occurs only in the Carradale district and only in oral tradition. Reppke noted two in 1943, that one and another near Sunadale, which he spelled phonetically '**Geo Chrocheral**'*. He noted that opinion was divided on the meaning of 'Geo Chaytch'. Angus Buchanan and Neil MacDougall – both native Gaelic speakers and both, incidentally, informants of Nils M. Holmer when he researched *The Gaelic of Kintyre* – told him that it meant 'the cats creek'.[334] The Wild Cat in place-names was also known as a 'beast' in Gaelic and invested with an unrealistically ferocious nature.

*Neil Shaw, An Commun Gàidhealach, suggested to Reppke the interpretation *Geòdha Chnoc-earail*, 'Creek of the warning (guarding) hill',[335] but no such hill is known.

There are Wild Cat stories connected with **Allt na Béiste** [773 303], the stream which forms both the boundary between Campbeltown and Saddell parishes and the march between High and Low Ugadale farms. A young soldier named Macniven, home in Kintyre following the Battle of the Boyne (1690), was supposed to have had the fight of his life against a big Wild Cat which confronted him as he crossed the burn. He had no sooner put his foot on the first stepping-stone when the cat leapt from a thicket on the opposite bank and faced him defiantly. Then it sprang on him and Macniven fell into the burn with the cat at his neck. A fierce struggle ensued, with claw and dagger exchanging blows, until Macniven, up to his chest in the rapid waters, finally killed the beast. He took it home, had it skinned and kept the skin.[336] In C1851, 'Altnabeast' appears as the name of a house there. D. J. Macdonald interpreted **Lag na béisd**, on Drumnamucklach farm, as 'Wild cat hollow';[337] the O.S. interpreted **Loch na Béiste** [765 546], south of Clachan, as 'Loch of the beast of prey'.[338]

Adam MacPhail, who farmed Skernish and was living in retirement in Glenbarr when I visited him in 1977, told me that the last Kintyre Wild Cat was shot in Barr Glen in the early 20th century. He gave me the name of the place, but at that time I didn't recognise it and left it for later, but later never came and the transcript is blank where the place-name should be. The creature was seen up a tree by Archie Galbraith, the Glenbarr Estate gamekeeper, but he had no gun with him and 'the cat had his eyes fixed on him and he had his eyes fixed on the cat, and he knew if he took them off, the cat could spring'. He sent the Estate handyman, John MacNeill, to fetch his gun, and waited until the gun was brought to him; then he shot the cat. Both men were engaged at the time in cutting back riverbank vegetation in preparation for the salmon-fishing season.[339]

According to Gibson and Colville, the last Wild Cat in Kintyre known to the historical record was shot near Loch Garasdale in 1910 and ended up stuffed in Largie Castle. The Wild Cat (*Felis silvestris*) was common throughout Kintyre, but as they remarked in 1975, 'As with the Pine Marten and the Polecat, the appointment of gamekeepers in 1842 was the beginning of the end for the Kintyre Wild Cats'. In 1975 they reported that the species was 'making something of a comeback' in Knapdale, and speculated that individuals might make their way down into Kintyre.[340] Within the past 20 years or so, reports have been received in Kintyre of Wild Cat sightings, but it is uncertain whether these are authentic or relate to domestic or farm cats, which often go wild, breed in the feral state and, as Gibson and Colville put it, 'sometimes grow to a remarkable size'. What is certain, however, is that the afforestation of Kintyre has provided impenetrable cover for many creatures, most of which we know about, but some of which we may not yet know about; and these may include the Wild Cat, or crossed versions of it, and even, as some reliable witnesses maintain, the fearsome 'Big Cat'.

CEANN is basically 'head'. **Kintyre**, the subject of this book, is from *Ceann Tìre*, 'head of land' or 'end of land' (see TÌR). The best known *ceann* place-name in Kintyre is now **Kennacraig** [818 625] – *Ceann-na-creige*, 'Head of the rock' – from which the Calmac ferry sails. The terminal was built by Western Ferries, whose newly launched *Sound of Islay* began running between there and Port Askaig, Islay, in April 1968.[341] Kennacraig is familiar to tens of thousands of people across the world who have travelled to Islay by sea, or sat in the West Coast Motors buses which stop at the ferry terminal to collect passengers; but in 1867, when the Ordnance Survey officers visited West Loch Tarbert, there was only the uninhabited rocky island, **Eilean Ceann na Creige**, and a house to the south named 'Ceann-na-Craige' [824 621].[342] The earliest record, in 1511, is 'Kynnacraig'.

Four hundred years ago, the pre-eminent *ceann* place-name, 'Kintyre' aside, would have been **Ceann-locha**, Gaelic for

Campbeltown and in historical records anglicised as 'Kinloch' and translated into Scots as 'Lochhead'.[343]

According to the Rev Angus J. MacVicar, 'The old folk of Kintyre always referred to Southend as *Ceann Siar*, "the west end"', and it puzzled him why the parish had not been called 'Westend' instead of **Southend**, a name which he ascribed to the influence of Elizabeth Tollemache, wife of Archibald Campbell, 1st Duke of Argyll.[344]

Perhaps as interesting as any of these, in its own way, is the field-name **Ceann Claidheamh** [760 259] on Kilkeddan. Duncan Colville noted it in 1929 from Ritchie McCallum, Peninver, and it is still known to Donald Armour, retired farmer at Kilkeddan, who described it as extending from the farm road to Lussa Water. Its meaning is 'sword-hilt',[345] from its shape, which must date it to a period when swords were familiar enough objects to suggest a place-name.

CÈARDACH is simply a 'smithy', and appears in **Camus na Cèardaich** (see under CAMUS), **Glenacardoch** [666 372], which represents *Gleann na cèardaich*, 'The smithy glen', and **Gortean na cèardaich**, 'The smithy field', on Beacharra farm.[346] In Gaelic *cèard* is 'a craftsman',[347] but the blacksmith was very seldom so termed – he was GOBHA or GOBHAINN, to which refer. The *cèard* was the Traveller, from his traditional role as tinsmith, or 'white smith', as opposed to his 'black' counterpart, who worked with iron. Hamish Henderson has suggested that Travellers are 'descendants of a very ancient caste of itinerant metal-workers whose status in tribal society was probably high'. He continues: 'One of the trades associated with them from early times was that of tin-smith, and it is clear that to primitive man the ability to use metals seemed very close to magic; consequently, both "black" and "white" smiths for long enjoyed immense prestige, not only as craftsmen but as wielders of secret powers.'[348] For an account of Traveller families in Kintyre, see my *An Historical and Genealogical Tour of Kilkerran Graveyard*, pp. 37-39.

CEATHRAMH, 'quarter', is a division of land in place-names. **Kerry** in Cowal was a name well known to Tarbert fishermen, who spoke of 'The Kerry Shore' (the coast from Otter to Ardlamont) and 'The Kerry Kyle' (the western strait of the Kyles of Bute). Watson considered this substantial 'Kerry' (*Ceathramh*) an 'old fourfold tribal division'.[349] Andrew McKerral dates *ceathramh* in Kintyre to 'purely Celtic times' and the gradual division of the BAILE into quarters and eighths and even smaller fractions.[350] The eighth part, *ochdamh*, is not represented in Kintyre place-names, but occurs in Islay and Jura as 'Octa-' or 'Octo-'.[351] In Kintyre, all *ceathramh* names are obsolescent or obsolete. **Kerrafuar**, 'Cold quarter' (see FUAR), is certainly of great antiquity. It appears in a charter of 1481 as 'Kerowsoyre'[352] and was possibly even then a well established name. In 1797 George Campbell had four horses at 'Kerafour', two of them classed as work horses and taxed at 2s each.[353] Of **Keramenach**, 'Middle quarter' (see also MEADHONACH), there appears to be no record earlier than 1605, when 'Keremanach' was documented at a court held at Knockbay (p. 47). At another kind of court in Campbeltown, John Campbell, farm worker at 'Kerrowmenach', was fined 10s in 1920 for riding a bicycle without lights.[354]

Deucheran, which gave its name to a hill and stream, comprised a 'big' farm, Deucheran Mór [776 433], and a 'little' one, Deucheran Beag [779 434], in close proximity to each other and both now ruinous. This name has been interpreted as 'Two quarterlands',[355] but a case could also be made for 'Black quarterlands', *Dubh cheathramhnan*. Old forms: 1502/07 'The Twa Dufquharanis' and 'The Twa Dowtorranis'; 1545 'Dowtorreneis'; 1564 'The Two Dufthorrenis'; 1596 'Tadowchreis'; 1605 'The twa Dowreis'; 1751 'Ducherinbeg' and 'Duchorenmore'. In 1888, as 'Duchrau', when advertised for let by Carradale Estate, it had 82 acres of 'good arable' and was capable of carrying 1600 black-face sheep and 25 cattle.[356] A photograph of Bella Campbell, 'Deuchran Farm', appeared in the *Scottish Farmer Album* – 'the publication par excellence of the agricultural year' – of 1920. She was one of the butter-makers who gained 98 per cent in the *Scottish Farmer*'s 'butter tests'.[357] For **Kirnashee** see under SÌTHICH and for **Kerran** under CAORUNN.

CILL is a common place-name element in Kintyre, and the names, taken as a group, are the richest in historical background. *Cill*, invariably anglicised 'Kil-', is Gaelic for a church and was originally the dative of *cell*, a borrowing from Latin *cella*, 'monastic cell'. No remains of Early Christian ecclesiastical buildings have been identified in Kintyre, but it is likely that many of the medieval and later churches and burial-grounds occupy early ecclesiastical sites.[358] 'Kil-' place-names – most of them are in South Kintyre, and Saddell and Skipness Parish has only two – are too numerous to examine individually, therefore I shall make a selection as representative of the whole and direct the reader to the Royal Commission on the Ancient and Historical Monuments of Scotland's inventory, *Argyll: Volume 1, Kintyre*, pp. 100-56, for a more comprehensive survey. The anglicised form 'Kil' may be deceptive in a few cases, since it can also stand for *coille*, 'wood', among other terms.

Cill Ainndreis [863 684], 'Andrew's Churchyard', the graveyard in Tarbert village, is something of an enigma. For a start, the name itself appears to have belonged in oral tradition until George Campbell Hay used it in his elegy to his MacMillan great-aunts, Elizabeth and Anne, *Cuimhneachan do Ealasaid agus Anna NicMhaoilein*, written in 1940. The spelling in that poem is *Cill Aindreis*, but in 'The Two Neighbours' (1946) it has become *Cill Ainndreis*, and by 1982 Hay had decided that the correct form was *Cill Ainndreann*, 'an old -*nn* genitive of *Ainndrea*: (Saint) Andrew'. He also knew of a **Sloc Aindreis**, 'Andrew's Pit', at the head of Tarbert harbour, which may not have been in Kilcalmonell Parish and, therefore, in Kintyre.[359] I wish I had asked Hay what his source for these names was, but I didn't. The history of the burial-ground itself is also obscure, but it does contain a pre-Reformation tombstone.[360] There is no chapel there, and, aside from a chapel associated with Tarbert Castle in the 14th century, the village lacked a place of worship until a church was built in 1775. According to Dugald Mitchell, the village graveyard replaced a burial-ground at Glenakill, West Loch Tarbert, which was ploughed up in the early 18th century. The perpetrators of this sacrilege naturally 'went from bad to worse, and died shortly afterwards'.[361]

Kilbride for *Cill Brìghde*, 'Church of [Saint] Bridget', occurs twice in South Kintyre, with no known chapel-site in either case. The one in Southend Parish [718 087] was a 'cot-house' which became a 'small farm' about 1866, and the one in Campbeltown Parish was also a farm, possibly the place later called **Laggs** [688 169].[362] **Cille Bhrìde** [829 623], near Kennacraig, contains a burial-enclosure which was used by the Campbells of Stonefield from the late 18th century until, in the following century, a mausoleum was erected north of the mansion at Stonefield.[363]

Kilchamaig [802 610] was interpreted by W. J. Watson as *Cill Chámaig*, 'Camoc's Church'. A dedication to a Saint Cormac has been generally accepted,[364] but records do not support that derivation, e.g., 1481 'Kilcamok'; 1539 'Kilcammak'; 1669 'Kilchamaig'. The O.S. in 1867 noted that no evidence of a chapel remained, though 'In the field S. of the farm house of Kilchamaig a considerable quantity of human remains were found in the course of levelling the ground for agricultural purposes'.[365]

Kilchattan [710 120] burial-ground, Southend, survives only as a 'small turf-covered mound of stones',[366] and the name survives only attached to a hill, which came into public prominence when an application to site a wind-farm there emerged in 2007. The application was rejected in 2012, but not before the name had been mispronounced hundreds of times. The 'c' is elided, and the correct pronunciation is that which appears in 19th century censuses, when there was still a settlement at 'Kilhatan'.[367] *Cill Chatáin* commemorates *Catán*, a 6th century Irish saint, who was an uncle of *Bláán*,[368] who is commemorated in the nearby farm of **Kilblaan** [702 098], *Cill-Bhlathain*,[369] a combination which also occurs on Bute.[370] The Kintyre surname McIllechattan, anglicised as Hattan and now vanished entirely, is *Mac Gille Chatain*, 'Son of the Servant of Catan'.[371] There is also a Kilchattan on Gigha.

11. CILL. Kilchousland Church, by T. P. White, reproduced from his Archaeological Sketches in Scotland, District of Kintyre, *Edinburgh 1873.*

Kilchousland [751 220] commemorates a 6th century saint, Constantine, who allegedly 'suffered martyrdom in Kintyre'.[372] Cameron Gillies gave the Gaelic form *Cill-Chuisilein* and doubted the Constantine link on linguistic grounds.[373] According to Peter MacIntosh, the church was named after Cusalan, 'daughter of the

king of Spain', who died aboard a 'Spanish man-of-war' in the
Kilbrannan Sound and was 'buried in this place'.[374] It's a romantic tale,
but doesn't work as history. The Parish of Kilchousland, extending
from Dalintober to Saddell Glen, was absorbed into Campbeltown
Parish, along with Kilkerran, Kilkivan and Kilmichael, in the post-
Reformation period. The Dalintober folk, indeed, were buried in
Kilchousland until the little graveyard filled up in the 20th century.
William McTaggart's evocative study of children at play, 'The Past
and the Present' (1860), was set in Kilchousland. Its background
is the medieval chapel, in which is buried the redoubtable Rev Dr
John Smith, Gaelic scholar and minister of the Gaelic Church in
Campbeltown until his death in 1807. In the last decade of his life
he lived at Kilchousland, where he had his glebe.[375] The sandy beach
below the picturesque churchyard was formerly a popular picnic
spot, particularly among Dalintober folk. 'Kilchousland' is the only
Kintyre 'Kil-' name which, in popular speech, has turned into 'Kirk-'.

12. CILL. Kilcolmkill from west, c. 1910, published by Martin Stationers.
Author's collection.

Kilcolmkill [673 077], *Cille-Choluim-Cille*, the former parish
and chapel, and continuing graveyard, at Southend, now known
simply as 'Keil', took its name from the greatest of all the Irish monks
who came to Scotland, *Colum Cille*, Saint Columba.[376] As with any

other *cill* name, it does not follow from the dedication that the saint was ever at the place, so, did Columba actually set foot in Southend? The tradition that he did is a tenacious one: the footprints cut in the rock from which he preached, the annual 'conventicle', or religious service, held at that spot in his name, and the argument that Southend would have been an obvious landfall for small boats setting out from the north of Ireland.

Gilbert Márkus is sceptical about these Columban traditions, which he suspects are no older than the mid-19th century and substantially dependent on George Buchanan's interpretation (1852) of Adamnan's statement that Columba went to Caput Regionis, which Buchanan suggested was a Latin calque on Kintyre, a suggestion which was accepted by other scholars, including Professor Watson. 'But it doesn't really work,' Márkus argues, 'because *regio* does not translate as *tìr*. *Regio* is not a piece of land, but a political territory, and *caput* is its head-place.'[377]

I have tried to establish the origin of the Columba tradition, but no clarity has yet emerged. The author of the *First Statistical Account of Southend* (1791), Rev David Campbell, makes no mention of it, but in the *Second Statistical Account* (1845) the Rev Donald Kelly refers to 'the tradition ... that St Columba landed here on his way from Ireland to the Hebrides'. Peter MacIntosh (1857) says that 'the gospel was preached in Kintyre, first of all, by St. Columb', with a footnote on 'Cummian and Adamnan, biographers of St. Columb', and, further, that Southend was Columba's 'first landing place' and the site of 'the first church he erected in Scotland'.[378] Captain T. P. White (1873), citing the place-name **Guala na pobuill** (see under GUALA/GUALANN) and Adamnan's *Life of Columba*, considers a landing at Southend 'by no means improbable'.[379]

The first Columban Conventicle at Keil was held in 1921 as a 'Columba Celebration'. It was organised by the Established Presbytery of Kintyre, and the service was presided over, significantly, by the Rev A. J. MacVicar, a lifelong admirer of Columba. An 'eloquent appreciation' of the saint was delivered by the Rev Donald Macmillan, D.D., LL.D., minister of Kelvinhaugh Parish Church, Glasgow, and a native of Skipness. The front page report in the *Campbeltown Courier* extended over three full columns, from which I quote only the introductory paragraph with its confident explanation of the event's significance:

It is an appropriate circumstance that the 1400th anniversary of the birth of St Columba, which falls upon the present year, should have had its first public celebration in Kintyre, for by a well-founded local tradition, it has been established that near the southern end of the peninsula Columba, while on his way from Ireland to the isle of Iona, first set foot on Scottish soil, thereby associating with this district a name that has made our native shire renowned for ever in the annals of the Church.[380]

An extraordinary feature of the old graveyard at Keil is the segregation of Gaelic and Lowland families, an arrangement which remains perfectly plain despite some later contrary burials. The Highland families are in the eastern part and the Lowland families in the western part. The reverse arrangement might have been more fitting, since the Lowlanders came from the east (Ayrshire), and the last stronghold of the Gaelic language in southern Kintyre was in the west (Glenbreackerie and the Mull). A writer in 1866 remembered that a tiny 'rill' which flowed through the graveyard was 'understood to be the boundary line separating the living as well as the dead ... Strange and indeed inexplicable is the feeling that the dead body would be more secure in the one corner of the church-yard than in the other'. The enmity existing between native and planter stock has its obvious parallel in the north of Ireland, where, however, the greater scale of the political initiatives produced greater and more lasting social consequences. In Southend, the two communities, which had been divided by 'differences in lineage and language', finally united through intermarriage, but that reconciliation took almost two hundred years to effect. In the early 19th century, 'for a lowland young man to marry a highland woman, however respectable she might be in regard to parentage, or character, or qualifications, was considered to be most disreputable. It was in fact losing caste as much as if the parties had been in India'.[381] The first interment in the thoroughly democratic extension of the burial-ground was that of Janet Paterson Andrew, wife of Alexander Ronald, Pennyseorach, in May 1916.[382]

Kildalloig is 'the Church of Dallóc', a name which Watson explains as 'a variant of *Dallán*, from *dall*, blind'.[383] John Cameron rendered the Gaelic *Cill Dalloig*, using the genitive form.[384] The site of a church has never been established, but the name 'Kildalloig' passed to an estate [753 188, mansion] which was associated from the 17th century until the early 20th century with the Campbell family which later succeeded to the Baronetcy of Auchinbreck in Cowal.[385]

Of **Kildavie** – *Cill-Do-Bhì*, 'Church of [St.] Bì' [386] – little has been written; indeed, little is known. The burial-ground, according to one who remembered it 'before it was ploughed over', was on the low side of the road beside the march-burn between Kildavie [724 105] and Chiskan. A 19th century tenant of Kildavie, by the name of Reid, removed the stones from the site without 'evil' consequences, but the cattle belonging to an earlier tenant died after he had 'attempted to interfere with the ground'.[387]

Kildonan [777 273] is *Cill Donnáin*, 'Church of Donnan', the Irish monk who founded a monastery on Eigg and was martyred there in 618.[388] The site is of little interest – nothing remains of either chapel or burial-ground – but the name is, because the farm named after it turned into 'Kildonald'. It was, until absorbed into Ballochgair in the 19th century, a two-merkland holding which enters the records in 1502 as 'Kildonane' and retains that form until around 1750, when 'Kildonald' took over.[389]

Kilkerran [728 193] is *Cill Chiaráin*, 'Church of Ciaran'. The Ciaran commemorated in Scottish place-names is assumed to be Ciaran of Clonmacnoise,[390] styled *Mac an t-Saoir*, 'Son of the Carpenter', who died c. 545, but no certainty is possible. Nothing remains of the medieval chapel which stood in the oldest part of the graveyard, and although it was abandoned to ruination in the 17th century and a replacement church built in 1642 beyond the east end of Kirk Street, the burial-ground continued in use. It has, since 1856, been extended westward until it can be extended no more,[391] and is now the largest and most attractive cemetery in Kintyre. The name 'Kilkerran' was also attached to the now ruined castle built around 1498 by King James IV opposite the graveyard gates and overlooking Campbeltown Loch.[392] South of Campbeltown, at the foot of Auchenhoan Head, **Saint Ciaran's Cave** [766 169] retains an atmosphere of sanctity. The religious relics there include a boulder incised with an Early Christian marigold design and a socket-stone in which a cross had probably been mounted.[393] This cave, which was possibly an anchorite's retreat, is traditionally associated with Saint Ciaran, as the name indicates. Professor Donald MacKinnon in 1887 remarked that Kintyre people said that Ciaran 'was tutor to Columba, and that it was he who persuaded the latter to undertake his famous mission' (*sic*).[394]

Kilkivan [651 201], the chapel and burial-ground between Drumlemble and Machrihanish, and also the name of a farm [656 203], probably represents *Cill Chaomháin*, 'Church of Kevin', saints of which name were numerous.[395] An often repeated tradition attaches to this church, that a priest, 'being much annoyed with delinquencies' – this I take to mean fornication – organised an annual assembly for 'all who were not satisfied with their wives or husbands'. In the darkened church, the participants were encouraged to grab another partner, and 'when the church was lighted again, whether the one they held was hunchbacked or crooklegged, they were obliged to put up with them till the next yearly meeting'.[396] In 1772, Dugald McEachern, 'dancing master' at Kilkivan, took Ronald McMurchy, son of William McMurchy, 'musicianer' in Campbeltown, to court, alleging that he had engaged McMurchy to play at his school for 20s a month and 'his victuals', but that McMurchy had deserted him for another dancing master at 'Knocknahall' (Knocknaha), and his pupils were threatening to leave owing to the lack of music at his school.[397]

There was another chapel dedicated to St Kevin at Macharioch [731 093], of which little remains. Burials there were discontinued by about the second quarter of the 19th century.[398] In 1924 a Southend man recollected having, with two others, 'carted stones for a whole day from the old churchyard' for the first improvements made to Macharioch House after the 8th Duke of Argyll acquired the estate in 1863.[399]

Of **Killarow** there are no material remains, but the present farm-steading is at 662 280. The dedication is to Maol Rubha of Applecross (640-722), whom Watson described as 'next to Colum Cille the most famous saint of the Scoto-Irish Church'.[400]

Killean, *Cill Eathain* [695 445], was dedicated to Saint John the Evangelist. The parish of Killean spanned the central area of the peninsula from west to east until 1753 when the districts of Saddell and Carradale were disjoined and formed into the new parish of Saddell. The old church, which is now a neglected ivy-smothered ruin, stands within its ancient burial-ground beside the busy A83. The building dates in part from the 12th century, but includes a remarkably elaborate 13th century chancel and a barrel-vaulted aisle added in the 15th century. It continued in use until 1770 when it was abruptly abandoned amid fears that it was structurally unsound. The minister, Mr Robert Thomson, was said to have had a premonition of the collapse of the roof. For the next 20 years, the congregation worshipped in the open fields until the completion of the handsome new parish church at A' Chleit[401] (see CLEIT).

Of **Killellan** chapel [683 148] very little remains. *Cill Fhaolàin* commemorates one Faolàn, an Irish personal name meaning 'little wolf', which was borne by several churchmen of the Irish 'Age of

Saints' (c. 500-c. 750).[402] The name also attached to an estate which belonged to the MacEachran family (see under EACH).

Only the turf-covered foundations remain of the chapel at **Killeonan** [687 181].[403] 'Killewnane' was valued in 1502/07 as a 17-merkland – a very substantial holding – and in 1751 as a 4-merkland. After the First World War, the land was divided into smallholdings for ex-servicemen. The name represents *Cill Adhamhnain*, 'Cell of Adamnan', the influential Donegal-born saint (627-704) who was ninth abbot of Iona and whose principal legacy is his *Life of Columba*. In 1928, the tenant, Sam Mitchell, knew two of the fields there as **Saint Adamnan's Field** and **Saint David's Field**.[404]

The site of **Kilmaluag**, Barr Glen, is at 700 379.[405] Captain T. P. White found only 'A small, half-effaced bank, enclosing a corner of a field, and two or three moss-grown slabs',[406] but D. J. Macdonald 30 years later noted that a well-known tenant-farmer in the parish, by name MacDougall, remembered an interment taking place there.[407] The name represents *Cill mo-Luáig*, 'Cell of Moluag', the Irish saint who founded the monastery of Lismore and died in 592.[408] The earliest forms on record are: 1502/07 'Kilmology', 1545 'Kilmoloig', and 1596 'Kilmaloag'. The Kintyre surname Milloy is a curious 'anglicisation' of *Mac Gille mo-Luáig*, 'Son of the Servant of Moluag', and early records of the name place these families in the area of the church and the farm [693 376] which took its name from the church, e.g. Gilnv (Gilnave) Mcilmaluag in Bar in 1653.[409] Adam MacPhail recalled, in 1977, hearing that Kilmaluag was a 'sacred burial-place' and 'never tae be touched', but that a tenant ploughed over it without seeing 'signs o' anythin' there'.[410]

Kilmichael – for *Cill Mhìcheil*, 'Michael's Church' – is on record thrice in Kintyre. Of Kilmichael in Carradale Glen, no ecclesiastical records have been found. 'Kilmichel' appears as a four-merkland holding in 1502, so the name is an old one, which survived as **Lag Kilmichael** [786 409] – the present steading clearly stands above a *lag*, or 'hollow', in the valley-bottom – and **Knock Kilmichael** or 'Knock' [786 405], a small division of the holding. Captain T. P. White remarked in 1873 that no remains of an 'ancient burial-place' had been identified nor any tradition 'met with hereabouts'. He allowed that Brackley burial-ground 'would have answered very well as to site',[411] but 'no tradition of antiquity' attaches to that site and the earliest legible stone is no older than 1734.[412] Charles Reppke in 1942 recorded 'a **St. Michaels well** in the hill between [Kilmichael] and Amod'.

The enclosure wall of Kilmichael [728 519] at the foot of Ballochroy Glen is now ruinous and there are few surviving monuments, the most interesting being a rough slab bearing a plain Latin cross carved in relief and probably dating to the early medieval period.[413] A more modern stone, which Captain White transcribed, commemorates a shipwreck fatality: 'John McNeil, Tobacconist at Inveraray, who was wrackt. and perished near Kilmichael, Kintyre, in Oct. 7th 1756, aged 30.'[414] The land-holding is on record as early as 1306-9 as 'Kyllmichill' and was latterly represented by a ruined township at 729 519.

Of the old parish church of Kilmichael [698 227], to the west of Campbeltown, nothing now remains, the stones having been removed for re-use as building material in the 18th century.[415] John Picken, who in 1776 divided Kilmichael farm with Daniel McMillan and took the west division,[416] was said to have made a road to his house through the graveyard. He 'gathered a basketful of bones, which he buried in the yard', but the earth which he 'stripped off the face of the kirk-yard' he spread on a field ... a big mistake! Nothing would grow there throughout his tenancy and 'nothing he put his hand to prospered'. In the end, Rev Donald Kelly remarked, 'he was roped [rouped] out ...'[417] The farm leases show that in 1787 Picken assigned his lease to Duncan Campbell, town clerk of Campbeltown.[418]

Kilwhipnach was tentatively interpreted *Cill Coibhdenach*, 'Church of St. Coibhdenach', by the K.A.S. place-names committee,[419] in disagreement with Watson's suggestion of '*Coidbenach*, bishop of Ard Sratha, who died in 707';[420] but they are variant spellings of the same saint's name, and the early forms favour *Coidbenach*:[421] 1502 'Kilcoubenach'; 1507 'Kilcowbenach'; 1596 'Kilcobenach'; 1605 'Kilcobenache'.[422] The Rev Donald Kelly recorded in 1838 that 40 years earlier, the tenant-farmers at Kilwhipnach eradicated the burial-ground. The account is rather confused, but Edward MacEachan appears to have built his steading over part of the cemetery, while the other tenant 'cleared away all the vestiges of the burying ground and had a kail-yard planted in its place'. When digging the foundations of the house, 'the men got a great many human bones'. The 'chapel' was reported as having been 'on the south side of the Strand'. What feature this name represents eludes me, but, since it was said to have earlier been a 'marsh',[423] it probably relates to the low ground below the present steading [674 165]. Whether that steading was built on the site of the earlier MacEachan steading is uncertain, but if it was, then the site of the burial-ground lies below it. Kelly's dates are in agreement with the period of MacEachan's tenancy. He got the lease of the south division of the farm in 1795, and it obliged him to work the limestone quarry and supply the Duke of Argyll's tenants with limestone at '2d per cart load'. The other tenant would have been Donald McQuilkan in Barr, who got the lease of North Kilwhipnach in the same year.[424]

CLACH is 'stone', the genitive is *cloiche* and *clachach* is 'stony', hence **Clachaig**, 'stony place', once an estate near Muasdale, with a mill, now ruined, and farms, Low [694 403] and High [700 406]. The field named Clachaig [637 205], west of Bayview housing scheme at Machrihanish, is also 'stony place', and so it should be since it lies on a raised beach. **Clachaig a' Bhorran** [625 205], the foreshore between Uisaed and the Galdrans, represents *Clachaig a' mhorghain*, 'Stony place of the shingle',[425] a double dose of the hard stuff.

The former farm of **Achnaglach** [693 150] is *Achadh nan clach*, 'Field of the stones'.[426] The mysterious **Totticlach** appears in a dispute in 1768 involving John McLean, tenant in Kilmaho, and Donald McKenzie, cottar in 'Totticlach'. McKenzie owed McLean £1 2s and gave him a wheel in part-payment, but 'Ugadale' – presumably the MacNeill laird – then had a warrant served on McKenzie claiming that the wheel was his. McLean had also taken legal action against Robert Hyman, sheriff officer, for the return of a black mare taken from him 'under pretence of poinding it on a decreet at the instance of Donald McKenzie'.[427] This was a complicated quarrel, the outcome of which is unknown, as is the location of 'Totticlach'.

Clachfin ('Clochfin' in the earliest records) is in Strathduie Glen and represents *Clach fhionn*, 'White stone', a feature [720 295] which the O.S. in 1866 described as 'pretty large'.[428] There was, however, also a small farm called Clachfin, the traces of which, Agnes Stewart was told by Archie McNicol, were in the vicinity of 714 294.[429] In 1686, among those summoned before the Justices of the Peace Court in Campbeltown for 'irregularities in church attendance' were John McIlbride, John McQuirrie and Duncan McSporran in 'Clochfin'.[430] In 1753, the tenant there, Duncan McTavish, obliged himself 'To make bullwarks with stones, creels and other matterials to ... divert the Water of Strathdowie from making further incroachments upon the said lands'.[431] Beside that Water, a century earlier, the Covenanting minister Rev John Cunison had made his home in a 'miserable dwelling', after being outed from the parish of Kilbride in Arran for nonconformity. There, it was said, he lived for seven years, subsisting largely on the trout he took from the burn. An account of his colourful life by D. J. Macdonald may be found in *Kintyre Magazine* No. 70. In a version of this story published in 1874, Clach fhionn appears as 'Clachfheoni', a garbled form of *feòil*, 'flesh', and is interpreted imaginatively as 'a spot where the flocks of cattle stood'.[432]

The Laggan farm **Clochkeil** [662 236] was admitted to be 'a name of some difficulty' by the K.A.S. place-names committee, with *Clach chaol*, 'narrow stone', finally suggested. The decision was influenced by John Cameron, who was told by a Miss McCorkindale, a native Gaelic speaker from Largieside, that the place was 'referred to in Gaelic as *A' Chlach Chéil*, which she interprets as The Narrow Stone (*céil* being the Kintyre form of *caol*)'. Old spellings include: 1481, 'Clagkeile', 1539 'Clachkeill' and 1629 'Clochekeill'.[433]

Rubha Clach an Tràghaidh [893 666] is on the coast between Tarbert and Skipness. It translates as 'Ebbing Stone Point', and the name was in use among 20th century Tarbert fishermen in that form.[434] **Clach na Breugach** [720 092] is the chambered cairn at Blasthill and has been translated as 'false or lying stones, i.e. not symbolic of Christianity'.[435] The boulder **Clach na Béiste** [907 619], north of Skipness, is 'Stone of the Beast'. For **Clach a' Ghèoidh** see under GÈADH, and for **Clach an t-Sagairt** under SAGART.

Clach is from Early Irish *cloch*,[436] the form retained in Irish place-names, and anglicised variously, e.g. 'Cloyfin', which is *Cloch Fionn*, or 'white stone',[437] as above. It is a certainty that very many *clach* names have been lost. Before the mapping of estates began in the late 18th century, land boundaries were a matter of local knowledge, passed on from generation to generation. Boundaries were marked by natural features, as far as these served, but man-made features such as dykes were also used, and cairns were purposely built. Rocks and boulders also served as reference points on the landscape, and, as such, were given names. A land dispute between John Macdonald of Largie and the 2nd Duke of Argyll in 1736 provides a detailed record of the boundary between Bellochgerran and Kilmory, based on oral testimony. The following stones with *clach* as the generic – spellings as in the legal document – were among the named features, starting at 'the West Sea' and ending at the 'Water of Glennadrochid': 'Clachoraistruaninunlaid', 'Clachviancnockouer', 'Clachleanin', 'Clachvrailickannicrouine', and 'Clachvraigleinchraignacuineg[438]. This class of place-name is clearly packed with precise descriptive elements – hill, craig, stream, valley – by which each rock could be identified and located.

If someone asked to be shown a typical *clach*, then I would choose a boulder [599 168] which has no name, though I am certain it once would have had. It is remarkably prominent, but its prominence owes little to size and much to situation. It can be seen as one descends the Inneans Glen into the Bay, on the skyline beyond the sheep-fank at Innean Beag. It marks, in fact, the corner where the old coast road turns north towards Craigaig, and as one walks that green track, which runs out in rocks before Earadale, looking back one can see, once again, the boulder silhouetted on the skyline. The first time I particularly noticed the rock, it was in a photograph Jimmy MacDonald took on Hogmanay 2008 of a Golden Eagle being mobbed by Ravens. The photograph (below) was taken in low light from the opposite side of the glen, but it is dramatic.

I once had a terrifying experience associated with a boulder. I was walking alone to Greenland on a sleety day in February 1999 when I noticed, on a knoll, a big stone I'd never seen there before. I went across to look at it, and, when almost up to it, was suddenly overcome by a suffocating sense of evil; but I have told the story before and it can be found in *By Hill and Shore in South Kintyre*, pp.122-24.

13. CLACH. Golden Eagle and Ravens at road-marker boulder, Innean Beag, 31/12/2008. Photograph by James MacDonald.

CLACHAN is generally translated 'kirk town', a place with a church, but it comes from *clach*, 'stone', and applied originally, as Irish *clochán*, to 'monastic stone-cells singly or in a group'. The word also refers, in Irish and Gaelic, to stepping-stones,[439] which was how Dugald Mitchell in 1908 chose to interpret Kintyre's only **Clachan** [764 561]: 'Like all *clachans*, the village has its burn and stepping stones (the name is derived from this circumstance), and the old village, with its church and churchyard, occupied the banks of the stream. Smart, modern cottages, appealing to the summer visitor, now line the highway.'[440] Peter MacIntosh, 50 years earlier, remarked that the village 'contains the parish church, school, grain mill, and smithy, all which are appropriate to render the name Clachan significant'.[441] Cuthbert Bede in 1861 described 'a large and pretty village in a valley, with a church and manse, inn, post-office, shop, grain-mill, and smithy'.[442] Duncan Reid, Gaelic educationalist, a founder-member of An Comunn Gàidhealach, and composer of *Suas leis a' Ghàidhlig*, the society's rallying song to this day, was born in Clachan in 1849 of Skipness stock. His father, also Duncan, helped out in the post office, and in 1868 helped himself to a £10 note from a letter, for which theft he was jailed.[443] 'The Clachan', according to Professor MacKinnon in 1887, was 'the common name in use among the Gaelic people for the parish of Kilcalmonell in Kintyre'.[444]

In *The Place-Names of the Parish of Campbeltown* (p 19), **Dalachlachan** is interpreted *Dail a' chlachain*, 'The field of the hamlet'. A pendicle attached to Knockhantymore, its location is now unknown, as is that of the 'hamlet', which I doubt ever existed. 'Dalaclachan' is marked on the Langlands map of 1793, and in 1797 Neil MacIntaggart had two horses at 'Dailclachan'.[445]

CLADH can signify a churchyard or a graveyard, but in Kintyre appears to apply to the latter. **Cladh nam Paitean** [663 346], which stands in stark and striking isolation on the machair north of Bellochantuy, was evidently in existence as early as 1699.[446] D. J. Macdonald interpreted the name as 'Burial ground of the humps'. The O.S. in 1867 had a more adventurous suggestion, from *bàth*, 'to drown', based on Peter MacIntosh's claim that the burial-ground was 'used as the resting place of some shipwrecked mariners' before adoption by 'the peasantry of the adjacent country'. The translation of the Gaelic form assembled to accommodate this tradition was the catchy 'The graves or mounds of the persons drowned'.[447] **Cladh**

Brìghde at Whitehouse is an alternative name for **Cill Brìghde**, to which refer as 'Kilbride' under CILL. In **Cladh Mhìcheil** [801 600], which was dedicated to Saint Michael, the earliest gravestones appear to date only from the mid-18th century.[448] Of **Cladh Bhadan** [c. 828 494], north of Cour, the O.S. in 1867 reported 'No vestige of former burying place now remains', and offered the interpretation 'Little grove burying ground'.[449] **Ach' nan Cladh** [700 379], 'Field of the Burial-grounds', which appeared on O.S. Sheet CCXLI.15, surveyed in 1867, pertains to Kilmaluag, to which refer under CILL.

CLÈIREACH, from Latin *clericus*, is a clerk or a cleric, but in Kintyre place-names is more likely to be the former; Gaelic *sagart*, 'priest', and *ministear*, 'minister', tend to cover the latter. A clerk in pre-Reformation times was an important functionary. Dugald Clerk, parish clerk of Kilkerran in 1505, had remission of rent for a merk of land for supervising the transport of the king's cattle to Stirling.[450] Such forms as 'McInclerich' and 'McA'Chlery', recorded in Kintyre from the 16th century, until the name was anglicised as 'Clark', represent *Mac a' chlèirich*, 'Son of the clerk'.[451] In post-Reformation place-names, the 'clerk' would have been of humbler status, e.g. a beadle.

In Southend, **Auchnacleirich** – *Achadh a' chlèirich*, 'The beadle's field' – was 'near old church, Kilblaan', said Archie McEachran, who contributed the name from oral tradition. He thought that **Dalaclerie** – *Dail a' chlèirich*, 'The beadle's field' again – which appears only in baptismal registers, might be the same place as the preceding or as **Achnaclary**, Langholm, which in 1841 was being farmed by Alexander McPhail with his wife Margaret, six children, two male servants and a female, the delightfully named 16-year-old Prudence Darmid. The local interpretation of this name was 'The field shaped like a pot-lid' (*clàr*).[452]

Dalachlarie [c. 764 573], a small farm near Clachan, is probably also *Dail a' chlèirich*. In 1841 two farmers and two weavers were in 'Dalclary', by 1861 only one house was occupied, and in 1867 the O.S. noted an 'old farm steading on farm of Corran'.[453] A stone in Clachan graveyard commemorates John Taylor, 'late tenant at Dalchlairy', who died in 1810, aged 62, and his wife Catherine Gilchrist, who died in 1828, aged 79. **Gortenclerich**, which is 'Little field [*goirtean*] of the clerk', appears near Putachan in C1851, when occupied by a cottar Janet MacFadyen and her four young children. In **Bailean-Cleirich** [889 571], Skipness, the generic is *baile*, and Captain T. P.

White considered it a 'probable relic of the days of episcopal rule'.[454] In 1851, Donald Hyndman was a cottar in 'Balanachlerach', but in 1867 the O.S. described 'The clerk's toun' as 'An old cot house in ruins'.[455] For **Arichlarie** in Campbeltown Parish see ÀIRIGH.

CLEIT, 'rocky eminence' or 'sea-rock', from Norse *klettr*, 'rock, cliff',[456] is rare in Kintyre. Had not the eminently picturesque parish church of Killean been built at **A' Chleit** [679 419] in the late 18th century, the word *cleit* would seldom be heard. D. J. Macdonald's interpretation of the name was the standard 'a rock or cliff', but his note, 'trap dykes at the place', elucidates the name's origin.[457] A' Chleit was formed some 60 million years ago during a period of major volcanic activity when 'thin sheets of molten rock were injected into Kintyre from below'. The promontory of A' Chleit is therefore an exposed volcanic dyke.[458] The other examples of the name are **Cleit Dhubh** [684 431], 'Black Sea-ridge', to the north, and the conglomerate ridges on the shore of Brunerican Bay, Southend, **Big Clet** [694 076] and **Little Clet** [693 076].[459]

14. CLEIT. The dyke at Cleit. Photograph by the late Hugh Ferguson, 1981.

CNOC, CNOCAN. *Cnoc*, sometimes anglicised as 'Knock', is 'hill', and *cnocan* is its diminutive, more or less. *Cnoc* is often defined only as 'hillock', and Gillies in *The Place-Names of Argyll* excludes it altogether from his round-up of hill-names, which runs to double figures, despite having earlier judged *cnoc* to be 'not infrequently a considerable hill'.[460] By no definition can **Cnoc Moy** [611 152] be considered a 'hillock'. At 1462 ft., it is the second-highest hill in Kintyre (see MAGH). **Cnoc a' Bhaile-Shios** [863 628] at 1383 ft. is the highest hill in northern Kintyre and was interpreted by the O.S. as 'Hill of the sloping farmstead'.[461] **Cnoc Buidhe** is 'Yellow Hill' and reaches 1023 ft. (see BUIDHE), while **Cnoc Donn**, 'Brown Hill', is higher still at 1335 ft. (see DONN). A selection of other *cnoc* examples, below a thousand feet, will suffice, while others will be found under their specifics, as above.

15. CNOC. Looking south to Cnoc Moy from Beinn na Faire, across the gorge of Inneans Glen and with Innean Mór sheep-fank part-visible to right. Photograph by the author, 3/5/2012.

Cnoc nan Iteag [718 492] is 'Hill of the Little Feathers'; **Cnoc Eòghainn** [717 352] 'Hugh's Hill'; **Cnoc a' Mhinisteir** [769 477] 'The Minister's Hill'; **Cnoc a' Chroicinn** [890 663] 'The Skin Hill'; **Cnoc nan Cnàmh** [877 661] 'Hill of the Bones'; **Cnoc an Fhreacadain** [859 651] 'The Witch Hill'; **Cnoc a' Mhór-fhir** [889

659] 'The Marquess's Hill'; **Cnoc an t-Samhlaidh** [798 493] 'The Apparition Hill'; **Cnoc Mòine Raibeirt** [901 591] 'Hill of Robert's Moss'; **Cnoc na Cluaise** [861 560] 'Hill of the Ear'; and **Cnoc na h-Àine** [778 403] 'Heated Knoll'. These names are intriguing. What did the little feathers signify? And the skin and the bones? Who were Hugh and Robert? Who was the minister and who was the witch, and the 'great man', or 'Marquess', who was he? Whose apparition or likeness appeared? What did the ear signify, and the heat? One may ask, but answers are unlikely to be forthcoming.

I had included **Cnoc Éibhleach** [714 078], 'Hill of Embers',[462] in the above list, but, as though to remind me of the folly of certitude, an answer came forth, in Ordnance Survey records: 'The name is derived from the dark appearance of the earth.' The interpretation 'Coal Hill, or Knoll',[463] while not literally correct – *éibhleach* has the sense of live or burning coals – certainly elucidates the primary allusion.

Just as meanings can be lost, so too can names themselves. Roy's mid-18th century map provides many examples, though, admittedly, the map's orthography as well as scale is unreliable. A group of three *cnoc* names in south-east Kintyre appears to be otherwise unrecorded. **Knocknacraig**, 'Hill of the rock', above Polliwilline, seems to correspond to the unnamed hill on O.S. maps at 739 108. **Knockmor**, 'Big hill', above Glenahervie, appears to be **The Bastard** [758 123], as it is now obscurely known, and **Knocknamoan**, which probably means 'Peat hill',[464] may represent the deviant O.S. **Cockalane** [740 119].

With the *cnocan* names, attached to knolls and hillocks, we enter different territory, and the place-names come to life. Or some of them do, thanks to D. J. Macdonald and to an enduring folk interest in the *sìthean*, or 'fairy knowes' (see under SÌTHICH) which dot the landscape like the huts of our ancestors. These knolls were once part of a well populated, intimately known and densely named landscape, and it is hardly surprising that the traditions attached to them persisted longer than those attached to many more remote features.

Cnocan nam piobairean [695 373], 'Hillock of the pipers', is near Blary. According to tradition, seven pipers, by the name of MacKeith or Keith, were buried there after being killed in a nearby 'engagement'.[465] **Cnocan a' Chrochadaire** [686 428] at Beachmenach is 'The Hangman's Hillock'. Described as a small mound, virtually levelled by ploughing, human bones were said to have been found there in the 19th century.[466] **Cnocan na-té-**

riabhaich [660 375], on Glenacardoch farm, may be translated 'Hillock of the grizzly one', though D. J. Macdonald, who collected a legend in connection with the place, suggested *tìr riabhach*, 'brindled or brown land'. However, he had his reasons for seeking to negate the human connotation. It is a cone-shaped hillock with the foundation of a house at its foot, and, according to a 'weird tale' collected by Macdonald, a woman lived there with seven husbands, 'each of whom entered the house by a private door'. He clearly disliked this example of sexual licence – 'the Tibetan matrimonial heresy', as he put it – in his parish, and was 'disposed to break a lance' in defence of 'a much maligned woman, in advance of her age and paying the penalty'. His argument was that the woman, an 'emancipated ... intellectual', had the house constructed 'to give free admission to the vital elements of earth, sea and sky, at a time when people lived in dark, unwholesome earth dwellings'. He speculates: 'Were her consorts spiritual and not social?'[467] His earnest analysis of a mere fragment of tradition might now seem as 'weird' as the story itself, but he was a man of his time and position. Neil Thomson, lobster-fisherman in Muasdale, had a simpler take on the woman. She was a witch who lived at Bealach a' Chaochain, and he interpreted *Cnocan na-té-riabhaich* as 'The Grey One's Knoll'. Indeed, the name was always with him because he used it when 'puttin marks on creels there'; that is, the 'dun' was one of many landmarks he used in the laying and lifting of his lobster-pots.[468] On the earliest O.S. map, surveyed in 1867, the knoll is named **Cnocan na Té Brice**, 'The Spotted Woman's Hillock',[469] with *breac* perhaps suggesting 'pock-marked'.

COILLE is a wood. The **Crock na Coilly** which appears on an old map of Sanda represents *Cnoc na coille*, 'Hill of the wood', which has become **Wood Hill** [723 045] on O.S. maps.[470] There is another Cnoc na Coille [769 422] west of Brackley, which, on the first O.S. map of the area, surveyed in 1867, has no trees anywhere near it. It happens, of course, that some place-names lose their meaning through landscape changes, and in this case the wood could have been cleared. If so, then Cnoc na Coille has recovered its original sense, because it is now covered by a coniferous plantation. **Coille Sheasg** [633 123] on Remuil Hill, Southend, is 'Dry Wood',[471] and on the earliest O.S. map (1866) is a bare slope. Again, it has been planted over. The O.S. defined it as 'The barren wood or grove' and explained that it 'was formerly a wood which has now entirely disappeared'.[472] **Coille Rubha Dhuibh** [862 554], 'Wood of the

Black Point', is the 'Black Wood' which Mrs Higginson claimed was infested with ghosts and fairies (see SÌTHICH).

The Southend farm **Coledrain** [727 088] may represent *Coille an droighinn*, 'The thorn wood', but *Cùil an droighinn*, 'The thorn nook', has also been suggested[473] and is preferred by Ian A. Fraser.[474] I have not found any spelling earlier than 1806 – on a gravestone in Kilcolmkill, erected to John McCoag in 'Cuildreghan', who died in March of that year – but this farm was one of the Lands of Saint Ninian, and **Culrachan** – in 1669 'Coulrachane' – which is listed with these Lands, and which has not been identified, may merit consideration. C1841 has 'Coulydrain', C1851 'Culydryan', and the O.S. in 1866 'Colydrain', without interpretation.[475] In a newspaper report of the grounding of the French brigantine *Eugenie Desiree* in 1881, the spelling is 'Collydrain'.[476] Strangely, in 1856, when the McMillans in 'Cuildryan and Knockmorran' offered to renew their lease, the Hon. Augustus Henry Macdonald Moreton of Largie refused money and insisted on the rent being paid half in cheese and half in meal. When ownership of the farms changed to the 8th Duke of Argyll, he agreed to a money rent of £265 instead. In a letter to the Duke, dated 17/1/1866, John McMillan stated that he agreed to the earlier rent only because his father and mother were 'old and frail and wished to end their days where they had spent most of their lives'.[477]

COIRCE, 'corn', 'oats' – see under ACHADH.

COIRE has been borrowed into English as 'corrie', for a circular hollow in a mountainside – cf. French *cirque* and Welsh *cwm* – but its original meaning was 'cauldron', and it is obvious how that image was transferred to the landscape. There were two farms named **Corrylach** in South Kintyre, but the interpretation of the name has proved difficult. The steading [645 126] of the one in Glenbreackerie has long been in ruins. John Cameron suggested *Corr-bhealach*, 'Steep or rugged pass', while the Rev. T. S. Macpherson advanced *coire* + *lach*, 'Corrie of the wild duck'.[478] Cameron Gillies considered *coire-chlach*, 'stony-corrie', but decided 'duck' was 'even better'.[479] Gilbert Márkus suspects *coire* + the locational suffix *-lach* = 'corrie place', adding: 'As this suffix is apparently no longer in use in modern Gaelic, it is not surprising that most modern speakers fail to recognise it fossilised in place-names.'[480]

For **Corrylach na Meine** [651 131] – 'a hollow formed by a landslip'[481] – about half-a-mile away, the preferred interpretation of '*na meine*' was 'of the mine', from *mèinn*, 'mine', 'ore'; but Ian A. Fraser considers *mèinn*, which occurs in several other Kintyre place-names, a 'problematic term', which he suspects applied to 'ore' rather than 'mine'. 'A number of burns which have reddish bottoms are called *Allt na Mèinn*, simply because of the colours, and without any mining operations being obvious.'[482] The Rev Colin Smith, whose Gaelic constructions I shall omit, offered a colourful choice: 'The corrie of the heroes of the Feine' and 'The corrie for the reckoning of the ore.'[483] For the other Corrylach [705 303], on the west side of Lussa Reservoir, a few 18th century spellings are available: 1736 'Coroloch and Row Coroloch'; 1764 'Coralach'; and 1790 'Rudh-Corralach'.[484] The present house was latterly a shepherd's steading.

Corriechrevie [739 538], north of Ballochroy, is *Coire Craobhaidh*, 'Corrie of the Place of the Tree'; cf. Corriecravie, Arran.[485] This name seems to have replaced Carnbeg (see under CÀRN), and the first record of it which I have is a baptism in 1785 at 'Corechrebhi'. **Coire nan Capull** [858 607], also in North Kintyre, is 'Corrie of the Mares'. The original sense of *coire*, as 'cauldron', was preserved in the Gaelic name for Salt Pans [632 207], **Na Coireacha(n) Salainn**,[486] where salt was industrially extracted from sea-water between 1670 and c. 1770.

One night, Calum MacGeachy had a supernatural experience when passing **Allt a' Choire** [726 272], 'Stream of the Corrie', which runs into Lussa River. He heard a voice, 'like the hoarse roaring of the sea', address him thrice: 'Ho! Calum!' To this uncanny greeting, the pious and intelligent Calum replied: 'I am Calum MacGeachy, and in the name of the blessed Trinity on my way home – what have you to say to me?' There was only silence. Peter MacIntosh, when a boy, heard that story and many others from the old man. Calum was born in Strathduie and lived in that glen until he became old and moved to Campbeltown, his wife having died and his family scattered abroad. Peter said of him that he was self-educated and 'could read a Gaelic book in English and an English book in Gaelic'.[487] I have to confess that when I noticed 'Alt-a-choire' in MacIntosh's book, it meant nothing to me and I had to consult my files to discover its location. I doubt if anyone alive could now put a name to that burn without first consulting a map, but it would have been well enough known for generations. McGeachy knew the name, and MacIntosh, having heard it as a child, remembered it into old age.

Through census records, I looked at the Southend Corrylach, which seemed to be full of strange and interesting people every ten years. It was clearly a remote place to which unstable paupers were sent. On 28/10/1850, the Parochial Board inspector at Campbeltown wrote to Neil Campbell, 'Corlach, Southend', asking him to 'send John Kelvie home on Tuesday or Wednesday as I have found a place for him in Greenock'.[488]

In 1841 Neil was farming there. His age was given as 35 and his wife Helen McMillan's as 31. The first of their children had appeared, one-year-old Mirren, who became 'Marjory' 10 years later. There was another Neil Campbell there, aged 15 and a farm worker. Catherine McMillan, a farm servant aged 27, was Helen's sister. Then there were Jean Fullarton (2); Flora McLarty (30), a 'pauper'; Angus McLarty, a baby, presumably Flora's; James Sinclair, a 20-year-old 'schoolmaster'; 80-year-old Catherine Tait; William Tait, 35, a farm worker – presumably her son – who will reappear later, and 77-year-old Betty Love.

In 1851 Neil and Helen have five children; Catherine, Neil's sister-in-law and a pauper, is there; Jean Fullarton is also still there, now a 'scholar', or schoolgirl; James Ryeburn, aged 50, is a pauper and lodger; Hugh Hamilton, aged 7, is also a lodger, and 14-year-old Peter Kelly is a 'visitor'. These last three were all born in Campbeltown Parish, as were Helen and Catherine. Neil Campbell himself belonged to Southend.

In 1861 Neil and Helen are there with four children, one of whom, Charlotte, was with her aunt Catherine, now in a cottage of her own. In the farmhouse, in addition to the family, there was a boarder, an Irish-born 'lunatic pauper', Fanny McIntyre, and Willie Tait, described as a visiting 'basket maker'. He was a colourful character whose frequent appearances in court were usually enlivened by some verbal outburst. In April 1871, exactly 10 years after he sat at Neil Campbell's peat-fire, he was in jail for 'theft of wearing apparel'. He got four months, but considered the sentence lenient, and as he was led out of court shouted in delight: 'Hoorah! Victorious, victorious, by the life of Pharoah!'[489]

In 1871 Neil and Helen were still at 'Corylach'. Charlotte, now aged 21, and son James, 19, were still with them, and a 6-year-old grandson, Neil C. McKinnon. There were two 'lunatics' now boarded at the farm, Jane McNaught from Southend and Duncan Galbraith from Campbeltown. Catherine was still in the cottage and still a pauper.

Ten years on, in 1881, the old Campbells were dead and son James was farming with the help of his nephew Neil McKinnon. Sixteen-year-old Susan McLean was a 'general servant' with them, Duncan Galbraith was still a boarder, and Catherine McMillan was still in the cottage. By 1891 no one was there. James died in Lochgilphead in 1924 at the age of 72.[490]

Willie Tait was a notorious thief, whose exploits entered local folklore and the records of the Lord Advocate's Department, Scottish Record Office. Calum Bannatyne had a rather improbable tale which implicated Willie in the theft of sovereigns from a public house at Lephenstrath Bridge, which was frequented by Irish lobster-fishermen who 'peyed their drink in gold'. After he had robbed the public house, he stole a boat from Glenbreackerie waterfoot and decided to escape to Canada by intercepting a liner outward bound from the Clyde. Unknown to him, while he was sitting in the bottom of the boat counting the money, 'the fellow at the mast-heid had his telescope on him'. When the ship drew alongside, Willie was asked if he wanted aboard, and he said that he wanted to go to Canada. 'They took the money off him, made him pey his wey across, ye see. But before he wis in Canada, he had his money stealt oot the till anyway, because he wis an expert at it. Ye see, there are some folk born tae steal.'[491]

16. CORR. *Corr nan Long from Crockan gate. Photograph by the author, 29/4/2012.*

CORR. There appear to be only two absolutely clear instances of this generic, both of them in Southend Parish: **Corr Bhàn** [599 103] and **Corr nan Long** [645 103]. In *The Place-Names of the Parish of Southend* (p 15), *corr* is interpreted as 'eminence', therefore 'Light-coloured Eminence' and 'Eminence of the Ships'. John MacQueen, in *Place-Names in the Rhinns of Galloway and Luce Valley* (p 84), notes that '*corr* in the sense "round hill" is found extensively in Ireland, but is unusual in Scotland'. D. and L. Flanagan in *Irish Place Names* (p 61) interpret *corr* as 'a "projection" of some kind or other, a "pointed hill"'. Much else lies between these poles of interpretation, but the main question from a local point of view – literally – is: what shapes do these hills have? Corr Bhàn, north of the Mull, is the higher, at 1212 ft., and is rounded. Corr nan Long (906 ft.), to the east, is more elongated and quite level-topped. Both, curiously, share latitude 103.

CORRAN. On the meanings of this element there has been disagreement. A popular derivation is from *corran*, 'sickle', referring to a curved bay, which was the O.S. interpretation in 1867: 'a shearing hook or sickle'.[492] Macbain took Gillies to task over his treatment of the Kintyre **Corran** [764 580]: '"Corran" means a point; the fem. is "corrag", finger; it is common in the Isles; what has corran, a sickle, to do with it? The root of corran, sickle, is "kerp, korp", to cut (Stokes).'[493] This is Gillies's offending passage, tortuous prose and all: '*Corran* is a diminutive formed from *còrr, excess, outgrowth*. The name is applied to small, blunt promontories at which the tidal current runs swift. Some have thought that the name has had origin from *Corran, a sickle*, and the shape of the various Corrans helped to support this view; so far as the *word* is, however, concerned, this must be given up, but as regards *the fact*, being descriptive, the error, if it is an error, is still a help. There is, indeed, no reason apparent why the two words may not have had a common origin. It is the same root we find in *Corr-ag, the thumb*.'[494] One has to wonder how a swift-running tide could have found its way into a definition of a promontory, and how he could have defined *corrag* as 'thumb'. Here is Professor Watson's definition of *corrán*: '... a low cape tapering symmetrically to a point, is from *corr*, "taper, peaked, rounded to a point", an adjective applied to a large variety of things – arrows, spears, blades of grass, eyes, fingers, goblets, etc.'[495] The Flanagans in *Irish Place Names* (p 62) had this to say of *corran*: 'Means basically an "angle", "corner" or even "sickle."' What does the topography of Corran at Clachan communicate? The present steading occupies a blunt promontory, and the big bay to the east, which might be seen as the 'sickle', is, in any case, the *lùb*, or 'bend', from which Loup took its name.

An Corran, Arran, Ian A. Fraser explains as '"The Sand Spit or Gravel Bank", from G. *corran* "sickle", "sickle-shaped sandbank"', formed before Machrie Water changed course.[496] **Corran**, on Glenramskill farm, was also a stream-related feature, described in a lease of 1808 as 'that small spot of ground upon the north side of the water'.[497] Likewise **Corran Mór**, a field on Dippen farm, Carradale, defined as 'Big Sickle', and formed by a bend of the river.[498] **Corranbuie**, near the head of West Loch Tarbert, is an error for Carnbuie (see CÀRN).

CRAOBH is simply a tree. **Eilean nan Craobh** [806 615] is 'Island of Trees' in West Loch Tarbert. **Tigh na Craoibhe** [897 575], 'House of the Tree', was a small 19th century settlement at the west end of Skipness village.[499] **Cnoc nan Craobh** [734 456], 'Hill of the Trees', rises to 1058 ft. east of Tayinloan, and has a cloak of trees on it now, if it hadn't before. **Allt na Craoibhe** [732 385], 'Stream of the Tree', flows into Barr Glen from the south. The burn south of Grogport which Carradale fishermen called **Allt Creeve** [808 427] most likely represents *Allt Craoibhe*, 'Tree Stream'. For **Lecknacreive** see under LEAC.

CREAG is 'rock' or 'crag', but can also mean 'cliff', 'precipice', 'quarry' and 'hill'.[500] Most of the *creag* features in Kintyre are not rocky hills, but rocks, some of them small, such as the tidal rock in Camus na Ban-tighearna, well known in Tarbert tradition as **Creag Eonaidh**, 'Johnny's Rock', or **Creag Mhic Cuilgein**, 'MacQuilkan's Rock'. In the beginnings of ring-netting, when the little 'trawls' would be set in a circle from the shore, with a man left ashore to haul that end of the net, Johnny was stationed on the rock when he saw that the net was full of herring. In his excitement, he began jumping and shouting *Tha mi beairtich gu bràth!* ('I am wealthy forever!'), and jumped so much that he flattened the rock.[501]

Davie MacFarlane, from whom I first heard the tale in 1975, claimed to have known Johnny MacQuilkan. He described him as a '*bodach*', a little old man, 'jeest there and no more', whom he would visit, in the company of one Duncan Johnston. They would sit with him in his 'wee single-end' at Springside and enjoy his 'crack', which was delivered in a mixture of 'broken English and Gaelic'.[502] MacQuilkan intrigued me and I decided to track him down. I was prepared for difficulties with the surname, because MacQuilkan, in common with many Gaelic names in Kintyre, was sometimes disguised in the anglicisation process and may appear as Wilkinson, Wilkison or Wilkie in the records. I checked the 1881, 1891 and 1901 censuses and found no trace of him. Davie himself was at Larkfield in 1901 as a boy of six years.

There are three recorded instances of **Creag Mhór**, 'Big Rock', in Saddell and Skipness Parish, one of which names was transferred to a settlement [c. 780 455], originally a one-merkland farm in Killean Parish and later a shepherd's house on the farm of Auchenbreck. Early forms include: 1576 'Craigmoir'; 1623 'Craigmor'; 1639 'Craigmor'; 1651 'Craigmoir' and 1683 'Craigmoire'. The house was deserted by the end of the 19th century.

Creag nan Cuilean [619 167] is 'Rock of the whelps', which may refer to fox-cubs.[503] Strictly, the name applies to a crag on the 1166-ft. hill extending from the Slate, but the whole hill now gets the name. In the 1920s, there was a post-box on the summit which allowed the McKendrick brothers, Dugald and Alexander, the former shepherd in Gleneadardacrock and the latter in Killypole, to exchange messages. Whenever a note had been left in the box, a wooden flag would be raised, which was visible on the skyline from both localities. Close to the box was the **Captain's Well**, named after Captain Hector Macneal of Lossit, who died in 1910. The well was a lunching place for grouse-shooters, and bottles of beer would be kept cool in its basin.[504]

17. *CREAG. Looking north to Craigaig Bay, with Dùn Bàn headland in distance, 3/5/2012. Photograph by the author.*

18. CREAG. Donald McKerral and wife Fiona McCallum outside the hut at Craigaig, c. 1955. Photograph courtesy of D. McKerral, Campbeltown.

Extensions of the word include *creagaig*, 'rocky place', anglicised as **Craigaig**, which is a township on the coast south of Machrihanish at 610 184. Though ruinous, it none the less retains much of its original integrity, and, if visited in winter or spring, when the bracken is down, presents a fair impression of how a typical late 18th/early 19th century township would appear, as to lay-out of dwellings and outbuildings; and, as a bonus, there is a corn-drying kiln nearby, skilfully made and nicely preserved. The township is beautifully located on a high terrace, with wonderful views south to the cliffy coastline of Kintyre and west to the Atlantic, with Islay and the northern coast of Ireland visible in the distance.

Natural beauty, however, does not always soothe the human spirit. John buie McGeachie and John McConnachie were feuding at Craigaig in 1686. McGeachie claimed that McConnachie had beaten and bloodied him. Neither men turned up in court on 15 December, and a constable was sent to bring them in. They were both fined for taking part in 'bloodwit and battery' and imprisoned until they paid and found caution to keep the peace. Two days later, McGeachie's son Patrick confessed to striking McConnachie and was also fined.[505]

In the latter half of the 18th century, Craigaig was tenanted by a McMath family. When Archibald McMath 'in Innenbeg' got the lease in 1758 from the 'Heirs of the deceast Duncan McMillan', one of its conditions was 'Not to harbour anyone accesseray to the late Rebellion, nor anyone in opposition to the Established Church'. When Archibald died in 1795, he left a wife and three children, Dugald, Jean and Archibald, who were helped on the farm by Malcolm and Donald Kelly, tenants in Machrihanish, who themselves got the lease in 1798.[506]   In 1813, Donald Kelly was involved in a dispute with 'Donald MacConochy or Campbell', Ballegroggan, over the road to Craigaig.[507]   On an Argyll Estate map of the farm drawn in 1836, the houses are described as 'ruined', but they were certainly occupied after then, for in 1853 an elderly widow, Flora MacKeagh (MacKeich), was recorded there, by which time the land itself had been turned over to sheep.[508]

Craigaig isn't named on O.S. maps; it should be. Like the Lake to the north and Inneans Bay to the south, it was a popular picnic spot in the 20th century, particularly for Drumlemble families. There was a wooden hut at the south end of the bay with a visitors' book in it. The entries would make nostalgic reading now, but the book is untraceable and the hut itself is gone.[509]

Creggan [869 563] near Claonaig is a diminutive of *creag*: *Creagan*, 'Little crag'. It was a farm of some antiquity and, as 'Craggan', is on record as far back as 1511. For **Balegreggan** and **Ballygreggan** see under BAILE, for **Creag an airgiod** under CRÙBAN, for **Glenairiecreggan** under ÀIRIGH, for **Creag Creamha** under CREAMH and for **Creagruadh** under RUADH.

CREAMH. Macbain gives only 'garlic' for this, but Dwelly adds gentian and Hart's tongue fern.[510] In Kintyre place-names I'd say it should relate to Wild Garlic, with one possible exception. The appearance of garlic leaves pushing through the earth in February is, for me, one of spring's first intimations. When chewed, the leaves make a peppery frontal assault on the taste-buds, but somehow fail to impart flavour when cooked. Some Kintyre woodlands are carpeted year after year with garlic leaves (the beautiful white star-like flowers are much later in coming). Wild garlic is therefore not a plant that can be missed in the landscape; even should the plant itself be overlooked, its strong odour may indicate its presence.

It is no surprise to find it in place-names, and there are three known in Kintyre, but **Lochan a' Chreibh** [807 548], above Clachan, is not, I believe, one of them. Wild garlic is essentially a woodland plant and that loch lies in high moorland. In April, 2012, my wife Judy and I walked out there to check the loch's margins. We didn't expect to find wild garlic there, and were not surprised by its absence. It might be argued, of course, that the plant could have been there two or three centuries ago, but I doubt that. I have never, anywhere, seen *Allium ursinum* grow in acid soil. 'Lochan a' Chreibh' is the current O.S. spelling, but 'Lochan Creamha' was the form recorded in 1867, with the interpretation 'Loch of the garlic'.[511] On a plan of Balinakill Estate, drawn in 1867, the spelling is 'Loch a' Chreamh', which I prefer, because it's a fair-sized body of water and no 'little loch'. The boundary of Kilcalmonell and Skipness parishes passes through its middle. John MacDonald, Campbeltown, tells me that the loch is known to anglers as the **Gull Loch**, from the gulls that nest there. **Allt nan Creamh** [680 298], 'Stream of the Wild Garlic', flows into the sea south of Bellochantuy. **Creag Creamha** (O.S. form) or **Creag a' Creamha** (local) is 'Rock of the Wild Garlic' and is south of Torrisdale at c. 798 352. Mrs Crystal Paterson, Port Rìgh, as a young girl some 75 years ago, heard the name from the Torrisdale Estate gamekeeper, and she remembered (30/10/2012) seeing 'a lot of wild garlic' there.

19. CREAMH. Loch a' Chreamh, 23/4/2012. Photograph by the author.

CRÌOCH is a boundary or march, dividing one land-holding from another. Before the mapping of estates, these boundaries were preserved in oral tradition (see CLACH). Streams (or their courses) were invaluable in the fixing of boundaries, having length and permanence, and **Allt Crìche**, 'March Burn', occurs at 886 571, 733 404, 792 344 and 633 153. At **Cnoc na Crìche** [755 281], 'Boundary Hill', the marches of three farms meet: Ardnacross, Kilkeddan and Ballochgair.[512] **Lean nan Tri Chrìoch** [902 602], north of Skipness, was interpreted by the O.S. as 'Meadow of the three marches' and described as 'a flat or hollow'.[513] '**Dounancrich**' is shown on the Langlands map of 1793 as, or on, the headland which forms the southern end of Cour Bay [826 484]. No *dùn*, or small fort, has been discovered there, and the name may represent *Dùnan Crìche*, 'Hillock of the boundary'.

CROIS is Gaelic for 'cross' and appears in several Kintyre place-names. **Crosshill** is a 270 ft. hill [715 194] to the south of Campbeltown. It gave its name to a farm, with the early spellings: 1545 'Crossall', 1605 'Croshall', 1678 'Crostall' and 1692 'Croshill'. It has been interpreted as Old Norse *Crossa fjall*, 'Hill of the cross',[514] but Rixson prefers *kross* + *vollr*, 'cross-field'.[515] **Crossibeg** [745 220], near Kilchousland, appears in early charters as: 1502 'Crossabeg', 1507 'Corsobeg', 1545 'Corsabeg', 1596 'Crosbeg' and 1629 'Crossibeg'. The name represents Gaelic *Croisean beaga*, 'Little crosses',[516] cf. Crossabeg (*Crosa Beaga*), County Wexford, identical meaning.[517] **Crossleggie** [683 147] has been interpreted *Crois shleachdaidh*, 'Cross of prostration'.[518] Dr Patrick H. Gillies in *Netherlorn* (1909) remarks on 'a steep defile' named *Bealach an t'sleuchdaich*, 'The Pass of prostration', half-a-mile from the mouth of the Euchar on the Melfort road, and a 'Cross of Prostration' near the head of Glen Aray, where the sacred island of Innishail in Loch Awe first appears in view.[519] **Ardnacross** [767 262], north of Peninver, is *Àrd na croise*, 'Height of the cross'.[520] In 1922, a party of Kintyre Antiquarians took Mr W. Mackay Mackenzie, Secretary of H. M. Commission on the Ancient and Historical Monuments (Scotland), to a location at Ardnacross 'popularly supposed' to be 'the site of a cross', but his opinion was that further investigation would probably reveal 'a place of ancient burial'.[521]

Since Crosshill overlooks Kilkerran, Crossibeg Kilchousland, Crossleggie Killellan, and Ardnacross Kildonan, it might not be entirely unreasonable to infer that the crosses enshrined in these names served as stations for prostration or genuflexion on the approach to the chapels.

Captain White speculated that **Port na Croise** [655 289], an inlet north of Westport, might have 'some early ecclesiastical association' with Kilchenzie.[522]

Crois Mhic Aoidh [734 350] is not a 'cross' in any sense, but a prehistoric standing stone on Arnicle farm, later incorporated into Kintyre Bruce lore. In 1306, tradition has it, the fugitive Robert Bruce landed at **Port Rìgh** [817 378], 'King's Port', from Arran. He was taken into Gilchrist MacKay's house at Ugadale, and, after some cryptic banter with MacKay's wife, went to bed in the barn, which is where, according to the version I have chosen, he watched the inspirational spider climb the baulks of the roof six times. In the morning, MacKay's son led him across the back of Kintyre towards the west side. When they parted at the stone, Bruce said to him: 'Look, my lad, and whatever length your sight can carry you, if I gain the victory you will get a right to that extent of land.' The boy replied: 'All I want is, that you give us the farm we left, and the farm we came down upon going across the country.'[523] So, the MacKays in 1329, after Bruce had become king, received a grant of the Crown lands of Ugadale and Arnicle.[524] The stone was also known as **Clach Mhic Aoidh**,[525] which makes more sense.

Crossaig [831 514] is difficult. Norman Newton in 1999 ventured a derivation from Norse *kross-vík*, 'cross-bay',[526] with which Ian A. Fraser tentatively agreed, 'even if a standing cross has not survived'.[527] Old spellings: 1502/07 'Crossak', 'Corshauch', 'Cressauch'; 1545 'Crossag'; 1596 'Crosak'.

CROIT is a borrowing into Gaelic of English 'croft'.[528] As a system of land-use, crofting was negligible in Kintyre, where the farm was the sole post-Improvement agricultural unit. Crofting townships, as found in the Hebrides, were therefore unknown. A 'croft' in Kintyre was usually a patch of land, or 'pendicle', apportioned to a sub-tenant or to a miller or blacksmith. *Croit*, however, is a rare form, which I have found only in Saddell and Skipness Parish; but in South Kintyre the Scots form 'craft' was in use.[529] See also DÒID, an equivalent term.

The 19th century 'land agitation' movements had relatively little impact on Kintyre, but a Kintyre branch of the radical Scottish Land Restoration League was certainly in existence in 1885, when it brought John Murdoch (1818-1903) to Kintyre for a week to address public meetings on the subject of 'The Land for the People'. Murdoch, who was brought up on Islay, became a nationalist while serving as an Inland Revenue officer in Dublin. Back in Scotland, he founded the influential *Highlander* newspaper and emerged as an anti-landlord campaigner of major political significance.[530] Murdoch was already familiar with Kintyre, having been stationed in the Largieside as an Inland Revenue officer. A report of his raids on illicit whisky-distillers, quite possibly written by himself, appeared in the *Campbeltown Journal* of 4/3/1852.[531] The main meeting in Kintyre was chaired by councillor Dugald Robertson, a local fisherman and boat-owner, who stated 'his honest conviction that the landed proprietors were now getting their reward; it was coming, they could not keep it back'.[532]

Garrachroit [808 447] at Grogport is *Garbh chroit*, 'Rough croft', which the O.S. explained as 'from the inferior quality of ground'. It appears to have been a small farm with crofts attached, and in C1851 was said to comprise 25 acres. In 1774, Alexander Curry, Malcolm McCallum and John and Iver McCoag in 'Garrachreit' appeared in a court case involving unauthorised wood-cutting.[533] In 1821 'Garachriot' was the scene of a disturbance which ended in the death of Duncan McPhee, crofter. Duncan's daughter Mary and Archibald McKeich had an 'agreement' to marry, and the meeting between them and their relations took place on the evening of 1 June. Archibald, John and Dugald Carmichael were charged with MacPhee's murder, but the charges were later dropped. The celebrants had been 'drinking till after daylight', and the violence appears to have stemmed from an earlier incident in which Duncan McPhee struck a brother of the Carmichaels' for calling him an 'Old Grey headed Buggar'. The precognitions, or preliminary examinations of witnesses, constitute an interesting, if incomplete, social and genealogical record of the community in that year. Eighteen named individuals are mentioned as living there. There were three Carmichael families: that of the accused, that of Duncan Carmichael, aged 60, 'Tenant and Constable', and Duncan Carmichael, aged 30, who explained that his relationship to the accused was 'not so near as second cousins', and that Duncan the constable was not 'in the most distant degree connected with them'. The other surnames, including wives', were Hyndman, McCallum, McKeich or 'McKee', McMurchy and McPhee or 'McFee'. As would be expected, there is evidence of a good deal of intermarriage among the families. All the young men were described as fishermen, except John and Dugald Carmichael who were boat-builders. The case having failed, Archibald and John – who was a fisherman in Campbeltown and had been back at Garrachroit having a boat repaired by his brothers – were released from prison; the third Carmichael brother, Dugald, had 'absconded' before legal proceedings began.[534] A headstone in Brackley commemorates Archibald Gilchrist, 'Garrachroit', who died in March 1819. See also Grogport under PORT.

Croit Bhrìdean [811 519] was described in 1867 as a ruinous 'old farm steading'.[535] It appears in 1654 as 'Croychtbridan' and on the 1801 Langlands map as 'Cretbridan'. As 'Cruitvridan' in 1852 it was advertised for let with North Crossaig and 'Achullin'.[536] The name now has to be interpreted as 'Oyster-catcher croft', after the wader *Haematopus ostralegus*; but 'oyster-catcher' properly belongs to the American species and is an absurdity here. The Scots name 'sea-piet', or sea-magpie, from its plumage, has regrettably now died out in Kintyre. *Brìdean* or *brìd-eun*, 'Bride's bird',[537] the Gaelic name in Kintyre, appears to commemorate the widely influential Saint Bridget. **Croit Bàgh** [918 615], north of Skipness, the O.S. interpreted as 'Bay (of the) field',[538] but 'Croft Bay' is more like it. The name presumably derived from the inland ruins marked **Croit** [915 615] on O.S. Sheet CCII, published in 1873; but that was the location of **Àirigh Fhuair** (see under FUAR).

CROMAN is a bird of prey, and the name derives from *crom*, 'bent',[539] alluding presumably to wing-shape in flight. The Red Kite (*Milvus milvus*) is the main candidate, though most dictionaries also gloss more vaguely as 'hawk' or 'small hawk', and, as an example of local variation, Eleanor MacDougall points out that '*croman* on the Ross of Mull is "buzzard", known elsewhere as *clamhan*'.[540] The Kite was once common in Kintyre, but probably became extinct as a breeding species in the 19th century, though in the past two decades it has reappeared as a visitor.[541] 'Kite' is not a certainty in all of the following place-names, but the general interpretation of *croman* in O.S. name-books is 'gled', which in Scots is primarily the Kite.[542]

In Southend, **Innean a' Chromain** [703 074], at the eastern extremity of Brunerican Bay, is 'Cove of the Kite', and **Creag a' Chromain** [631 117], 'The Kite's Rock', is a crag overlooking High Glenadale.[543] **Cnoc a' Chromain** [659 264], 'Hill of the Kite', opposite Westport, was inexplicably replaced on later O.S. maps by 'Cnoc a' Choirce', Hill of the Oats, and then 'Cnoc a' Choire', Hill of the Corrie. On Admiralty charts it is 'Crocnacroman or Gads Hill'. **Taychroman** [689 432] – *Tigh a' chromain*, 'House of the kite' – was a small settlement near Beacharr. Archibald Milloy was

a weaver at 'Tighcromman' in 1807, and Donald MacMillan farmer
at 'Taychroman' in 1855 when Duncan MacConachy allegedly bit
Hector MacLean during 'caelach' celebrations [544] (see CAILLEACH).
By C1891 it was uninhabited and by 1901 'in ruins'. **Loch a'
Chromain** [752 451], 'Loch of the Kite', is in the hills mid-way
between Tayinloan and Grogport. In 1738 and 1793 it was recorded
as 'Loch Croman', and on a map of Killean Estate in 1824 as 'Loch
a' chromain'. North of Skipness, **Eas a' Chromain** [900 609] is
'Waterfall of the Kite'.

CRUACH in place-names is 'hill', but is rather more than that.
The sense is essentially a 'heap' or 'stack', as applied to hay or peats.
Such stacks aren't exactly everyday sights any more, but the image is
of a bulky, fairly symmetrical mass, sometimes standing in isolation.
That is the linguistic template, but whether it matches all Kintyre
hills named *cruach* is a question which would make an interesting
topographical study, albeit one complicated by afforestation's having
modified the natural contours of the landscape.

20. *CRUACH. Robert McInnes's peat-stack* (cruach mhòine) *behind his
house at Stewarton, 1986. Photograph by Judy Martin.*

On 12/4/2012, I had a look at two, which stand close together above Killean, **Cruach an Eich**, 'The Horse Hill' (see under EACH), and **Cruach Mhic-an-t-Saoir** [743 429], 'MacIntyre's Hill'. The shape in each case clearly related not to the characteristically conical hay-stack, which had somehow imprinted itself on my imagination, but to the elongated peat-stack after the peats had been built into a neat pile for the winter.

The distribution of this place-name element appears to have a geological slant. In the whole of South Kintyre, there are only three hills named *cruach*. Southend Parish has only one, **A' Chruach** [612 108], standing at 1231 ft. near the Mull, and long and rounded in shape. In Campbeltown Parish there is another of the same name [712 245] and its neighbour **Skeroblin Cruach** [707 275], both close to the boundary with Kilchenzie Parish. For North Kintyre, my lists show a total of 32 hills with the generic *cruach*, half of them in Saddell and Skipness Parish; but that isn't the whole story.

21. CRUACH. *The elongated stack shape of Cruach Mhic-an-t-Saoir from Cruach an Eich, 12/4/2012. Photograph by the author.*

These are only the names preserved by the Ordnance Survey. For example, on a map of Killean Estate, drawn by Peter McQuistan in 1824, nine *cruach* names are recorded, only two of which, **Cruach a' Bhodaidh** [731 448] and Cruach an Eich (above), are known from

O.S. records. These names were transcribed by Latimer MacInnes, and I present them in the forms in which he recorded them. The 'English versions', he noted, are 'as per Map': Cruach Eoghan ('Ewen's pile or stack'); Cruach a' bhais ('Hill of Death'); Cruachan mor ('Big conical hill'); Cruach a' bhodaidh (Local: 'the bodach'); Cruach an Duidhe ('The blackening hill'); Cruach na Monadh Coill ('Hill of wooded moss'); Cruach nan Eich ('Horses' pile or stack'); Cruach an Stanard ('Hill of the Standard'), and Cruach da Mheal ('Hill of the two heaps').[545]

To these may be added two more from the crude McQuilkan sketch-map of Carradale Estate drawn in 1936 for Latimer MacInnes. 'Cruachnabiranach' is shown roughly west of Cruach nan Gabhar. A cairn is marked on the top, with a further significant note in MacInnes's hand: 'Wooden Pole & Cross at one time.' This may be 'Hill of the sticks or sharp points' (*bioranach*). 'Cruchnaean' should represent *Cruach nan eun*, 'Hill of the birds'. It is, significantly, marked to the north of Loch nan Eun, and may therefore be the unnamed hill at 754 431, but no certainty is possible. Roy's mid-18th century map contains further examples absent from modern maps, such as **Cruachnarachan** and **Cruach na Nina**.

I'll add several of the more interesting examples from Ordnance Survey maps. **Cruach Mhic Gougain** [754 502] and **Cruach Mhic Choinnich** [755 404] preserve the names of individuals who were in some way connected with the hills. The former is *Mac Guagain*, a surname found in Kintyre since the 16th century and anglicised as 'McGougan'.[546] The latter was interpreted by the O.S. as 'McKenneth Hill',[547] but 'Son of Kenneth' would be clearer, or the name may represent the surname MacKenzie, which, however, was rare in Kintyre before the 19th century.[548] **Cruach na Seilcheig** [766 521] is 'The Snail Hill', which I include because the smaller of the creatures with which we share the planet are seldom noticed in place-names. (**Raon nan cuilleag**, interpreted 'Fly plain' – midges may be involved! – is another, on Crubasdale farm.[549]) In Saddell and Skipness Parish, there are two hills [824 530 and 885 648] named **Cruach Bhreac**. The specific means 'speckled' – see BREAC – and both hills were described in the O.S. records as 'rocky',[550] which may account for the description, the rocks, in certain light, or when wet, creating a speckled or spotted effect.

Finally, to **Cruach an t-Sorchain** [875 653], a 1125-ft. hill south of Tarbert. The Ordnance Survey derived the specific from three boulders resting upon one another on the south side of the summit, *sorchan* signifying 'A rest or support – that on which anything leans or rests'.[551] George Campbell Hay accepted that the O.S. form was correct, 'it so happens', and acknowledged the standard meaning, 'footstool', which his friend, Calum Johnson, had confirmed. But George offered an alternative suggestion, which may not be apt: *an t-sorchain*, a term which he noticed in 'an old periodical', for the small pyramid of sand on which the shinty ball was placed at New Year's Day games. 'I was walking past Cruach an t-Sorchain in a summer evening after the War and I looked up and I saw this triangular bit, and that's the reason why it's called Cruach an t-Sorchain, it's like that, ye know, a shinty tee.'[552]

CRÙBAN is 'crab' in Gaelic. In Kintyre, the *crùban*, pronounced 'crooban', isn't just any crab, it's specifically the edible or 'red' crab, *Cancer pagurus*. Some of them grew to a great size. I use past tense, because nowadays there can't be many individuals survive the efforts of commercial fishermen and become giants. One which seized a baited hook dropped from a yacht in Campbeltown harbour in 1879 measured 14 by 7 inches and weighed almost nine pounds. Happily, it escaped the pot and travelled by steamer to Rothesay Aquarium,[553] where, presumably, it spent the rest of its life routinely fed and admired. Commercial creel-fishing probably began in Kintyre towards the mid-19th century,[554] but, to use modern jargon, the 'target species' was lobster, and crabs were merely a 'by-catch', to be taken home or given away.

Crabs could be captured by hand at low water on rocky coasts by those who knew where to find them. George McSporran remembers, as a boy, crab-hunting with his father along Keil shore, Southend. It was almost, for George, like watching a magician perform. His father would roll up a sleeve, insert his arm in a crevice, announce 'Here's one here', then pull it out; and he would keep the crab lairs in good order by clearing them of sand and stones.[555]

At Machrihanish, off Port nam Marbh, there is a rock which was known as **Bogha a' Chrùbain** [c. 629 208], 'Crab Rock'. There would have been no more than that to say about it, had it not been for James McNeill, who died in his native Machrihanish in 1956. He was headmaster of Drumlemble school and a keen antiquarian. In his retirement, he had the good sense to commit much of his knowledge to writing, his custom being to write a few pages after his daily walk. Ill health, however, prevented him from editing the manuscript as he would have wished, but it was published privately in 1976 as *Meanders in South Kintyre*, and reissued in 1997 by the Kintyre Antiquarian and Natural History Society.

In his book, McNeill explains that in Bogha a' Chrùbain there is an underwater cleft, known as a 'cruban feg', in which crabs lurked (and may still lurk). A local fisherman agreed to take a visitor out cod-fishing one Saturday afternoon, but, having no time to haul a creel for bait, he rowed over to the rock to seek alternative bait. 'Slipping his oars, he let the boat glide quietly alongside and jumped on to the rock. Lying on the rock with shirt sleeve rolled up to the shoulder, he groped with his hand in the feg. Almost instantly he withdrew it, holding a fine-sized crab by the large claw. With a sweeping movement he tossed it into the boat and proceeded to repeat the act a little further along the feg. Success in this operation needs skill and experience, for if the crab is disturbed by fumbling or hesitation, he plants his feet on the floor and presses his back so firmly against the roof of this feg that it is impossible to dislodge him.'[556]

While an old woman was gathering shellfish on Muasdale shore, she 'pulled out a crab from its crevice'; but she got more than the crustacean. Clutched in its claw was a shilling, and the rock was afterwards known as **Creag an airgiod**, 'The rock of the silver'.[557]

Off Carradale Point, there is a buoy known as **The Crooban**. In Charlie Reppke's place-names list, compiled in 1942, against 'The Cruban' he noted: 'Modern name [for] Carradale Point and Buoy.' It couldn't have been that modern, however, because '**Cruban Point**' appeared on a plan of Carradale Estate drawn in 1827, cited but not described by Duncan Colville.[558] I have to wonder, however, if the point in question wasn't actually the reef called the 'Cruban Rock', described below. In a newspaper account in 1915 on the death of Donald Cook, tailor in Airds, it was reported that he was 'proceeding to land on the Cruban Rock' in pursuit of guillemots and cormorants when his gun went off and shot him fatally in the head.[559] **Cruban Rock** can't be an offshore feature, and is presumably the reef at 820 367 which extends towards the buoy. Lacking any local tradition on the name, it is difficult to suggest a derivation. Is the meaning of *crùban* here actually 'crab', or was the primary sense of 'crouching' or 'squatting' operating on some feature? A final observation: the name migrated to Carradale Hotel, the public bar of which has been popularly known as 'The Cruban' for as long as I can remember.

CÙIL, 'nook' or 'corner', may be confused with CÙL, 'back'. Indeed, **Port na Cùile** [814 390], the sheltered inlet north of Carradale harbour, was interpreted 'The nook port' by the O.S., as the spelling shows, whereas Graham McKinlay, retired farmer at Whitestone, whose understanding of Gaelic place-names was sound, gave me 'Back Port'. There is also a minor and now forgotten Port na Cùile [624 204] at Pans, Machrihanish.[560] **Cùilgaineamh** [875 561], by 1867 a ruin on the farm of Auchnastrone, Claonaig, is 'Sandy corner'. **Culindrach** [919 593], the farm north of Skipness, is a difficult name, which may not even belong here, but the early spellings are: 1495 'Colintre'; 1511 'Cullintraith'; 1549 'Quhyllynoucht' & 'Cullynnouche'; 1631 'Cullenach'; 1751 'Cullintra'. When the Ordnance Survey was active in Skipness Parish in 1867, the farmer at Culindrach, William McNair, was among those consulted on the location of place-names and their meaning. William himself appeared in a place-name, though he may never have known that. Among Tarbert fishermen, a tree at Culindrach, whose silhouette could be seen in darkness when the steading itself was blotted out, was known as **McNair's Tree**.[561] For **Culinlongart** see LONGPHORT and for **Coledrain** see COILLE.

CUILIONN is Holly (*Ilex aquifolium*). **Port a' Chuilinn** [591 071], near the Mull of Kintyre, is 'The Holly Port', as it appears on O.S. maps, but see *The Place-Names of the Parish of Southend*, p 29, for an alternative interpretation. The O.S. in 1866 described it as 'A small landing place for small boats'.[562] **Auchachuillin** [838 530] represents 'Holly field', which the O.S. in 1867 reported as being in ruins.[563] In C1851, as 'Auchincullin', two houses there were inhabited, one by Marion McLellan, widow, pauper and 'formerly pedler'. She gave her birthplace as Greenock, her neighbour Duncan Crawford gave his as Kilberry, and his wife Mary gave hers as 'Auchehois'. In the following year, 'Achullin' was advertised for let with North Crossaig.[564] A 'bit of witchcraft' once troubled a Maclean woman who was living in Auchachuillin. She had been at a 'spinning match' (see LÌN) at Claonaig and was going home late with her spinning-wheel on her back. On the brae beyond Allt Romain bridge, a holly tree appeared before her, dancing on the road. It always kept ahead of her, and when she reached her own road-end, the tree wouldn't let her pass and she had to turn back and go to Escart for the night.[565] David MacFarlane, a Tarbert fisherman, considered **Culindrach** – see under CÙIL – 'The Place of Holly'.[566]

CÙL is 'back', as opposed to front, whereas DRUIM is 'back' as in 'ridge'. **Culfuar** [700 453], a farm in the Largieside, is *Cùl fuar*, 'Cold back place'. In the summer of 1872, a young boy, John Armour, son of the farmer at 'Kilafuar', drowned by falling into 'a linn of water of considerable depth, formed in the bottom of the river which runs through the farm'.[567] There was another 'Culfuar', on Oatfield Estate, near Achnaglach, which I have seen only in censuses. In 1841, the spelling was 'Culfure' and there were two families there, one of them consisting of Irish-born Samuel Gordon, wife Mary and daughter Catherine. He was a hand-loom weaver with eight acres of land. By 1861 he was a widower, aged 67 and alone. Another weaver's cottage, this one called only 'Cuil', and probably indeed *cùil* rather than *cùl*, appears between 'Isca' and 'Callyburn' in the 1841 Campbeltown census; Samuel McGeachy and family were there.

Cullindoun [699 168], a shepherd's house in ruins near Knocknaha, is *Cùl an dùin*, 'Back of the fort', and there is indeed, close by, at 699 170, the remains of a fort within which a dun was later built.[568] Ellen McDearmid, wife of John Jackson, shepherd, died young at 'Colondun' in 1869. John, originally from Langholm, Dumfries-shire, in 1871 married again, to Isabella McSporran, and himself died in 1883 of blood-poisoning from a sting by a 'day' nettle* in a harvest field.[569] The family's ill fortune didn't end then. John's son, William, who was born at 'Culindune' in 1868, lost all the fingers of his right hand while working at a steam thrashing-mill at Knocknaha in April 1889.[570]

*This appears to be the Common hemp-nettle (*Galeopsis tetrahit*). Dr Alexander McMillan, Campbeltown, seriously doubted if 'a simple nettle sting could have directly led to death, except in very rare allergic reactions', and suggested that the site of the sting could have become secondarily infected, or that another injury, perhaps minor, became infected and led to septicaemia (3/4/2012).

CURRACH. W. J. Watson defined this as a 'wet plain'.[571] Large scale afforestation notwithstanding, Kintyre still has plenty of bogland, but *currach* appears just twice in records. The main feature, **Currach Mór** [611 115], north-east of the Mull, was described in 1866 as 'An extensive piece of ground on the north side of A' Chruach'.[572] A walker in 1921 described his route 'over moors and mosses, past the Currachmore, an upland level, covered with rough grass and tufts of bog-cotton, and to the bottom of the glen where the waters of Altdoran and Altchapple meet'.[573]

There was another smaller bog, marked on an old map of Sanda which can probably be dated to the early 19th century, when improvement of estates was in full swing and land surveys were considered essential to the implementation of these improvements. The map (p. viii) shows a 'stone fence', and, joined on to it, the 'intended line of turf dyke'. In mid-island, just within the area of the projected dyke, is marked, at about 724 043, 'CURRAGH', and to the south of it 'BOG'.[574] In Ireland, *corrach/currach* was 'one of many Irish words for a "swamp" or "morass"'.[575]

22. CURRACH.   *The upland marshy plain of Currach Mór under the summit of A' Chruach. Photograph by the author, 15/7/2012.*

DAIL place-names require to be separated into two groups, Gaelic and Norse. In the Gaelic names the element comes first – e.g., Dalmore, Dalrioch, Dalavraddan and Dalbuie – whereas in Norse names the element is at the end, e.g. Carradale, Torrisdale, Rhonadale and Saddell. Gaelic *dail* has a range of meanings, which Dwelly listed as 'field, dale, meadow, plain',[576] and evidently derives not from Norse, but from Pictish (or British) *dol*, which equates with Welsh *dol*, 'meadow, field, pasture, oxbow'. The P-Celtic origin of *dail* explains its absence from Irish place-names (and Irish dictionaries) in spite of the vigorous occupation of much of Ireland by Norse-speakers.[577] Norse *dalr* is a 'valley'.

23. DAIL. Looking down Glenadale, Southend, with the roofless shepherd's cottage of High Glenadale in the foreground. Photograph by the author, 15/7/2102.

I shall look first at the Gaelic place-names, which mostly relate to fields. As Ian A. Fraser explains, 'The use of *dail* as a field name is widespread in Argyll and further up the coast, as far as Wester Ross; and in place-names in general, e.g. in the central and eastern part, and in Galloway, it almost invariably equates to the Scots haugh, water-meadow'.[578] In the case of **Glenadale**, Southend, the name appears to be of Norse construction and tautological, but the second element may be Gaelic *dail* in that sense of 'water-meadow': the glen, even now, is flat-bottomed and wet toward its eastern extremity. In pronunciation, the emphasis is firmly on *gleann*: 'gleena-dall'. On Roy's mid-18th century map, the cartographer somehow decided that enough was not enough and recorded 'Glen Glenedale'.

High Glenadale [627 115] was evidently last occupied in 1937 by James and Euphemia McLean.[579] When I went there on 15/7/2012 with my wife Judy, it was my first time back in 20 years. I was there for the first time on 7/5/1982, during a long hike from Machrihanish, to photograph the cottage for Robert McInnes, a friend who was born there in 1917. In my notebook I described High Glenadale as 'an unattractive building, though certainly attractively situated'. The interior of the cottage contained many names, dates and messages scraped or pencilled on the plaster of the walls. I'll record the ones I copied into my notebook that day, because the cottage is now roofless, not a scrap of plaster remains, and the entire living-room is deep in nettles: Neil McInnes, Ifferdale, 24/5/1958; A. Helm, Auchenhoan, 22/6/1958; Duncan Jackson, Ballygroggan, 24/6/1963; Jessie McCallum, J. McCallum, and Robert McInnes, 9/6/1968; Ranald Watson, Strone, Jan. 1970; Iain A. Ronald, Ormsary, 26/7/1974; J. McCallum, 24 Mill St., Jessie McCallum, New Quay Head, Margaret Cameron, Katy Goudie, 23/7/1976; Malcolm Docherty Jnr., Glasgow Art School, 1978. Most of these names belonged to members of shepherding families, most of whom are now dead. It was a rather sombre return for me, like entering a silent spirit world. Judy and I took a few photographs, ate supper beside the burn, then headed north towards Largiebaan, passing the ruins of old High Glenadale [624 119].

Low Glenadale [648 117] is now a dwelling-house close to the Glenbreackerie road, but was earlier a farm. 'Siol Chuinn', during his 'Wandering on the Moil Hills' in 1921, passed it on his way down the glen from Saint Catherine's Well: 'No dog barked, and beyond the cackling of the hens there was no sign of life – the hay field had claimed the inhabitants.'[580] Donald McQuisten, Donald Obrionn, and Gillecallim, Neil and Donald Odrean were recorded at 'Glennadillichtrache' – that is *iochdarach*, 'lower' – in a census taken c. 1636.[581]

Dailchoran is a place-name which has vanished. It appeared in 1793 under West Drumgarvie, Glen Lussa, in an Argyll Estate list of 'Situations in Kintyre most adapted for raising Trees upon', when described as a 'big water side called Dailchoran'.[582] The specific CORRAN here probably relates to sickle-shaped land formed by the stream.

There were many place-names in Kintyre with *dail* as the generic. Two became the names of villages which were later incorporated into the burgh of Campbeltown, **Dalaruan** and **Dalintober** (see under TOBAR). A dozen became the names of farms – half of these in Southend Parish – and the rest, with few exceptions, I suspect, lived and died as field-names.

The most interesting of the Southend settlement-names is **Dalmore** [695 108], which is just *Dail mór*, 'Big field'. That name, however, appears to have undergone a long linguistic journey to reach its simple state. As to why the earlier names should have been modified is a question which history cannot answer, but similar changes no doubt account for the disappearance of other early names from the records. Dalmore is absent from early charters, but evidence points to its having been '**Dachnaauchlisk**' and 'Dachnaachlysk' in 1505, '**Dalnaheccleis**' in 1562, 'Dalnahanslek' in 1596, and 'Dalnauchlesk' in 1605. The 'dach-' of the first two forms has been interpreted by Denis Rixson (5/5/2012) as the old land-measure *dabhach*, which equates with PEIGHINN. If correct, it stands as the only occurrence of the generic in Kintyre records. 'Dalnaheccleis' – a 4-merkland in 1562, and in 1596 a 2-merkland joined with the 1-merklands of 'Killquhattan' (Kilchattan) and 'Cristilloch' (Christlach) – clearly represents *Dail na h-eaglaise*, 'Field of the church'.[583]

Dalavraddan [683 104] has been interpreted *Dail a' bhradain*, 'Field of the salmon'. This interpretation might have strained the bounds of credulity, were it not for local testimony that the tributary of Glenbreackerie Water which flows past the farm had been 'known to overflow its banks and leave salmon stranded on the land'.[584] (This, incidentally, is the only instance in Kintyre place-names of Gaelic *bradan*, 'salmon', despite the former abundance of the fish and the economic importance of its fishery, both legal and illegal, but the salmon also appears in **Lussa**, from Norse *Laxá*, 'salmon river', which is the river, glen, and later reservoir, called Lussa Loch, which the North of Scotland Hydro-Electric Board created between 1948 and 1956.)

From among the pure field-names, **Dail-bhàite**, 'Field of flooding', alludes to a similar phenomenon. There is one at Machriemore smithy, Southend, one on Crubesdale and one on North Muasdale.[585] In D. J. Macdonald's 'West Kintyre Field Names' are listed 17 with the generics *dail*, *dal* and the peculiar *deile*, which is translated 'field' and may represent pronunciation, among them: **Deile spàgach**, 'Splay-footed field' (on High Dunashery), **Dal a' staca**, 'Steep hill or stack field' (Drumnamucklach), **Dail ghainmhidh**, 'Sandy field' (Lenaig), **Dail loisgte**, 'Burnt field' (Dalmore) and **Dail cruinneachd**, 'Wheat field' (Rosehill). The last-mentioned interpretation, with **Gortean na cruinneachd**, another 'Wheat field', on Kilmory farm,[586] is curious on historical grounds. Wheat was not a favoured crop in Kintyre, though tenaciously promoted by the 5th Duke of Argyll in the late 18th century. Kilmory was his at that time, and wheat-cultivation may have been tried there, but if it was the leases give no hint of it. See *Kintyre Instructions*, pp. 156-57.

Turning now to the Norse element, there are inconspicuous *-dalr* names throughout Kintyre, such as **Stockadil** [731 393], at the head of Barr Glen, which represents Norse *stokka dalr*, 'valley of stumps, logs'. The valley itself is not represented on any map and is therefore obscure, but the name was attached to a settlement, which is shown on the Langlands map of 1801. Old spellings include 1502 'Stokkadill' and 1545 'Stokadull'. In 1789 Donald Sinclair was baptised at 'Stockadile', and in 1796 John, son of Malcom McCallum, shoemaker in 'Stockadile', was also baptised there. John McLarty had four horses in 'Stockadel' in 1797.[587] By C1851, a shepherd, Archibald Mitchell, was there. Among 'lost' dale names, Denis Rixson includes **Loch Dirigadale** [722 459], **Loch Garasdale** [765 510] and **Loch Grunidel** (see **Black Loch** under LOCH), which now attach only to stretches of water,[588] to which may be added **Loch Freasdail** and **Lochorodale**, for both of which also see under LOCH.

Borgadale, to the east of the Mull of Kintyre, is wholly Norse, *Borgar-dalr*, 'Fort glen'. It takes its name from the dun – 'one of the best-preserved … in Kintyre' – at 625 061,[589] but to that Norse construct were later added Gaelic and English elements: the two farms were distinguished by *mór*, 'big', and *beag*, 'little', thus 'Borgadilmore' [630 063] and 'Borgadilbeg' [627 062]; and 'Glen', 'Water' and 'Point' were later added to the mix.[590]

There are two **Earadale** names in South Kintyre, one in Campbeltown Parish and one [745 124] in Southend. When *The Place-Names of the Parish of Southend* was first published in 1938, no attempt was made to interpret 'Erradil' (a variant). Edward Pursell, a member of the K.A.S. place-names committee, suggested 'Norse EYRRA + DAL-R = The dale of the gravelly beach', which was duly logged in the Schedules, with a note added by Duncan Colville: 'The place is situated inland at Glenehervie. The beach at foot of this glen is boulder strewn, not gravelly except in limited patches.' This is correct, but may not have been correct a thousand years ago; and since Glenahervie is a decent-sized valley, it may well have contained *dalr* in an earlier name. Early spellings include: 1481 'Eradall'; 1505 'Erredill' and 'Arredill'; 1545 'Aradull'; 1605 'Aradill'; 1751 'Erradil'.[591] MacKay ancestors of my own farmed Erradil in the late 18th and early 19th centuries and I have examined its history in *By Hill and Shore in South Kintyre*, pp. 60-62 and 72-74.

The other Earadale appears on O.S. maps as a 'Point' [596 173], with 'Port Erradil' [599 177], an earlier name – from an estate map of 1836 – attached to the inlet on the south side of Sròn Gharbh. In *The Place-Names of the Parish of Campbeltown* (1943), the derivation, 'Old Norse *Eyrar-dalr*, Dale of the shingly bank', emerges tentatively.

In that location, however, the derivation is even more problematic than that of the Southend name. First, the coast is decidedly boulder-strewn, in keeping with the steep terrain, though in that inlet south of Sròn Gharbh there are sea-rounded stones among the boulders. Second, there is nothing remotely resembling a valley until the Inneans Glen is reached. I am mindful of Macbain's remark, in the course of his savaging of Gillies's *The Place-Names of Argyll*, on 'that very much over-worked Norse word "eyrr", a beach'.[592]

Between Earadale Point and Sròn Gharbh lies an extent of land which has obviously been stone-cleared and cultivated in parts. In July of 2009, I took a party of archaeologists there, during a cursory survey of the coast between Ballygroggan and the Inneans. Dr Gary Robinson, University of Bangor, subsequently compiled a brief report, in which he wrote: 'At Earadale ... we were shown a series of circular mounds of stone located on a natural terrace of the hillside. On closer inspection, evidence of walling could be identified and it was clear that these mounds were the remains of roundhouses. Associated with these houses were field banks and small enclosures or paddocks. This site is particularly interesting as it may date to the Middle Bronze Age, an extremely rare find for Kintyre, and as we walked further north along the coastline, other similar circular stone structures were identified, in each instance associated with hill terraces.'[593] There is no evidence, physical or documentary, that Earadale was ever occupied within historical time, but there is clearly much to be uncovered about its prehistory.

DAMH is an ox or a stag, but 'ox' is the usual interpretation, and the only one which Holmer gave in *Studies on Argyllshire Gaelic* (p 150). **Ardnandamh** [834 507], a farm at Crossaig, was 'Airdnandamf' in C1841, and noted as 'ruins' in 1867 by the O.S., which defined it as 'Height of the oxen'.[594] In the case of **Creag an Daimh** [798 387], at Carradale, the O.S. interpretation was more specifically 'Stot's Rock',[595] 'stot' being Scots for a young castrated ox or a bullock, usually in its second year or older.[596] There are two other places named Creag an Daimh, in Campbeltown Parish. One, in the form 'Craigindeff', was taken from an old map, from which Duncan Colville calculated that it must have been a holding on the farm of Mulbuy, north or north-east of Bordadubh. The only description of the other one was that it lay 'between Ballygroggan and Largiebaan', which is a lot of ground. That one came from John McCallum and was interpreted 'The rock of the stag', but whether 'stag' was his term is unknown.[597] **Lag nan Damh** in 1545 formed a five-shilling land with 'Dalsmyrrell' (Dalsmeran), Southend. Old spellings: 1481 'Lagnadaise'; 1545 'Lagnodaf'; 1596 'Lagnandaw'. This holding seems to vanish from the record in the 17th century, but is represented by the feature [c. 635 123] from which its name derived, described in 1866 as a 'hollow or depression on the grazing of Amod ... caused by a land slip'. The O.S. definition 'Hollow of the Oxen' may be preferred to 'The Stags' Hollow', suggested in 1938.[598] For **Carraig an Daimh** see under MUC.

DÀPHEIGHINN was a 'two-penny land' in the old system which valued land in money rather by physical extent – which, anyway, wasn't accurately measureable until the late 18th century – and there are two such names in Kintyre. The better known example is **Dippen** at Carradale, a wide-ranging name embracing the existing farm [798 375], bay [799 363], hillock [794 369] and a now-abandoned settlement, South Dippen [800 366], also known as 'Ton Duppine', for which see under TÒN. The other one [835 643], north of Achnacarnan – in 1502/7 the 3-merkland of 'Duwpeyn' – was described in 1867 as 'several ruins, formerly farm steading'. When Duncan Colville went looking for it in 1938, he was told by the tenant in Achnacarnan that 'Duppen was by that time called Achatakye which he thought meant "Cows field"'. He was not a Gaelic speaker and had heard, in the specific, plural Scots for 'cow'. The O.S. recorded this name as **Achadacaie**, for which Captain T. P. White, surveyor in charge, ventured the improbable *achadh + dachaidh* = 'Field of the home or dwelling place'.[599] On Roy's mid-18th century map, the place on the west coast is rendered 'Dichpen' and that on the east 'Dupin'. See also LETH-PHEIGHINN and PEIGHINN.

DARACH is the Oak (*Quercus robur*) and, as an adjective, means 'oaken' or 'abounding in oaks', though, as with DOIRE place-names, the trees themselves may have long vanished. The Laggan farm **Darlochan** [East, 680 235, and West, 670 231] has been derived from *Dair lochan*, 'Oak loch', but there was another obscure holding grouped with it in a record of 1629, **Darrachan**, which is *Darachan*, 'Little place of the oak'. In that same record, a third farm completes the group to form a three-merkland holding, and that is yet another oak-related name, **Durry**,[600] for which see under DOIRE. Mid Darlochan was associated with a Kelly family from 1787 until 1844. When the original lessee, John Kelly, died in 1817, he left eight sons and four daughters. His eldest son, Andrew, claimed the remainder of the 1806 lease, but was rejected in favour of a younger son, Peter. Andrew, moreover, was forbidden even to occupy a cot-house on the farm.[601] This action on the part of the Argyll Estate chamberlain is unexplained. In 1815, four of John Kelly's sons had been implicated in the theft of timber from a brigantine, the *Saltcoats*, which stranded in Machrihanish Bay, but Andrew wasn't one of them and Peter was.[602] **Cnoc an Daraich** [744 456], in mid-Kintyre to the east of Tayinloan, is 'Hill of the Oakwood', and **Rubha Daraich** [802 365], 'Oak Point', is at Dippen, Carradale. For **Rubha Maol Daraich** see under MAOL.

DEARC is 'berry'. Macbain provides an interesting etymology for this word, the root of which is 'conspicuous';[603] *dearc*, 'eye', the berry being the 'eye' of the plant, is assumed to lurk here.[604] Since this is a general term, one can only guess at the fruit alluded to in the few place-names in which it occurs. Specifics there are aplenty in Gaelic for the different berries, but the only Kintyre one I have noticed is in Holmer's *The Gaelic of Kintyre* (p 71), *dearca dubh*, 'blackberries'. The main place-name, and it is an important one, even without the berries, is **Sliabh nan Dearc**, Skipness (see SLIABH). It may be translated 'moor-slope of the berries', and there are just two berry-bearing moorland plants common enough to merit discussion. The blaeberry (*Vaccinium myrtillus*) is the most abundant, plumpest and sweetest of all moorland berries and is typically found among heather. Its likely abundance in history would be hard to assess. On heavily grazed hills and moors, relatively few berries will reach ripeness, and these would quickly disappear inside birds. Until the mid-20th century spread of coniferous plantations – fenced off from sheep and deer, and having clearings, rides and roadsides on which blaeberries proliferate – pickings as a rule tended to be meagre. Now, in many forests – and Ben Gullion is certainly one of them – blaeberries can be gathered daily by the thousand throughout July and August. The darker-skinned crowberry (*Empetrum nigrum*) is generally less abundant, but is also edible, though smaller, less juicy and lacking in sweetness. It tends to favour a drier habitat than the blaeberry, and will typically form carpets on the slopes and tops of hills. **Cnoc nan Dearc** [874 667], south of Tarbert, is 'Hill of the Berries', and **Allt nan Dearc** [744 397], out beyond the head of Barr Glen, is 'Stream of the Berries'. The latter name also occurs on Arran; Neil Clark in Lochranza said people went there to gather juniper berries.[605]

DEARG, with RUADH, is 'red', and covers all degrees of the colour, but, compared with *ruadh*, it is rare in place-names. 'Deargallt' and 'Dearguillt' in the 1867 O.S. records refer to the same place, and represent 'Red Burn', elsewhere more conventionally formed as **Allt Dearg** [657 132]. **Dearg Allt** [807 463] flows from Loch Tana, and the bay [819 460] into which it falls, between Grogport and Cour, was, in the late 19th century, a popular camping-place for Campbeltown ring-net fishermen,[606] to whom the place was known corruptly as 'Jergal'. There was also a permanent settlement there, in C1841 two houses at 'Deargalt', occupied by farm labourers. **Bruach Dearg** [629 143], 'Red Brae', appears on no maps, but is the lower end of the steep earthen road from Glenahanty up to Largiebaan; the name comes from the colour of the earth. One of the caves at Largiebaan was known as **Beul Dearg** [595 149], 'Red Mouth'.[607]

DÌG is a drystone wall, or 'dyke', which is its origin in Scots,[608] but is also a 'ditch', and as such appears in **Dìg Ghorm** [877 641], 'Green Ditch', which forms part of the boundary between Kilcalmonell and Skipness parishes. The O.S. in 1867 described it as 'a drain rising about 10 chains [660 ft. or 201.17 m] to the W. of Cruach Doire Liath'.[609] **An dìg sheilich**, 'The willow ditch', is – or perhaps was – on the farm of Glenacardoch.[610] 'Dyke' in Kintyre was usually GÀRADH.

DÒID is a croft, defined by Macbain as 'a small farm, a "holding", from *dòid*, hand'.[611] D. J. Macdonald preferred the spelling *dòit*, which he defined as 'a small coin, a small portion of land, a croft', linking the agricultural use to 'a "doit" value or extent of land', and citing 'penny lands, merklands, etc.'[612] Macbain, however, defines *dòit* simply as 'a small coin less than a farthing', from Scots 'doit',[613] which was 'a small Dutch copper coin used in Scotland'.[614] I'll begin with Rev Macdonald's deviant harvest. On Beacharra, **An dòit**, simply 'The croft'; on Lenaig, **Dòit a' ghobha**, 'The Smith's croft'; and on High Clachaig, **Dòit a' mhuillin**, 'The mill croft'.[615] 'Dodvui' in the 1861 census of Kilcalmonell represents **Dòid Bhuidhe**, 'Yellow Croft'. It is now in ruins near Lagnascavach, Whitehouse, but in C1861 there were two houses there. One was occupied by a pauper who had been a merchant seaman, John McKinven, who gave his age as 62, and the other by a 78-year-old widow, Catherine McIntosh. She had with her – almost certainly as a helper and companion – an eight-year-old grand-daughter, Marion, described as a coal-miner's daughter, born in Ayrshire. If little Marion had no Gaelic when she arrived at her granny's croft, I daresay she'd have had plenty when she left! The 'cot house on Crossaig farm' recorded by the O.S. in 1867 as 'Toit Dubh' [835 519] – 'significance not known'[616] – should represent **Dòid Dhubh**, 'Black Croft', which, in translation, is exactly as the place appears in C1901. Local pronunciation is now 'Dodgie Doo'. **Dòid** [661 191], a three-quarter-acre patch of land below Rowantree Cottage, Drumlemble, is pronounced, by the very few locals who still know the name, 'Dodge'.[617] CROIT, to which refer, was another place-name element for 'croft'.

DOIRE is sometimes translated as 'grove', but 'oak-grove' – which is the standard Irish sense[618] – might be preferable. The Laggan farm **Durry** [686 224], which was largely reclaimed from heather moss, has been so derived. Early spellings are curiously lacking, but the forms of the name in all 18th century records which I have seen alternate between 'Durry' and 'Derry'.[619] See also **Durry Loch** under LOCH. The O.S. **Dorrie Burn** [603 122], south of Largiebaan, may also derive from *doire*, but John Cameron suggested *dobharaidh*: *dobhar*, 'water', and the locative termination *-aidh*.[620] In either case, the generic should be *allt*. 'Allt Dorie' was the name of a sheep heft in that area and also the name of a house, for which, according to tradition, divine intervention, in the form of a timely landslip, provided the necessary stone, thus enabling a newly-wed couple to secure their first home.[621] See 'Mulbuy' under MEALL for a possible location of this house. The O.S. interpretation of **Cruach Doire Leithe** [879 638], the 1236-ft. hill north of Skipness, was 'Hill of the grey thicket',[622] but see CRUACH. For **Doire na h-Earbaige** see under EILEIRG.

DOIRLINN/DOIRLING Professor Watson defined as 'an isthmus, usually covered at high water and connecting an *eilean tioram*, "dry island" (an island accessible at low tide) with the mainland or another isle',[623] which perfectly describes the two Kintyre *doirlinn* features.

By far the better known is the long dog-legged shingle bank which joins Davaar Island with the southern shore of Campbeltown Loch. In April 2012, while I was writing this book, I was on high ground at the back of Ben Gullion and looking down at the Dorlinn, which was brought into clear definition by a rising tide, and I suddenly realised just how remarkable a feature it is.

The curious claim was made in 1851 that what is now the flat tidal zone to the east of the Doirlinn was formerly arable land. The writer, 'W. B.', was told in his boyhood by an old man that the 'stackyard' of **Point** farm [745 193] 'stood, in his early days, where the Millmore is now'.[624] 'Millmore' is the beacon on the outer end of the Doirlinn (see under MEALL). This claim can be dated to the early to mid 18th century, but on Roy's map (1747-55) the shoreline is much as it is now. Erosion and inundation on the scale implied are certainly not unprecedented elsewhere, but the account is scarcely credible.

Since Archibald Mackinnon painted his Crucifixion in a cave on Davaar in 1887, innumerable visitors and locals – probably into six figures – have crossed to the island by the Doirlinn to view the rock-wall image. But the shingle-bank itself, which forms a barrier for Campbeltown harbour in south-easterly gales, is now much diminished except at its mid-point. Vessels leaving Campbeltown in ballast sometimes loaded up with Doirlinn sand and gravel to sell as building materials, an abuse which the Town Council introduced a bye-law to prevent. John Kane, master of the smack *Ann* of Dublin, was fined £3 3s in 1882 for removing from 'the Dorling' about eight tons of sand without the 'special consent' of the Council.[625]

Ships occasionally ran aground on the Doirlinn, having approached Campbeltown harbour between the south side of Davaar and the mainland, a stretch of sea known locally as the **Blin Soon**, or 'Blind Sound'. A French sailing ship, the *Esprigel*, grounded on 19/2/1867: 'Foreign vessels especially are liable to fall into the mistake of supposing the Dorlinn the entrance to the harbour, either from the old, or from the defective charts they use.'[626] The flat expanse of sand which extends eastward from the Doirlinn has for generations been a productive shell-fish gathering area at low water. Winkles, mussels, cockles and (formerly) oysters were gathered there, for line bait, for domestic consumption and for sale. Recently, commercial cockle-raking has been conducted there with alarming intensity.

An Doirlinn [814 367] is the neck of shore which at low tide connects Goat Island off Carradale Point to the mainland. **Port na Doirlinn**, 'Port of the tidal isthmus', is a little inlet on the west side of the Point. The Ordnance Survey spelling was originally 'Port na Darlain', but was amended.

DONN is 'brown', a modest adjective which hasn't attracted much attention to itself in Kintyre. **Cnocan donn** [917 592], 'Brown hillock', was a group of cottages near Culindrach, Skipness, which was ruinous by 1900.[627] By C1891, only Catherine Thomson was left there. **Cnoc Donn** [750 375], 'Brown Hill', stands at 1335 ft. between Barr Glen and the head of Torrisdale Glen, and the larger of two hills named **Meall Donn**, 'Brown Hill', in Saddell and Skipness Parish, rises to 1138 ft. to the east of it (see MEALL).

DROCHAID is 'bridge', before the existence of which the ford (see ÀTH) was the sole means of crossing rivers and burns, with stepping-stones provided if necessary. There are numerous old bridges in Kintyre, some redundant and some daily bearing loads – timber lorries, buses and agricultural machinery – which their builders could never have imagined. Murdo MacDonald tells me (21/10/2012) that the minutes of the Commissioners of Supply of Argyllshire, who administered the county's 'bridge money' fund, only survive from the year 1744, but that there were then already bridges at Machrimore, Barr, Crubasdale, Carradale and Strath. Curiously, however, I know of no bridge in Kintyre which carries the *drochaid* generic. **Gleann Drochaide** [755 445], 'Bridge Glen', is in the middle of Kintyre with no known road near it. **Tighnadrochit** [719 505] is *Tigh na drochaide*, 'Bridge house', and the late 18th/early 19th century bridge from which the house took its name is at 718 505. According to Neil 'P.O.' Thomson in 1977, **Ceann na Drochaide**, 'Bridgend', was an earlier name for Muasdale village, but this has not been substantiated and remains a curiosity. For **Sliabh na drochaid(e)** see under SLIABH, and for the building of the bridges over Allt na Dunach see under ALLT.

DRUIM, 'back' or 'ridge', is a common place-name element in Kintyre. I count 34 names in my files, most of them in the south. When these are examined, a particular characteristic emerges – the great majority survives as settlement-names and the topographical features referred to are obscure. There are too many to examine in detail, therefore I have restricted my choice to Campbeltown Parish.

Drumlemble applied originally to a land-holding and later transferred to the village which grew up around the mining industry. Since both farms, East [668 198] and West [661 198], are on the Laggan plain, the 'ridge' is elusive. The meaning of the name is also elusive. 'Old natives' in the early 20th century used the form 'Drumleman', and D. J. Macdonald postulated a derivation from *leamhan*, hence 'Ridge of the elm', which is now popularly accepted; but the earliest forms do not support that interpretation: 1502

'Drumlamele'; 1507 'Drumnamyll'; 1562 'Drummellennill'; 1596 'Drumlanbill'.[628] This place-name has, of course, travelled the world in Willie Mitchell's enduring song 'Road to Drumlemman'.

Drumore [707 220], on the outskirts of Campbeltown, is *Druim mór*, 'Big Ridge', but in 16th century charters it was 'Drummoirclannaye' and 'Drummorelannaye' – *Druim mór Chloinn Aoidh*, 'Big ridge of the MacKays' – presumably to distinguish it from Drumore na bodach,[629] for which see under BODACH.

Drumgarve [728 266] is *Druim garbh*, 'Rough ridge'. Though now a remote dwelling at the head of Glenlussa, this was once a four-merkland holding. By 1791, Thomas Templeton was tenant in West Drumgarve. He was married twice and had 21 children. His son James (1812-85) founded the Glasgow carpet-making business which by 1881 employed more than 1100 workers. In 1794, another descendant of a Lowland plantation family, Lt. Col. John Porter, got East Drumgarve, in the lease of which he was described as 'Major of the 2nd Battalion of Argyllshire Fencibles'. In that year, he was in his first term as Provost of Campbeltown, and four years later he distinguished himself at the head of his militia in the Irish Rebellion of 1798.[630]

Drumfin [c. 654 194] is *Druim fionn*, 'White ridge', and was a farm on Kilkivan hill, the steading of which is now in ruins. In C1851 'Drumphin' was occupied by a farm labourer, Alexander McMillan. His daughter Elizabeth died on 18 June of the previous year, aged 17, and is buried nearby in Kilkivan. **Drumban** [730 260], a hill in Glenlussa, is *Druim bàn*, 'Fair ridge' (but see BÀN), which name also attached to a house, now in ruins. **Drumathrottan** [752 239], on High Smerby, has been interpreted *Druim a' chroitein*, 'Ridge of the hummock', and is likewise ruinous.[631] In C1841, there were two farm workers and their families at 'Drimchrottan'.

DUBH is 'black', and one of its characteristic presences in place-names is as a descriptor of small peaty moorland lochs. All of these names are formed as **Dubh Loch**, in which the adjective precedes rather than follows the noun, 'a more archaic feature'.[632] On an 1833 map of High Smerby farm, an unidentified feature named 'Dulag' appears close to the march with Ballimenach. This is almost certainly a rock about 9 ft. square which Robert Clark, who was shepherd at Greenland, knew as 'The Doolach Rock' and described in 1929. It was close to the loch at Greenland, 'Black Loch' on O.S. maps, and may be a corrupt form of *Dubh Loch*. I suggest 745 244 as a rough approximation of its location.[633] Dubh Loch [713 398], north of Barr Glen, is 'Dou Loch' on the 1793 Langlands map and 'Dubhlochan' in MacIntosh (p 59). Another, 'Du Loch', appeared on that Langlands map to the east of Loch nam Breac [795 482], but is absent from O.S. maps and was perhaps drained. Yet another Dubh Loch [811 565] is in the hills between Clachan and Claonaig. See also **Black Loch** under LOCH. *Dubh* was commonly applied to a wide range of landscape features, from hills – four named **Cnoc Dubh** in Saddell and Skipness Parish alone: 786 371, 809 458, 829 493 and 839 543 **(nan Coileach)** – to fields, such as **Pairc dhubh**, 'Black park', at Glenbarr.[634] **Mullach Dubh** [784 555], a hill near Clachan, has for a generic *mullach*, 'top', which is very rare in Kintyre. (**Mullach Buidhe** [660 284], 'Yellow Top', is the other.) *Dorch*, 'dark', is also an extreme rarity in Kintyre place-names, but appears in **Druim dorchda**, 'Dark ridge', on Crubesdale farm.[635]

DÙN is a little word which sits on top of an immense heap of history, most of it out of reach. The standard interpretation is 'fort', but it can also apply to a castle, and 'castle' indeed was how these small structures were often defined to Ordnance Survey officers by local informants. Among Dwelly's definitions is 'hillock',[636] and this certainly applies to several Kintyre duns which bear no evidence of ever having been fortified. Some of these, from their location and flattened summits, look as though they should have been fortified, so perhaps the status was, in some cases, inferred. The typical non-archaeological dun in Kintyre is a rounded coastal headland.

Of the Kintyre castles on record – at Tarbert, Skipness, Largie, Airds, Saddell, Smerby, Lochhead, Kilkerran, Dunaverty, and perhaps also the fortified house on Tangy Loch – only Dunaverty, as the name shows, was designated a *dùn*. This, I suggest, is a matter of antiquity. The others are, in their origins, generally medieval structures, whereas **Dunaverty** [688 074] appears on record in the 8th century A.D. The name has been variously interpreted – 'Rock of Blood' being a lurid favourite – but almost certainly represents *Dùn Àbhartaigh*, 'Abhartach's Fort', which was besieged by one Sealbhach in 710.[637] Dunaverty would unquestionably be Kintyre's outstanding 'visitor attraction' – Robert Bruce was there in 1306 (in Barbour's epic poem, *Bruce*, the castle appears as 'Donavardyne'), John MacDonald of Dunyveg hanged King James IV's governor over the walls in 1494, and in 1647 the infamous massacre took place there – but for the fact that the castle itself was pulled down in 1685, at the time of the Earl of Argyll's rebellion, and only some inconspicuous stones and bits of defensive walling remain.

24. DÙN. Dunaverty, on which stood an ancient castle, pulled down in the late 17th century. The Rock is flanked by Dunaverty lifeboat house and the boat-house and slip. Postcard by Martin Stationers, Campbeltown, in author's collection.

Even without its castle, Dunaverty can exert a powerful stimulus on the imagination. The English poet and dramatist Gordon Bottomley – a close friend and correspondent of Edward Thomas – was one who succumbed. During a visit to Kintyre in 1932, he seized on an 'incident of the massacre' and turned it into a drama in verse, 'Dunaverty', which was published in *Choric Plays* in 1939. According to the tradition he adapted, a 'MacDonald woman' was 'promised freedom by the Campbells if she climbed the cliff on the northern side of the Rock'. She did just that, 'but as her hands appeared over the summit, a sentry cut them off with his sword and she hurtled back and down, a blood-stained thing, to the sand at the foot of the cliff'.[638] A tragic tale, of a familiar type, and almost certainly total invention. One would have thought that the massacre was bad enough without adding an innocent woman to the carnage.

Archaeologically, a 'dun' is considered to be a small fortified dwelling for a single family, whereas a 'fort' was spacious enough to accommodate a community. The distinction between a small fort and a large dun is blurred, but in place-names all are classed as duns. The important hill-top site at **Dunskeig** [757 571], near Clachan, actually contains three structures, a fort and two duns.[639] Duns were built with disproportionately thick drystone walls, usually to an oval plan and with average dimensions of about 50 ft. internal diameter. A few occupy elevated positions of natural defensive strength, but most were built near the seashore on slight knolls. They belong to the Iron Age (c. 600 B.C. - c. 400 A.D.) and 65 have been recorded in Kintyre.[640]

Of all the Kintyre parishes, Killean and Kilchenzie is richest in duns with associated traditions, D. J. Macdonald having taken the time to seek out his parish lore. While Dunaverty was clearly a fortification of major importance – on a naturally protected headland overlooking seaways to Ireland, the Hebrides and the Clyde – the status of these small northern fortifications can only be guessed at; but some, as legends hint at, may have been the strongholds of powerful men, perhaps tribal chiefs.

Dùn Ach' na h-àtha [673 386], 'Fort of the kiln field', at Muasdale, was reputed to have been occupied by the warrior-hero Fionn MacCumhaill himself (see FIONN). On one occasion, when absent 'for war or foray', he left the fort in charge of a henchman *Gille Cochull nan Craiceann*, 'The Lad of the Skin Hoods'. At dead of night, a monstrous bull-like beast descended on the fort down Eas-la-Cruit. The Lad placed himself at the gate of the fort to keep the beast out, but it went for him and 'when the combatants closed in deadly strife, you could hear the sound of their arms, as they clashed, beyond the seven bens and the seven glens and the seven moor mountains'. At length, the Lad sliced off the monster's head with his sword, but no sooner had he done so than the head 'descended, joined on to the colossal trunk, and up sprang the monster, fit as ever for the fray'. Again, he swept off the head and the same thing happened, but this time a voice came to the Lad. It told him to 'lay the flat of the sword against the marrow', which he instantly did, and 'down came the head like a thunder-bolt, but only to strike the ground, with a terrific thud, and sink deep into the earth'. So the lad survived his supernatural ordeal and gained fame, 'rivalling that of Fionn himself'.[641] Dun Ach' na h-àtha was indeed a fortification, but stone-robbing has reduced the wall to rubble.[642] One of D. J. Macdonald's parishioners told him that he had turned up two flint spear-heads while ploughing near the dun and broke one of them into fragments for use in lighting his pipe; the other one disappeared, probably in the course of house-cleaning.[643] The dun took its name from a small farm, Achnaha – see under ÀTH.

Dùn an Fhamhair [680 402], north of Muasdale, is 'The Giant's Fort', a short distance south of **Stac an Fhamhair**, 'The Giant's Stack'. In folklore, a giant and his family lived in the dun, but how they all managed to fit into such a small space remains inexplicable! The giant, unusually, was a 'pacifist', and had resisted repeated challenges from an aggressive neighbour on Islay. One day, however, the Muasdale giant's wife saw the Islay giant wading turbulently towards them. At last, a thundering noise at the door announced his arrival. The lady of the fort tip-toed to the door, a finger to her lips. 'Hush,' she whispered. 'Do not wake the child. He has had a bad night, teething and fractious all the time.' The Islay giant, peering inside, could see only an immense figure stretched from side to side of the room. 'I have come to fight your husband,' he said, 'but who may this be?' – 'Who but our child,' replied the wife. 'Well,' said the visitor to himself, 'if this is the child, I wonder what his father is like.' And to the woman: 'My compliments, good wife, to my brother giant. Say I am sorry I did not chance to find him at home. In the meantime, our contest can wait.' With that he turned for home, in greater haste than he had come.[644] No trace of the dun remains.[645] See also STAC.

Dùn Dòmhnuill [681 408], 'Donald's Fort', was built on the summit of an isolated stack north of Muasdale village. According to local tradition, 'the ancient Lords of Kintyre' held their 'courts of justice' there. 'Criminals sentenced to death were hurled down the sheer face of the rock, [and] despatched by executioners at the foot.' By another version, 'if the accused were not killed by their fall, they were pronounced innocent', but if the fall proved fatal, 'their guilt was supposed to have been established'.[646]

For **Dùn Fionn** see under FIONN and for **Dùn Bàn** under BÀN.

The diminutive *dùnan*, 'little fort' or 'little hill', is widespread in Kintyre. **An Dùnan** [897 576], 'The Little Hill', is a natural feature at the western end of Skipness village, but a 'doubtful legend', as Captain T. P. White described it, arose to explain the mound. One of the 'ancient Earls of Argyle' ordered 'criminals of a certain class (probably belonging to Skipness) to convey barrows of earth all the way to this spot from Inveraray, and Mr Fraser told me the mound had a Gaelic name signifying "Knoll of the Curse"'.[647] This 'Mr

Fraser' must have been a son of William Fraser, the notorious laird of Skipness from 1843. Fraser allegedly earned the enmity of his Skipness tenants by a policy of evictions, and antagonised fishermen by disputing their legal right to camp on foreshores. In 1848 he prosecuted John McMillan and several other fishermen for trespass. When his corpse was taken ashore at Tarbert, 'Gowrie' (W. Anderson Smith) recorded that 'the unseemly spectacle was presented of the fishermen cheering this evidence of his death', and Angus Graham alleged that 'after his death stones were thrown at his coffin'. Before he died, uncanny manifestations were seen at Skipness: fires 'which burned without leaving any mark on the ground'. In 1866, his son sold the estate to R. C. Graham.[648]

25. EACH. Loch an Eich, home to a mythical water-horse. Photograph by the author, 12/4/2012.

EACH is the horse, once indispensable in work and in war, but now a symbol of leisure on the margins of society. Kintyre's early historical link with the horse is well known, but the ground is worth covering again. Writing in the second century A.D., the Egyptian astronomer and geographer Ptolemy mentions a tribe called Epidii – from early Celtic *epos*, 'horse' – whose territory extended northward from the Epidion Akron, or 'Horse Point', i.e. the Mull of Kintyre.[649] An old Irish tale, *Aided Chonrói*, refers to *Aird Echddi i Cinn Tíre*.

Echde lived there, therefore the name may mean 'Echde's Point' or, alternatively, 'Horse Point' or the 'Epidian Point'. The story also mentions a 'tower', *Tor Echde*, presumably a fortification. As Ronald Black points out, the Epidii 'would have been Britons or possibly Picts'. He cites Alexander Macbain's theory that they took their tribal name from horsemanship, and Professor Watson's that they were probably horse-breeders and -breakers. Black, however, reckoned that there was something more beneath the surface: 'Horses lie so deep in the naming practices of Kintyre and some adjacent areas that one gets a strong whiff of totemism.'[650] Watson remarks that 'It is not without significance that Kintyre is the home of the MacEacherns, whose name is an "anglicization" of *MacEach-thighearna*, "Son of Horse-lord"'.[651]

I was surprised to find much of the above in 1913 in the *Campbeltown Courier*, which reprinted a letter to *The Times* from Professor Kuno Meyer (1858-1919) – the German scholar of Celtic philology and literature – along with a response in *The Scotsman* (13/2/1913) from W. J. Watson, 'High School of Edinburgh'. When Meyer told his Scottish friend, Professor W. P. Ker, of his discovery of the link between Ptolemy's 'Epidion Akron' and 'Ard Echdi' in 'ancient Irish literature', Ker's response was, 'This is solemn'. – 'And indeed it is,' Meyer concluded.[652] Ker, who died in 1923, was notably laconic. When told that the Celtic Twilighter William Sharp dressed himself entirely in women's clothing whenever he was preparing to write as 'Fiona Macleod', Ker's response was: 'Did he? The bitch!'[653]

Watson conveyed to Professor Meyer the gratitude of 'students of Celtic and of history' and averred: 'In this name we see before our eyes the old British *p* becoming replaced by the Gaelic *c*, thus proving that in Ptolemy's time (cir. 125 A.D.) the people of Cantyre spoke a language of the Cymric type, which later on was displaced by Gaelic. In view of the persistence of place-names, it would not be surprising if *Ard Echdi* were found to be still a living name in Kintyre.' (That final suggestion proved to be unfounded.) Watson here too referred to Kintyre as 'the original habitat of the MacEcherns'.[654]

MacEachran – now the universally preferred 'anglicisation' of the name in Kintyre – was an important family in Kintyre history, having been Mairs of Fee, or Crown officers, of South Kintyre. Colin MacEachran received a charter of Killellan from King James IV in 1499, and Angus MacEachran of Killellan was one of those executed at Dunaverty in 1647, after which the estate was briefly forfeited. The magnificent medieval cross in Campbeltown was carved for Ivor

MacEachern – probably parson at Kilkivan in the late 14th century – and a late 15th century cross-shaft in Kilkerran bears a dedication to Colin MacEachern of Killellan and his wife Katherine.[655]

Appropriately, MacEachran farriers had a high reputation in Kintyre, and Campbeltown-born Professor Duncan McEachran (1841-1924) of McGill University, Montreal, was a world authority in veterinary science, specialising in horse diseases. He was also a keen horse-breeder, and imported many Kintyre Clydesdales to his ranch on the Western Plains of Canada.[656] His career was paralleled by that of his younger half-brother Charles, who died in Montreal in 1919. A 'lover of fine horses', Charles was Professor of Contagious Disease in the Veterinary Faculty at Montreal and in 1914 was appointed to the British War Mission as Veterinary Examining Officer.[657] Their father David and brother John, links in an hereditary chain, were both smiths in Campbeltown. Another Kintyre family, MacEachan/ MacEachen, is sometimes confused with the MacEachrans (and other families besides), but its name represents *Mac Eachainn*, 'Son of Eachan'.[658] At its root, however, *Eachann* itself represents 'Horse-lord'. Anglicised as 'Hector', *Eachann* was traditionally a 'favourite name in the area from Kintyre north to Mull, Coll and Tiree'.[659]

But what of the horse in Kintyre place-names? Do any of the names hold faint voices from early history? The answer, sadly, is no. The horse in Kintyre place-names is principally the legendary *each-uisge*, 'water-horse', and there are merely two major names – one, in reality, since they are close together, high above Killean – **Loch an Eich** [742 437] and **Cruach an Eich** [741 434], the loch and the stack-shaped hill of the horse. This is D. J. Macdonald's version of the legend.

'At Braid is Loch an Eich. It is said that a horse on the way to market bolted, shook off the hems [hames] at Braid, the collar at Tigh an t-sergain and another part of its harness at Tigh an t-easgain, and disappeared into Loch an Eich. From that day to this, no trout are to be found in it. A proposal to restock the loch with trout was turned down on the plea that the horse would certainly consume them. A local shepherd averred that he had seen its footprints in the snow.'[660]

A version of the same story, from Neil Thomson, gamekeeper at Killean, appears in Holmer's *The Gaelic of Kintyre* as 'The "Water Kelpie": How Loch an Eich Got Its Name', with the places where the different parts of the harness dropped off named as 'an Bhràid', 'an Bhrigis', 'Tigh an t-Shùgain', and a tantalising 'etc'.[661] The story appears to be an exercise in linking parts of the horse's harness with local place-names, clever but now dated. *Braid* is the hames and *sùgan* a horse-collar, but how *brigis,* the breeching, worked in the scheme of the place-names, I don't know. This is the story: 'The farmer was going to Campbeltown, and when he looked into the stable, he found there a horse with harness on. And when he took the horse out, the horse went berserk, and left behind part of the harness: he lost the hames, the breeches, the saddle and the collar. And then he reached the loch and went into the loch.'[662]

Ian MacDonald heard a similar tale from his father Malcolm MacDonald, who was also one of Holmer's Gaelic informants. As Ian remembers the story, the horse was being 'broken in at Bradge', bolted and lost its collar at Tigh an t-Shùgain, 'House of the straw ropes or collar', lost its harness at Cruach an Eich, then 'turned up the hill and drowned in Loch an Eich'.[663]

A more characteristic account of the beast is preserved in the legend of **Loch an t-Saoir Carridh**, 'Loch of the Joiner Kerr', which lay somewhere east of Garveorine, Skipness, but disappeared through drainage. Kerr, who lived at Strone, was going across to the inn at Lagavulin with another man on a moonlit night. When they came to the lochside, they met a lone horse and Kerr thought that he would take the horse, so he got on its back and continued his journey while his companion returned to Strone. Kerr reached Lagavulin on the horse and left for home on its back, but his body was found at the side of the loch next morning 'mangled and torn', and the horse was 'never seen or heard of before or after that night'.[664]

Adam MacPhail had a story about illicit whisky-distillers at Upper Barr, which had a water-horse and a witch added in for good measure. The 'gaugers' (Excisemen) were lying in wait when someone came along on a white horse. The gaugers gave chase and the horse went right up the hill. They fired shots and struck the rider, but the horse carried on and went into a loch away above Kilmaluag hill. Afterwards, when the gaugers went into a house on Glenacardoch shore, they found an old woman lying on the bed with a wound in her leg. She was a witch and her man was one of the whisky-smugglers they were trying to catch. 'And that's the woman they fired on, so they say. They say that was quite true. And it was a family the name o' Toshes that wis doon in that cottage.'[665]

Lùb an Eich Chloimhich, 'The Mangy Horse Pool', near Kilmory, has been speculatively connected with a water-horse.[666] **Lòn nan each** on Lenaig farm is 'Meadow of the horses'.[667] **Clach Eich**, 'Horse Stone', came from Tarbert-born Rev Dr Duncan Blair, who described it as a 'white marble rock' in Camus na Cèardaich,[668] a bay north of Skipness; but it is the only record.

EAS is a waterfall, and, not surprisingly, given the abundance of burns in Kintyre, is a fairly common place-name element. A few examples will suffice. There are four in Lussa River alone, one of them, **Eas na Speireig** [708 281], constituting the only record in Kintyre of the Sparrowhawk (*Accipiter nisus*). **Eas a' Chromain**, north of Skipness, commemorates another raptor, the Red Kite (*Milvus milvus*), but see under CROMAN. **Eas Fhaolain** [908 581], north of Skipness, the Ordnance Survey interpreted, without explanation, as 'Fillan's Cataract',[669] but *faoileann*, 'gull', might be preferred to an Irish saint's name. **Easca** or Isca [721 282], a hill-farm in Glen Lussa, is surrounded by *eas* place-names, but the interpretation suggested in *The Place-Names of the Parish of Campbeltown* (p 23) is *easg*, 'ditch' or 'fen'. Ian A. Fraser considers the derivation a possibility, but remarks on its rarity and odd simplex form, having 'no specific to support it'.[670] Three families – Drean, McSporran and Smith, totalling 17 persons – were living there in 1792.[671]

EILEAN is Gaelic for 'island, isle, islet', and not even Edward Dwelly could pull anything more out of the bag. In Irish place-names, *inis* is preferred for 'island'. The biggest island off Kintyre – excluding Gigha, to which no justifiable claim can be made here – is **Sanda**, which has had a few names in history. One of them, **Eilean Abhainn**, is described in *The Place-Names of the Parish of Southend* as an 'ancient name for Sanda'. The principal suggestion, 'the stream island', was judged by John Cameron to be 'doubtful in the extreme', and a more satisfactory alternative, linking the specific to Norse *hafn*, 'haven' or 'harbour', was added. With **Eilean nan Caorach** [733 055], its smaller neighbour, there is no uncertainty. It represents 'Sheep Island', which is indeed its present name, and appears on Elphinstone's map of 1745 corrupted to 'Gorak',[672] a form which begs to be personified in a work of fantasy fiction.

Davaar [759 204] is probably the best known of the Kintyre islands, from its position at the mouth of Campbeltown Loch, its tidal accessibility across the Doirlinn shingle-bar, and its fame as the location of the crucifixion image, painted on the wall of a cave by Archibald Mackinnon in 1887. The name's derivation has been contentious. The obvious deduction has been *Eilean dà-bhàrr*, 'Island of two tops', which was Cameron Gillies's choice; yet, even he conceded that 'the real difficulty is in finding the reason for the name';[673] and that, indeed, was the crux of the problem. Looking from west or east, to catch the true profile of the island, there are three visible 'tops', the highest to the south and the lowest to the north. The two highest might be construed as representing the double in the place-name, but they don't appear to me to be conspicuous enough to inspire a place-name, though Moira Burgess remembers that, seen from the school bus from Machrihanish into town, the island 'does have two humps'.[674]

The problem's solution, in any case, was to be found in medieval charters, as T. P. White pointed out as early as 1873: 'Sanct Barr's Island.'[675] In *The Place-Names of the Parish of Campbeltown* (p 20), the matter was summarised thus: 'Before the year 1499, Alexander, Lord of the Isles, granted to the monks at Sagadull (Saddell) "the island of Sanct Barre with its pertinents lying at Loch Kilkerane". This would make the Gaelic name *Eilean Do-Bharr*, The island of Thy Barr, "thy" being used honorifically.' Professor Watson identified the saint as 'Barre, Barra, or Bairre of Cork', who died c. 610. The name is short for Findbarr, 'white crown'. 'At *Cill Bharr*, Kilbarr in Barra,' he continues, 'there was an image of the saint in [Martin] Martin's time (*fl.* 1700); here his anniversary was observed on Sept. 27. The proceedings were conducted on horseback, and concluded by three turns round St. Barr's church ...'[676]

Questions arise in relation to Davaar Island. What was the origin of the dedication to Findbarr? Was he venerated there, in a remoter time than Martin's, remembering, of course, that Catholicism was suppressed in Kintyre in the 17th century? White speculated that Findbarr might have had his 'cell' in one of the island caves,[677] but place-names evoking saints are not evidence that they were ever there. A quern with a cross carved on it was found on Davaar and ended up in Campbeltown Museum,[678] but Davaar has received only the scantest of attention archaeologically, and a comprehensive survey of the island is overdue. **MacRingan's Point** [754 213] points at Davaar across a short reach of sea and commemorates Saint Ninian, the honorific *mo* corrupted to 'mac';[679] but just as the Findbarr dedication is obscure, so too is that of its neighbour, attached to a rocky promontory without a trace of history on it.

Like its neighbour Ben Gullion, Davaar Island has become a symbol of home, particularly among expatriates. A song, 'Island Devarr', was composed in the 19th century by Maude Hepburn; a 19th century steamer was given the name, and a 20th century pub in

Dalintober; one of the 'houses' in Campbeltown Grammar School is 'Davaar'; a street in Campbeltown is 'Davaar Avenue'; and individual houses, too, one of them overlooking the island, but others dotted across the world: Betty McTaggart, a daughter of the artist William McTaggart, named her house in Longniddry 'Davaar';[680] and in South Island, New Zealand, 'Davaar' is the name of a farm belonging to a Macdonald family which emigrated from Kintyre in the early 20th century.[681]

Eilean a' Chòmhraig [886 675] is a small rocky island about a mile south of East Loch Tarbert. It means 'The Battle Isle', and so it appeared, as 'Battell yle', on the mid-17th century Gordon map. No tradition of a battle appears to have survived, but whatever affray occurred there must surely have involved boats. When I was collecting fishermen's place-names in Tarbert, my main informant, Hugh MacFarlane, maintained that the correct name was *Eilean na Corraig*, 'Isle of the Finger', from a tradition that one of the combatants sliced off his finger and threw it on to the island, so claiming it.[682] The story, or story-fragment, has parallels in Gaelic mythology, for example in the traditions of *Làbh Dhearg Uladh* ('The Red Hand of Ulster'). The Rev Dr Duncan Blair, who belonged to a Tarbert fishing family, explained the name by a 'local legend' of 'some combat for fishing rights between two uphill families'.[683] The bay south of the island was called **Bàgh na Còmhraig**, 'The Battle Bay'.[684]

Eilean da Gallaghan [834 658], in upper West Loch Tarbert, is closer to the Kilberry shore than to the Kilcalmonell shore, but was claimed for Kintyre by Duncan Colville. Dugald Mitchell interpreted the name obscurely as 'island of the two little ports or landing places' and made a case for it as an anchorage for 'boats trading with the Clyde'.[685] The O.S. recorded *Eilean dà Ghallagain* and decided that the name was obscure; then someone added 'Two Dogs Island' in red ink,[686] a derivation of doubtful merit. The notorious 16th century Maclean pirate *Ailean nan Sop*, 'Alan of the Straws', was said to have had a lair on the island. John Campbell MacLeod of Saddell noted in 1923 that 'the ruins of a house or fort' had stood on the island, but that fishermen and others had removed the stones for ballast. When he was last on the island, in July 1914, the foundations were still 'plain to the eye'.[687]

Most Kintyre *eilean* features are actually rocks in the sea, perhaps big ones, but rocks none the less. The distinction between an *eilean* and a *sgeir* or *bodha* seems to be that the first is surrounded by sea but the tide won't cover it, whereas the others are covered tidally if not actually submerged. Some of these rock-islands are mentioned elsewhere in this book – **Eilean Grianain** under GRIANAN, **E. nan Sgarbh** under SGARBH, **E. nan Gobhar** under GOBHAR, **E. Leathan** under LEATHAN and **E. na Tomain** under TOM – and a few other examples will suffice. There are two named **Eilean Carrach**, 'Rough Island', from their uneven, rocky shelves, one east of Carradale Quay [820 386] and the other off Skipness Point [913 572], which had its moment of glory as 'yl. Carroch' on the mid-17th century Robert Gordon map. **Island Ross** [785 272], as it appears on O.S. maps, is spoken as 'Isla Ross' and appears on Roy's map as 'Isle of the Ross' and on the Langlands 1793 map as 'Id. Ross'. It has been interpreted as 'Island of the promontory' (*Eilean an Rois*) and it does indeed lie off a point. It appears to be the only instance of *ros*, 'promontory', in Kintyre, unless **Rosshill/Rosehill** [669 376] may be included, but these names have a peculiar and largely obscure origin. In 'Jottings from West Kintyre' (p 65), D. J. Macdonald interpreted Rosshill as *Cnoc an Rois*, 'the hill of the point', but offered no evidence. The name appears to have emerged as 'Rosshill' in the 18th century, and in the first record of which I am aware, Roy's map, is simply 'Rosshill'. For a rather fanciful explanation of Rosehill see under BÀRR.

Mary MacEwan's Island [799 319], which is probably an anglicisation from Gaelic, is an offshore rock north of Pluck. The unfortunate girl was said to have fallen asleep after bathing in the sea, and 'the wilks or mussels got a hold o' her hair and kept her down while the tide drowned her'. Graham McKinlay, who gave me the little story in 1977 – with the afterthought, 'That's the kind o' fable that wis goin around'[688] – was wrong with the shellfish he named. Only limpets could accomplish the feat described, in the unlikely event that some supernatural motivation turned them from natural docility to communal malevolence! The story echoes other folk-tales, e.g. in Ireland, of foxes which in attempting to prise a limpet from a rock are clamped by the tongue until they drown.

Eilean applies also to inland features. **An t-Eilean**, 'The Island', is a rock outcrop in a shore-field on Whitestone farm,[689] while **Eilean na[n] Gobhar** [c. 712 280], 'The Goats' Island', sits in the River Lussa.[690] The final example is **Ellenlochnacanage** [695 279], the form the name took in a charter of the Lands of Skeirkenzie by John, Bishop of the Isles, to the Earl and Countess of Argyll in 1576: '*insula et fortalitium de Ellenlochnacanage*'. The name represents *Eilean*

loch na canaich, 'Island of the loch of cotton grass', which sits in
Tangy Loch, formerly **Loch nan Canach**, the Ordnance Survey's
interpretation of which was the poetic 'Loch of the mountain down'.[691]
There was a fortified house on the island – linked to the mainland
by a submerged stone causeway – which is marked on the Pont-
Gordon map of the second quarter of the 17th century, when Tangy
estate was in the possession of the MacEachan family.[692] According
to Peter MacIntosh, the date '1670' was carved on the house.[693] In
1786, the lessee of Tangy Mill, Lachlan Clark, was to raise the banks
of 'Lochnacanie' by at least 4 ft. and allow its water to power the
wool-mill as well as the meal-mill at Tangy.[694]

*26. EILEAN. Davaar Island from the Learside road, published by M. and
L. In author's collection.*

EILEIRG means 'deer-trap'. There are two in Kintyre, both in
Southend Parish, and their significance has slipped into obscurity.
W. J. Watson, in 1926, remarked of this place-name that it was 'not
uncommon in Galloway as Elrick; it is found in Argyll and in the east
from Inverness southwards, especially in Perthshire'.[695] Naturalist
and author Gavin Maxwell (1914-69) was raised in the village of Elrig,
Wigtonshire, which appears in the title of his memoir *The House of
Elrig* (1965) and is another form of *eileirg*. The word occurs in Old
Irish in the sense of 'ambush', but, significantly, is absent from Irish

place-names: *eileirg*, as 'deer-trap', derives from P-Celtic and may have entered Scottish Gaelic from Pictish or North British, or both.[696]

For a 'good description of the rather grisly type of hunt involved', Professor John MacQueen recommends lines 1150-73 of the Middle English poem *Sir Gawain and the Green Knight*,[697] while Professor Watson, discussing *eileag*, also a deer-trap, quotes a description in 1795, from Assynt, of a place where 'in times of old, the natives gathered deer, and when entangled, they killed them'.[698]

27. EILEIRG, the deer trap, at the Mull of Kintyre, looking east, from which direction the animals may have been driven. Photograph by the author, 29/4/2012.

The first **Eleric** [610 085] is over 1200 ft. and close to the Mull. My wife and I decided, at the end of April 2012, to investigate the feature. I had imagined it as a narrowing defile, but it wasn't. To be truthful, it looked insignificant, but after we had sat there for a while, eating our supper and looking around, we began to grasp the nature of the place. It is a kind of natural amphitheatre, the elevated sides of which offer ample cover for an ambush. I presume the deer would be driven into it from the open moorland in the east. This 'Eleric' appears to have survived only by the narrowest of margins.

How did it come to be recorded by the Ordnance Survey in 1866? The Mull townships were emptied in the latter part of the 18th century for the introduction of sheep. After the old native families had gone, who kept the name alive? It would appear from the O.S. name-book that 'Eleric' came from Archibald Todd, shepherd at Strone,[699] whose wife Agnes was one of the Amod MacNeills, a family which goes back many generations in Southend (see Amod under GLEANN).

Remarkably, Archibald was still at Strone when he died in 1923. The Todd family, though it originated in Dumfries-shire, was Gaelic-speaking from first to last in Kintyre, and was singularly connected with the Mull of Kintyre. Archibald's father George was shepherd in Balnamoil and fell to his death over a cliff in 1871.[700] Archibald and Agnes had six sons and two daughters, and celebrated their diamond wedding anniversary in 1919. When 'Siol Chuinn' visited them at Strone in 1921 during his hill-walking adventures, he remarked that they knew 'all that pertains to the past among the hill and glen folk'.[701] Three of the six Southend Gaelic speakers Nils M. Holmer mustered for his linguistic researches in the late 1930s were Todds: George, Katie and Jessie, children of Archibald and Agnes.[702] Calum Bannatyne, the retired shepherd I tape-recorded in the 1970s, had the greatest fund of folk-tales I met with in Kintyre. The bulk of Calum's stories were heard at Strone from Agnes Todd, and they constitute a record of events and personalities going back centuries. Without Calum's contact with old Agnes, the stories would have gone with her to the grave. But Archibald Todd appears not to have had any stories about Eleric, nor did the O.S. attempt to interpret the name.[703]

The other Eleric [712 146] is a ruined farm, north-west of Arinascavach. Since a settlement and the landscape feature it was named after do not always coincide topographically, the question arises: where exactly is this second deer-trap, which should represent 'a defile, natural or artificial ... into which the deer were driven, often in hundreds, and slain as they passed through'.[704] Since the hills around Eleric are now extensively afforested, identifying a suitable location would be no easy matter; but that location may well lie close to the ruined steading, since the holding was not a vast one. In 1499, 'Ellarig' was among the lands granted to Colin MacEachran from King James IV.[705] As 'Elarick', it appears in 1751 as a 1-merkland,[706] and in 1792, as 'Ellerick', was occupied by John McArthur, his wife Effy McCorqudall and their five children.[707] By C1841, as 'Alerak', it was no longer a working farm, but occupied by a farm labourer, Peter Black; and in 1851 a shepherd, Peter Clark, was in 'Ellerick' with his wife Catherine, five young children and two female servants.

In 1858, the holding was absorbed into Arinascavach, along with Knocknagreen and Dalbuy, when the lease passed from John McLean to Donald Macdonald, tenant of Arinarach and Arinascavach.[708]

One of Peter Clark's sons, Robert, who was born at 'Ellerick', contributed to Duncan Colville's place-names collection in 1929. He spent 40 years as shepherd in Gleneadardacrock (see under GLEANN), and in 1916, at the age of 65, received a silver medal and certificate from the Highland and Agricultural Society for long service.[709] He was at Gleneadardacrock in C1881, with his widowed mother, Catherine Bowie – he never married – a six-year-old nephew, Archibald Clark, and a 'general servant' William Watson.

Professor William Watson described the slaughter at the *eileirg* as 'the last stage in the great deer hunts which were once so common in Scotland and which survived in the north till the eighteenth century'.[710] The question naturally arises: how long ago were these deer-traps last used in Kintyre? Red Deer (*Cervus elaphus*), which is certainly the species in question, appear to have become extinct in Kintyre before the 16th century. The importance of deer-hunting in the Middle Ages is reflected in the sculpture of that period; for example, on the fragment of a 15th century Kilchousland cross, which is on display in Campbeltown Museum, a carving depicts a stag being chased by a hound. In the Gaelic poem *Marbhrainn Niall Òg Mhachra Shanuis* ('Elegy to Young Neil of Machrihanish'), which probably belongs to the late 16th century, the line occurs, 'and bring down the stag on the height', which may have a contemporaneous relevance to Kintyre or may not. Certainly, by about 1630, when the second volume of *Macfarlane's Geographical Collections* appeared, it was remarked of the Mull of Kintyre (p 188): 'There was abundance of deir in this mountaine of ancient tyme but now there is none to be sein nether in this Mountaine nor in the rest of the mountaines and lands of Kintyre.' To this was added (p 527): 'Dear and roes wonted to be heir, but now ther be none in all Cantyre.' Red Deer returned to Kintyre in small numbers in the 19th and 20th centuries, probably through Knapdale, and stags swimming between Arran and Kintyre have been recorded; on at least two occasions, individuals were captured and taken aboard fishing boats.[711]

Deer themselves appear in several place-names. In North Kintyre, **Cruach nam Fiadh** [821 566] is 'Hill of the Deer' and **Doire na h-Earbaige** [c. 736 355] 'Thicket of the young Roe'; **Allt na h-Earba** [651 143] on Achnaslisaig Hill, South Kintyre, is 'Stream of the Roe'; **Leum na h-earba**, on Barrmains farm, is 'The roe's leap'.[712]

A footnote: George McSporran remembered (23/2/2012) the late John Russell, Glenramskill, telling him that mountain hares would be driven through the Gap at the Mull to be shot at by waiting guns.

EIRBHE is a fence or a wall. In *The Place-Names of the Parish of Southend* (p 20), the southern Learside farm **Glenahervie** [747 107] is rendered *Gleann na h-eirbhe*, and interpreted 'Glen of the boundary', which, by extension, the fence or wall may have been. The specific of **Allt Harvie** [701 288], a burn at the south-west end of Lussa Loch, may also derive from *eirbhe* or may represent the surname Harvey.

EUN is a bird. **Gortinanane** [706 473], the farm north of Tayinloan, has been interpreted as *Goirtean nan eun*, 'The birds' paddock'.[713] The earliest records I have found are late 18th century baptisms there, spellings 'Gortenanean'. In 1797 William McKinnon owned two horses at 'Gortanein',[714] and in 1820 Dugald McDougall, 'Gortananain', took Donald Sellars, farmer in 'Coalfuar' (Culfuar), to court, alleging that Sellars had dismissed him 'for failing to clean the horses well enough' and had not paid him for the months that he worked.[715] In 1868, when Largie Estate advertised 'Gortinane' for let, it consisted of 195 acres of arable and 68 of pasture.[716] On Dalmore farm, Rev Macdonald recorded **Dail ghoirtean nan eun**, 'Bird paddock field',[717] which may owe its origin to the above. **Loch nan Eun** represents 'Loch of the Birds', and there are two [754 428 and 808 528] in Saddell and Skipness Parish. For **Suidhe nan Eun**, 'Sitting-place of the Birds', see under SUIDHE, and for **Allt Àirigh nan Eun**, 'Stream of the Birds' Sheiling', under ÀIRIGH.

FAD/FADA is 'long'. **Port Fada** [853 540], near Oragaig, is 'Long Port'. For **Bogha Fad**, 'Long Rock', at Machrihanish, see under BODHA/BOGHA, and for **Tòrr Fada**, 'Long Hill', under TÒRR. In the Largieside, D. J. Macdonald recorded a long rig, **An t-iomaire fada**, on Beacharra, and two long fields, **Ach' fada** on Tangy and **Ruighe fada** on Drumnamucklach,[718] the generic of which was left untranslated, but see under RUIGHE.

FAIRE is essentially 'watching' and was applied to look-out hills. **Beinn na Faire** – see also under BEINN – is in the south of the peninsula and the other three *faire* names are in the north, with *cnoc*, 'hill', as their generic. Watching what? The question is an obvious one, but the answers aren't quite so obvious and some speculation – dangerous ground for historians – will be necessary. These hill-tops – and no doubt many others which didn't get the name or later lost it – were places to which people went in expectation of seeing something This might have been something they wished to see, such as a boat or a person returning overdue or in bad weather. Or it might have been something they dreaded seeing, such as the approach of rumoured raiders, by land or by sea. In times of political or social unrest, or actual war, a watch-hill may have been manned for days or weeks on end. In more recent history, the enemy may have been Excisemen, or 'gaugers', on a raid to catch illicit distillers at work. James McNeill named two hills near Machrihanish on which fires would be lit to warn 'smugglers' of approaching danger.[719]

Do the positions of these hills communicate a sense of their function? The only one of them of which I have any intimate knowledge is **Beinn na Faire**, which stands at 923 ft. above the Inneans Bay, with clear views (on clear days) out to the north of Ireland and to Islay, both of great significant in Kintyre history. Ships could certainly be watched sailing north and south. Beinn na Faire is miles from any significant settlement, but folk of old thought little of walking great distances in one go. **Cnoc na Faire** [882 658], south of Tarbert and a mile inland, at 1000 ft. looks across lower Loch Fyne to Kerry Cowal. Another of the name [905 643], smaller at 480 ft., but close to the coast and prominent, overlooks Lagan Ròaig ruins from the north-east. The final Cnoc na Faire [878 567] is to the east of Claonaig, smaller still at 324 ft., but again close to the coast. Claonaig had a small fleet of fishing boats until the end of the 19th century, which may have some bearing on the hill's function.

As an aside, the house **Spion Kop** [838 607], on the Redhouse to Claonaig road, is Afrikaans *Spioenkop*, 'Spy hill', an imported 'look-out' name to add to the native ones. The name presumably commemorates the military engagement in January 1900, during the Second Boer War, in Natal, South Africa.

FAMHAIR/FOMHAIR is a 'giant', but unlike fairies, which inhabited a kind of parallel world with humankind and would cross over when it suited them – see SÌTHICH – giants belonged to a remote past and were known only through the stories told about them and the monuments which they left on the landscape, particularly the standing stones which were the missiles rivals hurled at one another over great distances when they quarrelled. Macbain, in his etymological dictionary, tracked *famhair* from Early Irish *fomór*, *fomórach*, 'a Fomorian, a mythic race of invaders of Ireland'.[720]

D. J. Macdonald recorded **Uaigh an fhamhair**, 'The giant's grave', on Beacharra farm, and I suspect it to be identical with **Leac an fhamhair**, which he interpreted as 'Giant's face'.[721] 'Face' (*leac*) here must represent 'hill-face', but in this instance might better equate with 'grave-stone' (see LEAC). He elsewhere described Leac an fhamhair as a 'pre-historic burying-ground' close to the Beacharra standing stone,[722] a reference to the Neolithic chambered cairn. For **Stac an Fhamhair**, 'The Giant's Stack', and **Dùn an Fhamhair**, 'The Giant's Fort', with a tale of a giant and his family attached to it, see under DÙN. For another giant tale see **Greanan Dheardruin** under GRIANAN. In **Altanopher Glen** [648 195] – *Allt an fhomhair*: 'Stream of the giant' – the march between Trodigal and Kilkivan farms, there was a rock with depressions in it which were believed to represent a giant's fingertips. In that stream, **The Foffar's Hole** or **Toll an fhomhair** [649 200], the original Gaelic, is a pool below a waterfall. Duncan Colville surmised, from having spoken with local people, that the story of a giant in the hole was concocted to keep children away from the dangerous gorge,[723] but it seems to me entirely possible that the tradition already existed. On the westernmost point of Sanda there was **Slochd an fhomhair**, 'The giant's pit'.[724]

Famhair is also a mole-catcher, and if the mole had been an earlier resident in Kintyre, that meaning might have entered the place-names nomenclature, but moles didn't make their appearance until the first half of the 19th century,[725] and mole-catchers weren't far behind. In 1863, Alexander McPhail, farmer in Drumgarve, was publicly recommending the services of Robert Walker, who had already trapped hundreds of 'this vermin which is rapidly spreading over the country'.[726]

FAOCHAG in Scots is 'wilk' and in English 'winkle'. There are several species of winkle, but the best known is *Littorina littorea*, not only because it is edible and abundant, but also because it has commercial value and has been an economic mainstay of the hardy and impecunious for generations. In *The Place-Names of the Parish of Southend* (p 19), the suggested derivation of the Learside name **Feochaig** [763 133] was *faochag*, but the connection was admitted to be 'obscure'. The holding appeared in the form 'Feachaig' as far back as 1481, and spellings thereafter were consistent with that. The place-names committee members fairly racked their brains over this one, and two of the suggestions were contradictory: the Rev Angus J. MacVicar put forward *feoch*, 'calm' + *uig*, 'bay' (but by 1965 he had decided that the name meant 'a place where whelks are gathered'.[730]) The Rev T. S. Macpherson advanced *fiadhaich*, 'wild' + *uig*. John Cameron threw in a terrestrial explanation, *féith-each-aig*, 'little boggy place',[727] while Cameron Gillies decided that the name was 'based upon the stem of *feoch-adan*, the corn thistle'.[728] I'll leave it there, drifting between land and sea, a reality in itself, but parentage uncertain. **The Faochag**, interpreted 'The Limpet', is a rock off the Arran coast.[729] **Port nam Faochag** on Gigha is 'Port of the winkles'.

FEANNAG is 'crow' and also, in agriculture, a 'rig'. The Raven – FITHEACH – is the biggest of the crow family and the most significant in both its spatial presence and its contribution to folklore. Since ornithology was unknown when the *feannag* place-names came into being, the question arises: which species of crow was meant? The Red-Billed Chough (*Pyrrhocorax pyrrhocorax*) bred in Kintyre until c. 1982,[731] and there is no reason to suppose that it wasn't resident for hundreds, or thousands, of years before then, but it has apparently left no trace in the Gaelic nomenclature of Kintyre. The Western Jackdaw (*Corvus monedula*) has left only one Gaelic place-name, **Cnoc nan Cadhag** [709 285], 'Hill of the Jackdaws', near Lussa Water.[732] The Rook (*Corvus frugilegus*) is now abundant in Kintyre, but nests communally in woodland and prefers to feed on grassland and is therefore an unlikely subject of place-names in remote parts. The Magpie – see **Allt na Pioghaid** under ALLT – is distinctive by its white markings and may be disregarded here, as may the Eurasian Jay (*Garrulus glandarius*), also for reasons of plumage and for its woodland rarity. Which leaves the Carrion Crow (*Corvus corone*) and Hooded Crow (*Corvus cornix*), which hybridise and were once assumed to be the same species. The status of the former in Kintyre is rather obscure, but it can be stated with certainty that in its pure form it is rare and possibly always was. The 'Hoodie', then, is the *feannag* of all, or most, of the Kintyre place-names. Macbain, indeed, defines the word only as 'hooded crow', while Dwelly has 'carrion crow' and 'rook', with the hoodie under *feannag-ghlas*,[733] 'grey crow', from its grey-on-black markings.

The 'Hoodie' population in Kintyre has increased greatly in recent decades, owing to an easing of persecution and the spread of forestry, in which the species finds unlimited nest-sites. Nests used to be found in remote spots, in a stunted tree in a moorland gully, say, and the birds themselves were seldom seen close to towns and villages, and rarely anywhere. Now they are common, but still hated by farmers and shepherds and still shot under licence.

Tobar na Feannaige [636 206], 'Well of the Crow', is in a field behind Seaview, Machrihanish.[734] **Allt Fheannag** [774 434] in Saddell and Skipness Parish was translated 'Crows Burn' by the O.S. in 1867.[735] **Gleann nam Feannag** [707 327], 'Valley of the Crows', is in Killean and Kilchenzie Parish. The farm **Strathnafanaig** [775 564], in Kilcalmonell Parish, may be *Srath na Feannaige*, 'Valley of the Crow', but *feannag* is also the term for a 'rig', and the context here may not preclude that meaning. **Cùl na Feannag**, a field on Largie Estate, D. J. Macdonald translated clumsily as 'Lazy beds back'.[736] Dwelly regarded the term 'lazy-bed' as 'merely a southern odium on the system of farming in Gaeldom'.[737] 'Lazy-beds' may be seen on unimproved Kintyre landscapes, notably on the coast between Machrihanish and the Mull, where they appear as patches of spade-formed ridges on steep or rocky ground on which no plough would run.

28. FEANNAG. *So-called lazy-beds at Innean Beithe, November 1977. Photograph by Agnes Stewart.*

FEÒIRLIN is 'farthing' in Gaelic, one of the 'fiscal names' which indicate 'extent' of land, and derives from Norse *fjording*, 'farthing';[738] but see PEIGHINN for more detail on the system. **Feorlan** [639 072], on the road to the Mull of Kintyre, was a farm and then a shepherd's house. Jon Mcintyre was in 'Feorling' c. 1636;[739] in 1711 Charles O Drain was a tenant of Malcolm MacNeill of Carskey's at 'ffeorlin'; in 1715 John Mc Camross and in 1739 Malcolm McCamross were there.[740] **Feorlinmolach** is marked on the Langlands map of 1801, very approximately between Whitehouse and Claonaig, and the parish in which it belonged is uncertain, let alone its actual location. It probably represents *Feòrlinn molach*, 'Rough farthingland'. **Garveoline** [846 579], the O.S. spelling in 1867, appears as 'Garvoine Township' in the Royal Commission on the Ancient and Historical Monuments of Scotland's inventory,[741] but Denis Rixson classifies it as a *feòrlin* name and suggests 'rough (*garbh*) farthingland',[742] which 'Garforling' in 1511 and 'Garforlin' in 1685 tend to support. **Ruigh' an fheòrlain** on Beacharra farm, Largieside, D. J. Macdonald interpreted as 'Firlot field'.[743] 'Firlot' is Scots for the fourth part of a boll (variable, but about 140 lbs) or a measure containing that amount.[744] Macbain relates *feòrlan*, 'firlot', to *feòirling*, the form he uses for 'farthing land'.[745]

FEUR is 'grass', and, as such, isn't noticed much. **Allt an Fheuraich** [688 416], which rises on Beachmore farm, is the form recorded by the O.S., which offered alternative interpretations, 'Stream of the Grass' and 'The pasture stream'.[746] **Feur Lochain** is 'grassy lochan', and there are two in North Kintyre, both of them smothered by vegetation and no longer showing blue on maps. One [776 510] is in mid-peninsula, west of Loch Garasdale, and the other [889 642] is north-east of Loch na Machrach Bige. George Campbell Hay was familiar with the latter, and set a late poem in Gaelic there, *Aig an Fheurlochan*, 'By the Feur Lochain'; but he wasn't there to write the poem, except in memory. While alone and 'lost in contemplation' by the little loch, a mysterious presence arrives at his side, touches him and then speaks – it is his Gaelic Muse, and, deeper in its nature and in the very nature of the wilderness which it now wanders, the indomitable spirit of the Gael. I quote the first two verses, translated by Michel Byrne:

> By the solitary Grassy Lochan,
> on my wanderings in the heather,

as I stood still for a while
lost in contemplation,
the hand lay on my shoulder,
kindly, gently.
I turned to look,
and saw no-one.

The hills and the uplands
stretched there, desolate.
I saw no movement
around me or beyond.
There was only the breath of the wind
in the heather, light and leisurely.
A sweet voice spoke in my ear,
and its sound I will never forget.[747]

FIONN, essentially, is 'white'. An adjective, it none the less appears as a first element in many compound place-names, and such is the case with **Fionnphort**. The best known example of this name is on the Ross of Mull, because a ferry to Iona operates from there. There are two 'white ports' in Kintyre, relating to a sandy shore or adjacent seabed (which, in the histories of storm and tide, are effectively one and the same). Of lesser significance is the inlet [625 201] just before the iron gate in the Galdrans. This was one of the place-names which Duncan Colville rescued from an old estate map at Lossit House.[748] The map spelling appears to have been 'Fionnaphort', representing the spoken form. I have never heard that name spoken, though Agnes Stewart has, but have heard the next one, which also has the excrescent 'a' sound, whose function is euphonious.

The other Fionnphort [902 648] is a bay between Tarbert and Skipness. The late Willie 'Tar' McDougall in Tarbert provided me with a vivid description of this port and its lore in 1979, when I was compiling maps of fishermen's place-names for *The Ring-Net Fishermen*. He described a 'fine green' there, about '100 yds. by 20', with a stream – 'Fionnaphort Burn', as Hugh MacFarlane named it[749] – flowing down at its south end. The skiff fishermen would moor their boats at a rock north of 'Fiannifort' and go ashore to fill their water-flasks and perhaps have a wash, since there was no place for personal hygiene at sea – water was precious and to be used only for drinking, cooking and tea-making.[750] The fishermen might amuse themselves at a game called 'rings'. As Willie explained, 'It was played with a wooden pin hammered into the ground and you threw a ring over the pin, something like pitch and toss'.[751]

Enthused by Willie's description of Fionn Phort, I resolved in 1980 to camp on its fine green foreshore and explore the surroundings. I set off with tent and provisions on 24 June, and by a remarkable coincidence actually met Willie. I was following the shore, and about three hours into my walk saw a man working from a small motor boat. I hailed him and he nosed his boat inshore and cut the engine. I had never met Willie, only corresponded with him, but I had a hunch that this was him and asked him. He affirmed that he was indeed Willie McDougall, and I, in turn, identified myself as his Campbeltown correspondent. We spoke for only about half-a-minute, by which time his boat was nudging the rocks. He later told me he regretted not having offered to transport me to Fionn Phort. Had he done so, I might actually have got there. As it happened, I pitched my tent in the wrong bay, which I later identified as Camus na Ban-tighearna.[752]

Dùn Fionn [657 306], which stands in Innean Mór below Killocraw steading, almost certainly represents 'Fionn's Fort', rather than 'White Fort'. This was the legendary hero, Fionn mac Cumhaill ('Fair-haired son of Cumhal'), whose warrior band was the Fianna. Fionn is known by various other names, including Finn, Finn MacCool, and Fingal. Indeed, Dùn Fionn was also known as 'Fingal's Fort'.[753] Fianna legends have been recorded in Kintyre, for example in connection with Dùn Ach' na h-àtha, Muasdale (see DÙN), which was occupied by the hero himself. Excavation of the dun on the rock of Dùn Fionn, or Dùn Fhinn – its other spelling – uncovered two distinct structural periods, one Iron Age and the other medieval. Artefacts from the first period included two bronze penannular brooches and two spindle-whorls (for wool-spinning), and from the second period a rotary quern, for the hand-grinding of corn.[754]

Loch Fionn-Ghleann [742 446], as 'Lochfinglein', was mentioned in a boundary dispute in 1736 (see CÀRN) and translates as 'Loch of the Fair Glen'. The location of the 'Fair Glen' now appears to be unknown, though D. J. Macdonald recorded it on 'Braide' as **Fionn a-ghleann** 'White or fair glen' [755] — cf. Fionnghleann, Breadalbane, of which W. J. Watson observed that it 'most probably means "holy glen"' [757] — but it won't be far from the loch. There is another loch which, by the look of its name, and since its tides ebb and flow off north-eastern Kintyre, should be in here; but the specific of **Loch Fyne** (*Loch Fìne*) is wine rather than water.[756] For **Clachfin** see under CLACH.

FITHEACH is the Common Raven (*Corvus corax*), the biggest, the fiercest and probably the brightest of native crows (which, as a family, are considered by many biologists and ornithologists to be among the most intellectually advanced and longest-lived of all birds). As I remarked in *Kintyre Birds* (p 52): 'Since Kintyre escaped neither the depredations nor, later, the cultural influence of the Vikings, it should be stated here that the Raven was Odin's bird. Supreme creator and god of war in Norse mythology, Odin had two Ravens, Huginn (Mind) and Muninn (Memory), who were his intelligence-seekers, returning from their world-ranging flights to perch on his shoulders and impart their knowledge.'

As I also remarked in *Kintyre Birds*, in Gaelic folklore the Raven is 'credited with knowledge which borders on the supernatural'; and in later reading I came across a remarkable example of that belief. Rev Fr. Allan McDonald (1859-1905) collected a Biblically-based tradition in South Uist, that the Raven was disliked because he did not return to the Ark but ate the carcasses he found floating. With the experience thus gained, he has ever since always known where to find meat. That intuition was proverbially known as *fios fithich*, 'raven's knowledge', and to bestow it on a child he should be given a drink from the dry skull of a Raven. He would afterwards always know where a missing beast had lain down to die and become food for Ravens.[758]

Dugald Macintyre was born in 1870 at Limecraigs, Campbeltown, the son of a gamekeeper, and great-grandson of the famous foxhunter, Allan Macintyre (see under SIONNACH). Dugald himself became a gamekeeper, but retired at the age of 55 and spent the rest of his life – he died in 1957 – writing articles and books on wildlife. As a boy, he had kept a pet Raven, and he admired its intelligence and was amused by its mischievousness, but warned of its treachery. As a gamekeeper, he was called upon to kill Ravens, and the conflict he felt between sentiment and duty is expressed movingly and memorably in the following account.

> The incident which I am about to relate affected me so much that I formed the idea that as long as I lived I would temper justice with mercy in dealing with the creatures named vermin. A keeper is rather in the position of a soldier in regard to vermin killing, for if either objects to killing he should adopt another profession.
> Shepherds occasionally brought me news of the bad doings of ravens I had thought of leaving alone, and I had news of such

a couple from a shepherd one day. No one could approach the nest, and the only chance of thinning out the family was after it had flown, when for one day the young may be stalked on the cliffs and shot. I found it easy to shoot three of the four young ravens, but not so the fourth which, a strong and lively bird, was warned by its parents every time I tried to stalk it. The day was near a close, and at my last stalk of the young raven one of the old birds brushed him from his perch as I drew near. The three ravens soared beautifully high in air near the parental cliff, when suddenly the two old ones uttered harsh croaks of alarm, and flew for the shelter of the cliff. The young bird did not understand what a distant black speck in air foreboded and continued to soar while an old female peregrine drew nearer. Back came the devoted old ravens to the young one and actually tried to drive him forcibly to cover in the cliff. He would not be driven, and the old birds left him as the peregrine's stoop began.

The hawk seemed to pass the young raven without touching him; but it had struck him in passing, for he fell to the ground as if shot. He recovered and took shelter in a low cliff, where (as I shall always regret) I stalked and shot at him. He was wounded, and flying to sea fell in the water. His parents croaked above him for a long time, then flew to their old nest and deliberately pulled it to pieces, hurling the sticks and debris of the nest down the cliffs, croaking dismally all the time. I make no comment, and it is pleasing to think that ravens are protected in most Scottish counties today.[759]

The Raven is now protected nationally, but may be shot in limited numbers under licence from the Scottish government. Some Kintyre farmers, in recent years, have availed themselves of that legal recourse, alleging a dramatic increase in incidences of Ravens' attacking sheep and lambs and causing mutilation and death. The allegation is fundamentally irrefutable, because, after decades of virtual immunity from persecution, Raven numbers have increased hugely, with communal roosting counts in Kintyre occasionally exceeding 100.[760] As an example, albeit arbitrary, of its past rarity, in the first six months of 1921 14 Ravens were recorded as among the avian 'vermin' killed in Kintyre, compared with 784 Black-Backed Gulls, 328 Rooks, 270 Jackdaws, 156 'hawks', 154 Hooded Crows and 16 Buzzards.[761]

Though they are now more numerous and may be seen and heard over towns and villages, the Raven remains, for those free to ignore the darker side of its nature, an embodiment, with the Golden Eagle, of wild places – moor, mountain and sea-cliff. Its croaking call from high overhead and thrilling aerial displays often enliven an otherwise uneventful moorland walk.

In early May 2009, after several hours in the Inneans, Jimmy MacDonald and I returned to Machrihanish by the rugged coast, and before we lost sight of the south, Jimmy pointed out **Binnein Fithich** [600 151], at the top of the Aignish and resembling a couple of knuckles on the skyline. I had never particularly noticed it, never linked the name on the map to the feature itself.[762] See also BINNEIN. There are several other place-names in Kintyre with the specific *fitheach*, most of them rocks and peaks on which Ravens habitually perched or nested – **Cnoc an Fhithich**, 'The Raven's Hill' [813 506 and 782 397], **Creag an Fhithich** [763 354 and 593 106] 'The Raven's Rock' – but Beinnein Fithich, 'Raven Hillock', is the most outstanding, towering at 1185 ft. I'll leave the Raven there, in its true element.

FLIUCH is 'wet'. **Refluich** [714 499] was interpreted by Cameron Gillies in 1900 as *ridhe fliuch*, 'the wet valley-bottom', and in 1906 as *ruighe fliuch*;[763] but see RUIGHE for definitions. Gillies, as far as I understand, never visited Kintyre during his researches, therefore his acquaintance with Refluich was only on paper. Ian A. Fraser considered *réidh*, 'plain, meadow', a possible alternative for the generic.[764] The farm was in Kilcalmonell Parish, but only just. For an account of the Stewart family of Refluich, see Ian MacDonald's 'Largieside and its People' in *Kintyre Magazine* No. 4, p 25. There appear to be no forms of the name earlier than the 18th century: 'Rifluck' on Roy's Map; 1785 'Rifluch'; 1787 'Righfluch'; 1809 'Reefluch';[765] C1871 'Reifliuch'.

Fliuchaig and **Fliuchach** both represent 'wet place'. The first [634 207] was 'The port where the fishing boats land at old Salt Pans',[766] but whether the name was applied to land or to sea is unclear. With the second one there is no doubt. The O.S. described it as 'A small place of shelter for fishing smacks', and on the first map it is marked in the sea just north of Sanda Lighthouse; but in the most recent map I have (2007), the name has migrated to a position south of the Lighthouse, which is not recommended for anyone desiring to shelter a smack. Admiralty charts more sensibly place 'Fliuchach' out in the bay. The O.S. interpretation in 1866 was delightfully imaginative: 'A place where rain clouds collect.'[767] On the old map of Sanda in C. & D. Mactaggart's office, Campbeltown (page viii), **Tobar Fliuchaig** is marked about a quarter of a mile north-east of the Lighthouse, or roughly at 728 040. In the Antiquarian Society Schedules, this was amended to *Tobar fliuchach* and interpreted as 'Wet well', but when the Southend booklet was published, 'Well of the wet place' had wisely been substituted.[768] For **Uamh Fhliuch** see under UAMH(A).

FRAOCH is 'heather', of which in Kintyre there are three noteworthy species, Ling (*Calluna vulgaris*), Cross-leaved heath (*Erica tetralix*) and Bell-heather (*Erica cinerea*), all of which (but especially the first) may produce the white flowers which are considered lucky. At the height of the grouse-shooting craze, from the mid-19th to early 20th century, heather moors were managed by systematic burning, but since then forestry plantations have eliminated much of that cover. Heather was used as a thatching material for houses, and John Smith, writing of Argyll in 1798, remarked that, 'Of old, most of our churches in this county were covered with heather'.[769]

The farm in Carradale Glen, **Auchenfraoch** [787 424], as spelt on the O.S. Explorer 356, is clearly meant to represent *Achadh a' fhraoich*, 'Heather field', but it was originally recorded as 'Auchenrioch', for *Achadh riabhach*, 'Brindled field'. Early spellings: 1500 'Auchinreauch'; 1502 'Auchinreich'; 1545 'Auchreych'. When Archibald McArthur died in 1916, he was a month short of his hundredth birthday and the oldest person in Kintyre. According to the *Argyllshire Herald* (14/10/1916), he died at 'Heatherfield, Carradale Glen', but in the *Campbeltown Courier* 'Auchenrioch' was the place. He was born at 'Cleonaig' and went to Craigmore as a shepherd. When he died, he had been 62 years at Auchenrioch and had 'lived under five lairds'. At the age of 97, he assisted in harvesting and thatched most of the stacks in the yard. He seldom travelled far, but wouldn't miss Tarbert Fair. One time at the fair, he heard a dealer boasting of having been there 24 years in succession, to which Archibald replied: 'Twenty-four years! Man, I havena missed Tarbert Fair but once for over eighty years, and that was a day when the boat didna call at Carradale.'[770] In the previous year, the *Courier* had published an interview with McArthur, which contains many more interesting anecdotes, including his involvement in illicit whisky-distilling and a resultant brush with 'gaugers' (Excisemen), and his conversion to the Haldane religious sect, which was brought to Kintyre in 1800 by Naomi Mitchison's great-grandfather, James Haldane, and his elder brother Robert. 'Mind the Haldians?' McArthur replied to the question. 'Of course I do. I joined them when I was young, and noo I'm the last in the glen. George Murray was the first Haldian minister and he did a loat o' good in this countryside.' Peter MacIntosh recalled the Carradale Glen 'Haldeans' and how the 'parish minister and proprietor raised a persecution against them'. Some of them, driven from the glen, drowned when their boat sank in a squall on passage to Campbeltown. Their persecutors naturally paid a heavy price. The minister was himself drowned and his body 'never found', and, as for the proprietor – presumably Campbell of Glencarradale – 'not a foot of the glen now belongs to [his] offspring'.[771] See also PUBULL.

Lochan Fraoich [814 551], on the boundary of Skipness and Kilcalmonell parishes, was originally named 'Loch Fraoich' by the O.S., but should perhaps be rendered *Loch an fhraoich*, 'The heather loch'. I visited it in 2012 and it is no *lochan*, or 'little loch'; nor did heather seem noticeably abundant there. **Tigh an Fhraoich** [809 605], south of Whitehouse, is 'The Heather House', called no doubt for the thatch on its roof, and there was another cottage of that name at Pennygown Bridge [687 140].[772] **Druim allt a' fhraoich**, 'Heather brook ridge', was on Barlea farm, and **Ach' a' fhraoich**, 'Heather field', on Rosshill farm.[773]

FUAR means 'cold'. **Àirigh Fhuair** [915 615], a ruined coastal farm north of Skipness, is 'Cold Shieling'. It was evidently a holding, and name, of some antiquity, and appears in 1511 as 'Aireour', which fairly represents the pronunciation, 'Arri oor'. In 1795 Neill Campbell was tenant in 'Ariuar' and in 1822 Peter McCallum,[774] but it appears to have been deserted by the time of the 1841 census. The mysterious 'Arion', advertised to let in 1872 with 'Glenskibble' and 'Altogalous' (Altagalvash), is actually Àirigh Fhuair in heavy disguise.[775] The Ordnance Survey does not acknowledge the ruin by name on its maps (see CROIT), though the stream **Allt Àirigh Fhuair** is named; but the Admiralty marked 'Areur' on its charts. Treasure was believed to have been found there in the 19th century – see under ULAIDH.

The name was well known to Tarbert herring-fishermen. Davie MacFarlane's simple interpretation was *Àirigh Ùr*, 'New milking-place'. He understood that the last occupants emigrated to Canada, and remarked that he had received, over the years, several enquiries about the place, even from Skipness.[776] George Campbell Hay, in his lovely poem to Kintyre, written in 1938, evoked Àirigh Fhuar in his 'litany' of 'names sweet to the mouth': 'Ròaig and Airigh Fhuar, / words from some fairy tale, / the Grianan and Davaar, / Carradale, Sunadale.'[777]

Kerrafuar [c. 680 145] represents *Ceathramh fuar*, 'cold quarter'. The farm-steading stood west of the A842 and north of Ballybrennan. The name appears, as 'Kerowsoyre', in a charter of 1481.[778] The generic is the land division CEATHRAMH. **Fuar Làrach** [811 544] is an 886-ft. hill which was on the grazing of Escart farm and has since been covered in coniferous forest. The O.S. in 1867 could make nothing of the name, but it looks as though it should represent 'Cold ruin'. **Clach Fhuair** [897 601], east of Glenskibble, Skipness, is 'Cold Stone'. For **Culfuar** see under CÙL.

GABHAR – see GOBHAR.

GAMHAIN, genitive **GAMHNA**, is a stirk, a one-year-old cow or bullock; from Early Irish *gamuin*, which is from *gam*, 'winter', therefore a winter old.[779] **Port nan Gamhna** [833 511], 'Port of the Stirks', at Crossaig, appears in C1901 as a croft, 'Portagabhnah'. **Allt Gamhna** [908 635], 'Stirk's Stream', runs south of Lagan Ròaig. A group of rocks between Kintyre and the north end of Gigha is known as **Gamhna Ghigha**, 'The Stirks of Gigha', and the Gigha folk were sometimes known as *Na Gamhna*, 'The Stirks'.[780]

GAOTH is 'wind', and, naturally, is usually connected with high, exposed places. In walking the hills of Kintyre, I have learned, over the years, a few lessons about wind-strength on the tops. I went out to Sliabh a' Bhiorain on Boxing Day, 2011, with George McSporran and three other companions. The wind was south-westerly and strong, but certainly not gale-force, and didn't bother us until we ventured on to the seaward side of the pinnacle and into a little gully, where the force of it almost blew us off our feet. We practically had to crawl into the lee of Sliabh a' Bhiorain, where, however, we sat quite comfortably and had lunch. Such wind-funnels in remote hill-country scarcely register now, since few humans walk the hills, but it was different in the past, when people frequently crossed Kintyre and herds were in the hills daily.

The highest of these named windy places is **Bealach na Gaoith** [742 428], 'Gap of the Wind'. It is below the summit of Cruach

Mhic-an-t-Saoir, which rises to 1127 ft. in the middle of Kintyre. A glance at the O.S. Explorer map will elucidate this name's origin. It is clearly a rocky defile and equally clearly a natural wind-funnel. This was a feature I was keen to visit and photograph, and my wife Judy and I went there on 21/4/2012, walking in from Killean. The pass ascends from the north-west, and we took that route, having, on our left, sheer walls of bare mica schist just below the summit. We had picked a sunny windless day for our visit, but the grim exposure of that place on days of rain-laden gales was not difficult to imagine. Looking at the surrounding topography from the summit of the hill, Judy reckoned that the pass must formerly have been of some importance in the criss-crossing of Kintyre. In 1868 a road between Carradale and Largie – 'a desideratum long felt to be a great convenience' – was surveyed, and three years later work began between Auchinbreck and Craigmore, but the project appears not to have been completed.[781]

29. GAOTH. Bealach na Gaoith, 21/4/2012. Photograph by Judy Martin.

30. GAOTH. The ruins of Innean Gaothach, with sheep-fank, looking west. Photograph by Agnes Stewart, spring 1981.

Innean Gaothach [595 133], south of Largiebaan, is 'Windy Cove' (but see INNEAN), for which a multitude of old spellings exists, e.g. 1505 'Innergy'; 1506 'Inyngergye'; 1605 'Innergye'; 1799 'Inengoich'; 1729 'Inengoey'; 1775 'Inengoich'.[782] It was the only one of the six innean-named townships to appear, as 'Inninnaghu', on the mid-17th century Gordon map. There was a small township there, which was leased to Campbells in the 17th and 18th centuries. In 1694 two hearths were recorded at 'Inangyth', which was occupied by Archibald Campbell.[783] On 27/9/1709 Margaret McCaimbrose and her son William Campbell got the lease of 'Innengeoch and Pubill', a 10s 5d land.[784] (See also PUBULL.) In January 1720, Malcolm MacNeill of Carskey entered in his accounts that he had paid 40 Scots merks to 'Georg Campbell in Inengaoch for tuo tydie Kows', to be delivered that May.[785] In 1792, a later George (22 years old), Ann (30), William (20), Flory (18) and Barbra (16) Campbell were recorded there, along with 50-year-old Catherine McMath, presumably their widowed mother.[786]

A George Campbell in Innean Gaothach was given the nickname *Deòrsa an Rum*, 'George of the Rum'. There are two stories to explain the name, in both of which the rum was plundered from a shipwreck: the liquor enlivened and prolonged young George's christening celebrations, or, alternatively, there was no water in the house and he was baptised instead with rum.[787]

When I visited it, with my wife Judy and Jimmy MacDonald, in June 2012, we walked in from the north, following the old coast road which leads to a smooth grassy terrace, cleared for cultivation – a rather startling vision in a landscape of mountain, cliff and scree. The township buildings had been demolished and a sheep-fank built on the site, of crude design and construction; but a corn-kiln still stands, to the east of the fank, proof, if proof were needed, that people once lived there and won a living from the land. To the south, and visible from Innean Gaothach, stands a neighbouring township, Innean Beithe, with its attendant sheep-fank. By 1798, these two holdings, plus Innean Coig Cailleiche, the next one south, were merged into a sheep-farm.[788]

On the Largieside farm of Low Clachaig, **Gortean na gaoith**, 'Windy field', was recorded.[789]

I shall cross to Arran now and look at a place-name which intrigued me as a youth fishing from Carradale. The Kintyre herring-fishermen had a sizeable store of place-names for the west side of Arran. These were fishing marks, named from the sea and for the most part unknown to the islanders themselves. I'll list just a few, from north to south: The Wuds, The Long (Stone) Dyke, The Schoolhouse Rock, Wattie Weir's, The Pintle, Jenny Lind's Bay, and The Sandy Point. There was one name which I often heard mentioned, and which sounded like 'Tunderguy', but it wasn't one of their own. I learned much later that it was a farm on the coast north of Pirnmill, and, much later still, that it represents Gaelic *Tòn ri Gaoithe*, 'Backside to the Wind'.[790]

GÀRADH is 'garden', as the form suggests, but can also be a wall. It is rare in surviving place-names, though it was no doubt common enough when the land was more densely populated and more intensively worked, and names existed for the merest of features. In the boundaries dispute of 1736, for example, ' ... an old Dyke called **Garvie Achavea**' is mentioned.[791] **Gàradh Dubh** [c. 680 077] is 'Black Dyke', but this one is geological: it applied to a reef projecting seaward at the west end of Dunaverty Bay.[792] **Garrygoor** [634 207] was garden ground near the old inn at Salt Pans, but the inn was demolished and the gardens built over. The meanings 'McGuire's garden' and 'The Smith's garden' were suggested.[793] For **Lagnagarach** see under LAG/LAGAN.

GARBH, 'rough', is common in Kintyre place-names and I'll mention just a few. **Garvalt** [652 077], a cottage on Carskey Estate, represents *Garbh allt*, 'Rough burn', though 'wild burn' brings forward the sense of noise and turbulence. It appears to be a relatively recent name, but Garvalt [719 389] in Barr Glen goes far back: 1502 'Garwald'; 1596 'Garvald'; 1685 'Garvall'; 1692 'Garvalt'. D. J. Macdonald's interpretation *Garadh mholt*, 'the wedder copse or den',[794] appears eccentric beside *Garbh allt*. Two streams named Garbh Allt were recorded in Saddell and Skipness Parish, at 775 405 and 879 610. On **Cnoc Garbh** [c. 688 090], 'Rough Hill', a notable volcanic plug has survived.[795] The old farm of **Garvachy** [686 169] at Oatfield is *Garbh achadh*, 'Rough field'. **Garbhachaidh** [815 515], a farm west of Crossaig, is the same. **Sròn Gharbh**, 'Rough Point', occurs twice in Kintyre: see under SRÒN. For **Garrachroit**, 'Rough croft', see under CROIT, for **Drumgarve**, 'Rough Ridge', under DRUIM, and for **Garbh Thòrr**, 'Rough Hill', under TÒRR.

31. GARBH. Sròn Gharbh in South Kintyre, from the south, 3/5/2012. The name, which means 'Rough Point', refers to its rock-strewn surface. Photograph by the author.

GART – see GORT.

GÈADH is 'goose', and the birds referred to in Kintyre place-names would almost certainly have been of the wild species from Iceland and Greenland, of which the main flocks are now White-fronts (*Anser albifrons*) and Greylags (*Anser anser*), which winter in the Laggan and at Rhunahaorine.[796]

Lag nan Gèadh [c. 669 194], 'Hollow of the Geese', is in the field between Ballygreggan farm-steading and the main road, near Drumlemble. The name came from Donald Paterson in 1929.[797] Geese may still be seen at times in or near that field, among them descendants, I dare say, of the birds which inspired the place-name. **Loch nan Gèadh** [814 533], 'Loch of the Geese', is a little loch in the hills north-west of Crossaig. It was once on the grazing of Escart farm, but is now inside a forest. How did its name arise? Was it one of the hill-lochs frequented as a nocturnal roost by geese from the flocks which fed at Rhunahaorine? Were they hunted there? There was another 'loch of the geese' in a field on Machrimore Mill farm, near Southend school, but it was drained; and close to Carskey steading there was a field known as **Druim a' ghèoidh**, 'Ridge of the goose'.[798] **Lagan Gèoidh** [895 582], 'Goose Hollow', at Skipness, is 'a great scar-bound cup carved out by the burn from a deposit of red boulder-clay'.[799] The house named after it was a ruin by 1867.[800]

Clach a' Ghèoidh [728 421], 'The Goose Stone', is in the hills beyond Clachaig Glen. It gave its name to a valley, **Gleann Clach a' Ghèoidh**, which in turn gave its name to a small farm [723 421], now in ruins. This cumbersome name gave endless difficulty in its spelling. The O.S. rendered it correctly in Gaelic, but attempts to anglicise it in other sources produced outlandish constructions: 'Glencochyary' in 1775, when Archibald McIlchallum there was accused of unauthorised wood-cutting on the lands of Col Charles Campbell of Barbreck;[801] 1801, 'Glenclachayhoigh', on the Langlands map; 1819, Colin Campbell, herd, 'Glencloichgeoi';[802] C1841, 'Glenclachyioich'; 1857, 'Glencloyoy' when advertised for let with Auchaglass, Stockadale and Garvalt;[803] 1888, 'Glen-Clach-a-Yoidh' when advertised for let again;[804] C1891, 'Glencloyoy', when occupied by John Campbell, shepherd.

GEAL, 'white', 'bright', and 'radiant', among other meanings,[805] is rare in Kintyre place-names. For **Geal Tràigh**, at the Galdrans, see under TRÀIGH. **Geal-shùileach**, which may be interpreted 'white-eyed', is 'a little above Glenehanty steading'. The name related to 'three holes caused by small waterfalls in the stream ...

which were supposed to be "the haunt of her"'. She, John McCallum told Duncan Colville, was a brownie, and he understood the name to mean 'white eyes'. Neil Mathieson, Glenahanty, spoke of the 'Mathieson brownie', which was believed to have haunted the glen for 'at least 500 years'.[806] This suggests that the Mathieson family, like the MacNeills of Carskey and the Macdonalds of Largie, had a brownie, or supernatural helper, attached to it. The Mathieson specimen, however, is otherwise unattested. The '500 years' appears to imply that the brownie came to Kintyre with the family, which was earlier *Mac Math(a)*, 'Son of Matthew', and, according to tradition, originated in Ross-shire. Certainly, MacMaths/Mathiesons farmed Glenahanty in unbroken succession from the 17th until the 20th century.[807] We may approach closer to the true significance of the name by comparing it with Glen-sulag, Lochaber, from Suileag river, which Macbain interprets as 'the river full of "eyes" or pools'.[808]

GLAC in Kintyre place-names is usually defined as a 'hollow', but an Early Irish sense, 'hand, handful' might better suggest the nature of the feature, as might Dwelly's 'hollow valley'.[809] As a generic, *glac* is quite common in Kintyre, particularly in the very north. **Glac Challtuinn** [881 680], 'Hazel Hollow', and **Glac Dhomhain** [882 682], 'Deep Hollow' – described by the O.S. as a 'rocky ravine'[810] – are close together south of Tarbert. **Glac Mhór** [865 666], 'Big Hollow', is a 'narrow valley' further to the south-west, while **Glac na h-Òrdaig** [852 672], 'Hollow of the Thumb', is near Escart farmhouse at West Loch Tarbert. These examples are all in Kilcalmonell Parish, which also has two *glac* settlement-names, **Glacandunan**, 'Hollow of the little fort', near Achanadrian, and **Glacantarry** [743 520], on the north side of Ballochroy Glen, which may represent *Glac an tairbh*, 'Hollow of the bull'.[811] The hill farm **Glecknahavil** [666 155] in Campbeltown Parish may be *Glac na h-abhaill*, 'Hollow of the apple tree', but, in any case, the name was given the chop and the farm is now known as Lochorodale.[812] It was once a substantial holding of three merklands. Around 1636, nine men were listed at 'Glaknalsaull', compared with only three at 'Lochourdill'.[813]

In the case of **Balnagleck** [680 250], in Kilchenzie Parish, *glac* is the specific: *Baile na glaice*, 'Township of the Hollow'. Thomas Paterson in 'Ballinagleck' was 'sent to the military' in the winter of 1757/58 for theft, but his mother must have been able to keep paying the rent because in 1765 Thomas Paterson in 'Balinagleck' was accused of beating his servant Christian McKiachan with a graip (dung-fork) for 'improperly' leading horses engaged in carting dung. That was Christian's allegation; witnesses would only swear to his having struck her with a rod.[814] There was an identical place-name in Southend, between Machribeg and Lephencorrach. Hugh McEachran, Kilblaan, recalled in 1937 'old people who used to take the short cut from Glenbreckerie to the village calling that part "The Glaik" or "Ballinaglaik"'.[815] This was originally a land-holding, on record as far back as 1502 as 'Glak'; c. 1636, Gilchreist and Jon dow McFarlane were recorded in 'Glak', next to Machribeg.[816] For **Glac an t' saic bhàin** at Muasdale, see under BÀN.

GLAS, like LIATH, is usually interpreted as 'grey', but isn't as simple as that; 'green', among other meanings, may also apply, and in Irish place-names the translation is usually 'grey-green'.[817] Gillies, in his analysis of *glas*, considered 'green' to be 'an old and reliable value of the word'.[818] Young saithe, when they attain a length of five inches or more, are locally known as 'gleshans' or 'glasans', from Gaelic *glasan*. Perhaps, if the reader is familiar with this fish (see SAIDHEAN), and can visualise its grey colouration and the green sheen on it which fades quickly after death, the subtlety here may be appreciated.

Achaglass [709 414], at the head of Clachaig Glen, is *Achadh Glas*, 'Grey Field'. John Mitchell occupied the small farm in 1867 when the Ordnance Survey men came calling.[819] The last tenants there were a family named Clark and the steading is now ruinous.[820] In the spring of 1920, one of the Clark children, Andrew, killed six adders basking together on 'Auchaglass Hill'.[821] The Southend farm **Dùnglas** [704 091] took its name from a dun [705 095] to the north of the steading. On a morning in November 1871, an elderly deaf mute Donald MacIsaac set off to herd cattle on Dunglas, his nephew's farm. When the cattle came home in the evening without him, a search party went out and found him 'lying at the side of a dyke quite dead'.[822] See also Dummy's Port under PORT. The name **Leonaglash**, for *Leana glas*, 'Green meadow', survived in a deed, dated 30/12/1632, by Lord Kintyre, granting three roods of land, believed to have lain to the west of Main Street, Campbeltown.[823] **Allt Àirighe Glaise** [645 149], 'Green shieling stream', runs off Achnaslishaig Hill.[824] **Cnoc Glas** [882 673], 'Grey Hill', is on the coast south of Tarbert. For **Innean Glas**, Southend, see under INNEAN.

GLEANN is a 'valley opening between two heights' or 'glen, dell, dale'.[825] Considering the generally hilly character of Kintyre, *gleann* is understandably a common place-name element, with 47 instances on record, counting only those in which *gleann* or 'glen', the anglicised spelling, forms the first element.

32. GLEANN. Gleneadardacrock ruins from east, 1986. The older ruin is to the right. Photograph by the author.

Perhaps the most curious example is **Gleneadardacrock** [621 156], which represents *Gleann eadar dà chnoc*, 'Glen between two hills'. At least, it has always seemed curious to me, since most of the glens I know are formed by the flanks of opposing hills. This one, however, lies between two big ones, Cnoc Moy at 1462 feet and The Slate at 1263 feet. Gleneadardacrock was on Lossit Estate, which at one time reached down through that glen to Glenahanty. It was first a farm and then a shepherd's house and was occupied well into the 20th century. Many locals, even, won't attempt a pronunciation of the name. For those in the know, it is 'The Glen Hoose', and in estate records it was 'the farm of Glen'.[826]

One day, in the late 19th century, John McCallum saw a man searching near Gleneadardacrock as though he had lost something. When John approached him, the man identified himself as belonging to the Ordnance Survey and explained that he was looking for a large stone which an earlier surveyor had bench-marked. John was able to tell him that the stone had been used in the construction of the house and could be seen there. It can still be seen, edging a window in the north-facing wall.[827]

Duncan Colville noted that anecdote from John McCallum in 1929. I wondered how and when the encounter might have come about. John was born at Gleneadardacrock, on 3/4/1857, and brought up there, but the O.S. didn't map South Kintyre until 1866, and by 1867 John was at Ballygroggan. In any case, the slate-roofed steading at Gleneadardacrock, where the bench-marked stone ended up, must have been built after 1866, and John would have been reared in the older drystone steading alongside. John's great-grandson and namesake had just the detail I required, and in his family history file I found that his great-grandfather had shepherded at Largiebaan from Whitsun 1877 to '79, then went back to Ballygroggan and herded there, for John McIntyre, from Whitsun '79 to '85. The meeting was probably in either of these periods – probably the latter – since both Largiebaan and Ballygroggan march with Gleneadardacrock.

Mrs Katie McNaughton, Campbeltown, was probably the last child 'born' in Gleneadardacrock, in 1925, except she wasn't actually born there, because her mother, Eliza Morrison, went to her own mother's house in Longrow, Campbeltown, to have her. Ten days after Katie's birth, she was taken to Gleneadardacrock, where her father, Dugald McKendrick, was shepherd. They afterwards moved to Kerran.[828]

I remember John Harvey in Gartnacopaig telling me in the early 1980s about an uncanny experience he had in Gleneadardacrock. One evening he smelt snow on the wind and set off with his collies to bring in sheep that were in the glen. The wind dropped away, snow began swirling down, and with it came profound silence. As John passed the ruined house, he distinctly heard the low tones of men conversing in a strange language. At once troubled and curious, he looked inside. There was nobody there. John was about as rational a person as ever I met – I'll say no more. A few years after he told me his story, he died under a car which fell on him while he was fixing it at Gartnacopaig.

Glemanuil is the O.S. spelling for the cottage – earlier a shepherd's place and still earlier a farm – at 641 071 on the road to the Mull. It has long been considered a problem name, and Duncan Colville's judgement was that 'The O.S. appear to have mis-spelt this name which is generally found in the form of Glenmanuilt';[829] but the bothersome 'glem-', or 'glam-', goes back further than the O.S: 'Glemnoull' in c. 1636, when Dounslaife odiman and Archibald and John McIntaggirt were there,[830] and 'Glamanuil' on Roy's mid-18th century map. The name vexed the K.A.S. place-names committee, but I give the last word to Angus Campbell, who addressed the subject in 1919, from Holmlea Public School, Cathcart. The 'phonetic rendering' he gave as 'Glaminool', adding: 'In my early boyhood days this charming spot was known as Gleann an uillt, i.e. the Glen of the streamlet – a name which is exactly descriptive of the place.'[831]

Glenrea [657 134], now in ruins, looks across the head of Glenbreackerie. The name – *Gleann réidh*, 'Smooth glen'[832] – survives in a satirical song, 'The Thatchers of Glenrea', written by an Irish thatcher, Hector 'Hecky' McIlfatrick, in the 19th century.[833] The target of his satire was a MacNeill, probably Archibald, who had been a farm servant and went to Glenrea to help his sister Margaret, widow of Dugald McMath who died c. 1830. Margaret herself died in October 1840, leaving two daughters, Isabella and Margaret, who subsequently emigrated to 'upper Canada'. Archibald, who was confirmed in the lease of Glenrea in 1837, married Margaret Armour. She died on 18/12/1855,[834] a week after Archibald, who was taking a short cut home from Campbeltown on 'some unfrequented bye-path' when his horse fell and rolled over him. He lingered in great pain for several days before death ended his suffering.[835] Neill and Neill 'moir' (big) McNeill were two of four tenants in 'Glenrae' c. 1636.[836]

33. *GLEANN. The east side of Glenramskill showing the ravine, 26/7/2012. Photograph by the author.*

In **Glenramskill**, *gleann-* is, of course, Gaelic, but the rest is Norse. The spelling in 1481 was 'Glenranskill' and in 1562 'Glenranskil', but after the 16th century the 'n' was replaced by 'm' and the name assumed its modern form. There has been general agreement that the final element is Norse *gil*, 'ravine'. A note in the 'Schedules' for *The Place-Names of the Parish of Campbeltown* (p 26) records that 'Professor Watson suggested Hrani's gil (Norse personal name)'. No source is provided, nor have I found any reference to Glenramskill in Watson's published work, therefore it would appear that the suggestion was noted by Colville during his meeting with Watson (p 214).

The Schedule for Glenramskill contains another intriguing entry, this one in Archie McEachran's hand: 'Professor Marstrander made the suggestion that it might be derived from the plant "wild garlic", and asked if this plant was abundant there.' Carl J. S. Marstrander (1883-1965) was Professor of Celtic Languages at the University of Oslo from 1913 to 1954. He and McEachran may have met in the summer of 1938, when Marstrander visited Kintyre. He was directing the Norwegian Linguistic Survey, for which Nils M. Holmer (p xxi) was a field-worker.[837] Holmer was certainly acquainted with Archie and his uncle Hugh McEachran,[838] and may have introduced them to his colleague. 'Wild garlic' in Kintyre Gaelic was CREAMH, but Marstrander presumably had in mind a Norse word for *Allium ursinum*, and no likely word has so far been found.[839] English 'Ramson's' and Scots 'Ramps' for this plant are suggestive, but the place-name is much too old for these to have had any influence.

Cameron Gillies suggested *ranis-gil*, 'the ravine of the hog-backed hill'. However he arrived at the construction – he almost certainly never set eyes on the glen – and whatever its linguistic merit, his derivation is topographically exact. The eastern flank of the glen is indeed hog-backed and its main distinguishing feature is the dramatic ravine at 739 183, which in wet weather conducts the waterfall known as the **Mare's Tail** [739 182].[840] Of the two farms, only Low Glenramskill [739 187] is now occupied. The other, smaller steading, High [734 184], was a shepherd's house, which has a picturesque view over Davaar Island to Arran.

Glenskibble [889 602] was interpreted in 1867 by the O.S. as *Gleann Sgiobail*, 'Valley of the barn or granary',[841] but Angus Graham, in his *Skipness* (p 4), suggested, on the advice of Professor W.F.H. Nicolaisen, that the second element derives from Norse *Skip dalr*, 'Ship valley'. Glenskibble – in 1511 'Glenskippaill' – was first a farm and then a shepherd's house.

In April 1982, I camped inside Glenskibble with a Carradale friend, Lachie Paterson. He had suffered a double fracture to an arm aboard a fishing boat and was recuperating ashore. We had set off from Tarbert, hoping to pick up the old track to Lagan Ròaig and spend the night in one of the little bays beloved of the Tarbert fishermen, but we went wrong at the very start by taking a forestry track which, as we later realised, led us inland. The rest of the afternoon was spent in slogging with heavy packs across ridge after ridge without sight of the sea. I remember our stopping, to rest and refresh ourselves, in the middle of what appeared to be infinite moorland; it was about to disappear under coniferous plantation, though we didn't know it at the time. We finally descended into a valley and found the ruin of Glenskibble, and by then it was time to pitch camp for the night. We rose at 10 o' clock the following morning, had breakfast and set off north to explore the coast which had eluded us the previous day.[842]

Neither of us knew at the time that, 70 years earlier, a terrible event had visited the shepherd and his family at Glenskibble. Neil Cameron and his wife Kate Maclean – both natives of Ardgour in North Argyll – had moved to Skipness from Moidart with their four children some time after 1907; a fifth child, John Hugh, was born in Skipness. Allan Cameron was their second child, born on 6/9/1900 at Glasgan, Acharacle, and 11 years old in January 1912.[843] On the 8th of that month, he accompanied his father to Tarbert by the seven-mile-long track, but when they left Tarbert to return to Skipness, the weather was 'threatening'. A blinding blizzard caught them on that open moor road and Allan was soon 'benumbed'. His father wrapped him in some of his own clothing and carried him for a while, but exhaustion forced him to leave the boy and return alone to Glenskibble. When the storm finally moderated, Neil Cameron returned to where he had left his son, and carried the boy's body home.[844] On the death certificate, Allan's death from 'exposure to cold' is estimated at between 1 and 2 a.m. The location of his death, 'Glensgibal Hill', suggests that he was not far from safety.[845] Allan is buried alone in Kilbrannan. How long his family remained in Skipness after his death, and where they went when they left, I don't know; but the place, with its cut-off memories of their lost boy, may, in the end, like the boy himself in his father's arms, have been too much to bear.

Both Glenbreackerie and Barr Glen have a farm named **Amod**, which, as far as I am aware, is unknown elsewhere in Argyll. It is from Norse *A-mot*, 'river-meet' or 'confluence',[846] definitions which are met in both cases. Leases show that the Southend Amod [643 125] was associated from 1776 until 1922 with MacNeills, though family tradition claimed a presence there of 'over three hundred years', which is possible if sub-tenancies earlier applied. The family claimed kinship with the Macneals of Lossit, and, according to tradition, one of them in 1647 warned the garrison at Dunaverty of the approach of General Leslie's army. Both the first known tenant and the last were named Lachlan. 'Siol Chuinn' visited the latter shortly before his death in 1921 and reminisced: 'Many delightful hours I have whiled away with him by the peat fire, in political argument or in memories of the countryside; and I can say that Lachie was a true type of the Highland gentleman.'[847]

The Barr Glen Amod [707 381] was the birthplace of William Gilchrist (1811-79), printer and lithographer in Glasgow and a friend of the Gaelic poet William Livingston (1808-70).[848] In 1694, John McMartin, Duncan McIlgurim and Neill McMillan were in 'Amod',[849] and in 1797 John Watson, Neil MacGill and Archibald MacNair each had two horses there.[850] In 1867, Amod was occupied by A. Mitchell, shepherd, and owned by Captain Macneal of Lossit.[851]

GOB can mean 'mouth', but represents 'beak' in the following place-names, describing a little point of land resembling a beak. **Gob an Lochain** [c. 899 655], 'Point of the Little Loch', is north of Lùb Dhubh on the Tarbert West Shore. Hugh MacFarlane, back in 1977, gave me a description of the feature, so detailed that he had clearly been ashore and looked around. He described the rock – 'aboot twinty yerds roond aboot' – as a 'neb', Scots for a bird's beak, with a pool of rainwater, the *lochan*, lying on it.[852] **Gob na Carraige** [840 665], 'Point of the Rock', is on the opposite coast of Kintyre, close to the head of West Loch Tarbert. **Gobagrennan** – in 1736 'Goubugrennan' – is now a house [705 285] south-west of Lussa Reservoir, but was originally a shepherd's house [708 295] until the steading was inundated when Lussa Reservoir was created in the late 1940s and early 1950s. The name suggests *Gob a' ghrianain*, 'The sunny point'.

GOBHA or **GOBHAINN** is a smith, whence the Gaelic surname *Mac a' Ghobhainn*, anglicised as 'MacGow(a)n' and 'Smith'. The blacksmiths' esteemed traditional role was in the making of armour and weapons, but latterly they served not martially-minded chiefs but, for the most part, farmers who needed implements made or mended or horses shod. In the accounts rendered to King Robert Bruce in 1326 for work on Tarbert Castle, Neil the smith was the best paid of all the skilled workmen, with 9d a day compared with the plumber on 8d and the carpenter on 6d.[853]

Blacksmiths were reputed to have powers to counter evil, and knowledge to understand and treat illnesses in horses and cattle. Some families, such as the Bannatynes, MacCallums and MacEachrans in Kintyre, produced generation after generation of smiths. The last traditional smith in Kintyre was Hector McMurchy, who died in 1981, some five years after he closed his smiddy at Kilkenzie. The local smiddy was a popular meeting-place, where men told stories and exchanged news. For more on blacksmiths and their work, refer to my *Kintyre Country Life*, pp. 120-22. See also CÈARDACH, 'smithy'.

Smiths would have the use of a patch of land for cultivation – 'the Smith's Acre' – and grazing for a cow or two, at a rent payable to the tenant-farmer from whose land the plot had been detached. In the lease of Bellochantuy for 1775, the incoming tenant, Charles McNeill, was obliged to let the smithy and six acres to the present blacksmith. When Drum farm was leased in 1812 to the brothers Alexander and John McWilliam, the house, garden and an acre of ground behind the steading were reserved for the blacksmith, who was to pay them £3 sterling a year in rent.[854]

The field-name **Dòit [Dòid] a' ghobha**, 'The smith's croft', on Lenaig farm, Largieside, preserved that custom,[855] while **Pennygown** [691 143], for *Peighinn a' ghobhainn*, 'The smith's pennyland', refers to a much larger unit of land (see PEIGHINN) and could date to the medieval period when the smith, as the valued maker and mender of armour and weaponry, might be favoured with a rent-free holding and other perquisites by his clan chief.[856] There are two streams of the smith, **Allt a' Ghobhainn**, at 817 500 and 598 074, and two smith's hills, **Cnoc a' Ghobhainn** [817 502] and **Tòrr a' Ghobhainn** [777 364].

The final name here, **An Gobhann** [601 069], is a curiosity which applies to terrain south-east of the Mull Lighthouse. The Ordnance Survey in 1866 described 'a very steep ridge of rock extending from Allt a' Ghobhainn eastward', and interpreted the name as 'a smith'. The main informant was Archibald Todd, shepherd in Strone.[857] **Allt a' Ghobhainn** nearby is 'The Smith's Stream' and is comprehensible as such, but does the specific really have anything to do with a smith? A Smith who wasn't really a Smith, but a MacLullich

– his outlawed Jacobite father changed the family name after the 1745 Rebellion[858] – was guided across the place by a shepherd in the 18th century. He was the Rev Dr John Smith, minister of the Gaelic Church in Campbeltown from 1781 until his death in 1807, and, as Peter MacIntosh concluded the story, 'The doctor was very angry at the guide for leading him over such a fearful place'. MacIntosh described the Goinnean – his spelling – as a 'precipice' with 'a narrow path across it, of an average breadth of fifteen inches', and explained that it 'makes the way shorter in travelling round the Moil'.[859] The place-names committee of the Kintyre Antiquarian Society offered no interpretation in its published work, but three of the committee, all ministers, offered suggestions. A. J. MacVicar saw *gob*, 'a point or jutting headland', in the name; T. S. Macpherson observed, rather pointlessly, that Welsh *cefn* 'would describe the whole neighbourhood of the Mull'; and Colin Smith suggested the root *gàbhadh*, 'danger'. Spellings on maps: 1750 'The Goien', 1789 'The Goign', 1793 and 1824 'Goyne'. A similar path on the Antrim coast, known as 'The Gobbins', was noted.[860]

An anonymous article, titled 'The Goings: An Awe-Inspiring Climb at the Mull', appeared in the *Campbeltown Courier* in 1933. The writer and his brother were guided by a 'young man whose experience of the pathway can be equalled only by the shepherd at the Mull'. This youth had 'crossed the path times without number, sometimes carrying rabbits, ferrets and a gun', and impressed upon them 'the legend of a convivial gentleman who, it is related, was successfully conveyed across the Goings by his sure-footed pony'. The route itself is described thus:

> The track, like a woman arguing, starts off gently, its initial lack of difficulty lulling one into a false sense of security. The hillside above and below, while steep, is not dangerous. But as we progressed we discovered that almost imperceptibly the hillside became a stony face and later that the stony face became a veritable cliff. Going towards the Mull the path rises gradually. At some parts it is extremely narrow, perhaps not more than a foot broad. Covered with loose stones, it presents the climber with an obvious hint to 'gang warily', for one false step would mean a swallow dive into eternity.
>
> The most difficult part of the path to my mind – though this opinion is not shared by all climbers – is at a point about three quarters of a mile from Bal-Montgomerie. Here we had to climb over an out-jutting boiler-plate rock overhanging a sheer

drop down to the narrow strip of green grass at the sea edge. As I circumvented this obstacle my back was turned resolutely to the seemingly limitless space behind me and beneath, and I confess to a distinct chill creeping upwards along my spine. I regained the path with a sigh of relief, rejoining my companions.[861]

34. GOBHAINN. George McSporran and Don McIvor crossing the Goings, 27/3/1988. Photograph by the author.

GOBHAR also occurs in place-names as *gabhar*, but the two forms have the same origin in Old Irish *gabor*.[862] This is the Goat (*Capra hircus*), once an important animal in the economy of Kintyre, but a victim of the agricultural 'improvements' of the 18th and 19th centuries, when its presence on the landscape was deemed inimical to the health of woodland plantations.

There were no native goats in Britain after the last glaciation, and the history of the goat in Scotland begins about 5000 years ago, with the arrival of migrant herdsmen and their livestock. Goats, like cattle, provided milk, meat, and skin, and in historical times were certainly a marketable commodity. In 18th century Campbeltown, for each goat slaughtered and brought to market, the town council levied a penny. In the 17th century, an increasing cash trade in black cattle exported to England had probably reduced the numbers of goats kept, but the most potent deterrent was certainly the restrictions mentioned above. Duncan Colville noted 83 Argyll Estate farms in Kintyre alone whose leases, between 1751 and 1857, forbade the keeping of goats. The penalty was 10s sterling per goat per annum, unless 'special liberty' had been granted. Goats, nevertheless, were kept on certain farms. In a manuscript dated 1769, three farms at the Mull were recorded as having goats: 'Ballin Mool' (*Baile na Maoile*) had 'a few', 'Inungouh' (*Innean Gaothach*) also had 'a few', and 'Ballahmakvicker' (*Baile Mhic a' Bhiocair*) had 20.[863] In 1686, Angus McMillan in 'Stuickeideill' (Stockadale) took Duncan McMillan in 'Duchorrain' (Deucheran) to court, claiming that he had stolen five goats from him.[864]

Since the coast from the Mull north to Machrihanish is virtually treeless, and has probably been so throughout the historical period, restrictions on goat-keeping may have been relaxed there. Certainly, that coast is now the last Kintyre stronghold of the 'Primitive Goat', the original breed with a history extending back to the introduction of livestock during the early Neolithic.[865] These flocks on Ballygroggan, Largiebaan and the Mull – probably fewer than 100 goats in total – are of national importance as survivals of genetically 'unimproved' stock, yet have absolutely no protection in law, since the wild goat is still classed as a domestic animal.

How did these goats come to be on that coast? There are several theories and no conclusive answers. During the late 18th and early 19th centuries, large numbers of goats were imported into Scotland through Kintyre, and 'even towards the end of the [19th] century it was not uncommon to see Irish goat-herds driving their Goats north through the peninsula'. Gibson and Colville (1975) were almost certain that goats which had escaped from Irish flocks and gone wild contributed to the Kintyre stocks.[866] My own theory, which I proposed in 1984, is that, in brief, some goats may have been left behind when the townships were abandoned in the late 18th and early 19th centuries; some may have been virtually wild, anyway, on what is a rough and precipitous terrain, for goats will comfortably graze where sheep might hesitate to venture; which is my final case, that shepherds introduced the goats – a practice not without precedent elsewhere – or tolerated those that were already there, on the principle that, as one shepherd, Duncan Jackson, explained to me: 'There would be no encouragement for the sheep to go down in dangerous places, because the sheep aren't as good among the rocks as the goats.'[867]

Cnocan Leum nan Gabhar [641 126], near Amod in Southend, is the 'Hillock of the Goats' Leap'. There was no doubt a tradition attached to the name, but it has been lost. **Slochd nan Gobhar**, 'Gully of the Goats', in Carradale Glen, was so named because sheep and goats fell into it and were lost. In a Gaelic story recorded by Nils M. Holmer from John Campbell in Torrisdale, a little girl gathering berries also fell into the gully, and the wooden bowl (*gogan*) she had for gathering the berries came out at Cnoc an Tobair, Torrisdale, nearly three miles away.[868] An earlier version of the story has a rather macabre conclusion – not only the bowl emerged from the well, but also 'a portion of a girl's breast'.[869] There are four hills named after goats, three as **Cnoc nan Gabhar** [899 599, 803 396, and 668 146] and one as **Cruach nan Gabhar** [750 419]; but the 'Cruach na Gour' on Roy's mid-18th century map appears to represent the Ordnance Survey's Cnoc nan Gabhar at 899 599, as above. '**Knokingoir**', which is perhaps *Cnoc an Gobhair*, 'The Goat Hill', appears in charters of 1556 and 1634 between Ballevain and Drumalea, and was later let with Ballevain, but its location is unknown. **Lephengaver** [673 096] represents *Leth-pheighinn gabhair*, 'Half-penny land of the goat', and was a farm in Southend, described in 1866 as 'a small cot house';[870] but see also LETH-PEIGHINN. **Bodach nan Gabhar** [605 086], a 1335-ft. hilltop at the Mull, is 'The Old Man of the Goats', but the significance of the name is now elusive and nothing about the hill's shape suggests an explanation. **Eilean nan Gobhar** [815 365] is 'Island of the Goats', known as 'Goat Island', off the end of Carradale Point. The goats there are of Saanen stock, a Swiss type. Naomi Mitchison told me in 1983 that they could have been introduced as far back as the 18th century, but they were certainly there in the 19th.[871] D. J. Macdonald interpreted **Creagan na' meann**, on Crubasdale farm, as 'Kid crags', reflecting poignantly that, 'The Ayrshire browses around the rocks on which the frisky creatures used to disport themselves'.[872]

GORT/GOIRTEAN.   *Gort* means 'standing corn', 'garden, field, enclosure', and 'crop of corn or grass', and its offshoot *gart* much the same. Its diminutive *goirtean* also means much the same: 'little corn-field', 'small patch of arable land', 'little field, enclosure' and also 'little farm'.[873] Though 'field' and 'little field' would be the simplest interpretations, behind these names, and central to their past identity, lie the senses 'arable' and, perhaps more specifically, 'cereal-yielding'.[874]   They come from Irish *gort*, 'cornfield', and *goirtean*, as the sound of it suggests, is related to English 'garden'.[875] Cameron Gillies is rather useful here with his observation: 'The nearest value of the present usage is "a fallow upland field", or a field or once-enclosed ground now gone out of cultivation, even if there is no enclosure now. In the old language *fér-gort*, "a grass garden", and *luib-gort*, "herb garden", are met with, which suggests that the two ideas of enclosure and cultivation are contained in the word.'[876]

There are very few surviving *gort* names in Kintyre compared with *goirtean* names, and merely two present themselves as being of interest. The first has actually turned into '**The Gortchan**' [702 214], but was earlier 'Gort na Glia' and variants, which have been interpreted as *Gort nan cliath*, 'Field of the hurdles', perhaps in the sense of a bridge or causeway, constructed of wickerwork or tree-branches across a stream or a marsh or deep bog.[877] This derivation certainly has the merit of relevance, since The Gortan or Gortchan, now at the western end of Campbeltown, stands on the edge of an area of bogland in which townsfolk had their 'moss rooms', or banks for cutting peat.[878] Cf. **Abhainn a' chliath**, 'Hurdle stream', on Kilmory farm, Largieside.[879] When the annual Kintyre Sheep Dog Trials were held at Gortchan in 1924, the local newspaper reported that 'dogs were not the only subject of argument'. The 'correct spelling' of the place-name was also under scrutiny: was it 'Gortan' or 'Gortchan', the latter being the general pronunciation? In the end, Cameron Gillies's *The Place-Names of Argyll* was consulted, and the 'correct rendering' *Goirtean* duly supplied, with meanings.[880] For **Gort na h-Ulaidhe**, the other, see under ULAIDH.

Gart as a generic is more common than *gort* in Kintyre settlement-names, 10 against 3 (all of these in Campbeltown Parish), but I'll look at only one, **Gartnacopaig** [627 145], which has many personal associations for me. In May 2000, my wife and I were at the Inneans with friends, Mike Smylie and John Brodie, and our route back took us through the field directly below Gartnacopaig steading. We noticed abundant clumps of dockens (*Rumex*) in the field, looking, as Judy remarked, as though they'd been neatly planted.[881] Since *Gart nan copag* is 'Field of the dockens', we were in a place which precisely matched the description in its name, not as common an occurrence as might be supposed. How many times in the farm's history had these 'weeds' been rooted out and returned? Or were they ever quite extirpated? *Copag* appears in no other Kintyre place-name, so it is highly fitting, I think, that dockens still grow where the name says they did.

Goirtean place-names, by contrast, were abundant, just as fields were abundant before agricultural changes in the 19th century led to the amalgamation of both farms and fields, while, in the uplands, innumerable patches of arable were abandoned to grazing as the holdings themselves were abandoned by their tenants. Coniferous forestry in the mid-20th century merely compounded the pattern of agrarian ruin. I have no doubt that hundreds of *goirtean* field-names have disappeared without trace during the past two or three centuries; still, too many survive to accommodate here, and I shall content myself with listing all those published by D. J. Macdonald in 1908. These, from his own parish of Killean and Kilchenzie, will at least impart a flavour of the entire, decayed fruit:

Goirtean cnapach: 'Hummocky field' (Kilmaluag);

Gortean an t-saimh (or an Daimh): 'Sorrel' or 'ox field' (Achadaduie);

Gortean na gaoith: 'Windy field' (Low Clachaig);

Gortean na cloich: 'Stonefield' (High Bellochantuy);

Gortean an aoireann: 'Ploughman's field' (Barrmains); [If 'ploughman's field', the spelling should be *an t-airein*; perhaps *aoireann*, 'raised beach' or 'ferry site', is more pertinent.[883]]

Gortean na cruinneachd: 'Wheat field' (Kilmory);

Gortean an t-seagail: 'Rye field' (Auchadaduie);

Gortean a' chàise: 'Cheese field' (Crubesdale);

Gortean na ceardaich: 'Smithy field' (Beacharra);

Gortean dubh: 'Black field' (Low Crubesdale);

Gortean na h-ullaidh: 'Treasure field' (Ballure);

Gortean a' bhodaich: 'Old man's little corn field' (Barruchdarach);

Gortean fàil (or na fàil): 'Paul's field' (Largie);

Gortean Mhicheil: 'Michael's field' (Low Crubesdale);

Gortean cruaidh: 'hard field' (Largie).[882]

Though *goirtean* place-names must have been born in little enclosures, some were elevated when their humble identity was elevated, by common usage, to the status of farm or croft. Few of these *goirtean* settlement-names appear to be of any great antiquity, but **Gortnafal**, north of Tayinloan, may be an exception. The earliest spellings, 'Gorttenafale' in 1502/7 and 'Gortnanofale' in 1545, may suggest 'Paul's field', but Ian A. Fraser suggested as an alternative *fàl*, 'pen-fold, divot', etc.[884] The earliest record of **Gortinanane**, also north of Tayinloan, appears to be 18th century (see under EUN).

In Skipness Parish, a few small farms or crofts with the generic *goirtean* were recorded. **Goirtean a' Bhealaich** [885 569] near Claonaig – 'Gortinvale' in 1541[885] – represents 'Little field of the Pass'. **Goirtean Cloiche**, near Cour, is 'Stony Field'. **Goirtean Eòrna** [892 571], south of Skipness, is 'Barley Field', and was originally a small farm, which appears on the Langlands map of 1801 as 'Gortaneorn'. **Goirtean an t-Sailleir** [818 471], between Cour and Sunadale, is an Ordnance Survey construction, interpreted as 'Salter's Croft',[886] but Carradale tradition suggests a link with a tailor there, therefore *Goirtean Tàilleir*. On the 1801 Langlands map, the spelling is 'Gortantaylor'. In 1812, William McFatter and Neil McGeachy in Achaglass claimed that money was owed to them for whisky supplied to Donald and John McClelland in 'Gortanataller'.[887]

35. *GOIRTEAN. Goirtean an t-Sailleir, south of Cour, late 1980s. The building is now roofless. Photograph by Iain McAlister.*

Goirtean Deocaidh [801 374] is the name – which I have never seen on any map – of the tiny cemetery beside the road into Waterfoot, Carradale. The traditions attached to the name seem rather contrived. By Charles Reppke's account, in 1943, 'the first person to be buried here was a low country horse dealer who was drowned coming ashore from a boat', while Donald McIntosh told me in 1980 that the cemetery was 'called after a jockey's body which was found on the beach'. The name is pronounced 'gortchan jocky'. *Goirtean* here is 'little enclosure', which the graveyard certainly is, but the second element is obscure, though cf. 'Gortonjocky' – *Goirtean Seocaidh*, 'Jock's Field' – on Arran.[888]

Place-names, like people, can turn up unexpectedly. One Sunday in November 2011, I was at Smerby sawing and splitting logs from a big ash branch which had washed ashore. On my way back to my bike, with rucksack and saw, I met Margaret McNair, heading out for a walk. She and her husband James had farmed Low Smerby until their retirement and still liked to walk the shore there. Seeing the saw, Margaret assumed that I had been clearing paths. I told her what I'd been doing and we began talking about the shore. During the conversation, she mentioned a small shore field, '**Gortchan**', and described its location. Two days later, I returned to Smerby for more wood and decided to look for the little field. Emerging from a hazel copse, I saw it ahead of me, overgrown with thistles and rushes. I sat and wrote a poem there and then, overlooking the field. Now and again, like a painter at his easel, I'd look from my notebook to the field, trying, I suppose, to gain a deeper appreciation of its nature. At High Smerby road-end, where I'd left my bike, I met James, whose McNair ancestors had farmed Smerby since the early 18th century, and asked him about Gortchan. He told me that the field hadn't been cultivated in his father's time, but that, in the 1970s, he took a notion to plough it, and planted potatoes and turnips there. He could reach it then by tractor along a track which later became overgrown. The plough turned up part of a broken quern-stone, which he took home and still has. Much of the preceding information went into the first two verses of the poem, which I titled 'Goirtean', so I shall quote only the final verse.

> I caught at once your Gaelic air
> little field or cornfield or enclosure
> and knew you for a timid ghost
> in plain and humble meaning dressed
> come to haunt this foreign time
> in the resurrection of your name.

36. GRIANAN. The shore crag on which Greanan Dheardruin fort was built at Largiebaan, looking towards the north coast of Antrim and Rathlin. Photograph by the author, 3/6/2012.

GRIANAN is from *grian*, 'the sun', and its main meaning as a place-name is 'sunny spot', though a Middle Irish sense, 'a resort for lovers',[889] cannot but delight the imagination. It has other significances which aren't so readily associated with the sun, including 'palace' and 'any royal seat'.[890] From an Irish perspective (which is not to imply significant cultural distinction) 'there is a strong indication that it may refer to a place with a view and that in some of the earlier examples it was used metaphorically to mean "important place"',[891] all of which may suggest an undercurrent of pre-Christian influence.

Tarbert historian Archie Smith's mother, Cathie Kerr, was brought up at Daisy Cottage, a croft south of Tarbert, which her father Archie Kerr worked until his death in 1933. Often, when she returned home from school, her mother – Barbara Milloy, a Gaelic-speaking farmer's daughter from Claonaig – would send her back out to herd the family cows, with the advice that she'd likely find them on a 'grianan'.[892]

It is, to me, not only a sweet-sounding word but also an evocative one. I recall summers in the hills of Kintyre and the way a beam of sunlight in late evening would sometimes linger on and transfigure a green hill or knoll. Once, on Crosshill in July 2007, I happened to look towards Knockbay, and the quarry hill had been picked out by an isolated shaft of sunlight. I quickly wrote a little poem, which I titled 'Grianan', and which ended with 'the little hill's familiar crown/ gleaming green from earlier rain/ and crowded with slender dappled cattle/ I'd say had gathered there to wear/ the final hours of sunlight on their skin'.[893] I thought of Cathie Kerr and the few cows she would find, basking in the warmth of an early evening, on some similar knoll near Tarbert Castle.

The published poem which followed that one also had 'grianan' in its title, but its focus was on the sea and fishing. It was written in 2006, but its origins lay in a conversation I had six years earlier with a retired Carradale skipper, Archie Paterson. In describing a catch of herring he took one morning, he mentioned where the shoal had been located, **Sgeir Bhuidhe Grianan**, and that name – 'lovely even in translation' – became the title of the poem. Archie's story, which can be found in my *Herring Fishermen of Kintyre and Ayrshire* (p 11), was slight in itself, but what impressed me more, years later, and drove the poem into being, was a powerful sense of not only his intimacy with the reef, but also his implicit guardianship of its name, which he spoke 'as though he were evoking/ the memory of someone who had lived'.[894]

Sgeir Bhuidhe translates as 'Yellow Reef' (see BUIDHE). There are four reefs so named on that stretch of coast north of Carradale, of which only two were acknowledged by Carradale fishermen, and distinguished, one from the other, as 'Sgeir Bhuidhe Grianan' and 'Sgeir Bhuidhe Crossaig'. Sgeir Bhuidhe Grianan took its identity from **Eilean Grianain** [812 419], a little rocky island to the north of which the reef lies, and the island in turn took its name from a coastal farm, **Grianan** [810 412], which became a shepherd's cottage in the 19th century and a ruin in the 20th; but it was once a holding of some note and appears on record as far back as 1545 in the form 'Grenane'. In Jim McAlister's earliest years as a forestry worker – he was taken on in 1959 – the interior of Grianan ruin was fitted with a tin-roofed stable, with tethering-ring and fodder-box, for the accommodation of a Forestry Commission pony, 'Bobby', who was employed in timber-extraction.[895]

The Tarbert fishermen also had their Grianan, with its satellite names too. It is on the coast between Tarbert and Skipness, the **West Shore**, which was the Tarbert men's home stretch. 'West' might seem odd in the name, since that coast is on the east of Kintyre, but theirs was a maritime perspective, and from lower Loch Fyne that coastline is to the west (with the **Kerry Shore** in the east). I have seen **Rubha Grianain** [913 633] translated both as 'Sunny spot point' and 'Sunny point', and there's a difference. If the former is correct, then there was a *grianan* somewhere near or on the point, from which the point took its name; but, if the latter is correct, then the point itself caught sunlight with such conspicuous success that its name still shines, albeit with the phosphorescent glow of decay. There is one certainty, however: whenever a blade of sunlight strikes that headland now, there will be few of our kind to remark on the vision, unless a passing yachtsman happens to notice it.

Since the West Shore was, for centuries, the main herring-fishing ground of Tarbert fishermen, attaining its zenith in the age of the ring-net, place-names are prolific along its rugged length. Most of these names attach to minor shore features – for example, rocks, and even specific bits of rock – and were the preserve of fishermen. No map contained them until in the 1970s I began to uncover them in the course of researching *The Ring-Net Fishermen* and put them on to a crude sketch at the end of the published book. Since the ring-net, or 'trawl', to give the net its earliest name, was originally hauled ashore – its deep-water application would evolve only after the general adoption of motor power around 1910 – an intimate knowledge of the coast was of vital importance to fishermen. They had to understand local tidal currents and had to know literally every rock and reef which might hinder fishing operations or even destroy the gear on which their livelihood depended. These minor names, therefore, gave expression to the 'marks' the fishermen required to judge precisely where they were in relation to the shore and to their prey.

Rubha Grianain has three satellite names, as I earlier described them. These three, well known to past generations of Tarbert fishermen, but virtually forgotten now, I dare say, were explained to me by Willie McDougall in 1980: **The Splits of the Grianan** are two conspicuous cracks in the rock-face on the north side of the point; **Grianan Rock** lies submerged off the headland; and **Grianan Bank** is an extensive area of peaked seabed, extending north-east towards Sgat Mór on the opposite side of Loch Fyne.

The sun also appears at the next headland north of Rubha Grianain. On a rock on the shore south of Rubha Lagan Ròaig, a group of quartz shapes brought forth, from some long-dead fisherman's imagination, the name **Roc an Sgadan Ghréine**, generally shortened to **Sgadan Gréine**.

On a summer morning, when the night's fishing was over, fresh-caught herring might be gutted and split, sprinkled liberally with salt and pepper, and spread on a board, with a cover of netting to keep gulls off them. On especially warm days, the fish would turn brown like kippers while the fishermen slept. These fish were considered such a delicacy among fishermen – who practically lived on herring at sea, as long as they were catching them – that batches would occasionally be prepared on a Friday for taking home next morning. The practice has died out, but is tenuously preserved in the name Roc an Sgadan Ghréine, 'Rock of the Sunned Herring'.

I first heard of that rock in 1976 from Hugh MacFarlane, a retired Tarbert fisherman of remarkable knowledge and intelligence. He introduced me to the name with the modest qualification, 'This'll no be any interest tae ye ...' Then he described it: 'If ye'll go intae a certain position at the shore in a boat in the waater, an look in at that, an it's square. Ye wid say it wis made. An the sgatan grenns [are] on that rock. Ye'll go in in a certain wey, an ye'll see the herrin split. An the herrin's all pure white stone – there'll be a dozen or more. That's what the ould folk named it, Sgadan Gréine, seein it, an it wis just resemblin it – jeest below Laggan Hoose. The herrin's in rows, pure white stone, the herrin.'[896]

When I asked George Campbell Hay in 1979 about *sgadan gréine* he knew of the practice and immediately responded with 'herring of the sun'; but when I mentioned Davie MacFarlane's tighter version, 'sunned herring', he acknowledged 'a good translation'. He knew about the rock, too, because his Gaelic mentor among fishermen, Calum Johnson, would talk about it, but George could never discover its exact location and incorrectly assumed it to be an underwater rock off 'Laggan Point', where 'nothing ebbs'.[897]

Knocknagreen [716 136] is *Cnoc na Gréine*, 'Sunny Hill', and lies near Arinascavach, a ruin amid the outrage of sitka spruce. This was the old farm Mary Galbraith, Polliwilline, knew as 'Crock' during her childhood at Arinascavach, and she remembered a stock of 120 ewes on it.[898] John McIlbreid was in 'Cnocknagrean' in 1694,[899] and Duncan McEachern kept three horses at 'Knocknagrein' in 1797,[900] before the sheep and then the forest.

There are two other *grianan* names in Southend Parish, at Largiebaan: **Grianan Ardrie** [595 147], which possibly represents *Grianan Àrd-ruighe*, 'Sunny high slope', and **Greanan Dheardruin** [593 147].[901] The former is the rocky slope which, if one approaches Largiebaan shore along the cliff edge descending towards the burn, bears the track which leads precipitously back north towards the caves, while the latter attaches to a prominent fortified rock. To my knowledge, that archaeological site has never been formally identified, but I took Norman Newton there on 2/8/1981, and he reckoned that we were looking at an Iron Age dun and, lower on the rock, an enclosure.[902]

These structures were clearly noticed hundreds of years ago and explained as 'the residence of a giant'. Dugald Macintyre – father of the writer Dugald – in 1885 referred to 'a large rock washed by the sea, with some building on it', about 'two hundred yards from the Largiebaan caves'. The 'Greenan giant', who lived by hunting and fishing, had a wife of whom a neighbouring giant, at 'Aonan More' (Innean Mór), became enamoured. He waited until the Greenan giant was away on a fishing trip and then visited his wife to try to persuade her to elope with him; but he waited too long and, when the husband returned, enraged, he fired an arrow after the fleeing suitor, which pierced him to the heart. 'The place where he fell is still called **Bealach a' Ghille Dhuibh** (The Pass of the Dark Lad).'[903]

The Rev Donald Kelly named that 'stern old tower' – which it is not, and never could have been – Grianan Dheardruin and attached to it a similar legend. The *Gille Dubh* – 'a dark-complexioned young man' – had his eye on a beautiful girl who had been abducted in Ireland by 'two brothers of the clan Usnoth' and was being held captive at the fort. Her life couldn't have been so bad, because she clearly preferred captivity to the prospect of a life with the Dark Lad, and duly informed the brothers of his designs on her. He had always been careful to visit when her captors were absent, but one day, as they returned, they saw him and killed him on the spot. 'The place where he was killed is called to this day Bealach a' ghille Dhuibh.'[904]

'Deardruin' no doubt represents 'Deirdre', Macpherson's 'Darthula', and the story itself may be a garbled version of the tragic tale of her elopement with her beloved Naoise and the subsequent murder of Naoise and his brothers by Conchobar, King of Ulster, to whom Deirdre had been betrothed.

The Ordnance Survey, unusually, had a story to explain **Bealach Ghillean Duibh** [596 148], the form which it recorded in 1866 and has stuck with ever since. The tale is a shortened version of the others. 'A swarthy lad [was] killed here while endeavouring to rescue a female prisoner from the hand of a man who kept her on Grianan Ardrie (*sic*).'[905]

GUALA/GUALANN is 'shoulder', but also 'elbow or corner of a mountain'.[906] As a generic, there appear to be only three examples in

Kintyre. **Guallan Mhór** [901 628], 'Big Shoulder', stands at 987 ft. north of Skipness. The O.S. in 1867 described it as 'a prominent hill on the grazing of Altagalvis',[907] but it was planted over with conifers in the mid-1980s.

Guala na pobuill (or **a' phobhuill**), 'Shoulder of the congregation', Captain White located on the knoll abutting the western wall of Kilcolmkill burial-ground, and associated with the legend of Saint Columba's preaching there – 'the voice of the sea-faring apostle went forth to the assembled multitude' – after landing at Southend during his voyage into exile on Iona.[908]

Ben Gullion is the 1000-ft. hill which overlooks Campbeltown from the south. The K.A.S. place-names committee, or Duncan Colville himself, interpreted this as 'Very probably *Beinn ghuaillean*, "Hill of shoulders"',[909] but the cautious phrasing is unnecessary, because the two shoulders, formed by a deep notch, are, from the north, as plain as the proverbial pikestaff, and, as the generality of place-names go, are defining features *par excellence*. 'The ben of the storm' (*Beinn ghaillinn*), which conjures a darkly romantic vision of turbulence on the heights, was the other main candidate, and the only local place-name mentioned by Professor Blackie during his lecture in Campbeltown in 1876 (p xvii). Folk etymology further back had it as *Beinn ghuil Eòghann*, 'Mountain of the lamentation for Hugh'. This Hugh was impossibly 'laird of Killeonan' at the time Saint Ciaran occupied the cave at Auchenhoan. The saint was blind and depended for his food on a beautiful deer which went about the country collecting alms on his behalf. The brutal Hugh one day put out the eyes of the deer for the fun of seeing it fall over the cliff at Auchenhoan on its way home to Ciaran, but Hugh himself, soon after, while sleeping on top of Ben Gullion wrapped in animal skins, was torn to pieces by his own hounds.[910]

Ordnance Survey maps place the name on a moorland hillock [726 176] where the triangulation pillar was erected in 1955, and well to the south-east of the shoulders. This eccentric positioning denies the hill not only its well-earned name, but, in consequence, any name at all. It has been a constant wonder to me that not a single place-name was recorded on Ben Gullion when Campbeltown Parish was surveyed in 1866, not even one of the burns which run off it. A couple of English names, **The Goat** and **The Hawk's Peak**, appeared later and have endured, without the assistance of a presence on maps, but surely the general features of a prominent hill, beside an ancient and populous settlement, had names? Having read the

O.S. name-book for Campbeltown Parish, my conclusion is that the officers consulted the wrong people. I have a special interest in Ben Gullion, going back to my childhood, but my relationship with the hill has been explored elsewhere, particularly in *By Hill and Shore in South Kintyre*, and I shall say nothing of it here.

INNEAN. The survival of a local place-name element, like the survival of a surname, can be a matter of chance. Just as some families in Kintyre were numerous in the 17th and 18th centuries and disappeared in the 19th or 20th, through migration or procreative failure, many place-names, familiar in the same period, also disappeared. *Innean* would have been one of those names consigned to virtual oblivion and known only to a few students of local history, from old maps and records, had it not been for the chance that two old townships, **Innean Mór** [601 162] and **Innean Beag** [605 166], were built above a beautiful bay in the high cliffy coast between Machrihanish and the Mull.

37. *INNEAN. The seaward end of Inneans Glen with Innean Beag sheep-fank in foreground and Innean Mór sheep-fank distant in the south. Photograph by the author, 3/5/2012.*

That bay, known as **The Inneans** after the two townships, became a ramblers' destination and then a popular camping spot, particularly for the mining communities of Drumlemble and Machrihanish after the new Argyll Colliery at West Trodigal opened in 1946. It is an ideal camping place, with an extensive level foreshore for tents, a spring on the south side of the bay, and a beach – sometimes of shingle, sometimes banked with sand – which gathers driftwood from the open Atlantic. Campbeltown singer, Alistair Moffat, in 2003 composed an evocative song in celebration of the bay, titled simply 'The Inneans'.

As the popularity of The Inneans spread, more and more visitors were drawn to it; I have met people from all over the world there. There are now thousands worldwide who are familiar with the name 'innean', through that bay, which, I am prepared to wager, makes it the best known innean in the world. Most of those who visit the bay, whether for a few hours' leisure or for a few days' camping, don't know what the name means, and don't care.

38. INNEAN. Inneans Bay, showing northern part of the 'amphitheatre', 15/5/2012. Photograph by the author.

Innean is from Early Irish *indeóin*/Old Irish *indéin*;[911] cf. the rare spellings 'inden' and 'indin', e.g. in 1692 'Twa Indens', i.e. Innean

Mór and Innean Beag.[912] The primary meaning is 'anvil', but 'rock' and 'hill' are among other, more pertinent, meanings given by Dwelly (p 542). There are, on the east coast of Arran, two innean features – Beag [047 324] and Mór [044 328] – for which Ian A. Fraser[913] offered no interpretation. On Rathlin, which is visible from many of the inneans on the south-west coast of Kintyre, *íneán* referred to 'a steep grassy path or access leading to the shore between two cliffs'.[914] This definition is certainly precise, but, in its very precision, it won't do here. An analysis of the Rathlin place-name 'Inannanooan' by Fiachra Mac Gabhann yielded *Ingeán na nUan*, 'cove of the lambs' as the preferred interpretation.[915]

'Cove' is close to the meaning arrived at by Duncan Colville and the K.A.S. place-names committee in the 1930s: ' … a grassy area on the coast bounded by steep rock-strewn slopes in the form of an amphitheatre'.[916] The Rev Angus J. MacVicar, minister in Southend (1910-57), a native of North Uist and an associate member of the committee, reported that 'The late Dr. Erskine Beveridge of Vallay in North Uist had a correspondence with me before his death. He made out that the word *Innean* was an old Irish Gaelic word – now quite obsolete – meaning a scoop in the face of a hill, and forming a holm or delta near the sea, i.e. as the scoop tapered into the sea'.[917] Many years later, in his *Book of Blaan*, the Rev Angus eccentrically defined *innean* as 'soil', e.g. Innean Beag, 'The little bit of soil' (p 73).

The form which Mac Gabhann settled for, however, was *ingeán*, based on the research of Gregory Toner, who argued that 'the masc. noun *íneán* represents in fact two distinct underlying words in Rathlin, both of which should be properly spelt *ingeán*. In those instances where it denotes "a green way down to the sea between rocks", it is derived from *eang* "track, trace". In some instances it is seen to denote "cove, harbour", however, and in these cases is derived from *eang* "a strip of land" (> "strip of land by the sea" > "cove, harbour")'.[918]

The question arises, is the Kintyre generic *innean* also suspect? Nils M. Holmer, in *The Gaelic of Kintyre*, uses 'aoinein (aonan)' – defined, without source, as a 'steep descent between rocks to a port' (p 42) – which forms relate to *aonach*,[919] among the definitions of which are 'hill, steep height' and 'green plain near the shore on a stony bottom'.[920] Another possible candidate is *aoineadh*, which Dwelly defines simply as 'steep promontory',[921] but which has been more specifically defined, in relation to Colonsay, as 'a grassy terrace open to the sea, and surrounded by rocky cliffs',[922] a description which matches the locations of some of the *innean* townships.

I had hoped that the Ordnance Survey name-books of 1866 might explain why *innean* had been selected to represent the spoken form, but was disappointed. And the definitions were simply 'hill' and 'rock', e.g. Innean Seilich, 'Willow Rock', and Innean Tioram – 'a rocky eminence on the seaside' – 'Dry hill'. Neither of these definitions is satisfactory. The extended entry for Innean Gaothach, however, suggests that the map-makers contemplated leaving out the names of the townships, and finally justified their inclusion on the ground that the names also, or primarily, related to natural features. But the reasoning is clumsily expressed: 'This name with several others, viz. Innean Beithe and Innean Coig Cailleiche, were formerly farm steadings of which nothing now remains. But the name which being pretty generally known and as Innean signifies a rock or hill, the names would be as applicable to the features as to the farms. Thus, being objects along the coast it would be better to retain them.'[923]

I conclude with the definition of *innean* given by retired shepherd Calum Bannatyne on 17/3/1977, when I asked him to recall the place-names on the coast between Carskey and Machrihanish. I didn't ask for a definition, but he gave me 'inlet', e.g. Innean Gaothach was 'Inlet of the Wind'. I have no idea whether he heard it or thought it out for himself, but it has much to commend it.

This, then, is an element, or elements, for which there is no simple interpretation. It may be a case of looking at features named *innean* and, from the accumulated images, arriving at a characteristic common to all. In Kintyre, fortunately, there is no scarcity of examples, and there must surely have been more which disappeared into oblivion along with hundreds of other place-names.

On an old map of Sanda, a relatively small island, four *innean* place-names were recorded, three on the west side and one on the east, and none of them now remembered. They are, with the interpretations suggested in *The Place-Names of the Parish of Southend* (p 22): **Inan-Airn** (*Innean Eirinn*, 'Irish Innean'); **Inan-nan-Gaune** (*Innean gaoithean*, 'Innean of the winds'); **Inanahapple** (*Innean a' chapuill*, 'Innean of the mare'); **Inanastouck** (*Innean nan stuc*, 'Innean of the pinnacles'). See page viii for a reproduction of a copy of the old Sanda map.

The distribution of the name *innean* is of interest. None occurs on the east side of Kintyre, though I have been in coves on the Learside – a kind of scaled-down version of the Mull coast – which perfectly match the main definition of a Kintyre innean, e.g. Johnson's Bay [768 158], immediately north of the Second Waters. So, the distribution would appear to be cultural rather than geological, unless such inneans as there may have been on the east side somehow eluded documentation. Could that cultural determinant have been proximity to the north Antrim coast and Rathlin? I leave that question for others better qualified than I.

The most northerly surviving example is **Innean an t-Sabhail**, 'Cove of the Barn', on the farm of High Bellochantuy. Its specific location is unknown, though it might be possible, by judicious deduction, to sniff out its lair. This one went into D. J. Macdonald's notebook in 1897 and was grouped with 'mythical or historical events' when read in 1908 to the Gaelic Society of Inverness (not by himself, as it happened, but by Mr W. J. Watson, Rector of Inverness Royal Academy and later Professor of Celtic at the University of Edinburgh and the pre-eminent Scottish place-names expert of his generation). Rev Macdonald translated *innean* simply as 'anvil', but, curiously perhaps, was uncertain about 'barn' for *sabhal*, understanding that 'a word having the same pronunciation means "fight"'.[924]

The one other northern outlier is **Innean Mór** [657 306], 'Big Cove', one of three so-named in Kintyre. It is on the farm of Killocraw and describes the scoop behind the raised beach in which Dùn Fhinn is located, on the landward side of the A83. For the preservation of this one credit goes to Duncan Colville, who noted it from 'Mr Armour, Killocraw', who was William Armour, tenant of the farm at that time.[925]

If there were other *innean* names on that coastline of raised beaches, they have not survived, and the name does not reappear until the Laggan is crossed and the Galdrans is reached. **Aonan nan gailleann** [625 203], 'Innean of the storms', is there. The name was given to Duncan Colville by Alex McGeachy, Anderston, 'whose parents and grandparents were Gaelic speakers, and lived at the Salt Pans, now Machrihanish'.[926] Although obsolete, the name was picked up and revived by Davie Robertson and Eddie Maguire and became the title of a now-popular song which they composed in 1993, 'Aonan nan Gaillean'.

South of the Galdrans, the high coast between Machrihanish and the Mull is gained, with eight *innean* names. The first is Innean Beag, where this entry began. Its ruins are on the northern flank of the Inneans Glen, close to the 19th century sheep-fank into which most of the township's stone disappeared. Innean Mór, built on a rough terrace south of the glen, is the next one. Its ruins are better preserved – one can almost imagine the place peopled and tilled – and the Kintyre Way passes through them.

In 1691, the lease of 'Indinmore' was granted to Malcolm and Alexander McConachie and that of 'Indinbeg' to Duncan Oig ('Young') McConachie.[927] Three years later, when the Hearth Tax list was compiled, John and Donald McConachie were listed in 'Innenbeg' and Alexander and Malcolm McConachie in 'Innenmor', which had 'ane cutag' (corn-kiln) attached.[928] More (Sarah) McConachie in 'Inanmore' was the wife of John 'Bocan' Weir, 'ane habitual Thief and Picker', who was hanged in Campbeltown in 1710 for sheep-stealing. With an accomplice, Neil MacIlglash in Inanbeg, he stole 13 sheep from Garvachie one night and drove them to Inanmore 'by the mountain way'.[929] By 1792 the McConachies were gone and 'Innanmore' was occupied by Peter McPherson and Donald McKellar and their families. Innanbeg was by then deserted,[930] as its neighbour too soon would be.

39. INNEAN. The township of Innean Beithe, between Largiebaan and the Mull, showing its terrace location, on and below which lazy-beds have been formed. The settlement was where the sheep-fank now is, at top left. Photograph by the author, 1986.

Records of Innean Mór and Beag do not appear to exist before the 17th century, but Duncan Colville made a case for a documentary appearance as early as the 15th century, in relation to a Kintyre charter of 1481 for the three-merkland of 'Kynethane and Henyng', granted to John of Islay. Neither of these place-names resembles any modern form, but after, I do not doubt, much deliberation, Duncan formed the opinion that 'Kynethane' represented Kilkivan (2 merklands) and 'Henyng' represented Innanmore (1 merkland).[931]

Next, in a string, as one heads south, are **Innean Seilich** [594 138], 'of the willow'; **Innean Tioram** [592 135], 'the dry one'; **Innean Gaothach** [595 133, a township in ruins], 'the windy one'; **Innean Beithe** [594 127, ruins], 'of the birch'; **Innean Coig Cailleiche** [596 120, ruins], 'of the five old women', and **Innean Dùnain** [595 115, ruins], 'of the little fort'.

The townships of Innean Mór and Innean Beag do not themselves occupy an innean. Their generic clearly derives from the bay which separates them, but are the others, above, as readily explainable? The settlements, likewise, are not shore features, as most inneans tend to be, but occupy elevated terraces. The connection between these settlements named 'innean' and a landscape feature which might satisfy a definition of 'innean' remains uncertain to me. I asked Agnes Stewart, whose knowledge of that coast is unrivalled, for her opinion on that group. She replied that all six do indeed satisfy the standard definition, being in or near an innean: 'Looking from Innean Gaothach towards the south, there is a large amphitheatre that includes Innean Beithe. Just north of Innean Gaothach, going towards Rubha Dùin Bhàin, there is another amphitheatre, where the *Dryas octopetala* grows, and Innean Seilich is in that one, with Innean Tioram more out on a nose. Further south, the other two, Coig Calleiche and Dùnain, are in another amphitheatre.'[932]

It is worth noticing that all six townships in the mid portion of the Machrihanish-Mull coast, between Craigaig in the north and Ballimacvicar in the south, have *innean* as their generic. There are no other settlements so named in Kintyre.

Of the above settlements, I'll look at only one here, Innean Coig Cailleiche (see under GAOTH for Innean Gaothach). The O.S. interpretation of the name was 'Rock of the five old women', from 'a large rock near which stood formerly a farmsteading'.[933] Most of what is known about this place was collected by the Rev Donald Kelly and published by his son Neil, who translated 'ianun' as 'cave'. The five old women of the name were supposed to have been bearded cave-dwellers who 'devoured raw flesh and fish'. To make matters worse, they were said to have been nuns 'who probably lived by working on the religious or superstitious feelings of the people, and in a manner repugnant to the ideas of all civilised people ...' Whence came these 'vestal sisters' to that inhospitable coast? They had been driven out of the 'nunnery of St. Catherine's' in Glenadale 'at the Reformation', except there never was a nunnery there, only the small chapel of **Caibeal Catrìona** with its holy well (see TOBAR).

There was also supposed to be a graveyard and chapel, called **Caepil Iunan co-Caillach**, which Kelly described as lying in a 'park enclosed with a stone dyke and about a gunshot from the houses ...' He reckoned that the burial-ground, in which 'the people in the Moil were buried in olden times', contained 40 graves, but if it existed, it has not yet been identified. A path leading to the shore passed a field known as **Lag na fidhleareachd**, 'Hollow of the fiddling', owing to strange, fiddle-like noises heard there by benighted travellers.[934]

In the Kintyre rentals of 1505, the 'Harper's Lands' – four rent-free merklands comprising six named holdings – included 'Innynkew Callache'. The Clan Donald harper in Kintyre at that time was Muriach (Murdoch) McMaschenach, a surname which has since become McShannon. Descendants were later proprietors of Lephenstrath Estate, which the family retained until 1819, and local McShannons have retained that musical tradition, as singers and pipers, until the present time.[935] Circa 1636 Donald McArracher was in 'Inoencallache'.[936]

No more inneans appear until another cluster forms east of Southend village, on the coast between Brunerican and Pennyseorach (and overlooking Sanda with its four examples): **Innean a' Chromain** [703 074], 'of the kite'; **Innean Glas** [705 074], 'the grey one'; **Innean Mór** [706 075], 'the big one', and **Innean Beag** [709 075], 'the little one'.[937]

Local pronunciation of the generic now alternates between 'eenyan' and 'eenan', the latter of which, I believe, is the more authentic. It corresponds more with what Holmer heard from George and Jessie Todd in Balnamoil,[938] to whom the township names would have been well known; and Archie McEachran in 1940 told Duncan Colville that 'the place-name Inandunan in Southend is mostly pronounced Eenan-donnan (as in donn = brown) but it means the "Inan" of the little fort'.[939]

I conclude with an alphabetical list of spellings collected over the years, proof, if proof were needed, of the intractability of the generic: aeion, aenan, aeonian, aoinean, aoinein, aonan, aonian, eanon, eenan, enan, enyn, eunan, inan, indan, inden, indin, inein,

inen, inin, innan, innean, innen, inon, inoen, inner, inni, innie, inin,
innin, inning, inyn, innyn, iunan, oinen, unan, unen.

INNIS is one of two Gaelic words for 'island', but is rare in
that sense, EILEAN having won the 'struggle for existence'. Its
main meaning in Scottish place-names is 'river-meadow', in Scots
'haugh',[940] but in the only certain instance of the generic in Kintyre*,
it has been interpreted as 'island'. **Inisroil** [698 084] was explained,
in *The Place-Names of the Parish of Southend* (p 23), as *Innis
Raonuill*, 'Ronald's Island', on the basis that 'At one time there was
an island in Conieglen Water at this point'. Ian A. Fraser suggests
that 'Ronald's meadow' might be preferable, adding that he has
always regarded *innis* as 'a piece of flat, arable land in an otherwise
difficult area', such as forest, scrub or bog.[941]

In 1775 'Inishroil' was a 'one fourth Merk Land' tenanted by Donald
McEachran;[942] 'Innishroill' appears as a farm on the Langlands map
of 1793; as 'Ishrael' was occupied in C1841 by a farm labourer, Neil
McGeachy; and in the Valuation Roll of 1933/34, as 'Inishrael', was
conjoined with Dunglas farm.

Archibald McCaig, who died in 1924, was probably the last
working tenant of the farm. He was born at Gartvain but brought up
at 'Inishrale', to the tenancy of which he succeeded after his father's
death. His four brothers all emigrated to America.[943] The progenitor of
the Southend McCaigs, according to Archie McEachran, was a 'weaver
... from Articlave in Co. Antrim'. He married Flora McCambridge,
who, Southend tradition relates, saved the life of Ranald, infant son
of Archibald Og MacDonald of Sanda, by smuggling him away from
Dunaverty and concealing him in a cave prior to the massacre in
1647. After the MacDonalds of Sanda were restored to the Pennyland
Estate in 1661, Flora's sons were given tenancies, and 'towards the
end of the 18th century there were McCaigs in Colidrain, Penlachtan,
Kilmashenachan and Pennyseorach'.[944]

*In C1851, near Strone, Southend, there seems to be another
one. I looked long and hard at the enumerator Archibald McNeill's
handwriting and he appears to have recorded 'Innishdush', the first
element clear and the second slightly doubtful.

IOLAIRE is 'eagle' and could represent the Golden (*Aquila
chrysaetos*) or the White-Tailed or Sea (*Haliaeetus albicilla*). **Creag
na h-Iolaire** [599 096], 'Rock of the Eagle', is above Balmacvicar on
the Mull and is probably the same feature as 'Craig-na-ti-iolairach',

which Neil Munro Kelly Robertson described as a 'steep range of rocks below Bailemacvicar'. He was born in 1823 and claimed to have seen White-tailed Eagles nesting there in his youth.[945] That species was exterminated in Kintyre in the 19th century, and the last in Scotland shot in 1918; but since the reintroduction of the species to north-west Scotland in 1975, breeding has resumed in Argyll,[946] and individual birds are increasingly being sighted in Kintyre, which may lead to their re-establishment as a breeding species on the coastal cliffs which they favour, an exciting prospect for ornithologists, but not, perhaps, for sheep-farmers. The Golden Eagle was never quite exterminated in Kintyre, and a few breeding pairs are well established.

On an old map of Sanda, the name '**Crocknahulirich**' represents *Cnoc na h-Iolaire*, or perhaps the variant *Cnoc na h-Iolarach*, 'Hill of the Eagle'; the location is uncertain, but 733 041 is approximate. **Creag na h-Iolaire** [767 383], once again 'Rock of the Eagle', is a steep rocky slope west of Carradale Glen.

In Campbeltown there is yet another Creag na h-Iolaire [729 212], in heavy disguise. This is 'Craighuller' or 'Craig na Heller' or 'Crock na Heilar' or **Crock na Heilan**, the final bizarre corruption to which I shall return. The name, which is virtually forgotten now, attached to the hill behind Bellgrove on High Askomil, the summit of which was occupied by a fort and later a dun. That name mysteriously migrated down to Low Askomil and attached itself to a spring in the sea-wall [726 207]. Perhaps its water originated, or was believed to originate, on the hill above.

Duncan Colville pursued this name – 'a lifelong problem' – for decades after *The Place-Names of the Parish of Campbeltown* was published. In an undated draft letter to Dr Kenneth Steer of the Royal Commission on the Ancient and Historical Monuments of Scotland, clearly written after its inventory on Kintyre was published in 1971, he asked Steer whence came the reference to the 'rocky boss, locally known as Craighuller', in the entry on the fort and dun.[947] Colville speculated that the spring 'found its way from the vicinity of Bellfield Farm', and reminisced on having enjoyed 'many refreshing drinks' from an iron cup on the end of a chain beside the spring, which was, he said, 'only about five minutes' walk from the house known as The Hall in which I was born'.[948]

My father used to speak of the spring's popularity among the Dalintober folk in his youth, and of how, in summer, he would fetch its cool water home. He maintained that it fell out of favour when a local doctor claimed it had become contaminated with sewage, yet Teddy

Lafferty, who was reared in Craigie Place, Dalaruan, frequently drank there in the mid-1950s. There was by then no receptacle, so he'd just 'sine', or rinse, his hands in the spring-water, and cup them to drink. He used to hear an acquaintance, Bertie Dalziel, complain: 'The tide's in – ye canna get a drink.'[949] The spring finally dried up about 1990, when Low Askomil was dug for the laying of sewage pipes.

The iron pipe – which emerges from the lower part of the wall – and the five stone steps set in the wall and leading down to the spout, can still be seen, though the bottom stone is broken. These steps were provided in 1875, on the initiative of Bailie Duncan Colville. 'Hitherto,' a report explained, 'the approach to this famed spring was by means of narrow fissures in the side of the wall, and much inconvenience and risk was thereby experienced, especially by females, in ascending and descending with their stoups and cans.' The Dalintober folk ascribed to its water 'rare medical and thirst-quenching qualities', and it was one of several springs and wells which supplied Dalintober until 1869 when the village was connected to the town reservoir at Crosshill, following repeated complaints of water shortage.[950]

The final corruption, Crock na Heilan, led to the popular etymology of *Cnoc na h-Eilean*, 'Hill of the Island' – no doubt with Davaar in mind – which was accorded some credence when a new-built bungalow on High Askomil was given the name.[951]

Port na h-Iolaire [c. 893 569], 'Eagle Port', an inlet on the coast below Goirtean Eòrna, Skipness, has a curious tradition attached to it. One harvest day, when shearers were busy at the corn in Goirtean Eòrna, they noticed a big bird flying over the sea from Catacol. As they watched it approach, they saw that it was an eagle, so they went down to the shore for a better look. It was carrying something in its talons, which it released when it alighted on a rock. That something was an infant girl, whom the people rescued. Not long afterwards, a boat was seen crossing from Arran. 'They found their child all right in Goirteaneorna. It happened that the Arran people were harvesting in the field, the mother wrapping the baby in a shawl and leaving it sleeping behind a stook of corn when the eagle snatched it away.'[952] Dugald Macintyre heard a similar yarn, but in reverse. An eagle lifted a baby from a harvest field in Southend and carried it to Arran, where, still wrapped in its mother's shawl, it was rescued by fishermen. The baby was adopted by one of the fishermen's wives, but eventually its mother heard of the incident and went to Arran to claim the child, which she able to do since the shawl was distinctively her own.[953]

Arnicle [710 381] in Barr Glen derives from Norse *arna*, 'eagle' + *gil*, 'ravine'. For the Bruce tradition associated with this place see **Crois Mhic Aoidh** under CROIS. Early spellings: 1502/1507 'Arnegyil', 'Ernegill' and 'Ardnegile'; 1545 'Arnegill'; 1596 'Arnekill'; 1685 'Arnikell'; 1688 'Eringill'.

LAG, LAGAN. *Lag* is 'hollow' and *lagan* 'little hollow'. The main place-name in Kintyre, in terms of the physical extent to which it applies, is **The Laggan**, the flat expanse to the west of Campbeltown, which reaches all the way to the Atlantic machair. The name appears to be recent, and its orgin is obscure. If it appears on any map, old or new, I haven't seen that map. Significantly, in the Schedules of *The Place-Names of the Parish of Campbeltown*, against 'WHERE OBTAINED' the only information is, 'Well known locally'. In the *Argyllshire Herald* of 23/9/1863, however, under 'GROUSE SHOOTINGS TO LET', 'The Laggan range of shootings ... bounded on each side by Roads leading to Campbeltown, [with] a road through the centre', is advertised. In 1876, William Galbraith, 7 Longrow, Campbeltown, was advertising 'A Few Articles made of Bog Oak from the Laggan of Kintyre'.[954] There is no earlier place-name in that entire area from which it might have come. The fitness of the name is also puzzling. Can that plain be perceived as a 'hollow', let alone the 'little hollow' suggested by its diminutive? I, for one, can't see it on the landscape, though Gilbert Márkus offers the suggestion that the name might derive from the 'hollow land form' in which a marsh typically forms, or from a nominative plural, *lagan*, 'the hollows', perhaps suggesting a place 'marked by several small hollows, rather than one particularly noticeable one'.[955]

There is another **Laggan**, in Glen Lussa, which is certainly an old name (see Baile mhic Mharcuis under BAILE). The holding was divided into three, 'East', 'Middle' and 'West', in the late 18th century, consolidated in 1856 – presumably for stocking with sheep[956] – then split again, into two holdings, East [740 257] and West [734 259], in 1921, under a Board of Agriculture scheme.[957] **Laggan Path** [729 234], fading now, ran from Auchalochy to Laggan farm and was the most direct route to and from Campbeltown for the population of Glen Lussa. **Laggan Pool** was a bathing spot in the River Lussa, below the waterfall Eas Bàn. The adjacent area [723 264], where the ruins of Kylipole/Calliburn mill are, was a popular picnic place in the first half of the 20th century. It was known as **The Laggan**, hence the name of the pool.[958]

40. LAG/LAGAN. Malcolm Smith, Tarbert, at Laggan Loch in the spring of 1957. Photograph by his brother, Archie K. Smith.

There is a large group of *lagan* place-names between Tarbert and Skipness, of which **Lagan Ròaig** [907 641], a coastal farm, is the main one. Ian A. Fraser considered *ròag* to be almost certainly Norse, perhaps *rá-vik*, 'roe-bay'.[959] The hollow itself, formerly cultivated, extends from the point, **Rubha Lagan Ròaig**, south towards Rubha Grianain.[960] Spellings include, 1511 'Roage' and 1785 'Lagan Roag', when Donald Duglass and Barbra Galbreth's daughter Jean was baptised on 16 July. On the 1801 Langlands map it appears as 'Laggan', as also in C1891, when occupied by Dugald Campbell, shepherd. **Laggan Heid** (Head) was the Tarbert fishermen's name for Rubha Lagan Ròaig; **Laggan Hole**, about 12 fathoms deep, lies close inshore and runs north from the headland, while **Laggan Rock** lies submerged still farther north, and **Laggan Bay** is below the ruined farm-steading.[961] For **Seanlagan**, or 'Old Lagan', which the steading at Lagan Ròaig replaced, see under SEAN. Seanlagan, Lagan Ròaig, Laggan and Laggan Head all recur in the poetry of George Campbell Hay, with too great a frequency to examine here; but, again, see SEAN. **Laggan Loch** is the Tarbert name for Loch na Machrach Bige [886 637], which lies to the west of Lagan Ròaig. Lagan Ròaig, as remarked above, occasionally appears on record shortened to 'Laggan', which might lead to confusion with the more southerly farm known as **Lagan** [908 588], but in the old parish records, certainly, the two are invariably distinguished as 'Lagan' and 'Lagan Roag'. Lagan steading lay below **Cruach Lagain** [908 597], 'Hill of the Hollow', in a sheltered hollow close to the old road to Culindrach. It was last inhabited about 1882 and its remains 'entirely removed'.[962] For **Lagan Gèoidh**, 'Goose Hollow', further to the west, see under GÈADH.

The exact location of **Lagavurich** is now unknown. It was on Borgadale farm, Southend, and was believed to be a small cemetery for unbaptised children, who, with suicides, were formerly denied burial in consecrated ground. If so, it is the only one of which I am aware in Kintyre. In Islay, in the late 19th century, when Hector MacLean went to look at a fort, he met an 80-year-old woman who said that when she was a young girl the old folk called the fort Dun Pruchrais. It had been 'converted into a burying ground for unchristened children', and she remembered burials there.[963] When Tim Robinson was mapping Connemara in the 1980s, he was shown some 40 children's burial-grounds, of which only a small number was marked on official maps or otherwise recorded.[964]

The name Lagavurich was given to Agnes Stewart by a Mrs Hunter, *née* Train, who was shown the graveyard by her father, and who described its location as 'between the sheep fanks and the road'.[965] The first Train in Kintyre, Thomas, was a shepherd from Carmichael, Lanarkshire. He was at Borgadelmore in 1798 and by then had been shepherding for more than 20 years at the Mull.[966] When Agnes and her husband Allister had a house built at Kilkerran Glebe in 1980, they named it 'Lagavurich'. The meaning has not survived, but Ian A. Fraser's 'bare' Gaelic derivation would be *Lag a' bhùirich*, 'Hollow of the roaring'. This term usually applies to the roaring of stags in rut, but, since red deer were effectively extinct in Kintyre by the 16th century (see EILEIRG), another explanation may be required. Dwelly gives 'wailing' and 'loud lament' as additional meanings, which might link with the burial-ground, but, as Mr Fraser points out, 'it would depend on Kintyre dialect, if *bùirich* was used for such'.[967]

Lag is numerous in Kintyre place-names and I shall mention only a few of the better-known settlements. **Lag na fada**, in Southend, is 'The long hollow' and became by translation **Langholm** [719 101] in Scots.[968] **Lagnacraig** [670 162] was a hill farm, its steading now in ruins. It represents *Lag na creige*, 'Hollow of the rock', and is now known as **Homeston**, another translation, in which 'home'

= Scots 'holm', a hollow.[969] Iver McLarty in 'Lagnacroig' erected a stone in Kilkivan to his daughter Florance, who died in 1794, aged 15. In C1851, Homeston and 'Lachnacraig' are enumerated together, the latter given over to an elderly Irish pauper, Robert Chambers, and his wife Catharine. **Lagnagarach** [713 217], near Drumore on the outskirts of Campbeltown, was described in 1943 as a 'farm',[970] but in the early 19th century consisted of 'two rows of little thatched houses, occupied for the most part by weavers'.[971] Owing to a lack of early spellings, the derivation of the name has proved difficult. Duncan Colville uncovered the form 'Lagnagare' in charters relating to Dalintober feu-duties, for which he provides no dates. While this suggests *Lag na geàrr*, 'The short hollow', it does not explain the full form of the name, for which John Cameron diffidently suggested *Lag na geàrr-fhaich*, 'Hollow of the short field', or *Lag nan gàrradh*, 'Hollow of the walls', neither of which was admitted into *The Place-Names of the Parish of Campbeltown*.[972] A derivation from *gàradh*, 'garden', seems more likely.[973]

In Killean and Kilchenzie, **Lagloskin** [726 468] represents *Lag losgainn*, 'Toad hollow'. For **Lagalgarve** [661 298, North, in ruins, 659 293, South] D. J. Macdonald offered *Lagan garbh*, 'the rough little hollow',[974] but Rixson, citing 'Lagolgarreiff' (1623), suggested Old Norse *lágr*, 'low/low-lying' + *vollr*, 'field', with Gaelic *garbh*, 'rough', tagged on.[975]

Lagloin [861 685], Kilcalmonell, was described by the O.S. in 1867 as 'a range of old dwelling houses a little W. of Tarbert', and the specific was taken to derive from *lonn*, 'a piece of timber put under a boat to facilitate launching',[976] i.e. a 'roller', one of Dwelly's definitions under the variant *lunn*.[977] But this place-name is identical with **Lag-luinge**, 'Ship hollow', which Dugald Mitchell associated with King Robert Bruce's military expedition to the west in 1315 and a tradition that one of his galleys, while being hauled over the isthmus, 'came to grief' at that place.[978] **Lag Kilmichael**, Carradale Glen, is the hollow of *Cill Mhìcheil*, but there is no evidence or tradition of a church at Kilmichael (see under CILL).

LAOGH is a calf. **Abhainn Laoigh** and **Gleann Laoigh** [785 486, both], 'Calf Stream' and 'Calf Valley', together form part of the boundary between Skipness and Kilcalmonell parishes. Here is Professor Watson, examining 'River Names' in *Celtic Place-Names of Scotland* (p 453): '*Laogh*, calf, is the stream of *Gleann Laoigh*, Glen Loy, in Lochaber and in Cowal; the latter is named in

Deirdre's lament on leaving Alba. A third Glen Loy is in Carradale, Kintyre. With these may be compared *Lóig les*, "vitulus civitatum" or "calf of the courts", the name of a well at Tara. There is a distinct mythological flavour about all these names.' There is a distinct nonsensical flavour about **Cnoc Laoighscan** [780 507] and **Loch Laoighscan** [784 507], as rendered on O.S. maps up to the present. That hill and its loch are north-west of Gleann Laoigh. **Allt Mór an Laoigh** [722 320] and **Allt Beag an Laoigh** [722 323], the big and little stream of the calf, run off Meall Buidhe into Strathduie Water to the north of Lussa Reservoir.

LÀRACH, for present purposes, is a ruin, or the site of a ruin, its mark on the ground. **Làrach mór**, in North Kintyre, is 'Big ruin', but I have so far not been able to locate it. Ian MacDonald (2011) described the settlement as 'Two sets of houses in the hills opposite Gartnagrenach. All in ruins. Originally part of Loup Estate'. The earliest record of it I have seen is 'Larachmore' in 1683. Donald McIlavoil was there in 1799,[979] and 'Larichmore' is marked on the 1801 Langlands map, in the area of **Larachmor Burn** [837 566], logically enough. Ruins are marked on both the north and south sides of the burn, with a set of two at 835 564. Angus Graham in *Skipness* (p 6) remarks on 'several crofts' associated with the burn. Archibald McArthur (see under FRAOCH) recalled a family at Larachmore, in the early 19th century, which he named 'the Iasgairs', or 'Fishers', a surname which certainly occurred in North Kintyre. Malcolm Fisher in 'Aremore' (Arivore) is on record in 1683,[980] and in C1881 Alexander Fisher was a Skipness-born Gaelic-speaking fisherman in Low Airds, Carradale. McArthur recalled a wether which 'had a hole in the rocks in the hill' from which no one could evict him until 'Iain Iasgair' came with his 'fine white doag' and 'soon managed tae turn him oot'.[981] **Bunlarie** [785 306] is *Bun làraich*, 'Foot of the ruin', in 1867 'an old cot house on farm of High Ugadale'.[982] The oddly named hill **Fuar Làrach** appears to mean 'Cold Ruin', but see under FUAR. For **Breaclaraich**, 'Speckled ruin', see under BREAC, and for **Lecknalarach** under LEAC.

LEAC is basically a flagstone or flat- or smooth-surfaced rock, natural or placed on a grave. It is prone to corruption and in Kintyre has turned into both 'lake' and 'leek'. The first corruption transformed **Leac Bhuidhe** [618 196], 'Yellow Slab', into 'The Lake'. This is a coastal feature south of the Galdrans, though some inattentive Ordnance Survey cartographer has recently shifted the name inland. In 1866, the O.S. correctly described the place – 'A rocky point of land' – but got the interpretation wrong: 'Yellow declivity'.[983] **The Lake** is a jumble of boulders on the shore and was a popular fishing spot, particularly for snaring crabs and lobsters in the tidal pools. There is one huge, flat, tilted rock there, which is the *leac* itself, I suspect. The 'yellow' may come from seaweed growth on the lower part of the stone, but I wouldn't be certain. I am certain, however, that the place-name itself is decidedly misleading. Once the specific dropped off, *leac* – pronounced 'leck', more or less – turned smoothly into 'lake', and its Gaelic identity was submerged in that lake. I was certain that I was not the only person who, hearing for the first time about 'The Lake' where people fished, imagined not a platform of weathered rock, but a body of water of some description, so I asked George McSporran for his recollection. He, too, had imagined that the name referred to water, but had a specific feature in mind – the biggest of the pools there.[984] In the summer of 1937, Alex McShannon, Lossit Cottages, got into difficulties in that pool during an afternoon swim. A newspaper report described how Malcolm Thomson plunged in fully clothed to rescue McShannon at 'a spot known as The Lake'.[985] For further information on this communal fishing and picnic spot see my *Kintyre: The Hidden Past*, pp. 151-52, and *Fish and Fisherfolk*, pp. 1-9.

41. LEAC. *Fiona McCallum (Mrs Donald McKerral) with a catch of lythe at The Lake, c. 1958. Photograph by and from Donald McKerral, Campbeltown.*

42. LEAC. *The coaster Glenfyne heading east past the Leek Rock, Mull of Kintyre, July 1971. Photograph by George McSporran.*

Left: Swimmer Mercedes Gleitze, from signed photograph given to Mrs Jane Russell, Sanda, and dated March 1930. Courtesy of Alex Russell, Campbeltown.

The **Leek Rock** [589 070] is in the sea below the fog signal south of the Mull Lighthouse. The name appears on no maps, and I am fairly certain it was perpetuated by fishermen. Its only appearance in print, as far as I am aware, was a reference in 1933 to the 'Leek Rock', from which Mercedes Gleitze set off on her unsuccessful attempts to swim the North Channel in 1929,[986] two years after she became the first woman to swim the English Channel. (The swim was finally accomplished by a South African, Wayne Soutter, on 26/8/2012.)

'Leek', like 'Lake', represents *leac*, and it is a significant name. **Rubha na Lice** [589 071], the 'point' which reaches out towards the rock, is certainly named after it, and **Tòrr na Lice**, the 'hill' – see under TÒRR – immediately to the north, almost certainly also relates to it. In the case of **Beinn na Lice**, 'hill' again and towering above both of these features at 1405 ft., there has to be doubt – the huge rock slab to the west of the summit cairn is a likelier contender. (*Lice* is the genitive of *leac* in all these cases.) It was Beinn na Lice into which a Chinook helicopter from Northern Ireland crashed on 2/6/1994, killing all 29 persons on board – most of them counter-terrorism experts – an event which thrust the Mull of Kintyre into world news.

George McSporran recalled his father telling him how Southend fisherman Archie Cameron would mischievously alarm visitors whom he took out in his boat to view the Mull. As the boat approached the Leek, Archie would feign preoccupation with matters other than navigation, gazing this way and that, anywhere, in fact, than in the direction of the ever-nearing rock. What he knew, and his increasingly frightened passengers didn't, was that the tide-race there would carry the boat swiftly and safely past the rock.[987] But don't try it, folks! I daresay timing was crucial, and Archie Graham allows that the rock can be struck. He remembers puffers lying in the 'bight' inside the *leac*, Port a' Chuillin, until tide or weather would moderate and let them round the Mull.[988]

No fewer than three farms in Campbeltown Parish had *leac* as their generic, but **Lecknahavil** is an odd case. It has been interpreted as *Leac na h-abhaill*, 'Flat stone of the apple tree (or orchard)', but appears to be the same place as **Glecknahavil** [666 155], for which the interpretation *Glac na h-abhaill*, 'Hollow of the apple tree', was suggested.   Whatever, Gleck/Lecknahavil became 'Lochorodale'. **Lecknacreive** [650 137] – *Leac nan craoibh*, 'Flagstone of the tree' – was further down the hill road from Lochorodale, but the ruined steading was demolished during road improvements, c. 1990.[989]

Leckavroan [727 214] is another curiosity. It was a hill farm and later a shepherd's place north of Campbeltown and is now known as **Summerhill** and unoccupied. In *The Place-Names of the Parish of Campbeltown*, no interpretation was offered aside from Cameron Gillies's suggestion *Leac a' bhròin*, 'Stone of lamentation', which, the committee added, 'may be related to the cup-marked standing stone [723 212] in an adjacent field'. This place-name prompts an inconsequential link with James Joyce in his use of the expression 'mavrone' – e.g. in *Ulysses*, 'And we to be there, mavrone, and you to be unbeknownst' – from Irish *mo bhrón*,[990] which has the same sense –'alas!' – as the Kintyre exclamation 'ochanee' (*ochan î*). For **Auchaleek** see under ACHADH.

Lecknalarach [712 331], north-west of Collusca, is *Leac na làraich*, 'Slab of the ruin'. It appears on Roy's mid-18th century map as 'Lochannalarg'. In 1775, when leased to Col. Charles Campbell of Barbreck, it was described as 'the shieling of Cloinagart', and, according to his proposal, dated Barr 3/11/1774, would be convenient for his 'muire and mountain cattle'.[991] In 1764, Flora, daughter of Hugh MacDonald, was born there.[992] Francis McCallum, adjutant of the 2nd Regiment of the Argyllshire Local Militia, got the lease in 1813. He considered 250 sheep, two cows and a horse a full stock for the farm, and made the offer 'for the purpose of having a healthy retirement in the summer season for the benefit of his wife's health'.[993] In fact, he predeceased his wife, Isabella McLean, in 1839, at the age of 65, and is buried in a walled enclosure in Kilkivan. In 1827 'Lechnalarach' was described as 'a mountain farm, and not much grain upon it ...'[994] When surveyed by the Ordnance Survey in 1867, it was marked as 'ruins'; when advertised for let in 1870 it was described as a sheep farm of about 638 acres;[995] and in 1927 it was one of five divisions comprising the sheep farm of Strathmollach.[996] There was a hill marked 'Cruachleckan' on the farm in a 19th century estate plan.[997]

Druimnaleck [784 566] near Clachan may represent plural *Druim nan leac*, 'Ridge of the flat stones', rather than *Druim na lice*. Old spellings include 1481 'Drummalaycht'. In Clachan churchyard: 'Here lies the corps of Archibald McCallum who lived in Drimnalek and died March 1722 aged 70.' In C1861, 'Drimnaleck' was described as a 100-acre farm. In 1876, the sale by public auction of tenant Archibald McPhail's stock, crops and implements provides a glimpse into small-scale farming: 6 tidy cows, 2 two-year-old queys (heifers), 3 stirks, 5 calves, 'all of the pure Highland Breed'; 1 horse, 1 cart, 1 pair harrows, 1 plough, 1 large chest, 5 stacks hay and 5 stacks oats.[998] In one of Duncan Colville's notebooks, he records a personal association with the place: 'John Gilchrist born there 19/7/1785 & married Margaret McBride, born at Tangie February 1786. Great-grandparents of Mrs Mary Fleming Colville.' Mary Gilchrist was his wife.

These are most of the main *leac* names, but there are many more, including some which describe a hillside. **Leac nan Gall** [854 664], close to the head of West Loch Tarbert, the O.S. in 1867 interpreted as 'Declivity of the Lowlanders'.[999] **Leac a' Chreachainn** [598 144] at Largiebaan provides an interesting little case for comparison of interpretations. The O.S. in 1866 decided on 'Declivity of the hard rocky surface', while in 1938 the Kintyre Antiquarian Society's committee came up with 'Hill face of the bare rocky height'.[1000]

The only shared descriptive term is 'rocky'. D. J. Macdonald, in 'West Kintyre Field Names', records six *leac* names, all of which he defines as 'face'; for **Tuath-leacan**, on High Bellochantuy, he gives 'North cheek'.[1001] Macbain defines *leac* first as 'a flag, flag-stone', then separately as 'a cheek', whence *leacainn*, 'a hillside'.[1002] Gillies confessed to being unfamiliar with *leac* as 'cheek', but offered this definition – or perhaps imaginative explanation – of *leacann* as 'a hillside, from a portion of which the earth has been washed away, exposing a smooth surface of flat rock'.[1003] In the matter of Gillies's ignorance of *leac* for 'cheek', Macbain administered a verbal caning in his review of *The Place-Names of Argyll*, ending with the advice: '... for its use in a school book see "Higher Gaelic Readings", p. 78.'[1004] In Ireland, *leaca/leacan* means 'any flat, sloping surface, like a cheek, and is generally construed as "hillside"'.[1005]

I conclude with a few more examples of *leacann*, offspring of *leac*. **Leacann Gharbh** [860 659] was defined by the O.S. as 'Rough Declivity' and described as 'A rocky hillside quarter of a mile S.E. of Cnoc Reamhar'.[1006] **Leacann Mhic Mhaolain** [652 104], Glenbreackerie, is 'MacMillan's Slope'.[1007] **Leacann an t-Seasgaich** [877 610], a hillside north of Skipness, was interpreted by the O.S. as 'Declivity of barrenness',[1008] from *seasg*, which carries a strong sense of cows' being dry.

LEACANN – see LEAC.

LÈAN(A) is a meadow or swampy plain. The farm **Lenaig** [707 486] at Rhunahaorine should be *Lèanag*, 'Little meadow', but the name has a slightly complicated history. The earlier form appears to have been **Lenagboyach**, which should represent *Lèanag bhòidheach*, 'Beautiful little meadow', though sometimes rendered 'Lenan-', as in 'Lenanboych' on the Langlands map of 1793. In C1841 and '51, 'Lenagboyach' and 'Lenag' were enumerated separately, the former occupied by a weaver and the latter by a farmer, but in 1861 'Lenagboyach' only is mentioned, as the farm. When Neil and Barbara McMurchy erected a gravestone in Kilkerran to their piper son Ronald in 1919, they were of 'Lenaig Farm'. **An Leana Mhór**, 'Great swamp or marsh', was recorded on Crubesdale farm.[1009] For **Lean nan Tri Chrìoch** see under CRÌOCH.

LEANNAN-SÌTH – see SÌTHICH.

LEARG has a range of topographical meanings, but is basically a slope. The best known *learg* place-name in Scotland is probably Largs, Ayrshire, which has taken an English plural.[1010] In 1915, old Archibald McArthur in Auchenrioch spoke of 'the Lairgs' as one of the Ayrshire ports to which Kintyre illicit whisky was smuggled in smacks.[1011] In Kintyre, the outstanding example is **Largie** and its offshoot **Largieside**. D. J. Macdonald, in whose parish Largie was, makes this case: 'The ruins of the old Castle of Largie stand over against the village of Rhunahaorine. The name by which the whole district is commonly known is derived from the sloping ground between the Castle and the road – "learg" – a little eminence or sloping declivity of a hill.'[1012] Nils M. Holmer gives the form 'Leargaich', from Leargach, 'sloping place'.[1013] Dealing with the Arran 'Largy' farms, Ian A. Fraser defines *leargaidh* as 'place of the green slope'.[1014]

The Macdonalds of Largie – one of the most important families in Kintyre history – descend from Ranald, a son of John Mor and Marjory Bisset of Antrim, and a grandson of John of Islay, 1st Lord of the Isles.[1015] By the late 19th century, Largie was the largest estate in Kintyre still owned by an old native family   in 1874 it comprised 12,775 acres with an annual rental of £4,024[1016] – but by then the surname had mutated confusingly by the introduction of the elements 'Lockhart' and 'Moreton'. The Macdonald name came to an end with the death of John in 1707. His successor, daughter Elizabeth, married Sir Charles Lockhart, whose name also died out. The estate passed to Mary Jane Macdonald Lockhart (died 1851), who married the Hon. Augustus Henry Moreton, second son of the first Earl of Ducie, who incorporated 'Macdonald', but not 'Lockhart', into his own name. John Ronald Moreton Macdonald of Largie, who died in 1921, was a son of Charles Moreton Macdonald (died 1879) and Elizabeth Hume Campbell of Glendaruel. An historian, educated at Eton and Magdalen College, John Ronald returned to live at Largie and was instrumental in the founding of the Kintyre Antiquarian Society in 1921, shortly before his death that year.[1017] 'Old Largie Castle' was sited at High Rhunahaorine [708 483], but little remained of it in 1867.[1018] See also **Ballochgerran** under BEALACH. Old spellings: 1685 'Largie'; 1788 'Lergy'. For 'Largieside', Holmer gives the form *Taobh na Leargaich*,[1019] the northern part of which is in Kilcalmonell Parish and the southern in Killean.[1020]

The twin farms **Largiemore** [677 257] and **Largiebeg** [672 258] represent respectively *Leargaidh mór*, 'Big sloping place', and *Leargaidh beag*, 'Little sloping place', but earlier forms of the name were sometimes prefixed by *baile*, 'township', giving such constructions as 'Bellinalaergziebeg' in 1683 and 'Ballylargiebeg' in 1827. For **Largiebaan** see under BÀN.

LEATHAN is 'broad'. **Rubha Leathan** [920 610], north of Skipness, is 'Broad Point', which looks like a contradiction in terms, but isn't, because a promontory can have a wide face and still appear elongated when approached in either direction by land or sea. **Eilean Leathan** [800 356], 'Broad Island', is actually a rock on the headland south of Torrisdale Bay. **Cnoc Leathan** [630 195], 'Broad Hill', is at High Lossit, **Leac Leathan** [c. 634 208], 'Broad flat rock', is off the Big Scone at Pans, and **Achadh Leathan**, 'Broad Field', was on Darlochan farm.[1021]

LETH is 'half'. The element is most prominent in the 'half-penny' settlement-names which are treated separately under LETH-PHEIGHINN. The rest are all minor features. **Leth-bhràgadh** was described as 'a terrace or slight slope' on the land of Eleric [712 146] and interpreted as 'half slope',[1022] but see BRÀGADH for standard definitions. D. J. Macdonald recorded two in the Largieside, **Leth-tràigh**, 'Half-shore', on South Muasdale, and **Acha' leth-ròid**, 'Half-road field', on Glenacardoch.[1023] The latter was near the 'Halfway Houses', enumerated between Rosehill and Barr Schoolhouse in C1901. An obituary of Neil Paterson, shoemaker in Glenbarr, who died aged 97 in 1921, refers to his brother-in-law Alex McIsaac, 'Halfway, Glenbarr'.[1024] **Leth-Uillt** [729 501], north-east of Rhunahaorine, is *Leth-allt*, 'half-burn', a concept which Cameron Gillies 'explained' as 'a single Burn, where, for natural reasons, two might be looked for'.[1025] Macbain, however, explained it thus: 'Leth-allt is a burn with one high bank, for the word originally meant "cliff, height" (Lat, *altus*)'.[1026] On the Admiralty chart of Gigha Sound, surveyed in 1849, 'Leath allt Bridge' is marked where the public road crosses the burn. Gillies includes **Lailt** [659 097] in Southend with *leth* place-names without explanation,[1027] but presumably he had *leth-allt* in mind. Macbain refers to 'Leault' in Badenoch and 'Lealt' in Skye, both from *Leth-allt*. The *Place-Names of the Parish of Southend* admitted the difficulty of 'Lailt' and offered no interpretation, but provided the early spellings, 1545 'Lyall', 1605 'Lyell', 1622 'Lailt', and 1751 'Lailt', to which may be added 'Lyelt' c. 1636.[1028] The pronunciation for at least the past century has been 'Laaltch', and 'Lalch' was the spelling on an 1830s map of 'Low Ballivenan'.[1029]

LETH-PHEIGHINN is 'half-pennyland' (see also PEIGHINN) from the Norse system of land valuation established in the Western Isles and then imported into Argyll. Place-names with the *leth-pheighinn* generic – anglicised as 'Lephen-' and 'Lephin-' – are all attached to habitations and confined to the parishes of Southend and Saddell.

First, the Southend names, all of which, excepting Lephenstrath, apply to habitations which are ruined or actually obliterated: **Lephenbeg** [c. 658 077] – *Leth-pheighinn beag*, 'Little half-penny land' – extended along the march with Lephenstrath as far as Cnoc Dubh, and consisted of seven fields, 86 acres in all;[1030] **Lephencorrach** [c. 670 093], *Leth-pheighinn-corrach*, 'Steep half-penny land', believed to be the same place as **Lephencarr**; **Lephenstrath** [662 084], *Leth-pheighinn na sratha*, 'Half-penny land strath', the strath presumably being Strathmore (see SRATH); **Lephengaver** [673 096], *Leth-pheighinn gobhair*, 'The goat's half-penny land',[1031] for which see under GOBHAR.

In Saddell: **Lephinbeag** [791 358], *Leth-pheighinn beag*, 'Little half-penny land', latterly a shepherd's house and now ruined; **Lephincorrach** [789 358], meaning as above, a farm, then a shepherd's house on Torrisdale Estate; **Lephinmore**, *Leth-pheighinn mór*, 'Big half-penny land', at 778 333 in Saddell Glen, but the name now attached to the farm previously known as Crockinreoch (see under RIABHACH). A second 'Lephinmore' shown on the 1801 Langlands map north-west of 'Lephinbeg', appears to be in error for Lephincorrach.

LEUM, however spelled, is a 'jump' or 'leap'. Instances are few, but interesting. See **Leamnamuic** under MUC and **Carraig an Leim** under CARRAIG.

LIATH is usually translated as 'grey' or 'hoary', but Professor MacKinnon gives 'light blue'.[1032] In some cases, this adjective may describe the natural colour of rocks, or rocks with a coat of grey lichen. The farm **Barlea** [666 369] represents *Bàrr liath*, 'grey top'. For the O.S. **Liath Allt** [885 597], 'Grey Burn', in Saddell and Skipness Parish, one wonders if *Leth-allt*, 'half-burn', might not have been correct (see under LETH). In his collection 'West Kintyre Field Names', D. J. Macdonald recorded **Càrnliath**, 'Grey cairn', on Low Clachaig farm, and **Am barliath**, 'Gray point' – his spelling and interpretation – on Barlea farm.[1033] For **Monyliadh** see MÒINE.

LÌON is lint, or flax, and also 'net', since lint was a traditional fibre in the hand-weaving of nets. The crop was grown on many Kintyre farms until the late 19th century, largely for the manufacture of linen, and it was a back-breaking business. For a start, the crop was pulled rather than cut. With grain crops, the head of the plant is the valuable part, but with lint the value was in the stalk, so the whole of it was wanted. To loosen the fibres, the stooks of lint were steeped in ponds until rotting (and stinking); then they were spread to dry before being beaten with a 'scutcher' to free the fibres for spinning.

After the women had spun what flax was needed for their own use, the rest was spun for sale, 'it being obligatory on servant girls to spin a certain quantity daily of market yarn'. Peter MacIntosh looked back nostalgically in 1857: 'Nothing could be more cheery than the whizzing of three or four spinning-wheels around a blazing peat fire, on a hearth placed on the floor of the kitchen, during a winter night, and the beautiful young girls, with their sweet voices, chanting a Gaelic song, far superior to the amusements of the present day.'[1034]

The redoubtable Mrs Higginson, in her memoir of life in 19th century Skipness, recalled that, in winter, women of all ages would go from house to house, competing with one another in 'spinning matches'. Oragaig and Escart, she said, were 'famed for their lint fields'. The lint was made into sheets, tablecloths, men's shirts and nets, but: 'There was more trouble and work with the lint than any other work. As in spinning matches the women foregathered and helped one another, first heckling with Heckles and then scutching it with the Scutches, then binding it with the lint tongs. I have heard it said that there might be twenty or more working at it in a barn, and they would make a terrible noise working with the Heckles and Scutches, and would be singing Gaelic songs; one would start a song and all the others would join in the chorus.'[1035]

In January 1737, Archibald MacNeill in 'Muilbuij' (see under MEALL) sold Malcolm MacNeill of Carskey nine pounds of lint at 6d per pound, not the only record of flax purchases in MacNeill's accounts.[1036]

English 'lint' survives in the place-name **Lintmill** [688 199], near Stewarton. A linen-mill was built there in 1792, with an associated field for the bleaching and drying of the cloth – hence the farm-name **Bleachfield** [681 207] – but the mill was converted to wool-production pre-1814. After the wool-mill closed around 1910, the little village which had grown around it, with its inn, grocery shop and joiner's shop, slipped into slow decline until completely abandoned. Of the entire village, only a broken wall now remains.[1037]

Allt an Lìn [871 685], south of Tarbert, is 'Stream of the Flax'. George Campbell Hay was told by his aunts, Elizabeth and Ann MacMillan, that women used to 'wash (*sic*) their flax' in the burn.[1038] Archie Smith remembers a 'large man-made pond' at the lower part of the burn, behind the houses, where presumably the flax was steeped.[1039] Graham McKinlay, discussing **Creag an Lìn** [790 340], 'Lint Rock', on Whitestone farm, recalled two pairs of circular depressions in the fields, where ponds had been for steeping the flax crop.[1040] **Na daman lìn**, 'Flax dams', a minor place-name on Glenacardoch farm, pertained to 'ponds here at one time in which flax used to be steeped'. Two more minor flax-related names on Largieside farms, **Cùl na lìn**, 'Flax back', a field on High Bellochantuy, and **Ruigh' a' lìn**, 'Flax ground', on High Dunashery, were noted by D. J. Macdonald.[1041] There are two instances of **Cnoc an Lìn**, 'Hill of the Lint', in Southend, recorded with the note that 'Lint was formerly spread out on hillocks to dry', and there may be a third if **Cockalane** [740 119], an O.S. form which raised the hackles of Cameron Gillies – see Polliwilline under MUILEANN – is indeed a corruption of *Cnoc an Lìn*.[1042] **Sgeirean Lìn**, near the head of West Loch Tarbert, a small reef 'visible at high water', but invisible on the maps I checked, was interpreted by the O.S. as 'The net rock'.[1043]

LOCH in English is 'lake', but that word sounds much too sedate for my Kintyre lochs. A wee loch is a *lochan* – *-an* is a diminutive in Gaelic, enlarging a word to shrink the image it conveys – and I have seen it translated as 'lakelet'. Cringe! I'll leave loch and lochan as they are, sounding as wild as they are in this part of the country.

There are but three sea-lochs in Kintyre, at Campbeltown and at Tarbert, East and West, though these two, I suppose, must be shared with Knapdale. Campbeltown Loch and East Loch Tarbert, the former capacious and the latter cramped, are both by any standards excellent harbours, and with that praise resounding across their waters I'll say goodbye to them and turn to their landlocked, freshwater brethren, which are kept alive by the rain that falls into them and by the burns that flow to them with their rainwater, both fresh and vintage from oozing bogs.

The first freshwater 'loch' I ever saw and the first I came to know well was Crosshill, except it isn't a natural loch, but a reservoir completed in 1852 to supply the expanding population of Campbeltown, for which the town wells and springs were no longer adequate. **Crosshill Loch** [715 192] was created by the damming of the glen between Crosshill and its bigger neighbour, Ben Gullion, and what remains of the glen, below the Dam, is known as **The Valley**, the only instance of that English place-name element known to me in Kintyre.

I take the opportunity here of correcting an unfortunate error in *By Hill and Shore in South Kintyre* (pp. 263-64), in which I state that four-year-old Margaret McEachran drowned in Crosshill Reservoir in 1919. She actually drowned in 'the small reservoir at Crosshill',[1044] later known as **Taddy Loch** [717 196] when it turned into a marsh in which frogs in abundance spawned, hence 'taddy' = tadpole.

Further south, at the back of Ben Gullion, lay another loch, small and shallow, known as the **Black Loch** [716 176], from its peat-dark waters. It too has its dam, a small construction at its eastern end, which would be opened to power the meal-mill at Knocknaha. This loch appears on Roy's mid-18th century map as **Loch Grunidel**, and as **Loch Grunidale** on a plan of Dalrioch, drawn for Argyll Estate by George Waterston in 1836.[1045] The second element is clearly Norse, and I referred it to Ian A. Fraser. He confirmed the generic as Norse *dalr*, 'valley', but there is no such valley-name anywhere near the loch, unless Tomaig Glen to the north or even Meal Kist Glen to the south-east was originally the *dalr*. As to the specific, Old Norse *groena*, 'green spot', or perhaps *grunna*, 'shallow', as in Tràigh Ghruineart, Islay, are possible.[1046] See also under DAIL.

Many Kintyre lochs have disappeared during the past two or three centuries through drainage schemes. Some, no doubt – the smallest of them, anyway – vanished quietly and took their names with them, while the names and descriptions of others survive in records. Southend Parish, remarkably, cannot now claim a single loch, large or small.

Lochorodale [657 163] is another valley-loch, but is also a settlement name, with a rather complicated history. The loch was drained in the 19th century and restored in the late 20th. The lease of 1755 obliged the tenant to 'use his utmost endeavours in draining the Bogs and the Loch ... and from time to time dress up and clear any ditches made for that purpose'. Since the lessee was the Rev David Campbell, minister in Southend,[1047] it is doubtful in the extreme that he himself would be dirtying his hands with any such labour, but the loch duly disappeared. The township – 'Lochoradill' in 1502 – was situated near the loch and part of it was rebuilt as a shepherd's house, but the name transferred to the roadside steading previously known as **Glecknahavil** [666 155].[1048] When the McCorkindale family moved to Lochorodale in 1938, all that remained of the loch was a marsh which was fenced to keep out livestock. The subsequent owner, 50 years later, dammed the marsh to restore the water level.[1049] Mrs Sheila Ross, Drumlemble, spent her first years in the shepherd's cottage. She was born in 1944 and moved in 1950, but not before starting school at Auchencorvie. She would walk to Kilwhipnach, where an older girl, Annie Millar, would meet her and escort her to school. The return journey was usually made in the postman Lewis McKechnie's van. Sheila doesn't recall hearing anything about the 'loch', but remembers the road to the cottage being a 'cart-track', hens being kept and peats cut.[1050] The cottage has since been restored as an occasional dwelling-house for the present owner.

The great plain of Laggan, between Campbeltown and Machrihanish, is now one of the prime farming districts of Kintyre, but until the agricultural improvements of the 18th century, it was largely a vast peat-bog nurturing lochs of all sizes. The Laggan was certainly ditched and drained during those improvements, but in wet seasons it is revisited by old ghosts, who lay themselves, as water sheets, across its expanse, an effect naturally best viewed from high ground.

There was a farm called **Lochsanish**, the substantial steading of which stood at 664 205, but scarcely a stone of it remains. The rubble was transported to fill four craters left on Parkfergus farm after the attempted Luftwaffe bombing raid on HMS *Landrail* airfield on 6/11/1940.[1051] The farm was named after a nearby loch, which, like the steading, has vanished. In Blaeu's mid-17th century *Atlas Novus*, the loch is represented as being vast, while Peter MacIntosh described it as having been 'about a mile in diameter'.[1052] When James Watt visited Kintyre in 1773 to survey the line of the projected coal canal, he described 'a lake called Lough Sanish now drained and turned into meadow land'.[1053] This assessment appears, however, to have been premature. In a lawsuit of 1826, the loch is described as 'partly drained and partly not yet',[1054] but MacIntosh in 1857 stated that it had been drained and that 'the land is excellent, yielding plentiful crops'.[1055] For the element 'sanish', see Machrihanish under MACHAIR.

According to a legend, which Peter MacIntosh preserved, the loch was the haunt of a tyrannical being known as 'The Black Fisherman of Loch Sanish'. He terrorised the district to such a degree that he must have been one of the giants who dominated the land before our own puny ancestors attained the wit and courage to extirpate the breed. Not only would no one live near him or dare fish the loch, but 'Largy' – a Macdonald laird of Largie, and as such a transposed historical personage – 'kept a guard of soldiers, lest the Fisherman should make an attack on him'. Daily, these soldiers would troop to the top of Balergy Cruach to see if the fisherman was on the loch, and if they saw him fishing they would return to Largie confident there would be no attack that day. A stranger – the hero of the tale – appeared at Largie's house one day and asked him why he kept the soldiers. He was told about the Fisher and accompanied the soldiers to the hilltop, from which he saw the Fisher on the loch. The stranger told the soldiers that he would go down to see the Fisher and that they might watch how he would get on. When he reached the loch, a fight to the death ensued, and it was the Fisher who fell. The stranger cut off his head, 'which was very heavy', left it at Largie's door, and 'went away, without telling his name'.[1056]

This legend survived into the 20th century, and, had the loch itself survived, the legend, too, like that of the Piper's Cave, might still linger in diminished form. Duncan MacPhee and Archibald Stewart, in Darlochan, told Duncan Colville of the **Black Fisherman's Well**, a spring in a field called Drumnaban on Darlochan farm. A cist, supposedly discovered close to the well, but not authenticated, was suggested as being the Black Fisherman's grave.[1057] During drainage of the loch, around 1790, a dug-out canoe was discovered,[1058] 'which, it was supposed, the Fisher fished in'.[1059]

Durry Loch [679 224], named 'Black Loch' on the Langlands map of 1793, was described in 1866 as 'now a marsh, this the effects of draining'.[1060] It probably took its name from a nearby *doire*, a little wood, characteristically of oak. On a Kintyre Antiquarian Society map, annotated by Duncan Colville, a group of oak and birch stumps, uncovered during peat-cutting operations, was marked just to the north-west of the loch. Peter MacIntosh in 1857 reported that, during drainage work, 'the remains of a house came into view ... built after the old fashion of the Kintyre houses – the hearthstone in the middle of the floor'.[1061] This appears to be a mistaken reference to the crannog, or lake-dwelling, excavated in 1892 by the Kintyre Scientific Association. It consisted of a substructure of branches and twigs covered with a layer of clay and stones, with, in the north-east part of the platform, a hearth containing ashes, burnt bones and hazel nuts.[1062]

Near Clachan there is another now-vanished crannog loch, **Lochan Dùghaill** [790 586], 'Dugald's Lochan', from a legendary figure. It was drained unsuccessfully in 1871, and again in 1890, when two crannogs were discovered. The larger one, when excavated by Dr Robert Munro in 1892, produced finds which included a flint scraper, two whetstones – for sharpening tools – a perforated stone disc, part of a bracelet made from cannel coal and a small clay crucible. Later archaeologists reckoned that the crannog could have been constructed around the 2nd century A.D., and, from the evidence of potsherds also uncovered on the site, reoccupied in medieval times.[1063] On the 1801 Langlands map, a settlement 'Lochanduil' is marked south-west of the loch. C1851 reveals two households there, one headed by a shoemaker, Duncan Cochran – actually the name MacEachran in disguise – and the other by Catherine McKechnie, a pauper and weaver's wife. The area was planted with conifers in 1959/60.[1064]

Crannogs were constructed with defence in mind, the chosen loch serving as a kind of ready-made moat, except that the dwelling itself, unlike a castle, was not fortified. The crannog – from *crannag*, 'a fortified island in a lake', a Gaelic word which passed into English – was accessible only by boat or by a secret causeway, and its immunity from attack was dependent on these facilities' being denied to hostile visitors.

Dugald Mitchell recorded a tradition which connects the loch with a warrior *Dugald Mac Gruamal* ('The Surly One'), who led a band of men from Ireland to Kintyre, slew Macalister of Loup, seized his lands, abducted his daughter and lived with her on a crannog. One day, 'King Fingal', chief of the MacDonalds, who lived in Saddell Castle, said to his natural son, 'Toothed Alexander': 'I am old, but if you will go and kill that Irishman on the island in the loch, and marry his wife, I will put you in the possession of the lands of Loup.' Alexander accepted the challenge and enlisted the help of Mac Gruamal's Irish blacksmith, who lived at Leum-na-Muic. Their chance to despatch the interloper came when the services of the smith's wife, a midwife, were required at the crannog. Alexander and the smith were able, by deception, to seize the all-important boat and reach the island. Mac Gruamal at once perceived the danger and attacked Alexander furiously and would have killed him had not the smith struck Mac Gruamal a fatal blow from behind with his sword. Alexander duly married the widow and took possession of Loup, but not before he had complied with three conditions: to build a church between two streams, a mill between two hills and a house between two woods.[1065]

A similar tradition survives to this day with Ian MacDonald. 'Dugald Gruamach' appears to have been a character in the mould of Robin Hood, robbing rich travellers of their money, goods and clothing, and distributing the plunder to 'the poor and oppressed in the neighbourhood'. His undoing came not through the treachery of a blacksmith, but of a tailor who lived at Clachan; and his crannog was invaded not by boat, but by his twisting and turning underwater causeway, the route of which the tailor revealed. So, Dugald was finally captured and put to death for his crimes.[1066]

Most, by far, of the Kintyre lochs are in the northern half of the peninsula, and several more may be mentioned in conclusion. **Loch nam Breac** [794 482] is 'Loch of the Trout', but see under BREAC. **Loch nan Gad** [783 571], north-east of Clachan, translates as 'Loch of the Withies', and a withy is a bendy stem of willow or suchlike. Cameron Gillies intuited that the name derived from the loch's 'good fishing', adding that 'We even yet say "*gad math*" for a good catch of fish'.[1067] (In Tarbert, in the 20th century, a 'gad' was a quantity of fish suspended from a wand or strung on twine through the gills.) The more prosaic explanation, however, may be that the withies were harvested nearby for basket-making (see SEILEACH). There was a habitation near the loch. On 29/4/1823, Betty, daughter of Neil MacRob and Flory McEachern, was born at 'Knoc du Lochnagad',[1068] quite a mouthful for a birthplace: 'Black hill [at the] loch of the withies'.

The O.S. interpretation of **Loch a' Ghatha** [778 516] was 'Loch of the Sting', from its 'sting like shape',[1069] and a look at a map will validate that interpretation. Gaelic *gath* is a 'sting' or 'dart'. **Loch Freasdail** [812 595], south of Whitehouse, was interpreted as 'Loch of supply' by the O.S.,[1070] and Gillies reached the same conclusion with his 'providence' (Gaelic *freasdal*), which he also attached to nearby **Glenreasdell**.[1071] Macbain dismissed these interpretations in favour of Norse 'Risdal', 'copse-dale'.[1072] There are no early spellings for the loch, which is locally pronounced 'Loch Restill',[1073] but the holding appears as: 1495 'Glenrestill', 1511 'Glenrysadill', 1669 'Glenristill', and 1685 'Glenreistle'.

Loch a' Chuirn [789 463], 'Loch of the Cairn', was described in 1867 as 'overgrown with rushes'.[1074] When visited by Duncan Colville, he found it 'drained recently by Forestry Commission who have planted the surrounding area'. He looked in vain for a cairn. Great caution was necessary in negotiating the bog, which once swallowed a Forestry Commission tractor engaged in deep-draining in the area at the time. The tractor was successfully recovered, but it had sunk to its exhaust, which in that old model was upright and the highest point of the vehicle.[1075]

'**Loch Creanach**', as reported in the *Argyllshire Herald* in 1866, puzzled me. The report is headed 'Two boys drowned at Clachan', and relates how Alex and Duncan Campbell set off on a March morning 'determined to go to a hill after sheep', and fell through ice on 'Loch Creanach'. When their dogs returned without them, a search was made and a break in the surface of the frozen loch was noticed. After the ice was cleared away, the tragic brothers were found 'drowned together'.[1076] I'd assumed that the name was a mis-spelling or a misprint, but when registers of deaths were checked, the boys were found in the Skipness register, with an identical spelling for the loch and the information that it lay 'in the farm of Garvorlin'.[1077] It is therefore **Loch Cruinn** [832 578], original O.S. form 'Loch Crinne', and 'Loch Crine' on Roy's map and in MacIntosh's *History of Kintyre* (p 59). The loch is in Skipness Parish, but the boundary with Kilcalmonell passes along its west side. The later O.S. *cruinn* suggests 'round', but the loch is long and narrow; the other forms suggest a derivation from *crìon*, perhaps with the sense of 'shrinking', but this is guesswork.

For **Loch nan Canach** refer to EILEAN.

I conclude with **Loch an t-Soluis** [635 191], 'Loch of the Light', which is actually a man-made reservoir on Lossit Estate, formed, using water piped from Killypole Loch, to power an estate electrification scheme initiated in 1904. It appears to have been the last Gaelic place-name coined in Kintyre and is still in use as 'Lochantolish'.[1078]

LODAN. Aside from a minor field-name on Clochkeil farm, **The Loadens**,[1079] the only recorded instance of this name is **The Loaden** [760 190], which is the sea-area between Davaar Island and Auchenhoan Head. The name suggests Gaelic *lod*, 'pool', with a diminutive ending, therefore 'little pool'; but it's anything but little and was once notable for its abundance of fish, both white and herring. Duncan McSporran in 1979 recalled having heard the name explained as 'Norwegian for fishpool', which is neat but baseless. George Campbell Hay heard the name, from Ayrshire fishermen, as 'The Loddins', which seemed to him to be Gaelic '*Na Lodain*, the Puddles'.[1080]

There appears to be no record of the name before the mid-19th century. In November 1860, a Campbeltown lawyer, in a complaint to the Fishery Board for Scotland about 'trawling' – an early name for ring-netting, which was then illegal – described 'the Loddan' as 'a range of Coast or Bay extending for miles'. It was then 'swarming with fish of every description', and 'in close proximity to the mainland and the adjacent shore of Davaar the trawlers are in the practice to take up their Station, and nightly – even this morning – four boats returned with from 40 to 50 stones each, including herring and fry'.[1081]

The earliest trawls – beach-seines, basically, though sometimes hauled to a boat – were tiny things. So were the boats: 6 ft. of beam, no longer than 25 ft., and light in the build for fast rowing and easy beaching. The Loaden was conveniently close to Campbeltown and Dalintober – clear the loch and head south around Davaar Island, and you're there. Along the northern shore of Kildalloig Bay were several sandy-bottomed corners where herring would sometimes gather, and these undoubtedly would have been among the favourite haunts of the trawl-fishermen. A few of these hauls – the **Long Point** [756 192] and the **Flet Rock** [c. 758 183] notably – retained their value even into the era of the evolved ring-net and the bigger, motorised skiffs. In the absence of natural 'appearances', or signs of herring, fishermen might trust to chance and slip the net into one of these tight, familiar corners. Now and again, they'd be rewarded with a bag of herring; at the least, they'd gather a 'rasher' of white fish or flats for the pan. Their nets were undoubtedly scraping patches of clean sea-bottom discovered, worked and named by their grandfathers and even great-grandfathers.

For incalculable generations – back, no doubt, to prehistory – the Loaden was a well-stocked larder. Into the 1950s, its whiting banks drew hand-line fishers, pursuing, in their little boats, a 'puckle' of gleaming fish for the pot, and enjoying the pleasures of companionship. But the scourge of unrestrained commercial operations – power-fishing backed by electronic wizardry in plotting grounds and hunting fish – has reduced the indigenous stocks to insignificance. Or so it appears to me, but other commentators advance different causes, including climate change.

If herring still frequent the Loaden, there are no local boats left to hunt them. On certain special evenings, as I walk the Learside road, returning from a day spent on that rugged coast, I'll stop before the final corner and look back towards the hazy blue headland of Auchenhoan, across the still and darkening reach of sea that remains the Loaden, and imagine a fleet of boats there, silent under sail, or those that I actually remember, engines throbbing and multi-coloured lights twinkling out of reach.

43. LODAN. The Loaden on a spring evening, looking south towards Auchenhoan Head. Photograph by the author, 2012.

LOISGTE, the past participle of *loisg*, is 'burnt, scorched, parched'. In most place-names with this word, the reference is probably to dry bits of land, the grass on which is prone to scorching in periods of drought. There are four 'burnt crags', **Creag Loisgte**: 642 115 in Southend and 725 508, 757 540 and 763 550 in Kilcalmonell. **Rubha Loisgte** [879 685], 'Burnt Point', is at the mouth of East Loch Tarbert, and **Dail loisgte**, 'Burnt field', is on Dalmore farm.[1082] **Gartluisk**, which is probably *Gart loisgte*, 'Scorched field', was evidently once a holding of some significance in Glen Lussa. It is recorded on Timothy Pont's map of the late 16th century approximately where Gartgreillan now is, but has been lost.[1083] This name might refer to burning off scrub to clear new fields or to restore overgrown fields.[1084]

LÒN, for our purposes, is a 'meadow' or 'marsh',[1085] but there are other definitions. **Tayinloan** [696 459] – *Tigh an lòin*, 'The marsh house' – is the main settlement of Largieside, and was described in 1861 as 'a pretty village, imbedded in trees, like many a village in the heart of England. Its whitewashed village inn and post-office, backed by a mass of foliage, and the trout-stream overhung with trees, made a pretty sketch ...' Then, as now, it provided 'a ferry and a post to Gigha'.[1086]

An annual fair was held there, on the 'ferry green', at or around Lammas (1 August). At the 1848 fair, four tents were raided by Excisemen and prosecutions for the sale of illicit whisky followed.[1087] In 1867, no buying or selling of cattle was conducted, nor was there any 'feeing' (hiring of farm servants), but several liquor tents were pitched near the ferry-house. There were also barrows 'well stocked with tempting confections', stands for the sale of apples, gooseberries and pears, and one 'devoted to the sale of ornamental cutlery'. There were shooting galleries, a three-year-old 'acrobatic performer', a Punch and Judy show 'inimitably performed by a select company of half a dozen blocks of wood and two or three cracked voices from parties rendered invisible by the cotton curtain', and a clown who 'kissed in the stereotyped fashion the oldest woman in the crowd, pretended to burn his nose at the pipe of a quiet farmer, made believe to pick a quarrel with a clamorous sailor, got whipped by the ring-master, sung a comic ditty, danced a comic break down, and in other respects exerted himself to the utmost in evoking the hearty mirth of the audience'. A 'photographic studio of primitively rude construction' brought to the event a touch of 'art', and 'science' was represented by 'a canvas polytechnic gallery in which a choice selection of models was exhibited'. The day being fine, the fair was well attended by visitors 'from considerable distances in all directions from Tayinloane' and from Gigha.[1088]

Two fields on Lenaig farm, near Tayinloan, **Lòn liath** and **Lòn gorm**, were interpreted 'Gray meadow' and 'Blue or green meadow' respectively by D. J. Macdonald.[1089]   **Lòn Dubh** [855 547], on Oragaig farm, was translated 'Black marsh' by the O.S. in 1867.[1090] There were five inhabited houses there in C1851.

Lonachan is one of those place-names, or rather places, which engage the imagination. It has disappeared, and no one knows, or ever will know, where it is; but somewhere in the south of Kintyre its vestiges remain – the faint outline of buildings and enclosures, and, in the earth itself, the leavings of unremembered generations: potsherds, scraps of metal from broken or discarded tools and weaponry, perhaps a lost bead or coin. The meaning of the name itself can only be conjectured. It appears on record for the first time in 1481 as 'Lonochane'; in 1505 it is 'Lonachan' and 'Lonochane'; in 1562 'Lenachan'; in 1596 'Lanaquhanye' and in 1605 'Lanaquhane'. Thereafter, it disappears from history except as a nominal part of other (occupied) holdings, including the Learside farm of Erradil [745 124], which is probably as close to a location as will ever be possible. The name, judging by its earliest forms, probably derives from *lòn*, therefore 'The little marshy place', unless the generic is *lèan*, 'meadow'.[1091]

LONGPHORT appears in only one Kintyre place-name, **Culinlongart** [652 119], the Southend farm, spelling c. 1636 'Collinlongphort'.[1092] *Celtic Place-Names of Scotland* (p 494) has *Cùil an Longairt* and *The Place-Names of the Parish of Southend* (p 16) has *Cùil an longphuirt*, both 'Nook of the fort'; and, indeed, there is a dun at 656 115, close to the steading.[1093] *Longphort*, from *long + port* = 'ship-port',[1094] has several meanings, including 'harbour', 'camp', 'garrison', 'palace', 'tent' and 'shieling-hut'.[1095] 'Encampment' is the primary sense in Irish, and *longphort* appears in the 9th century *Annals of Ulster* relating to the temporary beach camps of Viking raiders, with the meaning 'established or permanent stronghold' not emerging in annalistic sources until the 13th century.[1096]

Cameron Gillies devoted almost half-a-page to Culinlongart in *The Place-Names of Argyll* (p 25). He was aware of 'old Gaelic' *longphort*, yet hesitated to commit himself to it, explaining his caution thus: 'The supreme scholar in our time, not only of Gaelic but of all languages, has failed with the word, and I do not venture to be conclusive.' As to the identity of this linguistic giant, Gillies gave no clue, but Macbain, who may have been the target, informed him that the word had been 'explained in Inverness Gaelic Society Trans. fifteen years ago'.[1097]

LOSAID is represented by the forms **Lossit** and **Losset**. It means 'a kneading trough', which isn't exactly a familiar household article nowadays. P. W. Joyce, in *The Origin and History of Irish Names and Places*, gave this explanation: 'The allusion seems to be not so much to shape, as to use and production: for the word is applied to a well-tilled and productive field, or to good rich land. A farmer will call such a field a *losset*, because he sees it covered with rich produce, like a kneading trough with dough.'[1098] That said, other interpretations, such as 'shallow depression', clearly relate to the trough shape itself.[1099]

Losaid is a rare name anywhere in Scotland, and we in Kintyre should celebrate this jewel which glitters with antique charm. It is not, however, a hidden jewel. By chance, as it were, the name attained prominence as the chief residence of the Macneals, a major land-owning family in South Kintyre, descended from Lachlan

Buidhe in the 17th century (see Tirfergus under TÌR). Lossit Estate, at Machrihanish, was acquired by Lachlan in 1668 and remains in the Macneal family, though much diminished in extent. One can only guess at where the field which earned the description *losaid* lay. In addition to the farm, there is the mansion, Lossit House [633 202], built between 1820 and '26 by George Macneal to replace an earlier house at High Lossit [632 193], in the rubble of which, when demolished, was found another jewel, the Ugadale Brooch of Bruce legend, with its centrepiece of magical crystal, which had lain hidden behind a panel since the alarms of the 1745 Rebellion.[1100]

In Scotland, *losaid* as a place-name occurs twice in Islay, once in Kintyre – its first written appearance was in a charter of 1481[1101] – and once in Galloway, though John MacQueen indicated a fifth, minor and obscure, instance in Aberdeenshire, Losaid Beag ('little kneading trough'). Professor MacQueen makes a case for the Galloway Losset's being a name 'marking the early stage of Gaelic settlement'.[1102] The name is commoner in Ireland, but is still not common. Fiachra Mac Gabhann remarks on 'some 12 townlands of this name', all but two of them in Ulster.[1103]

LOSGANN is the Common Toad (*Bufo bufo*), though the name is also applied to the Frog; but since *losgann* is from *losgadh*, 'a burning', and was 'so named from the acrid secretions of its skin',[1104] the Frog is secondary, at least on etymological grounds. Among the features which distinguish toads from frogs are warts, and the irritants are secreted from these swellings. Some predators avoid toads, and others, such as the Hedgehog and the Buzzard, eat them with impunity. Crows take a middle approach – they tear the skin off them and eat what remains, excepting the bones. For several springs in succession, George McSporran and I found the remains of toads on Crosshill Dam. We'd see Hoodies patrolling the water's edge, but failed to see one actually catch a toad.[1105] Certain shallow lochs, in which toads congregate to breed, evince seasonal carnage.

I visited **Loch Losgainn** [747 431] on 12/4/2012 with my wife Judy, daughter Amelia and Murdo MacDonald, and found what I expected to find – decomposed toad or frog carcasses on the margins of the water. Barr Water begins its journey there, and despite Forestry Commission detritus on its western shore it remains a lovely little loch. **Auchaluskin**, a ruined settlement at Killean, is *Achadh an losgainn*, 'Toad field'. The minister of Killean had 'the grass of three cows on the lands of Auchaloiskin', an arrangement which ended in 1803.[1106] **Gartloskin**, behind Dalbuie, is *Gart losgainn*, another 'Toad field'. There were two farms there, High [696 139] and Low [695 132], and then none. The Ralston farming families in South Kintyre all descend from Gavin Ralston who was born at Gartloskin in 1823, as declared both on the gravestone he erected in Kilcolmkill for his first wife Jessie Dunlop, and on a second stone erected in Kilkerran.[1107] For **Lagloskin**, 'Toad Hollow', see under LAG/LAGAN.

44. LOSGANN. Judy and Amelia Martin at Loch Losgainn, 'Toad Loch', 12/4/2012. Photograph by the author.

LUACHAIR is 'rushes', of all species as far as I am aware. Macbain defines the word in Early Irish as 'light-maker',[1108] which illuminates its great importance in domestic culture. The pith of peeled rushes was used as wicks in the little oil-lamps called 'cruisies' until paraffin lamps were introduced in the mid-19th century. Rushes were also used for thatching corn-stacks, and sometimes the ropes that secured the stacks were twisted from the sharp-flowered rush or 'sprit' (*Juncus acutiflorus*). These 'sprits', which sometimes grew on outlying parts of hay meadows, were also cut and stacked for winter fodder,[1109] and rushes in general were used as bedding for livestock. Rushes thrive in damp, poorly drained land, and can now be seen in abundance in many Kintyre fields which were once under crops. This profusion is ironic, since rushes are now considered useless;

yet, country folk once took risks to secure them. In 1852, Duncan and Ann Turner, Achnaba, pled guilty to the theft of rushes from Kilmory Estate. Duncan was jailed for 48 hours in Lochgilphead, while Ann, on account of her youth, escaped with a 'severe reprimand'.[1110] Having stated my case, I now have to admit that the past importance of rushes isn't manifest in place-names. I know of only one in Kintyre, **Cnoc Àiridh Luachraich** [727 481], 'Hill of the Rushy Shieling', 814 ft. high and directly east of Rhunahaorine. The name relates to a long forgotten summer pasturage – see ÀIRIGH.

LÙB has many meanings, but in place-names is basically a 'bend' in the shore, in other words a bay. It is, therefore, similar in concept to CAMUS, which is also a bend, or curvature, in the coast. Contrast these with the deeper-indented BÀGH, and PORT, which may also be interpreted, in certain cases, as a bay. Hugh MacFarlane in Tarbert defined *lùb* poetically as 'a quiet bend of water'.[1111]

The best known *lùb* name in Kintyre is the unqualified **Loup** [777 583] near Clachan, in 1481 'Le Lowb'. The principal Macalister family in Kintyre occupied the estate of Loup, and Charles Macalister of Loup was appointed Crown Steward of Kintyre in 1481.[1112] The last battle in Kintyre was fought in 1689 at 'Loup Hill'. [1113]

Port Lùb na h-Uamha [656 291], on Tangytavil shore, is 'Port of the Bay of the Cave'; the O.S. in 1867 interpreted *lùb* as 'bend'.[1114]

Lùb Dhubh [899 653], 'Black Bay', between Tarbert and Skipness, was a favourite haunt of ring-net fishermen. As Hugh MacFarlane explained, 'It wis dark in below the hills, it was black for the herrin, and the herrin went in close'. Hugh pointed out to me that there was another Lùb Dhubh familiar to fishermen, below Erines House, north of Tarbert, known as **Lùb Dhubh na h-Aoireann**, 'Black Bend of the Foreland', to distinguish it.[1115]

Lùb Dhubh made an appearance in a Tarbert comic song, written by an unknown fisherman. When I showed it to Campbeltown-born author Moira Burgess, she spotted that it was a parody of 'Mockingbird Hill', first popularised in the U.S. in the early 1950s and released in the U.K. in 1964. The first two lines rhyme on corruptions. 'Lo Poo', which unfailingly suggests to me a Chinese poet – Li Po? – is how Lùb Dhubh was garbled by the post-Gaelic generation of fishermen, and 'Mary Deveroo' represents the Tarbert ring-netter *Mary Devereux*, the re-named *Golden Sheaf* of Maidens. 'Toga' was the nick-name of Robbie McNeill, who bought the boat from Duncan 'Matha' McDougall, her original Tarbert owner, in whose wife's family the unusual surname Devereux evidently occurred. Here are the two verses which were all that Robert Ross, Tarbert, could remember of the composition. I wish I could piece together the rest of the epic.

> The sun in the evening looks over Lo Poo
> And we are out fishing in the Mary Deveroo.
> An old Gardner engine in a leaky old boat –
> Toga got the lot for a five pound note.

> Tra la la, tra la lee lee, it gives me a thrill –
> A fine spot playing beneath Laggan Hill.
> We took them aboard and went on our way
> And shot once again in Skipness Bay. [1116]

LURGANN is 'shaft', 'shin', or 'leg', but can also be 'ridge of a hill extending gradually into a plain', as Dwelly very precisely explains it under *lurg*; [1117] in Ireland, 'ridge' appears to be adequate.[1118] There is only one **Lurgann** in Kintyre, at 764 458, out in the middle of the peninsula, at the head of Gleann Drochaide and not far from Narachan, an area now choked with coniferous forest. There was a little farm or croft there, which, confusingly, took a variety of names, including 'Lurgie' and 'Lorgie' (**Lorgie Hill**, to the south-west, alone preserves the name on modern maps). Although the settlement's affinities would appear to have been with the Carradale side of the peninsula, it is actually in Killean parish, but only just. Archibald McQuilkan and Flora Kelly were at 'Lurgan' in 1801, in which year the house and name appeared on the Langlands map. The last occupants were probably Ballygroggan-born Alex McConochy and his wife Mary Martin who were at 'Lurgie' for 14 years until, in 1850, 'Mrs Morton the Proprietor', who was 'desirous of taking possession of the plot of ground', offered McConachy £4 to remove to Campbeltown, which offer he accepted. The Inspector of Poor for Campbeltown Parish, writing to his counterpart in Killean on 22/4/1851, remarked of McConochy, whose 'strength [was] failing him': 'During his residence in Killean Parish he occupied a spot of ground called Lurgin which he cultivated by spade labours and by this means supported himself and wife and kept a cow or two and were in tolerable condition.' [1119] **An Luirgeann** on Arran – the stretch of coast from Lenimore to Whitefarland – is the same name.[1120] Peter MacIntosh mentions **Loch Luirgin(n)** as being a 'source of Carradale river', but offers no dimensions.[1121] The location of the loch can only be conjectured.

When Cameron Gillies was researching *The Place Names of Argyll*, his Kintyre investigations were conducted at a distance. The *Campbeltown Courier* published seven lengthy, speculative letters from him on the subject of Kintyre place-names. In his first letter, of 5/5/1900, he explained that the time he could devote to the work was 'extremely limited' and that he 'felt the need of assistance in more than one direction', particularly in such districts as Kintyre which he did not himself 'know intimately'. He was sure that not a few readers would be interested in 'a very delightful piece of work'. Dr Gillies acknowledged the published work of the Rev. D. J. Macdonald, 'a man of culture and understanding working on the spot', but considered some of his derivations 'open to doubt'. This is a large background to a small point, which is this. In his letter of 23/6/1900, Gillies suspected Lorgie 'to be the same as Largie, the small *lairig*', but added cautiously: 'I would not be sure of this, however.' By the time the book appeared, six years later, he preferred 'to take this from the form in -*ach* of *lorg*, the footprint of an animal, or a path'.[1122] This speculation demonstrates the danger of taking place-names at face value, and the necessity of uncovering, if possible, their historic forms.

I remember visiting Duncan Colville at his house in Machrihanish several years before his death in 1981. He was already in his nineties, but his mind was still sharp. My interest at that time was in fishing history and he looked out some material for me. The house was a veritable archive, with box upon box full of files and papers, all of it catalogued in his memory. When our conversation turned from fishing to general topics, he mentioned that in the early stages of his place-names research he had visited, in Edinburgh, W. J. Watson, the pre-eminent Scottish authority on the subject at the time. The Professor was initially somewhat sceptical about the project, but when Duncan produced his meticulously compiled lists of names from historical sources, the interview proceeded with greater ease.

MACHAIR, from MAGH, 'plain', has a variety of related meanings, but for simplicity's sake I'll plump for 'plain', that is low-lying, open country. But, as Tim Robinson pointed out on p 82 of *Listening to the wind*, the first of his trilogy of closely observed and impeccably written accounts of Connemara, 'Ecologists have borrowed the Scots Gaelic word *machair* for [the] type of habitat characterised by level expanses of closely grazed turf on a lime-rich soil derived from sea-sand'. That definition applies to the generality of Kintyre *machair* place-names, though two lochs and a hill south of Tarbert may be mentioned as preserving an inland feature, in the genitive case *machrach*: **Cruach na Machrach** [891 635], 'Stack-shaped hill of the plain', **Loch na Machrach Bige** [886 637] and **Loch na Machrach Móire** [884 631], the little and big loch 'of the plain'.

These lochs appear in a Gaelic poem George Campbell Hay wrote around 1960. The lovely title, *An t-Anmoch air a' Mhonadh*, 'Evening on the Moors', might suggest a homage-offering to his Kintyre, but the poem – a poor specimen of his art – is terse and full of mental disturbance, which he has projected on to the landscape. Darkness is coming, the wind is rising and he is alone in a desolate place from which he must escape. He had been discharged from hospital in 1960 and the poem would have been written in Edinburgh. He would have known the lochs, all right, before and after the war that damaged his spirit, but in this poem they appear at the end, like two dead eyes from his past.[1123]

By far the best known of the Kintyre *machair* place-names is **Machrihanish**, which covers a village – the much expanded settlement earlier known as **Salt Pans**, **Mary Pans** or **Pans** – a farm, the former RAF air base, two golf courses, a marine laboratory, and a bird observatory. Machrihanish is one of the few Kintyre place-names which W. J. Watson examined in depth in his *Celtic Place-Names of Scotland*, and I quote his analysis in its entirety: 'Machrihanish in Kintyre is for *Machair Shanais*, "plain of Sanas"; near it is Loch Sanish, on Blaeu's map "Loch Sannaish". An alternative name for it – perhaps the earlier name – was *Magh Sanais*: an elegy on "Niall Óg Mhachra Shanuis" contains the lines "sgaoil a fhréimh ó chian fa Shanuis," "his root (ancestors) spread from of old about Sanas," and "chaochail Magh Sanuis gu mór," "the plain of Sanas has greatly changed." There was another Magh Sanais in Connacht. *Sanas*, mas. or fem., ordinarily means "a whisper, a hint, a secret, a warning," and it may mean so here, but in some instances it seems to denote some kind of plant: *gass sanais* is "a stalk of *sanas*"; in the tale of the Battle of Ventry it is said, "we would form a Druidical host around thee of the stalklets of *sanas*" (*do na geosadánaibh sanaisi*). It is difficult to say whether the meaning here is "whispering stalks" or "stalks of a plant called *sanas*," and I find nothing really decisive: *Loch Sanais* may mean "whispering loch," and the plain may have been named after the loch'.[1124] John Cameron, 'with very great diffidence', in 1939 advanced a suggestion that 'the Norsemen' might have called 'the point at the head of the huge stretch of sandy beach' *Sand-nes*, or 'sand point', and explained how the 'd' would be 'assimilated'.[1125]

On the *machair* of Machrihanish itself there is a secondary feature, **Machair Uinnein** [643 208], a name which, to quote from *The Place-Names of the Parish of Campbeltown*, 'affords scope for conjecture'. The specific, at first sight, might suggest INNEAN, or one of the similar-sounding and competing topographical terms, but there is no steep cliff or cove nearby. Large scale O.S. maps carry the legend, 'Supposed Site of Battle between the Scots & Danes 10th Century', and, according to James McNeill, the specific (pronounced 'eenan') was 'supposed to be the name of some famous leader or chief who fell in battle fighting against an invading host'. The 'invading host' was, by his own account, a 'raiding party' which supposedly landed for water and cattle. This party belonged to one of King Hakon's longships, which were retreating to Gigha after the Battle of Largs (1263). A 'band of natives' attacked the Norsemen, and a few of the combatants were slain before the raiders retreated along the shore to Eilean an Tomain and were taken aboard a longship. 'Not many years ago,' Mr McNeill added, 'when the greenkeepers were making some alterations near the 18th green, they turned up bones which were certainly the remains of extra tall men. This certainly seems to bear out what the tradition has always asserted.'[1126] John Rae at Machrihanish told Duncan Colville that he had seen 'a dozen human skulls at this place'.[1127] According to a newspaper report in 1911, **Eilean Tomain** (see TOM) was where 'the last remnant of the Norse invaders is said to have been slaughtered'; and, to justify the dubious tradition, the rock's name was ludicrously interpreted as 'The Isle of the Last Man'.[1128]

The above traditions, if there is anything to them, are more likely to be connected with a raid on Kintyre by the punitive force which King Hakon IV sent from Norway in 1230 under one Uspik, who was already dead by the time Kintyre was attacked: 'They sailed north under Cantire and landed there, but the Scots came against them there and fought with them, and were in very loose array in the battle and ran to and fro. There fell many men on either side. But when the Northmen came to their ships, then the Scots had slain all their lads who were on shore to make ready meat, and all their meat kettles were away.'[1129]

The rest of the coastal machair names are in Southend Parish, though there are other shore lands in Kintyre, e.g. that from

Bellochantuy north, which qualify as machair but don't have the name. On the Admiralty chart of Gigha Sound, surveyed in 1849, south of Ballochroy is marked a tidal rock named **Machricarron Rock**. The name presumably relates to an onshore machair feature which is now unknown, but its second element rather resists interpretation.

The several farms of **Machrimore** along with **Machribeg** [686 084], the big (*mór*) and the little (*beag*), pertain to the strip of machair which fringes Dunaverty Bay, as did also **Macharie-castell** (see CAISTEAL). Shinty matches were played on the machair of Machribeg on Old New Year's Day, 12 January, until at least the early 19th century. An anonymous account of 'Southend Fifty Years Ago', published in 1867, relates how 'even the middle aged and the old' would turn out for the sport, 'each with his shinty [stick] well scraped and shining bright, having been laid aside in a careful place since the last occasion'. The young boys had a separate field for their own game: 'I remember how we would be up on that morning by two or three o' clock, scraping our shinties with glass for the twentieth time, that we might be ready for the sport as soon as daylight appeared.'

But there was another shinty match in Southend, and it was played further to the west, on the Strathmore of Carskey. Most of the participants were from Glenbreackerie and were Gaelic-speaking. 'The truth is that, with very few exceptions, the one beach was frequented by the Lowlanders, and the other by the Highlanders, and if parties of these came into contact with each other, when the blood was hot, there was usually a fight, the result being bleeding noses and cracked crowns ...'[1130] It was during the 'Highland' shinty match on Strathmore, on New Year's Day 1836, that a farm servant at Gartvain, John MacCaog, was fatally struck by a shinty-stick swung by Duncan MacDougall, during an off-field 'battle'. During the affray, Donald MacIlreavie, mason at Keil, denounced the crowd thus: 'I have often heard of the inhumanity of the Glenbreakry people, but now I see it when they can stand and witness such barbarous fighting.'[1131] His denunciation may have had some effect, if the existence by 1877 of the 'Glenbreckerie Literary Association'[1132] is anything to go by!

As the machair at Machrihanish has been tamed into golf courses, so the seaward edge of machair at Machribeg has been turned into a caravan site, and the same goes for the last of the names, **Macharioch** (*Machair riabhach*). The specific has been interpreted as 'brindled',[1133] but see RIABHACH.

Macharioch [733 093] was one of the extensive Lands of Saint Ninian, which originally belonged to the Priory of Whithorn. In a charter dated 1584, it is described as 'Six marks of Machrerioch with its shealing', the shieling presumed to be Gartnacopaig in distant Glenbreackerie; and in a charter of 1632, reference is made to 'the manor place of Machrerioch'.[1134] The estate of Macharioch was held by the MacDonald family of Sanda, which was founded by Angus MacDonald, a son of Sir John Cathanach MacDonald of Dunyveg, Islay, who in 1494 hanged King James IV's governor over the walls of Dunaverty Castle and was executed for treason two years later. Archibald Mór MacDonald of Sanda and his son Archibald were active on the Royalist side during the Civil War, and both paid with their lives in 1647, the father in the aftermath of the siege at Dunaverty and the son on the battlefield of Cnoc na nDos in Ireland. In 1650 the Sanda estates were forfeited, but on the Restoration of the Monarchy in 1660 were returned to the MacDonald family.[1135] In 1799, when the estate was sold, it comprised Macharioch itself, Achadaduie, Blasthill, Eden, Knockmorran, Cuildrain, Kilmashenachan, Penlachtan, Pennyseorach, Acharua, and Pennyland Mill. Its new owner was Donald MacDonald, who renamed it **Ballyshear** – *Baile Sear*, 'East township' – after his family estate on North Uist, but he soon afterwards drowned at Kirkbost, North Uist, and the estate passed to his son William, Professor of Natural History at the University of St Andrews, who in 1833 transferred it to trustees. It was acquired in 1844 by the Hon. Augustus Henry Macdonald Moreton of Largie. When he, in turn, sold the estate in 1863 to the 8th Duke of Argyll, George Douglas Campbell, the earlier name 'Macharioch' was restored.[1136]

If local tradition may be accepted, an eccentric action of William MacDonald's produced the minor place-name at Macharioch House, the **Gallows Tree**. MacDonald kept an 'expensive stable', and when one of his horses jumped a fence and got in among a field of growing corn, he gathered all his horses in the courtyard and hanged the 'lawbreaker' from the plane tree as 'a warning and a deterrent' to the other horses.[1137] D. J. Macdonald questioned the truth of the story,[1138] but a native of Southend claimed that a grand-uncle of his own was 'asked to do the hanging' and refused.[1139]

Macharioch House was given by the Duke to his son John, Marquess of Lorne, as part of his marriage settlement, when, in 1871, he wed Princess Louise, the artistic fourth daughter of Queen Victoria. The newly-weds, on their 'marriage tour', arrived in Campbeltown aboard the *Columba* on 21/9/1871, and on the following day were welcomed by the townsfolk. After a 'triumphal progress to the town boundary', they proceeded to Macharioch, where the estate tenantry was treated by Lorne to a dinner at the Home Farm. Princess Louise had been warned of the poor condition of Macharioch House – 'the roof was not even water-tight' – and she employed an architect, George Devey, to enlarge and modernise the building. She also set about improving the neglected grounds. Undergrowth was hacked down, walks cleared and gardens laid out so that 'the sea, which she loved, would be visible from every room of the house'. She planted a 'long fuchsia walk' from the house to the beach, a feature which survives to this day. She so much liked Macharioch, which she described as 'this curious lovely spot', that she and her husband remained there until 6 October;[1140] but she was never to return.

MADADH is a dog or any wild creature related to or resembling a dog. These other creatures, however, also have specific names, e.g. a wolf can be *madadh allaidh* ('wild dog'), a fox *madadh ruadh* ('red dog') and an otter *madadh donn* ('brown dog').[1141] When I look at a place-name such as **Dalivaddy** [677 199], I see, if I may risk absurdity, a hill clothed in mist except for the very top. That bare, visible tip is the name, and the invisible hill is the history underlying the name. Some place-names are explicable after hundreds or even thousands of years, but Dalivaddy is not. The Kintyre Antiquarian Society, for *Dail a' mhadaidh*, in 1943 offered 'The field of the hound (or wolf)',[1142] which is probably as close as we'll get to an understanding.

In 1975, more than 30 years later, Duncan Colville adjusted his position on the name's interpretation, for an account on Wolves in 'The Mammals of Kintyre', co-written with Dr Jack Gibson. 'Their former presence is recorded in local place names,' it was stated. 'One of the best known is Dalavaddy (=Dail a' mhadaidh) meaning "the field of the wolf."'[1143] I can only assume that, lacking any documentary evidence for Wolves in Kintyre, and in order to justify an entry on the Wolf, Duncan succumbed to temptation and upgraded *madadh* from possibility to certainty, a singularly uncharacteristic lapse on his part, I may add.

There was undoubtedly a tradition attached to the name Dalivaddy which would have explained it, but it has been lost. The farm is in the Laggan, between Stewarton and Drumlemble, and the earliest lease I can find for it dates only to 1776, when John McCoag 'in

Dailvaddy' had his tack renewed.[1144] In 1866 it was 'a row of thatched cottages in bad repair'.[1145] In that area of South Kintyre, the influx of Lowland settlers, beginning in the 17th century, hastened the decline of Gaelic, and, as the language disappeared, so too did its traditions.

On Arran, the interpretations of the *madadh* place-names admit only 'dog' and 'fox' into the frame,[1146] and in the case of **Allt a' Mhadaidh** [854 547], which rises north-east of Oragaig, near Skipness, the O.S. interpretation was simply 'Dog's burn'. Likewise, 'Dog's Hill' was the interpretation of **Cnoc a' Mhadaidh**, one [763 345] at the western extremity of Saddell Glen and another south of Torrisdale.[1147] **Creag a' Mhadaidh** [627 097], a 'conspicuous crag on the grazing of Keramenach', was 'The Dog Rock'.[1148] At the entrance to Tarbert harbour are two rocks [871 689], **Madadh Buidhe**, 'Yellow Dog', and **Madadh Maol**, 'Bald Dog',[1149] the former **Rubh' a' Mhadaidh Bhuidhe** on O.S. maps.

The domestic dog has been ever-present in human society for thousands of years, so that if 'hound' is assumed to be the specific, the dogs in question must have been involved in some notable events. As for the Wolf (*Canus lupis*), despite the abundance of 'last wolf' tales in various parts of Scotland, persisting into the 18th century, the species was declared extinct in Scotland in 1684, '20 years after the last official mention of them'.[1150] Gibson and Colville, assuming the existence of Wolves until historical times, 'when the peninsula was still well-wooded', considered unlikely their survival in Kintyre 'for very long into the 16th century'.[1151]

As a feared – and ruthlessly hunted – predator, the Wolf has certainly left its mark on history. In England alone, no fewer than 230 Wolf-related place-names (including field-names) have been identified, deriving from Old English *wulf* or Old Norse *ulfr*;[1152] but whether Dalivaddy is one of the Scottish number will never be known.

MAGH is a 'plain', a tract of level country. Tim Robinson, in the first of his compelling books on Connemara, considered *magh* to be 'indissolubly associated with Ireland's mythic dimensions'. Again and again in the legends, plains are named as 'sites of foundational events or aspects of the Otherworld', such as Magh Tuireadh, 'The plain of the pillars', where the 'epic battle of the magical Tuatha Dé Danaan and the demonic Fomhóire was fought'.[1153] We have the word in Kintyre place-names, but not the legends. Both *magh* place-names are in the south of the peninsula.

Moy [700 208, etc.] is a cluster of smallholdings between Campbeltown and Stewarton, but was an estate before being broken up. In a charter of 1545, it appears as 'Mye'.[1154] In 1797, at 'Mey', Robert Smith had five horses and William MacMurchy six.[1155] The estate was held by the Greenlees distilling family in the late 19th century and the name *Moy* was given to a schooner built for the Dalaruan and Hazelburn distillery companies. She was the first vessel built by the Campbeltown Shipbuilding Company at Trench Point, and her launch, on 20/3/1878, attracted more than 3000 spectators; but almost six years later, on 23/1/1884, she foundered within sight of Campbeltown in a snow-squall, with the loss of her captain, John Walker, and all hands.[1156]

Moy's location, close to the apex of the plain called Laggan, certainly satisfies the definition of *magh*, but was there more to the name? That plain is huge. Roughly, it extends triangularly from Campbeltown to the Atlantic seaboard, framed by two roads, the B843 in the south and the A83 in the north, with another smaller triangle of flat land south of the B843 between Stewarton and Drumlemble. There is no satisfactory name for that plain. 'Laggan' is the name it gets, but it makes little sense to me there – see LAG/ LAGAN. Did 'Moy' originally cover a greater area and shrink to one farm? Is it possible, therefore, that *magh* could have been applied to the entire plain, which, however, was largely a swamp until drained and brought into cultivation in the post-medieval period? Watson suggested significantly that *Magh Sanais* may have been an earlier name for Machrihanish[1157] (see under MACHAIR).

Cnoc Moy [611 152], the second-highest hill in Kintyre, is number two and should represent *Cnoc Maighe*, 'Hill of the Plain'. In *The Place-Names of the Parish of Campbeltown* (p 16), the question is asked: 'Does this refer to the Laggan?' Put the two features together and, hypothetically, there is a kind of match: the biggest hill in South Kintyre and the biggest area of flat land in all Kintyre. For me, however, the match is problematic. Were it the case that the hill stood directly above the plain, the relationship would be clear, but it doesn't. It stands about six miles to the south-west, and only the north-western area of the plain is visible from Cnoc Moy, and vice-versa; but distant perspective may be the key to an understanding. Viewed from the north and from the sea, the 'big picture' is indeed of a land-mass, with Cnoc Moy as its crown, sloping to a flat, or 'plain'. The Ordnance Survey in 1866 decided that the specific represented *maoidh*, 'threaten', and offered the ingenious explanation that, from its being the highest hill in the district, mist was more liable to 'rest upon it ... thus giving the appearance of "threatening" to rain'.[1158] Peter MacIntosh stated in 1857 that from Cnoc Moy's summit on a clear day, the Isle of Man, Ben Nevis, and Tory Island can be seen with a 'good telescope', and, with the naked eye, Mull, Scarba, Jura, Islay, Sliabh Gaoil in Knapdale, Cowal, Arran, Ayrshire, Wigtonshire, and the Irish coast.[1159]

45. MAOL. Approaching the Mull of Kintyre from the east. Photograph taken by the author from the Waverley *paddle-steamer, 1/6/2012.*

MAOL, as a topographical descriptor, is defined by Dwelly as 'brow of a rock, cape, promontory, mull, great bare rounded hill',[1160] but the primary meaning is 'bald'.[1161] **Maol Chinntìre** is 'Mull of Kintyre', which translates roughly as '(bald) cape of the headland' or '... of land's end' (see TÌR). Kintyre, of course, is now the entire peninsula, but was originally the end of land, as seen from the north of Ireland and the sea. The Mull, or 'Moil', is more specifically the bare south-western face of that land-mass. Just as the name *Ceann Tìre*, 'Cantire' or 'Kintyre', migrated northwards, so too has 'Mull of Kintyre', which now equates in many minds with the peninsula itself. Some folk complain about how 'Mull of Kintyre' as a name has been made to work harder than ever before, but that's progress! Paul McCartney's massive chart success with the song 'Mull of Kintyre' in

1977 helped muddle the geography further, and I believe that the Isle of Mull's tourism benefited by the confusion! The lighthouse at the Mull, which became operational in 1788, was a difficult engineering project owing to the comparative inaccessibility of its location,[1162] but an outrageously impractical proposal was published in 1868, by two 'eminent civil engineers', to create a railway tunnel between the Mull and Fair Head on the north coast of Ireland. 'This scheme when completed would cost 75 millions, and take six years to complete.'[1163] Needless to say, nothing more was heard of it.

46. MEALL. Millmore (Meall Mór) Beacon, also known as 'The Winky', on the crook of the Doirlinn, Campbeltown Loch. The caption on this postcard, published by A. & C. Ralston, Stationers, Campbeltown, is ' "King Edward" passing Dhorling, Campbeltown', but the back of the card states: 'This is really "Queen Alexandra." ' From the author's collection.

There is another *maol* at the opposite end of the peninsula. 'Mealdarroch Point' [889 683] is the O.S. spelling for the headland south of East Loch Tarbert, but it is wrong, as local pronunciation proves, and should be **Rubha Maol Daraich** (or *Daraigh*, the softer form which George Campbell Hay preferred), 'Point of the oaken head'. MEALL for *maol* is a recurring confusion on Ordnance Survey maps, which only local pronunciation or topographical familiarity can resolve. A township there [879 682] took the name and appears on the 1801 Langlands map as 'Muldarrach', which better represents the correct form. In 1750 it was described as a 'pendicle', or subsidiary holding, on the lands of Archibald Macalister of Tarbert, and is believed to have been deserted around 1845. The settlement was also known as **Beldarroch**, 'Bel-' presumably representing *baile*, 'township'. It appears as 'Beldarich' on Roy's military map (1747-55), and in C1841 there were four occupied houses at 'Beldarroch'. See A.O.M. Clark, 'The Deserted Settlement of Beldarroch', in *Kist* No. 48, pp. 1-7. For Mulbuy see MEALL.

MARBH is 'dead'. **Port nam Marbh** [c. 629 207], 'Port of the Dead', is a little bay at the old lifeboat shed, Machrihanish. James McNeill suggested that unidentifiable corpses from the sea could have been buried there, rather than in consecrated ground, 'in case they might not have been Christians',[1164] which as speculation is fair enough. Two human skeletons were uncovered there by storm action in February, 1936, thus appearing to validate the place-name. Behind the *Campbeltown Courier* report may be heard the promptings of Duncan Colville: 'The discovery should prove of particular interest to the Kintyre Antiquarian Society which, at present, is conducting an exhaustive enquiry into the origin of local place-names ... The discovery, too, provides confirmation of the contention of the antropologists [*sic*] that folk lore is always based on a foundation of solid truth.'[1165] Folklore, in this case, had nothing to contribute to the debate. There was another Port nam Marbh [654 271] north of Westport, which, owing to its proximity to Kilchenzie, Captain T. P. White thought might have 'some early ecclesiastical association'; and the same with nearby **Port na Croise**.[1166] Ian A. Fraser, in his paper 'The Place-Names of Argyll', associated Port nam Marbh place-names with bodies' being 'carried ashore for burial'.[1167] Captain White connected **Bealach na' Marbh** [786 321], 'Pass of the Dead', with 'the fact that in early times, on account of the place's great sanctity, the dead were frequently brought long distances to Saddell'.[1168] The pass is certainly between the Abbey and the coast, from which, in medieval times and beyond, most visitors – living and dead – would arrive.

MEADHONACH is 'middle' and is most commonly applied to divided settlements. There are three farms named **Ballimenach** in Kintyre, one at Kildalloig [754 183], one near Smerby [750 227] and one at Carradale [812 387], all *Baile meadhonach*, 'Middle farm'. **Keramenach** [638 098] in Southend is *Ceathramh-meadhonach*, 'Middle quarter' (see CEATHRAMH), and **Auchameanach** [882

568] at Skipness is *Achadh meadhonach*, 'Middle field.' On Tangy farm, D. J. Macdonald recorded **Sliabh meadhonach**, which he translated as 'Middle hill',[1169] but see SLIABH. For **Beachmenach** see BEITH.

MEALL is basically a 'lump', and the word was applied to some big hills in Kintyre. **Meall Buidhe** [735 325] is 'Yellow Hill' and stands at 1228 ft. There was a farm, **Mulbuy**, which lay to the east of Bordadubh and took its name from the hill. Though far from Darlochan, in the 18th century it was a 'grass pendicle' of that farm. In 1720, Malcolm McNeill got the lease of Darlochan 'with the 20/- land of Monchuill or Mulbuy'. In the 19th century, it was let with **Alltanteirve** – *Allt an tairbh*, 'Stream of the bull' – which was closer to it. James Haldane Stewart, youngest son of Duncan Stewart of Glenbuckie, Argyll Estates chamberlain in Kintyre, got the combined lease in 1827, but on his death it passed to his brother, Charles Stewart in Poonah, Bombay, who renounced it in 1837.[1170]

There was another Mulbuy, spellt 'Mulbuij' and 'Muilbuij' in the rental book of Malcolm MacNeill of Carskey, who noted on 28/11/1734 that he had received from Duncan Campbell there 'in Cash One pound & three shill sterll money', and in February 1741 that Patrick McMath paid him 'Seven marks Scots being in his proportion for the Sumer herding of the Cattle in Muilbuij'. This name has been interpreted as *Maol Buidhe* – see MAOL. Duncan MacNeill, who had farmed Low Glenadale and by 1937 was in Dalsmeran, told Archie McEachran that Mulbuy was situated on the south side of Glenadale Water, not far from Saint Catherine's Chapel. Similarly, Elizabeth Marrison (2008) believed that Mulbuy might lie at 631 113, which corresponds to the location on the map accompanying *MacNeill of Carskey: His Estate Journal, 1703-1743*. McEachran himself noted the ruins of a steading on the west bank of Allt Dorrie, about 800 yards east-south-east of Sliabh a' Bhiorain. No one could tell him the name of it and he speculated that it might be Mulbuy, but see Allt Dorie house under DOIRE.[1171]

Mealbaan was another steading the location of which is uncertain. It represents *Meall bàn*, 'Light-coloured hill', and, since the area of 641 190 on Lossit is still known as 'Mealbaan' to the farmer, Adam Armour, the name is likely to have applied to one of the now nameless adjacent hills.[1172] It appears as 'Meaullbaan' on the Langlands map of 1793 and as 'Malbaan' in 1797, when Alex MacConachy's two horses were noted there.[1173] **Meall Mór** [736

170], 'Big Hill', overlooks the head of Glenramskill at just over 1000 ft. Meall Mór [744 200] was also the name of the beacon on the crook of the Doirlinn, and **Meall Beag** [738 203] the name of the neighbouring beacon at Trench Point. These may be interpreted as the 'big' and 'little' lump or heap and could relate to a seabed feature or features.[1174] The generic is absent from Southend, Killean and Kilchenzie and Kilcalmonell parishes, but three names occur in Saddell and Skipness, **Meall Buidhe** [781 413], again 'Yellow Hill', and twice [777 376 and 887 615] **Meall Donn**, 'Brown Hill'.

MÒINE is defined by Macbain as simply 'peat, moss',[1175] but it applies not only to the substance that was dug, spread, dried and burned extensively until the mid-20th century, but also to the source of the fuel, the peat-bog itself. The once boggy plain between Campbeltown and Machrihanish was known as the 'Moss' – Scots for boggy ground, moorland and for peat itself – as well as the Laggan, and huge quantities of peat were extracted there for domestic use and for the distilleries of Campbeltown. The name is preserved in the **Moss Road** – often corrupted to 'Morse Road' – which intersects the Laggan, south to north.

Mòine Ruadh, a settlement-name both in Southend and Carradale, is 'Red Moss'. In Southend, the anglicised form is 'Muneroy', which fairly accurately represents local pronunciation. The name is still alive, attached to the village store and tearoom [691 084], but there is no longer any indication of moor or bog there. A lease first appears for 'the half mark land of Monroy' in 1770, and with it 'the right and privelidge of Ferrying from the said lands to the Coast of Ireland as now and formerly in use'. Archibald Lamont had the lease, followed by John Dillon and Dugald Campbell, and in 1822 by Donald MacKay.[1176] In 1867, a native of Southend remembered 'Monerua' 50 years earlier as 'a row of low thatched cottages' and a 'lowly hostelrie' run by John Dillon, an Irishman. At that time, there was a great deal of traffic between Dunaverty Waterfoot and the ports of County Antrim, and he recalled seeing herds of 40 or 50 ponies grazing near the public house.[1177] **Moine Ruadh** at Carradale has two settlements, High at 795 383 and Low at 794 382.

Druimnamòine [646 121] is a small ruin on Amod farm, Southend, recorded in 1866 by the O.S., which interpreted the name 'Ridge of the peats or turf'.[1178] 'Siol Chuinn', during his rambles in the summer of 1921, refers to leaving Low Glenadale and passing 'on across "the Odle" and over "Drumonie"' to Amod.[1179]   The

'Odle' is presumably Glenadale Water and 'Drumonie' is certainly Druimnamòine.

Monimore [694 463] at Tayinloan is *A Mhòine Mhór*, 'The Big Moss'. In 1867, the settlement consisted of two cottages with 'a small pendicle of land attached'.[1180] At C1871, 'Monimore Hamlet' consisted of six occupied houses. The settlement no longer exists, the stone from the ruins having been used to fill in a big drain which ran to the sea.[1181] **Monyguail** was a peat-moor near Tayinloan, referred to in a dispute between John Macdonald of Largie and the 2nd Duke of Argyll. John MacIlchattan, Bellochgerran, stated that '... about eight Years ago, he interrupted James Montgomery, who then lived in Killean, from casting Peats upon that part of Monyguail belonging to Bellochgerran, by sending him and his Servants from the Moss, until he undertook to pay them for the Liberty, if they would demand it'.[1182] The name almost certainly represents *Mòine a' ghuail*, 'Peat-moss of the coal', possibly alluding to production of charcoal from peat.[1183]

Monyliadh [c. 785 582], a ruined croft north-east of Clachan, represents *Mòine Liath*, 'Grey or Hoary Moss'. **Moncbeg**, also near Clachan, at Loch Ciaran, is *Mòine Beag*, 'Little Moss'. In 1840, Donald McAllister there was 'a Cottar and pays the Croft rent and has one cow';[1184] in C1841 'Moniveg' was occupied by cottar Lachlan Black, wife Effy, and six children. The specific of **Monybachach** [905 580] at Skipness is probably *bàcach*, 'rugged', which can apply to ground which is difficult to work.[1185]

Monadh, a distinct term, is defined as 'a mountain range' by Macbain , who noted it as being 'rare in Argyle topography',[1186] but it has lesser meanings such as 'moor' and 'hill'.[1187] Even with these, it is rare, so rare, in fact, that I can find only two examples, and these, from the similarity to *mòine*, are suspect. They are **A' mhonadh mhòr** and **Monadh brìdean** (or **brìdcheann**) in the Largieside. The first specific is 'big' and the second presumably refers to the Oyster-catcher (see under CROIT); but in both cases the generic was unhelpfully left untranslated.[1188]

MOLACH is 'rough' or 'hairy'. Cameron Gillies, examining **Barmollach** [808 438] – ' ... very difficult to express in English, though it is very simple Gaelic' – offered these notes towards an understanding of the name: 'Barr is *a summit* and molach is *hairy*, but by secondary meaning it is abundant grass or crop.'[1189] See also under BÀRR. **Strathmollach** [715 304] – *Srath molach* – has been interpreted as 'shaggy strath'.[1190]   It was once a sheep farm, and the ruined steading is now on the shore of Lussa Reservoir. For **Feorlinmolach**, 'Rough farthingland', see FEÒIRLIN.

MÓR is 'big' and is a recurrent element throughout this book. Here, however, are two examples of interest. **Diolloid Mhór** [772 396], which stands to the north of Rhonadale, is 'Big Saddle', from a resemblance to that article of equestrian gear; but it is tree-covered now. **Creag Dhòmhnuill Mhóir** [c. 634 208], at Machrihanish, is 'Big Donald's Rock', from his habit of fishing from it.[1191]

MUC is a pig. **Leum na Muice** [790 595], between Clachan and Whitehouse, is 'The Pig's Leap', and is associated with the Ossianic legend of the ill-fated lovers Diarmaid and Gráinne. The Tarbert author, Dugald Mitchell, published a version of the tale in 1908, but since a variant appears in the account of **Beinn an Tuirc**, under TORC, I shall draw selectively from it here. The lovers fled from Ireland to Kintyre, where at **Carraig an Daimh** (see under CARRAIG) 'the unfaithful Grainne – unfaithful still – fell in love with Old Ciofach Mac a' Ghoill (the son of the stranger), whom Diarmaid slew after a determined struggle'. Diarmaid then left Kintyre and proceeded to the great mountain ridge north of Tarbert, **Sliabh Gaoil**, 'Hill of Love', whence he was followed by Gráinne. Still later came the boar-hunt which ended in Diarmaid's death. From Beinn an Tuirc, according to tradition, Diarmaid pursued the chase through glens and over hills to Leum na Muice, 'where two rocks are shown, across which the boar leapt', then round the head of West Loch Tarbert until at **Tòrr an Tuirc** – 'Hill of the Boar' – the beast was finally killed.[1192]

Glenamucklach [705 123], Southend, has been interpreted *Gleann na muclach*, 'The glen of the pig-kind':[1193] 'Glen of the piggery' would be simpler. **Lag na Muice** [720 110], 'Hollow of the Pig', isn't very far away. For **Drumnamucklach** [696 439], Largieside, D. J. Macdonald suggested *Druim nam mulc chlach*, 'the ridge of the stone lumps',[1194] which Cameron Gillies dismissed in favour of *Druim na muc-lach*,[1195] cf. Glenamucklach above. Earliest forms: 1556 'Drumnamwkloche'; 1634 'Drumnamuckloch'; 1709 Janet Cameron, relict of Dugall Campbell in 'Drumnamucklach'.[1196] **Allt na Muice** [741 391], Barr Glen, is 'The Pig's Stream'. **Cnoc na Muice**, 'Hill of the Pig', is now **Whinhill** [709 206], on the outskirts of Campbeltown.[1197]   For **Oitir na Muice**, 'The Pig's

Shoal', see under OITIR. **Mucklach**, for *muclach*, was a pendicle of Largiebeg, described by Ian MacDonald (2011) as 'a weavers' place near Kilkenzie', but its precise location is unknown to me. There was another Mucklach [645 095] in Strone Glen, Southend, which is on record as early as 1545 as a 1-merkland and which has been defined as 'The piggery'.[1198]

MUILEANN is 'mill', for the grinding of grain into meal. As with English 'mill', it derives from Latin *molina*.[1199] In prehistory, milling was done by hand using a quern or a knocking-stone, but when water-driven mills came into existence, the traditional methods were discouraged by lairds, who built and leased the mills and recovered their costs and paid the millers by the 'multure' or milling charge. Tenants, therefore, were bound, or 'thirled', to particular mills, but some ignored these regulations and took their corn elsewhere, often to a more conveniently situated mill, which led on occasion to legal wrangles between landowners, e.g., in 1736, John Macdonald of Largie and the Duke of Argyll, over Tangy Mill, and, in 1819, George Macneal of Ugadale and Charles Rowatt of Kilkivan, over Knocknaha Mill. The earliest records of Kintyre mills appear in the 17th century, but there were no doubt mills in operation earlier, some perhaps of simple horizontal construction, for which see Balmacvicar under BAILE.[1200]

The village of **Whitehouse** [816 612] was earlier **Lag a' Mhuilinn**, 'Mill Hollow', in 1785 'Lagabhuilin'.[1201] In Southend, **Drumavoulin** [670 091] represents *Druim a' Mhuilinn*, 'Mill Ridge'. The name was evidently chosen in 1777 by the English settler Robert Makepeace, who wished to set up a mill there,[1202] but there is no evidence it was ever built. **Polliwilline** [735 100] is *Poll a' mhuilinn*, 'The mill pool'. It shares with **Ballywilline** [712 224], *Baile a' mhuilinn*, 'The mill farm', the corrupt-looking '-willine' ending, but that, or at least 'willin', is the spoken form. Cameron Gillies, in a rant against the Ordnance Survey over its 'most contorted and ignorant and careless' treatment of Kintyre place-names, singled out 'Cockalane' and 'Pollywillin' as 'comically stupid renderings'.[1203] He had a point, of course, but my impression is that with settlement-names the O.S. preferred anglicised spellings to Gaelic spellings. The name-books reveal that little or no effort was made to establish the meaning of farm-names, and if a spelling already existed – in rentals or estate maps, or wherever – it would be adopted. The O.S., therefore, did not invent these 'stupid' forms. In the case of 'Polliwilline', similar forms go back centuries before the Survey was founded. In 1596 it appears as 'Poldowilling', in 1692 as 'Polwilling' and in 1720 as 'Polwillin'.[1204] These, certainly, co-existed with other spellings more in keeping with 'standard' Gaelic, but they appear to represent actual local pronunciation, presumably through the influence of Ireland, just across the North Channel; cf. Drumawillin (*Droim an Mhuilinn*, 'Ridge of the mill') in the parish of Ramoan, County Antrim, and 'Portawillin' (*Port an Mhuilinn*, 'Port of the mill') on Rathlin Island.[1205]

Allt a' Mhuilinn [704 362], 'The Mill Stream', is a remote burn south of Barr Glen, and **Loch a' Mhuilinn** [797 480], 'The Mill Loch' – in the Langlands 1793 map, 'Loch Vuline' – is in the hills west of Cour. These two, like most of the surviving *muileann* place-names, are difficult to connect with any known sites of mills, and probably relate to earlier and more primitive arrangements. **Tòit [Dòit] a' mhuilinn**, a field-name on Clachaig farm, is 'The mill croft',[1206] and preserves the custom of the miller's having a patch of land to cultivate, as part of his lease, as was generally also the case with blacksmiths (see GOBHA/GOBHAINN).

47. *MUILEANN. An old millstone, one of a pair, at Killean Gate Lodge, 21/4/2012. Photograph by the author.*

NATHAIR is a 'serpent' or 'snake', which in Kintyre is truly represented only by the adder (*Lacerta vivipara*), since the slow-worm (*Anguis fragilis*) is properly a legless lizard, though such a distinction would have been unknown when Gaelic place-names were being coined. In recent history, adders, whose venom can kill children and the sick and elderly, have been much persecuted.[1207] Local newspapers in the 19th and early 20th centuries reported their routine destruction, and much interest was shown in the dates of killings – spring, when the reptiles emerge sluggishly from hibernation, was the prime time – and also in the length and colouration of specimens.

48. NATHAIR. Arinarach Hill (R.) and head of the Meal Kist Glen (L.) from the south slope of Ben Gullion, 27/4/2012. Photograph by the author.

The only local fatality of which I am aware was a two-year-old girl, daughter of Duncan McMillan, weaver at Craigs, West Loch Tarbert, who was bitten in the foot in September 1851 in a hay-field and died before Dr Hugh Campbell could reach her, about nine hours later.[1208] In May 1865, Charles McFadyen, 'Kerafuer', was bitten in the ankle 'whilst putting off his shoes on the bank of the river'. The leg quickly swelled up, but he received medical attention and recovered.[1209] Three weeks later, his shepherd father, John McFadyen, killed two adders on 'the hill face of Homeston', each of them about 26 inches long. 'Observing that the circumference of the one was much greater than the other, he cut it open, and to his surprise found three young grouse in its stomach.'[1210] The father-son relationship was not referred to in the newspaper report, but the two appear together in the 1871 census of Southend at 'Kerifuar Shepherd's Cottage', John aged 65 and Charles aged 17. John McFadyen was a native of Torosay, Mull, and the progenitor of the family of building and haulage contractors in Campbeltown.[1211] In no sense would the killing of the two adders have been an act of revenge on the father's part: the slaughter was routine throughout society. In July 1911, a Campbeltown fisherman, Dugald Robertson, stretching his legs on the shore at Cour, 'unexpectantly trod on an adder, which he killed'. It was 'in the act of devouring a young linnet at the time, and its victim was tightly held in its mouth'. The adder, which was 21 inches long, was 'preserved with its prey' by Donald McKinlay at Campbeltown Museum, 'the combination being rather uncommon'.[1212]

Peter MacIntosh records a curious belief concerning **Tirfergus Glen**, that no 'Serpents' were found there because the young trees 'were taken from Ireland'.[1213] This, of course, is a reference to the absence of snakes in Ireland; St Patrick was credited with banishing them.

There are two Kintyre place-names containing *nathair*. **Arinarach Hill** [731 161] takes its name from a long-abandoned farm, Arinarach [724 150], which represents *Àirigh nathrach*, 'serpent shieling'. The farm itself must have taken its name from a nearby shieling, or summer grazing (see ÀIRIGH). The name is an old one – it appears as 'Arenarroch', joined with 'Ellerich', in a charter of 1481, and as the one-merkland of 'Harrenarroch' in a charter of 1545.[1214] The occupiers then are unknown, but in 1792 John McMichael and Cathrine McArthur were there with their five young children, Mary, Barbra, Cathrine, Dugald and Helen, and two servant-girls, Isobell Campbell, aged 20, and Peggy Galbreath, 16.[1215] In 1797 Duncan McCallum in 'Arinaroch' owned two horses,[1216] and in the oldest part of Kilkerran graveyard there is a stone erected to Donald McMillan, tenant in Arinarach, who died in 1833.

The original 'serpent shieling' must have been infested to an extraordinary degree to have warranted its name, unless there is some underlying but forgotten significance. The north side of Arinarach Hill faces on to the back slope of Ben Gullion, which was once the lair of an immense and powerful serpent. This mythical creature, which was a terror to man and beast alike, remained invincible until a hero named MacMurchy appeared. He lured it to a trap, in which, with agonised writhings and hissings, it was roasted to death.[1217]

A similar legend – improbably dated to 'some time in the seventeenth century' – was attached to Altagalvas north of Skipness.

In the hills at Ashens near Tarbert there was a monstrous serpent which had 'stung' people and killed cattle and sheep. It could fly like a bird and no one could destroy it until it arrived at Altagalvas where another hero was waiting. His name was Thomson and he found the serpent asleep in the burn and killed it. He hid the lethal sword below a rock overhanging the burn and afterwards went abroad. When he returned some 20 years later, he went to the burn to see if the sword was still there and found it where he had left it. It was very rusty so he wet his finger and was rubbing at the rust. He died a few hours later from the poison on the old sword.[1218]

49. *NATHAIR. Narachan ruin in a snow-whitened landscape, c. 1995. Photograph by Iain McAlister.*

Narachan ostensibly represents *nathrachan*, 'a place infested with serpents', but Ian A. Fraser, considering Narachan on Arran, observed that 'The name usually applies to a situation beside a meandering, serpentine stream',[1219] which certainly suits the Kintyre case. Narachan [768 465], like its near-neighbour Lurgann, was an interior hill farm, and only just in Killean Parish. In fact, the parish boundaries of Killean, Kilcalmonell and Skipness all meet nearby. As with many remote holdings, Narachan was originally a farm, was then adapted as a shepherd's cottage, and finally abandoned. Its earliest appearance on record was evidently in 1502, as the 'Twa Narachanis'.

By 1798 the occupant was a shepherd, John McNabb.[1220] In C1901, John McCallum was shepherd there with his widowed mother Jane and sister Maggie. John was just 20 years old and Maggie 19, and one might wonder at the nature of the lives they led there, miles from 'civilisation'. No doubt they were inured to solitude and hardship, but the time was fast approaching when the kind of life possible in such a place as Narachan would be rejected. The McAlisters in Grogport received from a family leaving Narachan – perhaps the last to live there – a big German-made wall-clock which has been dated to c. 1870. It is now in the possession of Iain McAlister, who lives in Campbeltown. He had it repaired and it again keeps time,[1221] as it once did at Narachan, where time meant less than it does now. Narachan, the place of serpents or the place beside a winding stream, is now a ruin enclosed by forest.

Naomi Mitchison walked the track between Auchenbreck and Largie, and back, in May 1941 to discuss a play with Mrs Macdonald of Largie, an adventure described at length in *Among You Taking Notes* (pp. 148-50). She refers to 'the deserted village of Narrachan', and in a poem, published in September of the following year in the *Scots Magazine*, tells the 'Ghosts at Narrachan' (the poem's title): 'Sheep are over your garden/ And where the road was.'[1222]

Since then, sheep have been displaced by trees. Agnes Stewart was about 12 years old when her father Willie Mitchell took her to Narachan, and she remembers nearby hills being ploughed for afforestation at the time. The year would have been 1949 or 1950 and the month was June, with cuckoos calling all day. She remembers a 'gorgeous day', such as 'seemed to fill long-ago summers'. She and her father cycled from Campbeltown to Auchenbreck and followed the burn from there up to Narachan, but they returned by the hill and the going was difficult over the ploughed ground.[1223]

Jim McAlister was involved in fencing and then planting the area adjacent to Narachan on the east side of the burn. In fact, it was his and Alistair Strang's first job when they joined the Forestry Commission in March 1959. Jim remembers that Narachan still had a tin roof on it and that shepherds from 'the west side' would occasionally spend a night there.[1224]

The first time I was at Narachan was in 1985, with my wife Judy and Lachie Paterson. I returned with Judy in August 2012 to photograph the ruin, and we both felt alienated there. It seemed as though the history had been squeezed out of the place by the press of the trees, some still standing, some uprooted by gales and others felled and replaced with saplings among the stumps and litter of brashings. In short, a once-attractive steading with cultivated garden and fields now decays in a wasteland.

ODHAR is a colour, but, as with RIABHACH, how should it be seen? Of course, landscapes may change in the space of years, let alone centuries. A hill once judged to be red-looking or speckled or rough is going to be green when a plantation of Sitka spruce begins to rise on its flanks, and whatever perception informed its Gaelic name will be erased, if it hadn't already been erased by earlier changes in land use. The standard interpretation of *odhar* is 'dun', but, as Cameron Gillies pointed out, dun itself, 'brown', is a loan-word in English from Irish and Gaelic DONN. Gillies considered *odhar* 'one of the most difficult words in Gaelic to translate into English', and, in an effort to clarify its meaning, suggested 'a colour frequent in cattle, but rare in horses, in which *donn* is the prevailing colour';[1225] but whether that distinction generally makes much sense in the 21st century is arguable. I turn to Dwelly, who gave the following definitions, 'dun, dun-coloured, pale, sallow, drab, dapple, yellowish'.[1226] Take your pick!

The summit of **Cnoc Odhar** [667 129] is in Southend Parish, but only just, because the boundary with Campbeltown Parish passes immediately to its west. It stands at 907 ft. in a commanding position and must have afforded spectacular all-round views before its western slopes were planted with conifers; but the view east remains unobstructed across Southend to Sanda, Ailsa Craig and Arran. The summit can be reached by taking the forest track which ascends past Glenrea, and cutting through the trees at the track's highest point. From the forest's eastern edge, across a fence, a lovely moorland ridge rises, with the panorama beyond.

There are two hills named Cnoc Odhar in Killean Parish, one at 701 425 and the other at 707 438, called Cnoc Odhar Auchaluskin to distinguish it. The two were referred to in evidence taken in 1736 during the land dispute between John Macdonald of Largie and the 2nd Duke of Argyll. John MacIlchattan, Bellochgerran, stated: 'That at the time the people of Bellochgerran and Kilmory built the Dyke betwixt the two Cnockouers, there arose a Dispute betwixt the people of both Towns about the March ...'[1227]

OITIR has a range of meanings. Among those recorded by Dwelly are: 'bank or ridge in the sea', 'shoal, shallow', and 'low promontory jutting into the sea, rock projecting into the sea',[1228] to which may be added, as a further example, 'a fishing ground with sandy bottom in a sound or channel', recorded in South Uist in the late 19th century.[1229] The best known example of the name is attached to the mile-long sand-spit which juts out from the eastern shore of Loch Fyne. Just north of that spit, ferry-boats crossed the narrow upper loch between East Otter and West Otter, from at least the 16th century until the mid-20th century.[1230]

50. OITIR. Oitir Mór (upper left) and Oitir na Muice (below it, mid-left) bared at low tide, April 1996. Photograph by the author.

There are seven Kintyre *oitir* names, all of them on the south-east of the peninsula, and all, with one possible exception, matching the definition 'shoal, shallow'. The one exception is the northernmost of the seven, **Otter Ard**, off Smerby. Since it is submerged – some 10 ft. deep at the lowest ebb – and about a mile offshore, I assume that it was named by fishermen. It rarely reveals itself, and the late James MacDonald, in a lifetime as a fisherman, saw it 'blow' just twice, on both occasions with the combination of a spring tide and a southerly gale. He described as 'awesome' the sight of great seas breaking on the fleetingly bared rocks.[1231] Otter Ard has been interpreted as 'High shoal or sea-bank'.[1232] Since I have never seen it, I have no opinion to express.

The next one south is **Ootir Buie** [761 206], the sprawling rock-shelf below Davaar Lighthouse. It represents Gaelic *Oitir Buidhe*, 'Yellow Shoal' (see BUIDHE). It was not recorded by the Ordnance Survey and I heard of it first from Campbeltown and Dalintober fishermen I was tape-recording in the 1970s. Before motor power revolutionised the fishing industry, that shelf was one of the spots where fishermen could clamber ashore from a skiff and jam an anchor into a rock crevice to moor the skiff for the hauling of the ring-net. My uncle, Henry Martin, pronounced Oitir Buidhe 'ooter buie', which is exactly what you'd get if you translated 'outer buoy' into Scots; and he supposed that the name referred to a former navigation buoy, 'outer' in relation to a buoy which was moored off **Donal Stott's Broo** on the north side of Davaar Island, still within Campbeltown Loch and therefore 'inner'. *Oitir*, conventionally pronounced, was sometimes confused with the Otter (*Lutra lutra*), particularly in connection with the Otter Rock, below, because Otters do land on particular rocks to deal with catches, and opened shells of razor-fish and the remains of crabs litter these rocks, along with Otter excreta.

The next one south is **Oitir Carrach** [754 194], 'Rough or Rocky Shoal', which forms the ebbing point below Davaar House, then there is **The Otter** or **Otter Point** [768 164], a rock-shelf immediately north of the First Waters, with an attendant **Otter Rock**, in a disputed location. This one gave me much vexation, as related in *By Hill and Shore in South Kintyre*. I began to think about the place-name in the summer of 1998 while transcribing, for a second time, and more thoroughly, the tape-recordings I'd made of Kintyre and Ayrshire fishermen in the mid-1970s: 'Davie McLean, during the course of an anecdote, asked me if I knew where the Otter Point was, and, to my horror, I heard myself replying that I did. Well, I may have known its approximate location at that time, and I did have it noted, from the information of Duncan Newlands, on a map of fishermen's place-names I was compiling then; but I most certainly did not know precisely where it was. Davie was about to explain that to me, but I was no doubt keener to keep him on the narrative of his tale. Twenty-odd years on, it now struck me how worthless a name is if the feature it applies to is no longer recognised. But I was very lucky with the Otter Point ... James MacDonald was able to identify its location without hesitation ... which just goes to show that oral tradition can be a resilient agent, given the right circumstances.'[1233] An elderly woman, who, as a child, was taken by her father on picnics to the Learside, also knew its location, and I was keen that she too should identify it. Her verbal description was too ambiguous to be of value, so I asked her son, who had both a car and a camera, to drive her down the Learside and photograph the feature she would point out to him, but he never did, and she died with that scrap of knowledge I craved from her.

There are two more off Polliwilline, **Oitir Mór** [744 090] – in the middle of which the **Arranman's Barrels** sit – which translates as 'Big Shoal', and closer to shore **Oitir na Muice** [743 096], 'The Pig's Shoal', which might relate to a whale, which in Gaelic is *muc-mhara*, or 'sea-pig', at times shortened to *muc*, 'pig'. The last of them is another **Oitir Buidhe**, or 'Yellow Shoal', at the mouth of Sanda harbour.[1234]

It has been pointed out to me, concerning the article on Kintyre *oitir* place-names in *By Hill and Shore in South Kintyre*, that *oitir* is 'a feminine noun and aspirates the succeeding adjective, so *Oitir Mhór, Oitir Bhuidhe* ...' My response was that in local pronunciation and on Ordnance Survey maps, *oitir* in Kintyre would appear to be masculine, but Gilbert Márkus has considered the question and suggests that the lenition of feminine adjectives, where it is not represented graphically in written forms, might shift the local pronunciation of a place-name. 'This,' he adds, 'doesn't mean that the noun itself is locally treated in general as a masculine noun ... Something peculiar is going on between written forms, or very familiar elements, and their representation in place-names.'[1235]

PAIRC is 'park' and derives from English,[1236] but its standard application in Gaelic is not to a large open space, but to an enclosed field. It is, therefore, primarily a field-name, but there are a few examples of *pairc*/park habitation-names in Kintyre.

The farm of **Parkfergus** is in the Laggan. Only West [659 209] remains; East Parkfergus, also known as **The Rhue**, stood at 669 213, but was demolished. The construction of the name is Gaelic, but there is no record of it before the 19th century.[1237] Fergus (Gaelic, *Fearghas*), which also appears in the much older place-name Tirfergus (see TÌR), was not a common forename in Kintyre in recent centuries, though there were families named *Mac Fhearghuis* – anglicised as Ferguson – from the 17th century.[1238]

The names **High Park** [694 257] and **Low Park** [706 257], neighbouring hill farms north of Campbeltown, were in use by the late 18th century, but **Skeroblinraid** was the earlier name. Well into the 19th century, however, the names were in use interchangeably, a confusing business made all the more confusing by there being a nearby holding named **Skeroblingarry**. This muddle emerged in 1827 during evidence given in the Tangy Mill thirlage dispute.

Alexander McLean, Kilmaco: 'By Skerobline the depondent means Skeroblingary: That Skeroblineraid, which comprehends the High Park and the Low Park, was never bound to any mill.'

Alexander Ballantine, Achalochy: 'By Skeroblin the deponent means Skeroblingarry; but he does not know whether the Laigh [Low] Park is called Skeroblinraid or not.'

John Fleming, Ballivain: 'That Skeroblineraid or the Parks was understood not to be thirled to Tangie.'

Donald McBride, Drumelea: 'That the farm which the deponent has named Skeroblin in the above enumeration, is the farm now called Skeroblingarry.'[1239]

Even on the most modern of O.S. maps, Low Park appears as Skeroblinraid, a name I have never heard spoken in my entire life. When Paul McCartney bought High Park in June 1966, as a member of the Beatles he was one of the most famous men in the world, and the intense media interest brought Kintyre and that obscure little sheep-farm to international prominence. He later added Low Park and several other neighbouring farms to his Kintyre property, but since the death of his first wife, Linda Eastman, in 1998, his visits to Kintyre have been rarer. A memorial garden to Linda McCartney was created in the grounds of Campbeltown Museum, its centrepiece a life-sized bronze sculpture of Linda by Jane Robbins.

As examples of *pairc* field-names in Kintyre as a whole, I list all those collected by D. J. Macdonald:

A' phairc chùil: 'back park' (Rosshill);
Pairc a' Bharr: 'Barr park' (Portavorrain);
Pairc nam bà : 'cow park' (Largie);
Pairc dhubh: 'black park' (Glenbarr);
Pairc Fhionnlaidh: 'Finlay's park' (Portavorrain);
Pairc Mhòr: 'big park' (Drumnamucklach).[1240]

I shall add one more from his parish, which he appears to have missed. **Pairc Ailein** is 'Allan's Park', near Barr village. Latimer MacInnes received the name from an informant of his, A. McMurchy. The field was named after Allan Macintyre (1745-1840), foxhunter and bard. His *Gaelic Songs* was published in 1829 while he was at Barr.[1241] See SIONNACH.

PEIGHINN is Gaelic 'penny', early Irish *pinginn*, from Anglo Saxon *pending* and Norse *penningr*, now English *penny*.[1242]   For a sound analysis of old land values, refer to Andrew McKerral's *Kintyre in the Seventeenth Century*, Appendix III, in which he states that there is 'only one authentic instance of the use of the *pennyland* as a practical measure of land in Kintyre', that being the charter of Ugadale which King Robert the Bruce granted to Gilchrist Mackay in 1329.   The grant was for four pennylands, which were named and must equate to individual holdings, but the names are now unrecognisable.[1243]

All five *peighinn* names have been anglicised 'pen' or 'penny' and are in South Kintyre.   **Pennygown** is the 'Smith's pennyland', for which see under GOBHA/GOBHAINN.   **Peninver**, now a seaside village, was merely a 'few cottages with a schoolhouse' in 1866.[1244] The name may represent *Peighinn Ibhir*, 'Ivor's pennyland', as local pronunciation suggests, but Gillies decided on *Peighinn an inbhir*, 'the Inver penny-land',[1245] *inbhir* being a confluence of waters.   The earliest spellings are: 1502 'Peyningvir' and 'Pennynimir'; 1507 'Pennynymire'; 1545 'Peyninver'; 1596 'Penneneir'. [1246]

In Southend, the *peighinn* names are all problematic, none more so than **Pennysearach** [712 078], which was one of the Lands of Saint Ninian.   Its first appearance is probably as 'Pennanshelach' in 1584, followed by 'Pendinserak' in 1620.   In 1745 (Sanda rentals) and in late 18th and 19th century spellings, the specific is rendered '-surach', but local pronunciation is '-sairach'.   On Turner family headstones in Kilcolmkill, the specific is '-sorach' in 1796 and '-saragh' in 1857.   Census enumerators, being resident, sometimes provide spellings which, one suspects, capture local pronunciation with reasonable accuracy.   The spelling in 1841 was 'Pennysurach' and in 1851 'Penasaorach', but these constitute no advance on Roy's 'Pennysarach' or Langlands' 'Pennysurach'.   The O.S. was of no assistance linguistically, but noted improvements going on in 1866 at 'Pennysearach' – 'removing the old fences with a view to increase the size of enclosures'.[1247]   On the shore of this farm, there is a small rock pillar, the **Rat Stane** [711 074], into which steel pins were formerly driven by tenants to ensure the fertility of the land and the cattle on it.[1248]   Gillies suggested *Peighinn nan Searrach*, 'Pennyland of the foals',[1249] while the K.A.S. place-names committee tentatively offered *Peighinn saothrach* or *Peighinn na saothrach*, 'The toilsome pennyland', but not without a good deal of energetic debate, which also threw up, from among its Gaelic-speaking clergy: 'The cheap (or free) pennyland', 'The pennyland of plenty' and 'The pennyland abounding in primroses'.

For **Penlaughton** [719 082], which lay near Kilmashenachan and was also one of the Lands of Saint Ninian, old forms include: 1584 'Penlachna'; 1632 'Pendlachna'; 1751 'Penlachline' and 1793 'Penlaughton'. The interpretation in *The Place-Names of the Parish of Southend* is *Peighinn Lachdunn*, 'Dun-coloured pennyland', though the personal name Lachlan, which Dugald Macintyre Snr. preferred in *Peighinn Lachluinn*, was considered. About **Pennyland Mill** [710 095], now known simply as 'Pennyland', nothing apart from the name and three lines on land division appeared in *The Place-Names of the Parish of Southend*. If there was ever a mill there, I haven't heard or read about it, but Macharioch Estate appears to have been known as 'The Pennyland Estate' before becoming 'Ballyshear'. The charming but mysterious **Pingina** has been interpreted as *Na peighinnean*, 'The pennylands', and linked speculatively with both Machrimore (see **Tigh-Amorirna** under TIGH) and Macharioch.[1250] In *Reliquiae Celticae*[1251] there appears 'John Mor, Laird of Pingina in Kintyre'.

PLOC has a wide range of meanings, but in relation to place-names 'any round mass'[1252] is applicable. As 'plock', block of wood and potato-masher, I heard it from Kintyre Gaelic speakers or individuals brought up in Gaelic-speaking families; and 'plook' – Scots for a pimple, and still in use in Campbeltown – is also related.

The main place-name is **Pluck**, the round-headed point north of Saddell Bay [797 317], which appears as 'Ploc' on the Gordon map of c. 1644. A now-ruinous cottage [796 333] north of the point was also known as 'Pluck', and the name was revived in 2011 when a house built close to the top of Saddell Brae was named 'High Pluck'. Duncan Reid, roadman, was recorded at 'Saddell Pluck' in C1851, and he was followed by John Morrison, fisherman, who was there when the 1861 Census was taken.

From that family's residence there, the stretch of shore on which the cottage stood was known to fishermen as **Morrison's Bay** [797 334]. John Morrison and his family had moved to Saddell from Campbeltown, but his son Neil returned to Campbeltown. To him was given the honour of representing the Campbeltown fishermen at the opening ceremony of the great Fisheries Exhibition in London in 1883,[1253] and in partnership with his nephew, Daniel Morrison, he had a pair of skiffs, the *Agnes* and the *Elizabeth*, which latter was popularly known as 'Neil Morrison's Flying Machine', from her fast-sailing reputation.[1254]   His passion for speed appears to have been ingrained. As a side-show of the 1874 fishermen's regatta at Campbeltown, Neil – still living at Saddell – challenged any 23 ft. skiff to sail against his *Janet*, an early product of the Carradale self-taught boat-builder, Matthew McDougall. William Cook, with his *Jessie*, accepted the challenge but lost the race – and the £3 wager – by 23 seconds.[1255]

I recall the late Robert 'Bob' Morrison telling me that his father Daniel, as a boy at Saddell, was sent to Carradale on an errand, and when he returned to report that the article wasn't to be had there, his mother promptly despatched him to Campbeltown for it. That would be a total distance, on foot, of some 30 miles. Agnes Stewart was told that Daniel once walked from Saddell to Southend to attend a dance, an even longer round trip. I don't doubt the truth of these stories. Until the advent of the bicycle and, later, the motor car, such distances on foot were a fact of life in country places.

Agnes, traditional singer, local historian and latterly a Reader in the Church of Scotland, is descended from that Morrison family on her maternal line. Her mother, Agnes Rowatt Morrison, was the second-youngest of the nine children born to Daniel Morrison and Agnes Morrison Rowatt, who were second cousins and married in 1882, and she married Willie Mitchell, musician, poet, and song-collector, best remembered now for his much recorded composition, 'Road to Drumlemman'. Bob Morrison, above, was an uncle of Agnes Stewart's, and Dan Morrison, barber in Campbeltown, whose indefatigable *bonhomie* ensured him a niche in local memory, was her second cousin once removed.[1256]

There are two other examples of this element. The O.S. defined **Am Plocach** [684 130] as 'Abounding in turf', and described 'a mossy portion of ground'[1257] on Kilirvan farm, Southend, while the K.A.S. place-names committee plumped for 'The Humped Hill'.[1258] **Ploc Sgolaig** is a tidal rock at Sgolaig [916 622], a bay north of Skipness where fishermen formerly drew their boats ashore and camped. The rock formed part of a breakwater constructed with boulders cleared from the ebb.[1259]

POLL is a pool or hole. Its main appearance in Kintyre place-names is the Southend farm **Polliwilline**, which is *Poll a' mhuilinn*, 'Mill pond', dealt with in detail under **MUILEANN**. **Poll na Bó Dearg**, 'Hole of the Red Cow', is a rock cavity at Skipness.[1260] **Poll**

Bàn [c. 633 208], 'White fishing ground', to the west of Sgonn Mór at Machrihanish, was believed by Duncan Colville's informant to apply to a rock, but John Cameron corrected that misapprehension: '*Poll* is applied to a patch of sand among rocks where cod etc. are fished. Such spots are, in my experience, in fairly deep water (those nearer the shore are *bric*). The probability is that the fishing ground has given its name to an adjacent rock.'[1261] The popular fishing spot north of Port Rìgh which, in researching *The Ring-Net Fishermen* (p 247), I was given to understand was 'Balfadyen' (*Baile Phàidein*, 'Paidean's Farm'), was noted in 1942 by Charles Reppke as '**Polfadge**', therefore *poll* seems the likelier generic, which makes more sense there. For **Pollan Breac** see under BREAC.

PORT in any language is a little word, but it is heavy with significances. Most of the Kintyre 'ports' were in use for thousands of years, though archaeological proof would be difficult to find. The entire coast of Kintyre was populated until the 19th century, and boats were the simplest means of moving goods and people until the 20th century with its improved roads and motorised transport. For coast-dwellers, boats were almost the equivalent of cars nowadays. Fishermen, many of whom worked seasonally, were to be found not only in present-day fishing centres like Tarbert, Carradale and Campbeltown, but also in Skipness, Claonaig, Grogport, Port Rìgh, Torrisdale, Saddell, Southend, Pans, Bellochantuy and Muasdale, and scattered along the coast in isolated stations. Commerce with Ireland and Ayrshire and elsewhere was conducted not only from the larger population centres, but also from remoter harbours, particularly trade in illicit goods.

The vast majority of 'ports' in Kintyre were named in Gaelic, but some, which appeared in the 18th or 19th century, are clearly of Scots/English origin. In Gaelic, *port* will derive from Old Irish *port*, 'a place, a haven', which is ultimately Latin *portum*, 'a harbour, haven, port'. In Dwelly's Gaelic dictionary, *port* has many meanings, but Nils M. Holmer, in *Studies on Argyllshire Gaelic*, gives two definitions, 'small inlet or natural harbour',[1262] which will suffice here, except that in some cases a port may be man-made.

I have noticed such 'ports' on the Learside, notably on Glenahervie and Corphin shores. They are passageways, for the beaching and launching of small boats, and were created by the clearance of boulders from the ebb. They are clearly the work of fishermen, whose stone huts will be found nearby. Perhaps they all had names once, but I know of only one, the **Dummy's Port** [771 143], north of Ru Stafnish. The 'Dummy' was Donald MacIsaac, a brother of John MacIsaac, tenant of Corphin farm, now ruinous on the hillside above the port. There are actually two ports immediately north of the single-roomed stone house which Donald – a deaf mute – occupied as a summer fishing station.[1263] For Donald's fate, see Dunglas under GLAS.

There is also a man-made port at Smerby, which leads to a rough-built jetty known as the **Quay Rocks** [758 230]. It looks as though the boulders cleared away to create the channel went into the making of the jetty, which makes perfect sense. The jetty was used in shipping Smerby potato crops in the 19th century. There is little room for manoeuvre at the jetty itself, and I was told by James McNair that 'flat-bottomed boats' would come in and load up; the smack itself would presumably anchor offshore. **Smerby** is a purely Norse name, representing *smjorr*, 'butter' + *by-r*, 'farm'. It is a quiet spot now, but was once a thriving community with a cluster of farms, a meal-mill, a wool-fulling mill and, earlier, a medieval castle perched on the promontory of **Isla Muller** [756 224], 'Miller's Isle', which is linked to the mainland by an eroding causeway.[1264]

51. PORT. Looking into Port na h-Olainn, 'The Wool Port', summer of 1980. Photograph by Agnes Stewart.

Port is one of the commonest of place-name elements in Kintyre, thanks to the peninsula's long indented coastline. In my lists, I have counted 100 port names, 42 of them in Saddell and Skipness parish and only one, Portachoillan, in Kilcalmonell; but there would certainly have been many more which were never recorded and have disappeared from memory.

52. PORT. *A smack beached at Port Crannaig, c. 1920, with net-drying poles and Carradale fishermen's sheds along Shore Road. Author's collection.*

Port na h-Olainn [592 131], north of the Mull, translates as 'The Wool Port'. Agnes Stewart vaguely remembers hearing about wool-smuggling between Kintyre and Rathlin, and, as she remarks, 'that wee port is ideally situated for a quick trip to Rathlin in favourable weather conditions'. The foundation of the smuggling tradition is clear enough, though. When the tenants in the old run-rig farms east and north of the Mull were being ousted to make way for sheep in the late 18th century, the incoming sheep-farmers were forbidden to export their wool. When the 5th Duke of Argyll leased 'Inendounan' and 'Innencocallach' in 1775 to Colin and John Campbell and Colin McEachran, 'Graziers in Kintyre', they were to 'occupy the lands entirely as a sheep farm and not export wool produced to Ireland, but to sell the whole of it in Kintyre'.[1265] In 1773, Edward and John

Murray petitioned the Justices of the Peace Court in Campbeltown for the return of a 'parcel of wool' seized from them at Carskey by Lauchland McNeall, Surveyor of the Customs, and 'taken to Campbeltown on suspicion that it was to be taken to Ireland'.[1266] There is one certainty – no one in his right mind would choose to use Port na h-Olainn if there was a better alternative, which lends some credence to the smuggling tradition. The terrain above the port is steep and rocky, and the port itself, exposed as it is to the full weight of the open Atlantic, is a treacherous spot. Agnes and her husband, Allister, descended to the shore in 1980 and found 'a fairly deep inlet in the rocks', accessible by small boats, but only in calm weather.[1267]

53. PORT. Port na Cusaig, or should that be Portan Àluinn? Photograph by George McSporran, April 1970.

From sheep to cattle. **Port a' Chruidh** [920 585] is a small shingly inlet north of Skipness which translates as 'The Cattle Port'. Angus Graham, in his *Skipness* (p 10), remarks that the port was used by 'ordinary traffic', destined for Ayrshire, as well as by cattle-drovers, and noted 'at least one hole, for a mooring-rope ... bored through the rock on the south'. Its use as a port was superseded in 1838 when a harbour was built a little to the north, at the **Red Wharf** [920 589], as fishermen called that quay, from its red sandstone blocks. There was a settlement, now in ruins, on a bluff above the landing-place at Port a' Chruidh, which in 1855 contained three tenants.

Perhaps the most puzzling of all the *port* names is **Grogport** [809 442], attached to the tiny village north of Carradale. 'Grogport', in any form, is absent from the Langlands maps of 1793 and 1801, signifying that it had not yet come into existence. It seems to me a possibility that Grogport was an outgrowth of nearby **Garrachroit**, which was more inland than coastal. In Mary McMurchy's testimony after the violent death of Duncan McPhee in 1821, she said that she was 'met in the village of Garrochriot' by Flory McCallum, wife of her brother Edward Hyndman.[1268] Whether 'village' was the word she used is certainly conjectural – her evidence may have been translated from Gaelic – but Garrachroit was a sizeable community at that time (see CROIT). Most of the men there were fishermen, and it may have been that some families decided they could operate more conveniently from houses built along the shore. Certainly, by C1851 there were five households at Grogport and only a farmer and a fisherman, both named Stalker, left at 'Garchroit'. The first mention of Grogport which I have been able to find dates to 1840, the birth of Mary McPhee, daughter of Donald McPhee and Christina McKellar, 'Grogport', who was born and baptised on the same day, 11 October.[1269] McPhee was one of the half-dozen names recorded in Garachroit in 1821.

Various derivations have been suggested for 'Grogport', but the name continues to resist a definitive explanation. In 1943, however, Charles Reppke submitted two interesting local traditions to the Kintyre Antiquarian Society: 'Opinion is divided regarding the meaning. Illicit still whisky was shipped from this place but it is also suggested that the name should be "Crockport", the port of Cnoc na Coileach, a hill above the village.' To these notes may be added my own. 1. 'Grog' has no clear connection to whisky, but has several meanings relating to alcohol, the most common of which equates it with naval rum, and the term would have been familiar to generations of local seamen. 2. 'Cnoc na Coileach' has not been recorded elsewhere, and was probably meant for **Cnoc na Coille** (see under COILLE). 3. Had the port taken its name from a *cnoc*, the result, given that the people there in the 19th century were Gaelic-speaking, would more likely have taken a Gaelic form, say *Port a' Chnoc*.[1270] In Brackley graveyard, an unusual slate monument dated 1855 poignantly commemorates the 'departed children' of 'Archd Carmichael Boat Man Grogport'.

All down that east coast in the 19th century there were boatmen for ferrying passengers and goods to and from sailing vessels and, later, Clyde steamers. Donald Taylor, 'boat man in Skipness', raised a stone in Kilbrannan for his father Archibald, 'croft man in Skipness', who died in 1817 aged 61 and was 'much lemented by his sorraufull widow Christian McKinven'.

Lachie's Port [790 312] at Saddell – **Port na Cuthaig** on O.S. maps – was a fishermen's place-name and commemorates Lachlan Galbraith, Gigha-born ferryman there in the early 20th century.[1271] In the first half of the 19th century, Dugald McMillan was ferryman at **Port Crannaig** [819 386], across which Carradale Quay is now built.   His daughter Elizabeth was baptised at 'Portchranaig' on 9/12/1820, and in C1851 his was the only house recorded there. By 1869 he was a widower in Port Rìgh, his 10 surviving children dispersed across Scotland or abroad, except for son Donald, a fisherman living at home.[1272] The O.S. form of the name was 'Port Crannaich', for which the derivation 'plough-shaped' was offered,[1273] but this seems highly unlikely, and Graham McKinlay's suggestion of *crannag*, 'pulpit', in 1977, may be preferred, particularly since the harbour is overlooked by a rocky height known as **Dùn Crannaig** [820 385]. However interpreted, the specific appears to be *crannag*, from *crann*, 'tree', which also gives the loan-word into English, 'crannog', a lake-dwelling (see under LOCH).

Port MacCùca is 'MacCook's Port' and attached to the bay where the first MacCook, or Cook, was said to have landed as a fugitive from Arran. The location of the port is now unknown, but Angus Cook in Crossaig, who gave the story to Nils M. Holmer more than 70 years ago, would certainly have been able to point it out. The full Gaelic text of 'How the Cooks Came to Kintyre' is in *The Gaelic of Kintyre* (pp. 137 & 139), and I published an abridged English version in *Kintyre: The Hidden Past* (p 209). This, further reduced, is the story. Cook and his son, who lived at Pirnmill, were expert bowmen and were killing deer. When the king of Arran, *Glas nan Cailleach* ('Grey One of the Old Women'), heard of the killings, he hanged Cook's son, and would have hanged Cook, too, but the old man, when summoned before the king, tricked him into removing his helmet and split his skull with a concealed axe. He escaped to Kintyre in a waiting boat, landed at the bay later given his name, was granted the protection of Clan Donald and prospered.

Some of the little ports have charming associations. One such is **Port nam Maighdeag** [634 208] at Machrihanish. Duncan Colville rescued this name from Dugald Fraser in 1928.[1274] Its meaning is 'port of the cowries', and I guess that *maighdeag* is related to *maighdeann*, 'virgin, maiden', because the underside of the cowrie shell, with its slit, greatly resembles the vulva, and cowries were formerly locally known as 'maiden-shells'. Two species of cowrie can be found on Kintyre beaches, *Trivia monacha* and *Trivia arctica*, which are similar in appearance but easily distinguishable since the former has spots on the upper part of its shell. Cowries are among the most attractive of native sea-shells, but I am not aware that they had any decorative uses in Kintyre. As a child, I enjoyed hunting for them on the few shores where I knew I could find them, particularly the shingly beach west of Dunaverty Bay. On 6/2/2012, my 60th birthday, my wife Judy and I travelled out to Machrihanish by bus, to celebrate my retirement and qualification for a travel pass. It was a fine sunny day and we picnicked at Uisaed and then walked the length of the Galdrans. While waiting for the evening bus home, I decided to search Port nam Maighdeag for cowries. Having had no success, I began scraping the shingle back and eventually found one shell before the bus arrived. It was enough to validate the name and I returned home, content, with that solitary cowrie in a pocket.

54. *PORT. A bracken-filled fishermen's hut, abutting a rock, at Port Mìn/ Glemanuill Port/ Port na Maoile, October 1982. Photograph by the author.*

Port Mean [643 065] is *Port Mìn*, 'Smooth or Calm Port', which seems an odd description for an inlet on the exposed south coast of Kintyre; but the sense is no doubt 'relative', and in any case

Glemanuill Port was the preferred local name by the 20th century, and **Port na Maoile**, 'Port of the Mull', the name given to it by the Islay fishermen who used it.[1275] **Port Garbh** [645 067], just to the east, is 'Rough Port', and the contrast was probably intentional. In 1866, the original O.S. interpretation was 'Little Port', which suggests that the specific was taken to be English; but a later hand queried this eccentricity: 'Should it not be "Port Mìn", smooth port in contradistinction to Port Garbh?'[1276] Port Mean's relative calm – or perhaps cleanness of seabed – is confirmed by its having been a fishing station for Rhinns of Islay handline fishermen who prosecuted a summer cod fishery at the Mull until 1915. They lived in turf-and-stone huts, which may still be seen, and kept their boats hauled up on the shore. They'd use the ebb tide to get them to the Mull, fish during slack water, and return on flood tide to the port, where they'd clean and salt the fish and spread them on rocks to dry. The bulk of their catch was taken to Ireland for sale at the Ballycastle Lammas Fair in August.[1277] Fish sold locally were landed either at Dunaverty or at a rocky creek west of Dunaverty Bay, which is still remembered as the **Islaymen's Port** [681 077].[1278]

Just west of that port is another, **Keil Port** [678 077], which the Ordnance Survey in 1866 described as 'a small landing port for boats facing Keil Mansion house'.[1279] In 1774 Archibald Lamont, lessee of the public house and ferry at Monirua, complained that Angus McMillan, cottar in Carrine, was ferrying passengers to Ireland, and asked for £10 in damages plus legal costs. McMillan contended that he had not interfered with Lamont's ferry and that his own 'wherry' was kept 'at the Carskiey water and sailed either there or at the port of Kilcolmkill'.[1280]

Portan Àluinn [655 071], below Garvalt on the Mull road, translates as 'Beautiful Little Port',[1281] but I am not the only person to wonder if the Ordnance Survey got the location right. The nearby bay named **Port na Cusaig** [652 072] on maps is startlingly beautiful, with its curve of white sand, while one would pass by Portan Àluinn without giving it a second glance (unless the aesthetic judgement was formed from seaward). The O.S. name-book, however, confirms the geographical relationship: Portan Àluinn, 'Pretty port', a 'landing place for boats', is indeed 'east of Port na Cusaig', which is defined as 'Port of the wild mustard'.[1282] *The Place-Names of the Parish of Southend* (p 29) preferred *Port na cuiseige*, 'Port of the couch-grass'. A township **Ballanancusag** – *Baile nan cuiseige*, 'Township of the couch-grass'[1283] – stood nearby. It appears on Roy's map as 'Ballnagushag'.

In July 2012, while I was still pondering these seeming incongruities, a friend in Linlithgow, Bob Smith, former curator of Auchindrain Museum and a dedicated angler, wrote to me advising caution with O.S. maps. His examples were not ports, but lochs: 'I came across two lochans, on the hill between lochs Fyne and Awe, which were on the map as "Lochan Garbh" (Rough Lochan) and "Lochan nam Breac Buidhe" (Lochan of the Yellow Trout). When you fished them both, you discovered that they had been mis-named – and I think I know exactly how that came about, an O.S. surveyor taking directions from a native, only without an on-the-spot confirmation. The lochan named as the "Lochan of the Yellow Trout" is as rough as a bothy cat, shallow with a rock-bound shore and with scores of boulders sticking up all over it, its trout wee black things. Half-a-mile away, the "Rough Lochan" is something from a picture postcard, its trout fat and beautiful golden creatures, well-besprinkled with big red spots. So there.'[1284]

The Champion Port, north of Carradale harbour, was a latecomer, perhaps the last of the port names. The bay was named by Carradale fishermen after a motor smack, the *Champion* of Ayr, was wrecked there with a cargo of timber in October 1916.[1285] A solitary inland example, **Black Fisher's Port**, appears on a revised map of Machrihanish, dated 1829, near the steading of Strabane [661 222]. See under LOCH for the Black Fisherman himself. For **Port Rìgh** see Crois Mhic Aoidh under CROIS and for **Port Sgadain** under SGADAN.

PUBULL comes through Old Irish *pupall* from Latin *papilio*, 'butterfly, tent'[1286] and essentially means a tent, or a booth. In Kintyre, the name survives only in **Puball Burn** [712 262]. When revising *The Place-Names of the Parish of Campbeltown*, I postulated (p 39) an association with outdoor religious assembly and referred to Sir David Wilkie's 'Tent Preaching at Kilmartin', drawn in 1817. Later, when examining the Ordnance Survey name-books, I found the **Circle of Puball** [712 262], an oval earthwork close to Puball Burn, described by Mr Buchanan in East Skeroblingarry and Mr McPherson in Gobagrennan as 'a place where worship was wont to be held in troublesome times'.[1287]

When the brothers James and Robert Haldane, itinerant evangelists, came to Kintyre in 1800, they were preaching up to four sermons a day in different places, and at Campbeltown drew congregations of over a thousand to 'the green slope of a hill'. The local ministers they condemned as being 'deeply immersed in farming, fishing or trading in sheep or cattle'. Robert Haldane was a great-grandfather of Naomi Haldane, who, with her husband, Dick Mitchison, bought Carradale Estate in 1938.[1288] Cuthbert Bede was an 'accidental witness' to an open-air Gaelic service at Barr, which he described in *Glencreggan* (Vol. II, pp. 222-26) and sketched the following morning from memory. Of course, outdoor assemblies predate Christianity, never mind Protestant evangelism! See also FRAOCH.

55. PUBULL. *'Open-air preaching in Cantire' by Cuthbert Bede, c. 1859. From Glencreggan, Vol. II, p 223.*

Another **Pubill** appears conjoined with **Innean Gaothach** (see GAOTH) in leases, e.g. in 1605 and 1709.[1289] The location of this Pubill is unknown, but Duncan MacNeill, Dalsmeran, told Archie

McEachran that an 'old ruin on the north side of Glenadale had a name which he couldn't remember, but which resembled Fiunvall to the best of his recollection'. An ancestor of MacNeill's died in that place 'at the time of the great plague'[1290] (c. 1647). Was 'Fiunvall' a distorted echo of 'Pubill'? The one is as obscure as the other.

Denis Rixson has suggested that both of these 'pubull' names might incorporate Old Norse *ból*, a 'farm'. For the latter he cites an early form 'Bugill' in 1596, as well as the 1605 'Pubill' and another 'Pubill' in 1678.[1291]

RAINEACH is 'fern', of which bracken (*Pteridium aquilinum*) is the most conspicuous of the many species. In fact, it is now rampant in Kintyre. In the early 19th century, 'forests' of bracken grew towards the south end of Sanda. They 'all but overtopped a man' and were 'as thick as your finger', descriptions which contemporary hill-walkers will recognise. These Sanda brackens served 'as padding on the beam athwart ship, in which the fishing rods were inserted',[1292] a somewhat arcane use, it appears to me. In general, bracken was used as thatch for roofs and as bedding for animals. Bizarre though it now seems, in 1792 five 'servant maids' were each ordered to pay 12s damages for 'cutting and stealing away' 40 cartloads of bracken which Dugald Campbell of Kilmartin had intended for thatch.[1293] **Ranachan**, a hill and two farms [High 704 243, Low 697 245] near Campbeltown, has been interpreted *raineachan*, 'little ferny place'.[1294] John McLean, tenant in Low Ranachan, stated in a memorial dated 14/9/1830 that his 'great-grandfather, grandfather, and his father all occupied and died on the farm of Ranachan where the memorialist himself has resided from his birth till his present advanced age of 70 years'.[1295] The family was certainly there in 1686, when John McLean in Ranachan was summoned before the Justices of the Peace Court for 'irregularities in church attendance'.[1296] **Creagan Rainich** [789 345] on Whitestone was interpreted 'Ferny Craig' by the O.S. in 1867.[1297]

REAMHAR is basically 'fat', from Early Irish *remor*, 'thick'.[1298] In place-names, this adjective is attached to hills, and 'fat' is often used to translate it. The concept, topographically, is perhaps hard to grasp, but there are other recognised meanings which might better suit: 'plump', 'big', 'great', 'thick', 'gross, of great circumference'.[1299] In all Kintyre instances the generic is *cnoc*, thus **Cnoc Reamhar**. There is none in Campbeltown Parish; one in Southend at 615 113;

two in Killean and Kilchenzie, at 704 352 and (collected by D. J. Macdonald) on Tangy farm; one in Kilcalmonell at c. 859 662, and three in Saddell and Skipness, 839 540, 797 428, and 779 461.

RIABHACH is a common adjective in place-names, and Kintyre has its share, but its meanings do not translate well. I'll list those in Dwelly's dictionary: 'brindled', 'greyish', 'grizzled', 'brown', and 'drab'.[1300] In Irish, 'striped' or 'tabby', but 'often translated as "grey" in place-names'.[1301] Professor MacKinnon offers 'heather-colour', 'brindled', and 'brown'.[1302] Cameron Gillies devotes a paragraph to *riabhach* in his introduction to *The Place-Names of Argyll*. He notes that the usual translation is 'brindled', a word which is worth defining, because it isn't exactly in common use now. From the *Concise Oxford Dictionary*: 'Brownish or tawny with streaks of other colour.' Gillies, however, provides a short-cut to comprehension with an ornithological example: 'The most exact meaning, however, is that it is the colour of the lark – the *riabhag*.'[1303] I have watched skylarks, as dots in the air, for most of my life, but can't say that I have ever been close enough to one to notice its plumage; but I know from illustrations that it is browny-drab, like that of sparrows, and that's as far as I'm going to get; but it isn't far enough to enable me to look at a hill or field, once deemed *riabhach*, and see what Gaelic speakers hundreds of years ago saw and named with confidence. In short, a once-comprehensible word-picture eludes this observer for whom the language of his ancestors has become a store-house with some of the rooms locked. I asked a friend in Lewis, Donald MacLeod, who is a native Gaelic speaker, to define the word for me, and he obligingly provided a package from which I have selected bits relative to landscape: 'I'm not sure that any one English word will cover its meanings. A drab mixture of colours, usually a dark brown background streaked with greys, or vice-versa. Often applied to moorland, particularly a drab autumn/winter mixture of dark browns and faded greens.'[1304]

A few examples of Kintyre place-names will suffice. **Knockrioch**, near Stewarton, is *Cnoc riabhach*, 'Brindled hill', with the High farm at 701 197, the Low at 694 200 and the Little at 694 197. **Tonrioch** [692 198], nearby, represents *Tòn riabhach*, which is translated in *The Place-Names of the Parish of Campbeltown* as 'The brindled bluff',[1305] but 'backside' or 'arse' for *tòn* might nowadays be preferred. **Maysreoch** has been interpreted similarly as 'The brindled or speckled hump', *Màs riabhach*, but the straightforward meaning of *màs* is 'the buttock'.[1306] As a place-name, Maysreoch has disappeared, but in 16th century charters it was linked with Balegreggan and may later have been given the unrelated name **Whitehill** [716 222].[1307] **Crockinreoch** [786 326] was a farm at the foot of Saddell Glen, but the name was changed to 'Lephinmore', evidently after an alleged murder there in 1936.[1308] It represents *Cnocan Riabhach*, 'Brindled Hillock'. **Rubha Riabhach** [834 495], 'Brindled Point', a headland north of Cour, has a namesake for a near-neighbour south-east across the Kilbrannan Sound at Pirnmill.[1309]

ROC. The generic *roc* for 'rock' in Kintyre appears to be confined to the Tarbert area. **Roc a' Chaisteil**, 'The Castle Rock', isn't in Kintyre. It's in the sea north of Kintyre – see the map of Tarbert fishermen's place-names in *The Ring-Net Fishermen*, p 245 – but refers to Tarbert Castle, which is in Kintyre. The castle was the 'mark' which line-fishermen employed to get their boats above the rock. When they had gone a certain distance north from Tarbert harbour – about 200 yards past the Horse's Bight, Hugh MacFarlane reckoned – they would 'open' (bring into view) the castle 'on' (over) Carvel Point, and the rock was seven or eight fathoms below, with its congregation of whitings, haddocks and cod.[1310] **Roc an Sgadan Ghréine**, 'Rock of the Sunned Herring', is examined under GRIANAN, and on the north shore of Tarbert harbour there was also the O.S. 'Roc nam Buitseach', which George Campbell Hay considered incorrect and amended to **Roc a' Bhuidse**, 'The Wizard's Rock'.[1311] When I mentioned Roc a' Chaisteil to Rev Donald Mackenzie, Auchterarder, in 1979, he wondered at that borrowing from English, 'since there are already in Gaelic so many precise terms for different kinds of rock, e.g. *sgeir*, *bodha*, *creag*, etc'.[1312]

ROS, 'promontory' – see under EILEAN.

RUADH, like DEARG, is 'red', and Gillies remarks that between the two words – from the pale tones of the Roe Deer, or *ruadhag*, to 'intensest scarlet' – 'the gradation is practically infinite'.[1313] **Dalaruan**, once a village but absorbed into Campbeltown in the 19th century, and **Knock Ruan/Loch Ruan**, to the north of town, may or may not derive from *ruadh*. See *The Place-Names of the Parish of Campbeltown* and Schedules for the cold rags which once clothed a heated debate, and compare, for example, with Irish Drumaroan, *Droim an Ruáin*, 'Ridge of the red place'.[1314]

Creag Ruadh [691 436], 'Red Rock', is south of Killean. As 'Cregruadh' it was described in C1851 as a farm occupied by 'Dougd Currie'. In 1915 the *Scottish Farmer* published a 'fine snapshot of the Tayinloan rams' which belonged to Neil Currie, 'Craigrua', who 'took the highest average at the Ardrishaig sale this season'. Neil collapsed and died at the age of 60 in November 1920 while giving a neighbour 'a day' discharging a coal-boat on Killean shore.[1315] A grandfather of Neil Thomson in Muasdale told him, when he was a boy, about a mysterious hand-mill at Creag Ruadh. 'The grindin-stone would start goin; they could hear it and they always were at the old man about this, that the grindin-stone was goin again without anybody with it. "Yes," he says, "I hear it of'en enough, but I've never come on it goin."'[1316]

Allt Ruadh [872 605], 'Red Burn', flows into Abhainn Leim nam Meann south of Cruach Tarsuinn, **Cruach Ruadh** [787 451], north of Carradale Glen, is '"Red Hill", from colour of ground', and **Peileir Ruadh** [777 423], 'Red Ball', is a little knoll, now covered in coniferous forest, described in 1867 as 'the source of Allt a' chaoruinn'.[1317] For **Ballochroy** see under BEALACH.

RUBHA, often spelled *Rudha* or shortened to *Rubh'*, is a point or promontory, usually on the coast and usually, among surviving place-names at any rate, attached to a prominent feature. It occurs along the entire coast of Kintyre, from West Loch to East Loch Tarbert, sometimes tautologically. On O.S. maps, **Rhu Point** [825 638], north of Kennacraig, is an example of Gaelic *rubha* having an English equivalent unwittingly tagged on to it. In the case of **Ru Stafnish** [772 138], on the Learside, the earlier Norse name for the point, *Stafa-nes*, 'Headland of the precipice', had *rudha* added to it,[1318] presumably after Norse influence had waned in Kintyre and the name had become obscure. On the mid-17th century Gordon map, however, only the garbled Norse form 'Staphanich' appears; *rubha* is absent. The name contains the same element as in Staffa, which is usually defined as 'stave-island' from the volcanic pillar-rocks there.[1319]

The best-known *rubha* place-name in Kintyre is **Rhunahaorine**, because a village [707 484] grew up close to the point [689 493] and took its name. The O.S. in 1867 ventured the derivation *Rudha na h-Airne*, 'The Point or Promontory of the Sloes'.[1320] D. J. Macdonald more sensibly suggested *Rudha na aoireann*, 'the point of the beach or of the low-lying land near the sea ...'[1321] See also AOIREANN. In his analysis of the 'growth' of the name, Cameron Gillies speculates that 'when the English Survey-man came, he named the promontory upon the farm, and called it Rhunahaoirine *Point*'.[1322] In fact, the tautology pre-dated the arrival of the Ordnance Survey in 1867. In the *Argyllshire Herald* of 23/9/1863, for instance, the let of 'the Farm of RHUNAHAORINE POINT' is advertised. Many linguistic crimes are ascribed to the Ordnance Survey, some justified and some not, as in the above case. The fact is that the Survey accurately recorded numerous minor place-names which would otherwise have been lost. Old spellings include: 1502-7 'Rynahierin', 'Rynnaheryng', and 'Rinahierine'; 1627 'Rownahearin'; 1675 'Rownaherring'.

Rhunahaorine was once a populous settlement. In the work horse tax list of 1797-8, nine horse-owners are named at 'Runaherin', with a total of 21 animals.[1323] C1841 records 30 occupied houses at 'Runehorine', and the O.S. in 1867 describes a 'small village' in which 'The majority of the houses are in indifferent repair, and occupied by labourers'.[1324] Neil 'PO' Thomson in Muasdale had this to say in 1977: 'I used tae hear ma grandfather tellin about the number of people that was in Rhunahaorine, and he used tae have two names that always surprised me and stuck in ma mind, was "High Street" and "Shore Street", so there must've been a row of houses, or rows of houses, and that there was twelve tailors, so there were quite a number of people.' Ian MacDonald in 2010 told me that these houses occupied both sides of the present A83 road. Rhunahaorine is also remembered for the skirmish on the Moss there, on 24/5/1647, between General David Leslie's Covenanting army and the Royalist force under Alasdair MacColla (Lieut-General Sir Alexander MacDonald), which precipitated MacColla's flight to Ireland and culminated in the massacre at Dunaverty. Willie McGougan said that the fighting began at Rhunahaorine Dun [709 485] and 'carried on right down to the wood', and that many of the rebel dead were supposed to be buried near the end of the wood, at a place he called **Cnocan Dùn Mór**, 'Hillock of the Big Fort'.[1325] 'Old Largie Castle', seat of the Macdonalds of Largie, was at High Rhunahaorine [708 483], but little remained of it by the mid-19th century. Nowadays, one can pass Rhunahaorine without noticing the least sign of its past. The population there, largely a seasonal one, is now concentrated in Point Sands caravan site.

There are 32 recorded *rubha* place-names on the coasts of Kintyre, by my reckoning, and, skulking inland, a possible 33rd, **The Rhue** [669 213], which was the alternative name for East Parkfergus;[1326] but, since that farm was merged with West Parkfergus and its steading demolished, 'The Rhue' is a name now seldom heard. As mentioned earlier, most *rubha* names attach to prominent coastal features, but two, for minor rock features on the west side of Uisaed, were marked on an old Lossit Estate map which Duncan Colville examined some 80 years ago: **Rubha Dubh** [625 207] 'Black Point', and **Rubha Mór** [625 200] 'Big Point'.[1327]

I conclude with another minor name, **Rubha Bhàltair** [888 671], which George Campbell Hay mentioned in 1979. No one had spoken of it to me before and I never heard of it again, but that does not surprise me because a minor place-name, in its final years of survival, might be preserved by only a few individuals. I presume he heard it from one of the fishermen – Calum Johnson or his like – with whom he went to sea in the 1930s. It means 'Walter's Point' and is the little point between the shingly 'port' into which Allt Beithe runs and the next port south of that one. George was also told of an **Uamh Bhàltair** – 'Walter's Cave' – on the hillside above, but was unable to find it. 'Walter' might, at first sight, seem a rather strange name in Kintyre, but it featured prominently in the Campbells of Skipness from the 16th century on, and was adopted by the Campbell commonalty and persists in Carradale and beyond, having been transferred to other families, in particular the McConnachies (arguably Campbells themselves, anyway) through marriage. For **Rubha Clach an Tràghaidh** see under CLACH.

56. *RUBHA. Ru Stafnish from the* Waverley *paddle-steamer, 1/6/2012. Photograph by the author.*

RUIGHE is, assuredly, a mild, retiring element, which has never enjoyed prominence in Kintyre, but local interpretations are interesting in their diversity. First, to Alexander Macbain for a look inside the engine of the name. It is 'an arm, forearm', and then 'the outstretched part or base of a mountain, shealing ground'. As to etymology: Irish *righ*, Early Irish *rige*, *rigid*, 'a reach, reaches', from the root *reg*, 'stretch'.[1328] If the foregoing still hold good, a perception begins to take shape, which I shan't blur with additional definitions. What were the local interpretations? I turn first to D. J. Macdonald's treasure-house, 'West Kintyre Field Names'. He records 10 *ruighe* names, 5 of which he defines as 'field', 2 of which as 'ground' and 3 of which he omitted or declined to define.[1329] Whether these definitions were based on physical observation, local information, or scholarly deduction is unclear. In *The Place-Names of the Parish of Southend*, for which the main Gaelic authority was John Cameron, the standard interpretations of *ruighe* are 'slope' and 'sloping field', as in **Ruighe Gorm** [c. 763 133], which was a croft, of which no trace remains, directly below Feochaig steading, and interpreted as 'the green slope'.[1330] D. J. Macdonald's **Ruighe gorm** he interpreted as 'Blue field', but there is no conflict. As far as is known, *ruighe* in Kintyre was not used to denote a 'shieling', which was invariably ÀIRIGH.

Ruighe, in its sense of 'arm' or 'forearm', may be classed among those anatomical terms in Gaelic which have transferred to topographical features. Some, such as *màm* and *cìoch*, both a woman's breast and applied to rounded hills, do not occur in Kintyre place-names, but several others do, including GUALANN, 'shoulder', LURGANN, 'shin', SRÒN, 'nose', TEANGA, 'tongue', TÒN, 'backside', and UCHD, 'breast'. **Glunimore** [742 050], the rocky island near Sanda, has been interpreted as 'A great knee' and 'Big knee' – *glùn*, 'knee' + *mór*, 'big'[1331] – which, if its appearance is anything to judge by, is absolutely sound. An old tradition in Southend held that 'if two sheep were put upon it they would die of fatness, and if four were put upon it they would die of hunger'.[1332]

SABHAL is a barn, a roofed building in which grain was stored and winnowed in the through-draft between facing doors. Barns were invariably built across the prevailing wind, and dwelling-houses end-on to the wind, useful points in the identification of ruins.[1333] There were two farms named **Auchnasavil** – *Achadh an t-sabhail*, 'Field of the barn' – one in Carradale Glen [790 394] and the other near Carskey. **Cnoc Sabhail** [636 204], a distinctive flat-topped hillock at Lossit, is 'Barn Hill', explained in 1866 as 'a hill where the grain in olden times were (*sic*) sifted from the chaff'.[1334] On a chart of the Firth of Clyde, dated 1846, it is named 'Consaval', which corresponds to local pronunciation in the early part of the 20th century, 'Consafell'.[1335] **Cnoc an t-sabhail**, 'Barn hillock', is on High Bellochantuy farm.[1336]

SAGART is a priest, and the word is familiar, even if disguised, in the local surname MacTaggart, which represents *Mac an t-sagairt*, 'Son of the priest'. This was one of the ecclesiastical surnames cited by Professor MacKinnon as being 'frequently brought forward to prove that celibacy was never enforced in the Gaelic church'.[1337] The Catholic religion was effectively eradicated in Kintyre in the 17th century, notwithstanding the efforts of Irish Franciscan missionaries to preserve it. Anna ncDonald, 'ane obstinat papist' in Kintyre, refused to relinquish her religion and in 1652 was excommunicated by the Protestant Synod of Argyll.[1338]

Clach an t-sagairt [830 518], near Crossaig, is 'The priest's stone', also known as 'The Priest's Chair', from its resemblance to a chair. It is actually a prehistoric cup-marked stone.[1339] **Tùr an t-Sagairt** [908 577], 'The Priest's Tower', is referred to in the *Second Statistical Account* in 1843 as a tower at the north-east end of Skipness Castle. No tradition is recorded, but there was a 13th century chapel nearby, dedicated to Saint Columba, which was later incorporated within the castle walls.[1340] **Glebe an t-Sagairt**, near Clachan, is 'Glebe of the Priest': English 'glebe', church land, with the Gaelic specific. The record was transcribed from the Benefice Register of the Presbytery of Kintyre by Duncan Colville: 'There is a large extent of land at Loch Kiaran side which was once Church property, and may possibly still be claimed as such. The land ... is called "Glebe an t-Sagairt" = the Priest's Glebe.' This is probably the same place as **Reighn Taggart** 'above Clachan', where an illicit distiller John McStocar operated in 1815.[1341] **Bealach an t-sagairt**, 'Pass of the priest', was in Saddell Parish, perhaps near the monastery, but its precise location is unknown. The name appears in old parish registers in the following forms: in 1781 and 1796 'Bealachantagairt', and in 1815 'Bealachintagirt'. **Dunan Sagairt** [666 328], 'Priest's Knoll', is the O.S. spelling for a 'knob or neck' of land north of Bellochantuy.[1342] For **Tobar an t-Sagairt**, 'The Priest's Well', at Kilchenzie, see under TOBAR. **Tavantaggart** [703 466], a house north of Tayinloan, is *Tàmh an t-sagairt*, 'The priest's rest'. G.W.S.

Barrow cited the name in his study of '"Tabhnach" (Tannoch etc.) in Scottish place-names as an indicator of early Gaelic-speaking settlement',[1343] but in fact it is no older than 1895, when the scholarly John Ronald Moreton Macdonald of Largie built it as a retreat for his friend Cosmo Lang (1864-1945), who would become Archbishop of Canterbury in 1928, seven years after Macdonald's death.[1344]

SAIDHEAN is the Saithe (*Pollachius virens*), from its former abundance a most important fish to the folk of Kintyre. Remarkably, however, **Port nan Saidhean** [629 207], 'Port of the Saithe', a little bay at Machrihanish,[1345] is the only surviving place-name in Kintyre which mentions the species. Macbain derives *saidhean* from Norse and notes it as an Argyll usage,[1346] and Dwelly defines it as a 'Coal-fish in 2nd. and 3rd. years';[1347] but, except for that record, the word is unknown to me. There were five other common Gaelic names for the saithe in Kintyre, each marking a stage in its growth – see my *Fish and Fisherfolk*, p 52 – and collectively testifying to its economic importance. It was, however, of little commercial significance until the mid-20th century, and the generality of fishermen, who had choicer fish to eat, despised its flesh. Country folk, however, enthusiastically fished for saithe, with rod and line from boats and rocks, and with bag-nets or small seine-nets – see Carraig na h-Oidhche under CARRAIG – and ate them fresh or, late in the year, salted and dried them for winter provisions.[1348] Calum Bannatyne told the story of an old woman in Innean Gaothach who would put a pot of potatoes on the fire, then go down to the rocks with her fishing rod and cast for a few 'gleshans' (small saithe) to add to the already bubbling pot. 'An' that's what they had for their dinner that day. An' they thocht they were in Heaven, ye know.'[1349]

SAMH. The name of the field below the sluice at Auchalochy reservoir, as provided by Archie Kelly in Whitehill farm in 1927, was **Savanach** [723 222].[1350] A farm of the same name near Killocraw is recorded as 'Savanach' on the Langlands map of 1801 and appears in the earliest registers of Killean and Kilchenzie Parish, e.g. Archibald, son of John McMillan in 'Sabhnach', baptised 22/9/1763. W. J. Watson advised Duncan Colville that *samhanach* meant 'abounding in clover',[1351] but Common Sorrel (*Rumex acetosa*) appears to be the main candidate,[1352] hence, I suppose, 'abounding in sorrel'. That *samh* for 'sorrel' was known in Kintyre is confirmed in D. J. Macdonald's interpretation of **Gortean an t-saimh** (see list in

GORT/GOIRTEAN). Common Sorrel is known locally in Scots as 'soorucks'. As a child, I chewed its leaves for their tart, refreshing juices, and no doubt people have been chewing them for thousands of years. Sometimes when I pass that field at Auchalochy, I remember the name 'Savanach' and speak it to myself. It is beautiful-sounding, with an exotic suggestion to it, perhaps an echo of the tropical 'savannah', a meadow-plain. Dwelly (p 786) gives *samhnach*, 'deer-park', but in relation to Kintyre such a connection seems highly improbable.

57. SAMH. The field called Savanach to the south of Auchalochy reservoir dam, from Knock Scalbert, 30/4/2012. Photograph by the author.

SEAN is 'old'. I still hear 'shennar' – *seanair*, 'grandfather' – used occasionally, even in Campbeltown; and *seanachaidh* – for a story-teller, a custodian of clan or community history and genealogy – is quite well-known outwith the Gaelic language itself. Indeed, the first place-name here is identically pronounced.

Sheanachie [751 124] is on the Learside. When *The Place Names of the Parish of Southend* was published in 1938, the place was described as a shepherd's house, but it is now privately owned. It appears as 'Sheanachie', with sheep-fold attached, on the first O.S. map, surveyed in 1866. I understand that the name was originally attached to the line of ruins at 753 122, by the roadside south-east of the present house. There was certainly a school there – Ewan McMaster was its teacher in 1821 – and possibly an inn too. Flory Loynachan, for whom a well-known song, packed with local dialect, was composed, was born there in 1810. The song is still sung locally and might have gained wider popularity had its vocabulary been less intractable. Her sister, Mary Loynachan MacDougall, attained her 100th birthday on 18/6/1913 in Canada, where she had emigrated in 1838. The derivation of the name is *Sean-achadh*, 'old field'.[1353]

Seanlagan [899 647], on the coast between Tarbert and Skipness, also has literary associations. It translates as 'Old Lagan' – see LAG, LAGAN – in contrast with nearby **Lagan Ròaig**, the steading which replaced it. In 1867, it belonged to Stonefield Estate and was already a ruin.[1354] Seanlagan and its neighbour were haunts of George Campbell Hay in his wanderings. They put their mark on his poetry, and he cherished their memory until the end of his life. Seanlagan appears as *An Lagan*, 'The Hollow', in George's poem of that name; but there are really two poems. The first was conceived in innocence, as it were, and celebrates the hollow as a beautiful and tranquil refuge from human strife. The strength of his connection with the place is nowhere more explicit than in the line: ' ... consecrated is each stalk of grass in it.' The second part, grafted on eight years later, in 1945, in a mood of clinical realism, rocks with the sights and sounds of war, and appears to shroud that first vision; but at the very end he returns in memory to his peaceful hollow with a question which could only be answered in the time left to him, and perhaps never was. I quote the first and last verses, in his own translation, which appeared with the Gaelic original in *Fuaran Sleibh* (1948):

Who saw the silent hollow,
with the early sun upon its flank,
gilding the smooth sweep of the lower slope,
that did not lose his heart as he looked?

The thunder of the waves and the years is between
me and the one who made the praise, beyond them.
After them will I find in the hollow
that part of my soul which I left there?

In prose, this evocation from him: 'Seanlagan, the Old Hollow, above a clean, white, shore and at the foot of an amphitheatre of gracious, sheltered slopes, where the roe-deer go calling in the fresh stillness of the morning – a wild land's quiet and secret sanctuary ...'[1355]

In **Sheneval** [809 382], *Seana-bhaile*, 'Old township', a field on Carradale Estate, there is yet another literary association, with Naomi Mitchison (1897-1999), writer and social activist, who bought Carradale Estate with her husband in 1938.[1356] She was no high-minded onlooker in the management of her estate, but engaged enthusiastically in the practicalities of farming, not least during the war years, when local food production was vital to the war effort. In 1944 she wrote: 'But if I did not plough here, and if I am to keep up my acreage, as we are all pressed to do by the War Agricultural Executive Committee, I should have had to plough Sheneval, my one good pasture field, or else take in another piece of the bay, ground that is almost pure sand.' In 1952 she contributed an entire article on 'Sheneval' to the *Manchester Guardian*, opening the piece with the statement, 'This was the first year we took a crop off Sheneval', and then speculating on the significance of the name, which she thought might be 'the old village'. Finally, in 'Thoughts on Growing Grass', published in 1955 in *The New Statesman and Nation*, she describes Sheneval, 'the field which was sown out last year', as having 'a beautiful, wind-rippling thick hay crop, but not as tall or as ripe as the grass has been at this time in most other years'.[1357]

Two fields on Carskey Estate were named **Senachrea** and **Shentalive**, which have been interpreted (the first tentatively) as *Seana chrè*, 'old clay', and *Seana talamh*, 'old ground'.[1358] Finally, there is **Sheanakill** [765 562], the site of a burial-ground at Clachan, which Dugald Mitchell interpreted as 'The ancient cell or church' (*Seanachill*); but when the site was visited in 1962 by archaeologists, no remains were apparent.[1359] For **Glenahanty** and **Knockhanty** see under TIGH.

SEASGAN is 'a fenny country, marsh',[1360] from which derive the two Kintyre farm-names **Chiskan**, one in Southend Parish [730 102], which was also known as 'West Polliwilline',[1361] and the other in Campbeltown Parish [680 189],[1362] near the southern edge of the Laggan, which was once a boggy expanse and still floods after prolonged heavy rains. In February 1871, a 'heavy flood on the Lagan' swept away 16 tons of turnips at Chiskan.[1363] The spelling 'Shescan' appears for the Laggan farm in 1761.[1364] Shiskine (*an t-Seasgunn*) in Arran is 'a boggy, marshy or sedgy place',[1365] and in Ireland *seisceann*, 'a swamp or marsh', is most commonly anglicised as 'seskan', 'seskin' or 'sheskin', and occurs throughout the country, sometimes qualified – as in Sheskinshule, County Tyrone: *Seisceann Siúil*, 'moving swamp' – and sometimes not,[1366] as in Kintyre.

SEILEACH is the Willow (*Salix*), or rather Willows, for there are many forms: sallows, osiers and a third less definable group, comprising crack-willow, white-willow and bay willow.[1367] The main products of willow are its wands, which were used extensively in wickerwork, for baskets, creels, and much else. **Coursheileach** [751 513], near Loch Garasdale, was interpreted by the O.S. in 1867 as 'Dell of the willow',[1368] presumably from *cùrr*, which can mean 'pit'.[1369] In 1900, Gillies reached the same conclusion – 'the willow pit or hollow'[1370] – without, however, having access to old forms of the name, which are: 1545 'Carsellocht (the two)'; 1627 'Little Corschelache', let with Carnbeg, and 'Muckle Corschelache', let with Carnmor; 1675 'Corshealloch'. **Cnoc an t-seilich** [733 399], 'Hill of the willow', stands over the head of Barr Glen at 814 ft. **Cnoc Achadh nan Seilich** [855 675] is 'Hill of the Willows' Field', at Escart, West Loch Tarbert. **Allt Seilich** [643 153], 'Willow Stream', is near the Slate. For **Innean Seilich** see under INNEAN, for **Arisheloch** under ÀIRIGH and for **An dìg sheilich** under DÌG.

SGADAN is the herring, *Clupea harengus*, the most important of fish in the history of Kintyre. Remarkably, it appears in just two minor place-names. **Port Sgadain** [799 357], 'Herring Port', the O.S. form,[1371] is a creek on the south shore of Torrisdale Bay. The O.S. offered no explanation, and I doubt if anyone could offer one now. Perhaps, if I may indulge in a little guesswork, herring were shipped there. In the late 18th century, there was a 'Redherring House' in operation near the mouth of Torrisdale Burn, as marked on the Langlands map of 1801, and therefore close to the port. Port Sgadain may, therefore, have been the port into which catches of herring were landed and red herring shipped out. The salting and smoking process for red herring was a lengthy one, not to be confused with kippering, which came later; but see *Kintyre Instructions*, pp. 157-59, for a brief history of that establishment.

In C1891, there were two fishermen and their families living at 'Portasgadain', and in 1901 only one, Alexander Campbell. Graham McKinlay, who farmed Whitestone and took a keen interest in the activities of his neighbours up the shore, had a little story about a family which lived at **Port Bàn**, by which the cottages at Port Sgadain were also known (the two ports are next to each other). Some of the men in the family 'fell out very sore', and in the ensuing hostilities one of them was chased by the others and climbed into the branches of a Scots fir to escape. Not to be outdone, his pursuers 'went for a double-ended saw' and felled the tree to get their hands on him.[1372]

Naomi Mitchison's 1950 novel, *The Big House*, is set in Carradale, which she called 'Port-na-Sgadan' – a form which corresponds more to local pronunciation: *Port na(n) Sgadan*, 'Port of the Herrings' – not a fictitious name, but one unlikely to be recognised by many readers outwith Carradale itself. She used the name again, in the form 'Portnasgadan', as the setting for her play *Spindrift*, co-written with her friend, the Carradale fisherman Denis Macintosh, and produced at Glasgow Citizens' Theatre in 1951.[1373]

The other place-name, **Roc an Sgadan Ghréine**, on the shore south of Rubha Lagan Ròaig, can be found under GRIANAN.

58. *SGADAN. Looking south from Torrisdale Bay towards Port Bàn and Port Sgadain. Photograph by the author, 6/8/2012.*

SGARBH applies both to the Great Cormorant (*Phalacrocorax carbo*) and the Shag (*Phalacrocorax aristotelis*), just as, in Kintyre Scots, both species are covered by a single name, 'scart'. Gaelic and Scots both derive from Old Norse *skarfr*.[1374] Since the word was adopted a thousand years ago, more or less, the failure to distinguish the two species – Shags have a forward-pointing crest, which the larger Cormorants lack – may be excused. Whatever interest the birds excited then would have been related more to human survival than to ornithology, for both species were eaten, and continued to be eaten in Kintyre, particularly in the fishing communities, well into the 20th century. The birds would be shot and then wrapped in cloth and buried for a few days, to mitigate the fishy flavour. Both species breed locally – the Cormorant in comparatively small numbers – particularly on the Sanda islands.[1375]

Skarfr is imitative of the birds' harsh call, but many localised names allude to the black plumage. Indeed, the Latin specific *carbo* means 'black', and 'Cormorant' itself has a Latin origin as 'sea raven'. Unlike other seabirds, Cormorants' and Shags' feathers are not waterproof and require to be periodically dried, which the birds do by perching on rocks and characteristically stretching their wings.[1376] And so they may be seen, primitive and prominent, on certain promontories and islands on the Kintyre coast (though the Cormorant will visit inland lochs and rivers to fish).

Rubha nan Sgarbh [800 340], below Whitestone farmhouse, is the 'Point of the Cormorants', and **Eilean na Sgarbh** [637 208], off the car-park at Machrihanish village, is 'Scart Isle',[1377] though Moira Burgess, in her childhood at Machrihanish, heard only 'Scart Rock'.[1378] In William McTaggart's 1883 painting, 'A Message from the Sea', Eilean na Sgarbh occupies the top right-hand corner of the canvas. A wave is breaking over the rock, throwing spray, and perched on mid-crest of the rock can be seen the unmistakable forms of two cormorants.

SGEIR is from Old Norse *sker*, 'a rock in the sea'.[1379] I have a total of 26 *sgeir* names on record for Kintyre, excluding debatable inland cases, which are considered later. Saddell and Skipness Parish has the most names, 11, while Southend Parish has none. Along a coastline which extends from Largiebaan, in the west, round to the Second Waters, in the east, no *sgeir* name existed or, if it did exist, survived. The inter-tidal and offshore rock-features of that coast took the generic OITIR, which applied to shelves or platforms of rock, most of them sandstone, and quite different in character from the hard reef or rock described by *sgeir*. The word, for 'reef', survived in the vocabulary of Kintyre fishermen into the present century. I last heard it in 2003 from Lawrence Robertson in Campbeltown – 'Ye can go inside that skerr here, A know that for sure' – but it probably remains active.

On the west of Kintyre, the most northerly *sgeir* is in West Loch Tarbert: **Sgeiran Dubh** [805 616], 'Little Black Reef'. There are others further up the loch, but these are more on the north side and properly belong to Kilberry Parish, rather than Kilcalmonell. In Killean and Kilchenzie Parish, seven out of the eight names are close to Muasdale. The most southerly of these is **Sgeir a' Bhlàir**, a 'sea-girt skerry', as D. J. Macdonald described it, nicely but unnecessarily. It translates as 'The Battle Rock' and is off **Port an Dùin**, which took its name from the dun at 659 375, directly onshore. According to Macdonald, when 'the enemy' attacked the dun, they shot their arrows from the rock.[1380] Neil 'P.O.' Thomson in Muasdale gave me the same name and translation, but his description – 'the big rock that makes the point down there', i.e. Glencardoch Point – would place it further north at 658 379.[1381] All evidence considered, the former location is likelier to be the correct one.

A look at a map, or an observant journey south from Bellochantuy to Westport, will present one with a succession of skerries, but none has any known identification, and the next with a name is **Skerryvore**, which lies off the south end of Machrihanish Bay. This is *Sgeir mhór*, 'Big reef', and its presence matches the description. In storm, it shows as a cauldron of boiling water and spray, and even on days of relative calm, its lair is betrayed by crested undulations. There are actually two reefs there, with the **Caolas**, or 'strait', between them, which 'only an experienced fisherman would attempt to go through'.[1382] Perhaps the strangest of its victims was the smack *Mystery*, lost in May 1869. She left Campbeltown and rounded the Mull on passage to the Minch herring fishery. The weather was fine, but she struck the reef and foundered, and her skipper Dugald Mathieson and crew of six all drowned before anyone knew of the mishap.[1383]

The next one south is also the last on the west coast, the last indeed until Carradale on the east coast. **Sgeir nan Gall** [596 166], 'Reef of the Strangers', lies to the north of the Inneans Bay and was not noted by the Ordnance Survey, though it appears on Admiralty charts and was known in oral tradition. James McMillan, a fisherman in Machrihanish, told me in 1977 that the rectangular feature in the north-west corner of the Inneans Bay was a mass grave for the 'seamen that came in off a wreck on the Sgeir nan Gall', but that tradition is not consistent with the nature of the feature, which is almost certainly a stock-enclosure.[1384]

The element *sgeir* reappears in Carradale harbour. **Sgeir a' Bhogha** [815 390] is at the south end of Port na Cùile. The O.S. in 1867 defined it as 'The bow rock';[1385] *bogha* can mean 'bow' and 'bend', or 'bulge', as in a badly built wall.[1386] At the north end of Port na Cùile is **Sgeir Bhuidhe** [814 391], 'Yellow Reef', and, still further north, another of that name [812 421], at Eilean Grianain, known to Carradale fishermen as 'Sgeir Bhuidhe Grianan', to distinguish it from yet another reef of the name at Crossaig, 'Sgeir Bhuidhe Crossaig' [838 518]. In fact, there are four yellow reefs on that stretch of coast, the fourth being below Barmollach [811 438]. And if Sgeir Bhuidhe [922 594] at Culindrach and another [868 690] in East Loch Tarbert are included, that makes six. See also BUIDHE for remarks on colouration.

Sgeir Ghiobach, to my knowledge, is not on any map, but George Campbell Hay marked it at 877 686, on the south shore of East Loch Tarbert. I heard the name defined in Tarbert as 'ragged reef', but he gave me 'hairy reef', and explained it in terms of its seaweed cover.[1387]

There are five inland 'sker-' place-names, all near Campbeltown, and a sixth, the **Lands of Skeirkenzie**, which is redundant. (**Skernish** in Barr Glen is a name imported from Skye: see BARR.) Skierchanzie, to use Andrew McKerral's spelling, comprised church lands belonging to Iona, which in 1576 passed to the Campbells of Argyll.[1388] These lands, significantly, lay mostly in the parish of Kilkenzie, and included **Skeroblingarry** [West 708 267, East 709 267] and **Skeroblinraid**, one of which [694 257] became **High Park** and the other [705 257] **Low Park** (see under PAIRC). **Skerry Fell** [640 183], its neighbour **Skerry Fell Fad** [636 182] and **Skerry Fell Cruin** [642 194] are similarly-shaped hills above Machrihanish. The local pronunciation of 'Skerry Fell' is 'Skarafeld' in all cases, with the third-mentioned popularly known as 'Low' or 'Wee Skarafeld'.[1389] The O.S. in 1866 interpreted Skerry Fell Fad as 'Long rocky hill'.[1390]

These, in the main, are difficult names. This is not the place to analyse them, nor am I equipped to do so. The generic is what interests me here. Can *sgeir* translate from sea to land? Dealing with Skeroblingarry and the three fells – from Norse *fjall*, 'hill' – the K.A.S. place-names committee opted for *sgeir*, 'skerry'. John Cameron, who was present at the discussion of the names, but not at the meeting when the interpretations were adopted, disagreed with the decision. He wrote on 14/2/1939 to Duncan Colville to reiterate his objections, which were gently stated but clearly impassioned. He was, he said, convinced that the names were Norse, but he was also convinced that their origin was 'quite distinct from "sgeir", a rock in the sea'. He cited *sgeir-mhòna*, 'peat-bank, or rather the trench made in cutting peats', and proposed Norse *skura*, 'scar', giving 'Skurafell, Scarred hill'. He continued: 'I was strengthened in my belief when I found that Capt. Thomas in The Place-Names of Islay [F.W.L. Thomas, 'On Islay Place-Names'] had long ago come to this conclusion, viz. that "sker" means a scar or score or trench.'[1391]

Ian A. Fraser remarks that the 'skerry fells' sound Norse, 'one possibility being the personal name *Skari*, or even an obscure Norse topographic term like Old Norse *skerf*, "a hard place where rock is exposed"'. He encountered the latter term in John Stewart's *Shetland Place-Names* (1987, p 248), but considers its occurrence in Kintyre as unlikely. The 'skeroblin-' names he likewise considered 'extremely tough',[1392] but perhaps some scholar of Norse will ultimately chew them over long enough to render them digestible.

SGRÌODAN, from Norse *skritha*, is a landslip or scree, the English form it assumed. Rockfalls and carpets of small stones – difficult to keep one's footing on – are common enough sights in the more rugged parts of Kintyre, particularly on the cliffy coast between Machrihanish and the Mull, but the word appears only once in the place-names record, in **Sgreadan Hill** [741 295], which stands at 1298 ft. north of Glenlussa.[1393] The O.S. interpretation in 1866, 'Noisy hill',[1394] is eccentric, but comprehensible. **The Riddlings** or **Devil's Riddlings** [761 205] referred to scree on the south face of Davaar Island; fishermen listening for herring on still nights might hear stones dislodging and falling.[1395]

SIONNACH is the Fox (*Vulpes vulpes*), though he is also known as *madadh-ruadh* (see MADADH). The Scots word for fox, 'tod', appears in **Tod Hill** [721 117], also called 'Tod Muntan'.[1396] John Brolichan, a farm worker, was recorded at 'Tod Mountain' in the 1841 Southend census.

Allt na Sionnach [747 542] belongs to that group of place-names comprising the once-important and since-forgotten. Dr Colin M. MacDonald, who was Director of Education for Argyll and author of a *History of Argyll* (1950), hunted down this 'stream of the fox' and in 1955 published the results in an obscure little magazine, *Mactalla*, produced for Argyll teachers. I'll quote at length from his article, 'An Old Kintyre Boundary'.

One of the most interesting streams in Argyll, at least from the point of view of History if not Geography, is the Burn of the Foxes or, in its Gaelic name, Allt-na-Sionnaich, which separated old Kintyre from old Knapdale.

Prior to the year 1481 the lands of North and South Knapdale formed part of the vast possessions of the MacDonald Lords of the Isles, South Knapdale extending beyond the modern village of Clachan but not so far South as the village of Tayinloan because the boundary with Kintyre lay somewhere between these villages. Old charters made frequent reference to the boundary Burn when grants or transfers of land were made. But where did this important Burn run and how did it get its intriguing name? The simplest explanation may be the best – it was merely the stream at which the observant old inhabitants had seen foxes quench their thirst! But where exactly was it and where is it?

The present writer was anxious for reasons of history to know the course of this stream. He made many enquiries. He consulted ministers, teachers, lawyers, farmers, factors and lairds but met invariably with negative shakes of the head. He looked up maps. He knew that it was shown on Pont's old map. He saw it in the map of Kintyre published by Cosmo Innes in his erudite compilation, *Origines Parochiales Scotiae*, a mine of information to those interested in their native localities, but it was impossible to identify which particular one of the small streams hurrying to the sea was actually intended. Burn after Burn was considered as a candidate for the honour but still the stream continued its evasive course!

Finally certainty was achieved through the kindness of Mr John MacDougall, M.A., of Dunskeig by Clachan. He stated that at a short distance North of the 25th milestone from Campbeltown and the 13th milestone from Tarbert a small Burn runs down to the sea. To most of the present-day inhabitants of the district it is a Burn without a name but old natives reported that their parents long ago told them that it was known by the name of 'Allt-na-Sionnaich'.

Surely, however, it may be suggested, the early Ordnance Survey Maps would have showed (sic) where this stream flowed! The common Maps available to the general public were of no service but with Mr MacDougall's clue as guide a large-scale Ordnance Survey Map was consulted and then with the aid of a magnifying glass the name of the long-forgotten Burn in its microscopic printing leapt into view! [1397]

It's a dramatic narrative, but I can't help wondering why Dr MacDonald didn't carefully check an O.S. 'large scale' map in the first place, with or without the magnifying-glass; also, whether, as he suggests, the stream's name derived from foxes' drinking there is entirely conjectural.

The Fox was formerly common in Kintyre and is again common, but was probably exterminated as a resident species by about 1800, largely through the efforts of Allan Macintyre (1745-1840).[1398] He was known as *Ailean nan Sionnach*, 'Allan of the Foxes', and he makes an appearance in Colonel Walter Campbell's *My Indian Journal*, published in 1864.

When I had learnt to handle a rifle (which I did as soon as I was strong enough to hold one to my shoulder) I took to deer-stalking under the guidance of old Allan Macintyre, the fox-hunter and bard of our district. The old fox-hunter has long been superseded by the modern gamekeeper. Like the Red Indian he has been superseded by the tide of advancing civilisation. But, in the days of my boyhood when gamekeepers were almost unknown, and hardly needed, the fox-hunter of a Highland district was a person of no small importance. He was paid so much a year by each proprietor, and wandered about from house to house, always a welcome guest, slaying eagles, foxes, wild cats and other vermin, and receiving a certain gratuity from every farmer for every fox or eagle he could produce ...

My friend Allan Macintyre was a specimen of the thoroughbred old Highlander rarely met with nowadays. He was a tall, wiry, active-looking man of about fifty, with strikingly handsome features, and the grave expression and dignified manner of an American Indian chief. His bow, when saluting a lady, would have done credit to a courtier. He had studied in the great book of Nature, and not in vain, for it had made him a naturalist and a poet. From the stag to the stoat he was as familiar with the habits and instincts of the wild animals of the Highlands as a shepherd is with the habits of his sheep, or the instincts of his collie dog. And during his long, solitary rambles among the hills, he beguiled the time by composing Gaelic songs and poems worthy of Ossian. Many a pleasant evening have I spent listening to them, as we sat over a peat fire in a lonely bothie, and rested our weary limbs after a successful day's stalking. [1399]

Allan Macintyre is credited with having killed the last fox in Kintyre, which, considering his occupation, is probably a reasonable claim. The tradition is still alive; I had it from Ian MacDonald in 2011. By his version, Allan hunted that fox from Glenbarr to Largiebaan, where he discovered his lead hounds dead below the cliffs. Looking over, he saw that the fox had gripped a small rowan and swung into a cave which had an inland exit. Allan cut part-way through the rowan, and on the next hunt found the tree snapped and the fox dead at the bottom of the cliffs. He was reputed to have remarked afterwards: 'It was the worst thing I ever did. It cost me my job.'

A version of that story was told to Nils M. Holmer by John Campbell in Seaside Cottage, Torrisdale, around 1939. I'll mention only a few of the details by which it differs from the above. The fox was a 'bobtailed' (*cutach*) bitch, and would kill every dog-fox she had. She was about to have pups, and if she'd had her brood, Allan said, the hunters would never have rid Kintyre of foxes.[1400]

Dugald Macintyre, Allan's great-grandson, in 1922 related that Allan relied solely on his 'long gun' and his 'pack of terriers, all noted and scarred veterans in battle with fox, otter and wild cat'. Allan composed a Gaelic song, the title of which in translation is 'Song of the Fox on the Mull of Kintyre', and Dugald said that he had heard it sung 'by an old lady in Mull recently'. The first verse, in translation, goes:

Every hand is now against me, chased about on every side,
A thief I am, and not ashamed o't, still I make my wile my guide.
One friend I have, he in the lighthouse, oft he sees my
    children play
Round the Goin in early morning, and he drives them not
    away. [1401]

Just as the Fox's extermination was facilitated by the sparsity of woodland in Kintyre, its re-establishment as a breeding species was facilitated by Forestry Commission plantations. By the early 1940s, Foxes were once more breeding in North Kintyre, and local farmers blamed these plantations for 'giving sanctuary to stragglers coming down from Knapdale'. In 1948, the Carradale branch of the National Farmers' Union complained: 'More plantations, more foxes in Carradale.' Foxes are now firmly established throughout Kintyre. They continue to be hunted, but the virtual disappearance of shooting estates and the gamekeepers employed for 'vermin' control, has eased persecution. The Kintyre Foxhunting Society was formed in 1955 and paid bounties on an average of around 90 adults and cubs annually between 1965 and 1975.[1402]

One could debate endlessly the rights and wrongs of Foxes and Fox-hunting, but in the end the argument may be reduced to this: they are abhorred by those – farmers, shepherds, and shooters – who believe they stand to lose by the Fox's predations, and admired by those who watch them in the wild without thought as to how they feed themselves and their young.

SÌTHICH is 'fairy', but the Gaelic fairy bears no resemblance to the English fairy as portrayed in popular culture. Indeed, the translation 'fairy' for *sìthich*, though pretty universal, conveys an altogether misleading impression of that malign subterranean race which seems to have vanished. The subject is immense, therefore I can only touch on it here. The first point to be made is that the existence of 'fairies' was a common belief, which, when one thinks about it, was no more strange than belief in invisible gods. I never met anyone in Kintyre who believed in fairies, but I met people who were familiar with the lore of fairies.

Donald McCallum, born in 1900 at High Glenadale, was one of them. As a boy, he heard older folk talking about **Crock Shee** [618 144] – *Cnoc Sìth*, 'Fairy Hill' – a green knoll on the road up to Largiebaan, but they would mock the traditions. In earlier generations, people going home in the dark would avoid the place in case 'the wee folk' would be out or their voices could be heard underground. By his reckoning, belief in fairies died out in his grandparents' or perhaps great-grandparents' generation, that is in the early to mid-19th century.[1403]

Mrs Higginson in Skipness was in no doubt that fairies had been 'very numerous in the district'. People had seen them in the Black Wood between Oragaig and Creggan, at Rubha Dubh, and 'strong-minded men fought shy of passing through it at night'. It was customary to stick a darning-needle in the bonnet as 'a good protection against ghosts and fairies'. The following are some of Mrs Higginson's stories, in all of which, remarkably, the protagonists are identified by name and location.

Gilbert Taylor in Goirtean Eòrna was going through the Black Wood one night when he heard a great noise behind him, so he left the road to let the company pass. It was a crowd of fairies on little white ponies, tiny men and women dressed in green and all speaking

Gaelic. They dismounted beside him and he ran off in fear, with the fairies in pursuit, shouting one to another, 'Stop him up and stop him down, and drive him up to the Ear Hill' (Cnoc na Cluaise). He got away, however, by running down through Rockfield until he found himself standing in the sea below Claonaig. He managed to make his way home and later emigrated with his family to America.

Another young man, Archibald Hyndman, met a fairy company at High Claonaig one summer night on his way home to Skipness. They escorted him to the top of the old road above Skipness, playing the bagpipes and chattering to one another, but never interfered with him.

The wife of the farmer in Londubh, John MacBride, was 'taken away with the fairies' in about 1820 and remained with them for seven years. She would sometimes come to the house after sunset and 'pass by like a shadow'. One harvest night, John was out late and chanced to meet her. She told him to be at the wooden gate in the stone wall above Oragaig on a certain night and to have her wedding dress with him, and when she would pass to throw it to her and that would break the spell. He was there on the night and she appeared with a band of fairies riding on little ponies, and as she was passing he threw the dress to her and got her and brought her back home. She told him that she had been living with the fairies in the 'Rocky Hill' (Cruach Oragaig) and that they had been kind to her, but she did not live long after her homecoming.

One summer evening, a woman named MacKinnon who lived in Glenbuie went to the hill to bring home her cow. The mist was thick and she lost her way, but she saw a bright light and was heading towards it when she heard the sounds of music and dancing. She went into the light and joined the company. She did not know anyone, but everyone seemed to know her and called her by her name. They were fairies and pressed food and drink upon her, but she refused all the offerings, though she danced with them. She was in the middle of a reel when she heard the cocks crowing at Glenbuie, and when she turned around she saw that she was standing near her own house and that her new pair of shoes were worn out with the dancing. It was said that after that night she had a 'great twist in her mouth'.

Robert Campbell, who lived at Crossaig, was walking home from Tarbert one night at harvest-time. As he was passing below Oragaig, there was a long narrow field of growing corn on his right hand, and it was full of fairies busily shearing. They were very merry and calling to one another: 'Poor little narrow field, we will shear it no more, we will shear it no more, shear it, shear it, shear it no more.'[1404]

By the time I began collecting folklore in Kintyre, in the 1970s, little remained of fairy traditions. Neil 'P.O.' Thomson in Muasdale, who was born in 1904, heard about how 'two or three young men would sit up for two or three nights after the baby was born in case there'd be any changeling business'.[1405] Edward Dwelly explained the 'changeling business' succinctly: 'The sìthich is the most active sprite of Highland mythology. It is a dexterous child-stealer and is particularly intrusive on women in travail. At births many covert and cunning ceremonies are still used to baffle the fairies' power; otherwise, the new-born infant would be taken off to fairy-land, and a withered brat laid in its stead.'[1406]

D. J. Macdonald collected a Gaelic tale about **Cnocan nam ban** near Charlottan in Barr Glen. I quote it in full, as translated by the Rev Macdonald himself. I find it not only compelling, but almost convincing, and had I heard it as a child, told at the fireside of some lonely cottage, I would have believed all of it. The detail is what lends the story its authenticity: a man whittling a piece of wood to make a ring for a pail and so keep himself awake during his anxious vigil to thwart the powers of evil. Thanks to Macdonald's fidelity to the original, the story has a narrative simplicity and strength which Cuthbert Bede would have sacrificed in a turgid revision.

> There was a woman here that had a child. One or two of the children which she had were taken away by the fairies. The children used to be watched then for fear that they would be taken away. The man of the house said that he would not let anyone watch on that night but himself. To keep himself wakeful, he took a wooden pail, and he got a knife and began whittling a ring to put on it. And he heard the sweetest music he ever heard. He could not keep himself awake for the music. The music was lulling him to sleep. The knife went into his hand, and that woke him, and he went to the door and was listening to the music at the door. 'It is good for you that it was I that had the arrow,' said one of the fairies to him, 'else you had not been there tonight, and as a sign,' said he, 'look and you will see the cock dead on the perch.' The man went and took a light, and he found as was said to him – the cock was dead. They never troubled that family again, as the man himself had watched.[1407]

In keeping with the above tradition, Macdonald refers to Cnocan nam ban in another source as having been 'so named because newly-born children were spirited away by fairies'; but the name is clearly 'The women's hillock'. Were the women those mothers whose babies had been taken? The link is obscure, though Macdonald does also describe Cnocan nam Ban as 'this fairy hill'.[1408] Willie McGougan, Largie, associated the name with 'old wives' and mentioned traditions of folk going up the glen late at night and seeing 'old weemen dancin oot in the field' – witches, presumably.[1409]

Close to Cnocan nam Ban is another fairy hill, **Cnocan na Cainntearachd**, and the fairies were believed to have been able to travel between the two using 'secret ways'. Cnocan na Cainntearachd was 'so called from the sound of discourse or music which the quick ear of imagination heard proceeding from the knowe'. 'One wonders,' Macdonald adds, 'whether the eloquence and music with which fairy hills were supposed to be replete accounts for the saying, *Cho glic ri cnoc*, "as wise as a hillock."'[1410] Macdonald had theories about the origins of the fairies and of their name, *sìthichean*. He certainly rejected the popular derivation from *sìth*, 'peace': 'As a matter of fact, the Sìthichean were not peaceful people at all. They were quite the opposite. Malicious, malevolent, tricky, mischievous, thieving beings.' **Cnocan nan sìthichean**, 'a long narrow ridge' between Blary and Auchaduie, is 'Hillock of the fairies'.[1411]

Fairy hillocks were small, rounded, green and not at all sinister in appearance. There is a nice one at Machrihanish, which is identifiable by its name, **Cnocan Sìthein** [644 206], 'Fairy Knoll'. It is actually a Neolithic burial-cairn and therefore man-made. It has existed for over 4000 years, largely unmolested, and now stands between two bungalows on the roadside. Near Gartgunnel, Tangy, there is another Cnocan Sìthein,[1412] and **Sìthean Mór** and **Sìthean Beag**, the big and little fairy knowes, are hillocks on Kilblaan Hill.[1413]

'Fairy hills' are often prehistoric burial-mounds and were venerated for that very reason, as Robert Kirk, minister at Aberfoyle, observed in *The Secret Commonwealth* (c. 1691): 'There be many Places called Fairie-Hills, which the Mountain People [Highlanders] think impious and dangerous to peel or discover, by taking Earth or Wood from them; superstitiously believing the Souls of their Predicessors to dwell there.' Editing Kirk's text two centuries later, Andrew Lang dismissed the then-current theory that 'fairies' are a folk-memory of an actual race of underground dwellers, Neolithic or Bronze Age people, or perhaps Picts, who lived in the mounds now called 'fairy hills'; but he recognised these as tumuli or barrows (hence, to some extent, the legends of 'fairy gold', from the finding of grave goods) and suggested that 'fairies' equate to ancestral spirits.[1414]

Kirnashie was a farm north of Carradale, for which the following early forms are available: 1500 'Keironasche'; 1545 'Carrefysche'; 1564 'Kerenasy'; 1596 'Kirknache'; 1605 'Kirknache'; 1751 'Keronshee'; 1756 'Cearanashi'; 1776 'Kerranashi'; 1836 'Kerrynasith'; 1839 'Corrinasith';[1415] C1851 'Kirranashee'; C1861 'Kernashee'. Cameron Gillies had a stab at explaining the name in 1906, having deemed it 'troublesome' in 1900.[1416] 'Is this,' he asked, 'the beautiful *Coire na sìth* of Gaelic tales; it looks like it – *the fairy corrie*, or *the corrie of peace!*'[1417] It may not look so much like it in the earlier forms of the name! Ian A. Fraser remarks on 'the complex history of the old forms', but, focusing on 'Keiro-', 'Kere-', 'Kirri-' and 'Ceara-', etc., suggests that the generic may be *ceathramh*, 'quarter-land'. If this is correct, then Kirnashie represents the fourth *ceathramh* place-name known in Kintyre (see CEATHRAMH). As for the specific, *sìth* is probably correct.[1418] I have not been able to locate the settlement on any map, but the Hill [800 416] and Wood [793 407] named 'Kirnashie' indicate the general area.

Still in Carradale, the motif of the fairy hill recurs throughout the writings of Naomi Mitchison, in fiction, poetry and autobiography, over at least 30 years, during which period her concept of the hill, or of the 'country' inside it, changes. In the short story, 'Mirk, Mirk Night' (1936), it is a place of artificial and superficial attraction, contrasted with the real world of human relationships. In the children's novel, *The Big House* (1950), it is as real as real life, for so long as that suits the fairies. In her African memoir, *Return to the Fairy Hill* (1966), it is a type of ideal society. As Moira Burgess points out, other Scottish writers, such as Neil M. Gunn and George Mackay Brown, also use the myth, 'but none as consistently as Mitchison'. For a fuller discussion of the subject, see Dr Burgess's *Mitchison's Ghosts*.[1419]

Allt Leannan-Sìthe [617 158], 'Burn of the Fairy Lover' – the O.S. in 1866 suggested 'Burn of the fairy meadow'[1420] – is close to the head of Gleneadardacrock. I have already written at length on the name in *By Hill and Shore in South Kintyre* (pp. 233-34), so will limit my treatment of it here. *Leannan-sìthe* is a 'fairy lover', and the place-name, attached to an otherwise insignificant stream running off the side of Cnoc Moy, begs more questions than can be answered. What tradition could lie behind it? The 'fairy lover', in essence, was one who enjoyed the sexual favours of mortal women, and the male child of such a union was *Dubh-Sìth*, 'Black Fairy'. One such in Kintyre was a dwarf known as *Sìtheach*, 'Fairy Man'. According to Willie McGougan, the dwarf offered martial service to Sir Lachlan MacLean of Duart on the eve of the Battle of Tràigh Ghruineart (1598), but MacLean spurned the offer. The mercenary *Sìtheach* then approached MacLean's rival, Sir James MacDonald, who tested his prowess with bow and arrow and then engaged him. *Sìtheach* fittingly killed Sir Lachlan with an arrow, and the MacLeans fled the battlefield.[1421]

Ronald Black, in his introduction to *The Gaelic Otherworld* (2005), an edition of John Gregorson Campbell's collection of Highland folklore, suggests that fairy traditions may have served to explain, or excuse, 'a spectrum of social issues'. His list is long, from 'the fears and perils of marriage' to 'purgatory', and, while unintended pregnancy isn't specifically on the list, in the event it would have been 'handy to have the possibility of a *leannan-sìthe* up by the burn', as Moira Burgess remarks.[1422]

SLABHRAIDH was the chain, with pot-hook attached, which hung above the open fires in old houses. It appears in only one place-name in Kintyre, and that is **Allt na Slabhraidhe** [646 109], a burn which flows south from Glenadale, near Caibeal Catrìona. No tradition is known about the origin of the name. In houses without a chimney, the chain would have been suspended from the underside of the roof, but in later houses built with chimneys, the chain was attached to a 'bolt' – this was the term I heard in Gaelic – which was fixed into the stonework of the chimney. When cooking, the height of the pot-hook above the fire could be adjusted, to lessen or to increase heat, by raising or lowering it a link on the chain.[1423] One of these bolts may still be seen in the east-facing gable of Gleneadardacrock house, where the stonework of the outer face of the chimney has broken off, leaving a hole.

SLIABH is a name which I heard pronounced in Kintyre only once in my lifetime, in 1983. I was researching wild goats at the time, and visited a Machrihanish man, John McMillan, to ask him about the goats he kept at Mingary from 1942 to 1944. I had decided not to use a tape-recorder, because the subject was a small one and would be covered quickly, so I was scribbling his information into a notebook. Somehow the place-name 'Sliabh' came up and I noted it too, though I wasn't at the time particularly interested in where the place was or what he knew about it. Unfortunately, however, I recognised the name and spelled it '*sliabh*' rather than phonetically, and so missed my chance of preserving – as a tape-recording would also have done – the pronunciation of the word from the mouth of a Kintyre native.

I was never again to hear the name authentically spoken, but I was to encounter it again – for the very same place – written phonetically by Mrs Hector Galbraith, Polliwilline, and I included it, as 'The Sliabh', in my supplement to *The Place-Names of the Parish of Southend*. It had already been collected by Duncan Colville, from Archie McEachran in Kilblaan, but for some reason Duncan excluded it from the published compilation. It slumbered in the Society's 'Schedules' – the bound volume of parish source materials – in which it was described as lying 'North of Cnoc na Greine, Arinascavach, about a mile north-east of Gartloskin Hill'.

By then, I had already published, in *The Kintyre Magazine* No. 45, Mary Galbraith's memoir, pieced together from jotters she had filled before her death in 1995. Her earliest years, as Mary Balloch, were spent at Arinascavach, which she remembered as comprising, additionally, the old holdings 'Crock', 'Arinarach' and 'Sleof'. So, there it was again, and its existence was confirmed in a lease of Elerick granted to John Turner in 1793 by the 5th Duke of Argyll: ' ... as soon as a division of the Muir called Sleave being a common muir betwixt his farm of Elerick and the farms of Cnocnagrain and Arinascavach takes place ...' That entire area of southern Kintyre is now covered in coniferous forest and 'the Muir called Sleave' torn up and lost from view; but, having considered all the evidence, I offered an approximate location of 718 148.[1424]

There are many interpretations of *sliabh*. Dwelly[1425] lists the following: '1. Mountain of the first magnitude. 2. Extended heath, alpine plain, moorish ground. 3. Extensive tract of dry moorland. 4. Mountain grass, moor bent grass. 5. Face of a hill.' There are merely two *sliabh* names recorded in Kintyre on O.S. maps, **Sliabh nan Dearc** [906 592], north of Skipness, and **Sliabh a' Bhiorain** [601 124], south of Largiebaan, and these are on the map of Scotland showing the distribution of names containing *sliabh* in W. F. H. Nicolaisen's *Scottish Place-Names* (p 43).

What, however, is the status of the hill named '**The Slate**' [633 164] south of Machrihanish? It is a broad, rounded mass, pleasing to the eye, and at 1263 ft. is big in the scale of Kintyre hills. Visible from various parts of Campbeltown, particularly the higher land in the north, on hazy evenings The Slate wears a blue coat of tranquillity, alluring to anyone who knows it from nearer. The Langlands map of 1793 shows 'Slate', Peter MacIntosh in 1857 gave 'Sleit', 'Sleibhte' and 'Sleit Mountain',[1426] while Cuthbert Bede in 1861 had 'Sleit, or Sliabh'.[1427] The O.S. in 1866 suggested a derivation 'from "Sleibhte", an extended heath or Alpine plain, by which name [i.e. the Gaelic form] it is also known'.[1428] The K.A.S. place-names committee, after considering the name, plumped for *Na Sléibhte(an)*, 'The Hill moor'.[1429] Dwelly[1430] gives *sléibhte* and *sléibhtean* as plurals of *sliabh*, and MacKinnon interprets Sleat in Skye as '*sleibhte*, a plural form, literally "the mountain slopes"'.[1431] The pronunciation among country folk in Kintyre, as I heard it in the latter half of the 20th century, was 'slaitch'.

The O.S. in 1867 interpreted Sliabh nan Dearc as 'Alpine plain of the berries',[1432] but 'moor-slope of the berries' – which were presumably blaeberries – might nowadays be preferred. Its translation of Sliabh a' Bhiorain was 'Heath or Alpine plain of the sticks';[1433] *The Place-Names of the Parish of Southend* (p 32) offered 'The slope of the pinnacle'. That pinnacle stands in clear definition from the north – indeed, Allister and Agnes Stewart would use it as a landmark when walking from Largiebaan to Innean Coig Calleiche and Innean Dunain[1434] – but as one approaches closer to it, the point, by a trick of perspective, vanishes, and one would almost wonder if one were looking at the same feature.

Not so very far from Sliabh a' Bhiorain there was another, which, like 'The Sliabh', has never appeared on any map. Towards the end of 2011, I handed my wife Judy a copy of *The Kintyre Magazine* No. 5, which contains an article by Dr F. S. Mackenna on 'Old Kintyre Roads'. I supposed that it would interest her, and it did; but I should have read it carefully myself years before, because she soon brought it back to me and pointed out, on page 18, a minute of the Commissioners of Supply, dated 2/5/1759 and reporting a petition from 'the Tennants of Glenbreckry in Kintyre' complaining that the high road from the 'Maoll of Kintyre to Campbeltown' had been neglected and was now almost impassable where it crossed 'a bad Muir called **Sliavnabodiry**'. Here was another *sliabh* place-name in South Kintyre, and I asked Ian A. Fraser if he was able to interpret it. He was uncertain about the specific, but suggested that it might be *bothair*, 'lane' or 'road', with an *-aidh* ending, giving 'moor of the place of the road' or some similar allusion.[1435]

Where was that 'Muir called Sliavnabodiry'? In the Langlands map of 1801, there is no direct track shown between the Mull and Glenbreackerie, only: 1. The coastal track linking the townships between Carskey in the south and Lossit in the north. 2. A track running north from Carskey to Keprigan. 3. A branch of that following the line of Glenbreackerie and running out at Gleneadardacrock. 4. Another branch heading north at Achnaslishaig and coming on to the main road at Auchincorvie, as is still the case. My guess is that the bad bit was on that last track, which then, as now, would be the shortest route to Campbeltown from Glenbreackerie. So perhaps 'Sliavnabodiry' was on the moor west of Cnoc nan Gabhar, before the road dips to Lochorodale. I helped Robert McInnes cut peats there in the late 1970s and early '80s, and experienced its capricious watery ways. But this is total conjecture.

On Roy's mid-18th century map, **Slioch Chrannie** represents another *sliabh* name (Sliabh nan Dearc appears as 'Slioch na Deark' on the same map.) Marked west of Loch Dirigadale, it almost certainly refers to the unnamed 821-ft. hill on O.S. maps at 719 459.

In Macdonald's 'West Kintyre Field Names', his interpretation of *sliabh* is 'hill' (thrice) and 'field' (once), with one blank: **An Sliabh**, 'The hill' (Glenacardoch); **Sliabh meadhonach**, 'Middle hill' (Tangy); **Sliabh na drochaid**, 'Bridge hill' (Barrmains); **Sliabh na saighead**, 'Arrow field' (Rosshill); **Sliabh mór** (Barlea).[1436]

SLOC (or SLOCHD, the older alternative) is a pit or gully. This place-name element was most common around Carradale. **Slochd nan Gobhar**, 'Gully of the Goats', has already been remarked on under GOBHAR, but there were half-a-dozen others, including **Slochd na Cloiche**, 'Pit of the Stone', one at Carradale Point, recorded by Charles Reppke in 1942, and another south of Grogport, a seabed hole known to fishermen, who also called it the **Minister's Sloak**, from the manse at Barmollach. **Slochd a' Chapuill**, 'The Mare's Pit', was at Torrisdale,[1437] and the same name was recorded at Uisaed [626 208] on an old map at Lossit House.[1438] That one is the only record for the whole of Campbeltown Parish. In Southend Parish there were three, two on Sanda Island and one on Sheep Island, all, as above, taken from an old map. **Slochd-an-offar** – *Slochd an fhomhair*, 'The giant's pit' – has been looked at under FAMHAIR/FOMHAIR. The other on Sanda was **Slockdou**, for *Slochd dubh*, 'Black gully'. **Uave Slocknaboak**, on the south side of Sheep Island, has been interpreted as *Uamh sloc nam boc*, 'Cave of the gully of the he-goats'.[1439] For **Sloc Aindreis** see under CILL. The final one is the most interesting. It was given to George Campbell Hay by a Tarbert fisherman, Calum Johnson. **Sloc a' Chaibeil Bhàin** [876 687] was a gully on the south side of East Loch Tarbert, believed to be buried under the road now. Campbell Hay interpreted it as 'Pit of the White or Blessed Chapel' and considered it 'important', but had heard no tradition attaching to it.[1440]

SOCACH. *Soc* is a 'snout' or 'nose', hence *socach*, 'snouted promontory',[1441] and is akin to TEANGA, a 'tongue' of land. The O.S. Kintyre name-books generally define *socach* as a point of land between two streams.[1442] **Allt an t-Socaich** [871 589], 'Stream of the Snout', is near Skipness. Graham McKinlay told me that there were two fields named **Socach** on Whitestone farm, a north one and a south one.[1443] In Campbeltown Parish: **Socach** on a hill on Low Tirfergus, on a hill on Low Ugadale, and in a field [687 181] at Killeonan.[1444] In Southend Parish, east of Knockstapple, **Socach Meadhonach** [715 121], 'Middle Snout', with **An Socach** [714 110], 'The Snout', directly south of it, suggesting a further *socach* place-name, now lost, to the north of the middle one; **Socach Planting**, a wood on Macharioch farm, west of St. Coivan's Chapel. Finally, there is **Socach** [744 128], with a glen named after it, and one of a cluster of ruins near Glenahervie, the others being Cantaig, Erradil, and the earlier Sheanachie. This was a farm, which appears in the Valued Rent Roll of 1751 as the one-merkland of 'Soccoth'. In 1792 'Succoth' was occupied by Donald Cameron, his wife More Olynachan and their six children; in 1828 it was merged with Cantaig, and by 1852 its lands were part of 'one monotonous solitary sheepwalk'.[1445]

SRATH, simply defined, is 'valley', but there is more to it than that, as a look at *srath* locations in Kintyre will suggest. Dwelly includes, among his definitions, 'valley through which a river runs'; 'low-lying or flat part of a valley district or farm'; 'any low-lying country along a river, strath'; 'the low, inhabited part of a country, in contra-distinction to its hilly ground'; 'plain beside a river'.[1446] Watson, having cited exceptions, declares that in Gaelic place-names the standard use of the term denotes 'the lower ground on both sides of a stream', and that 'a strath differs from a glen in being as a rule wider and, perhaps always, smoother'.[1447] In Irish it 'basically means "valley-bottom", or a "flat place", e.g. beside a river or lake, a "holm"'.[1448] To appreciate what, in my opinion, is a classic Kintyre strath, visit the top end of Lussa Reservoir and look north towards

Strathduie. I had wondered whether that watery valley-bottom related to Strathduie or to Strathmollach, further south, but the 1851 Killean and Kilchenzie Census enumerator's concluding remark – having covered 'Coliska', 'Gobagrennan', 'Corrilach' and 'Bordaduh' – may satisfactorily dispose of that doubt: 'End of the detailed glen of Strathduie.'

Strathduie [718 319] is indeed a valley, and a broad one, at the upper reaches of Lussa Water. It appears as 'Stradowich' on Pont's map of 1610 along with 'Loch na Dowich', which corresponds to the location of the present **Arnicle Loch**. The strath does not appear on O.S. maps, but 'Strathduie Water', which flows through it to the north end of Lussa Reservoir, does. The name has been interpreted as *Srath dubhaidh*, 'Gloomy strath'.[1449] Peter MacIntosh told a story of two farmers in 'Straduie Glen' who were digging potatoes one day and boasting of their strength. One said to the other, 'Put that sack on my back', and, when he had the sack properly balanced, gave three leaps on one foot, threw it off and asked his neighbour to do the same. The sack weighed 400 lbs. and his neighbour declined the challenge.[1450]

59. SRATH. Strathduie Glen, April 2012. Photograph by the author.

Strabane [661 222] was a farm in the Laggan, and any terrain in Kintyre less likely to have a valley of any description in it would be hard to imagine; nor was there any stream, let alone river, close by.

It might be supposed that the name was formed at a time when the topography was different, but it does not appear in any record until 1866 when the Ordnance Survey described it as 'A newly built farm house and offices, the property of John Colvill Esqr. of Burnside Street, Campbeltown', while failing to address the name itself.[1451] In an advertisement of the estate of Machrihanish in 1813 the farm is apparently named 'Langlands'.[1452] In C1841 the holding was called **Links** and was occupied by eight farm labourers and their families. In 1851, it is 'Links No. 1' and 'No. 2', the latter 70 acres in extent and farmed by Donald McSporran. It seems likely that the name was adopted from elsewhere, just as Skernish in Barr Glen was called for a place in Skye. Whatever, Strabane – *Srath bàn*, 'Fair' or 'White Strath' – was associated during its brief history with a McSporran family. James McSporran started his working life in farm service, but, with 'enterprise and energy beyond the common', got the tenancy of 'Strathbane' in the 1870s and worked it until his death in 1920 at the age of 73. Potatoes were his main crop, for which the 'Links' were especially suited. He and his wife, Jane Blue, raised a family there, and two of his sons moved to Gigha to farm, hence the family of that name on the island.[1453] During World War II, the land was commandeered for an air station and the steading demolished. The aerodrome, though commissioned as HMS *Landrail*, was also called Royal Naval Air Station Strabane, but that name was quickly changed by the Admiralty to R.N.A.S. Machrihanish when it emerged that stores and personnel were ending up at Strabane in Northern Ireland, a costly misunderstanding.[1454] The station was taken over by the Royal Air Force in 1963 and is now community-owned.

Strathmore [666 079], the triangular stretch of level ground on the farm of Gartavaigh, bounded by river, road and sea, is *Srath mór*, 'Big strath'. New Year's Day shinty matches were played there (see under MACHAIR). 'Stramore' was one of the early names of the Laggan farm now called simply **Strath**, but see under UACHDAR. There appear to be merely two *srath* place-names in North Kintyre, **Strathnafanaig**, for which see under FEANNAG, and the difficult **Strahatildy**, as it appears on the Langlands map of 1801, well inland of Oragaig and south of Larachmore; in 1796, the deceased Charles MacNicoll was referred to as a 'drover in Strathadalty',[1455] the same place. For **Strathmollach** see under MOLACH, for **Lephenstrath** see under LETH-PHEIGHINN, and for all other straths refer to the place-names booklets for Southend and Campbeltown parishes.

SRÒN is 'nose', and topographically a 'point' or 'promontory'. It is a fairly common element in Kintyre place-names, from large scale to small. At the upper end, there is the rocky headland **Sròn Gharbh** [600 178], south of Machrihanish, which has the specific 'rough', and anyone who has scaled its flank will vouch for that description; there is another of the name at the mouth of East Loch Tarbert [875 681].

60. *SRÒN. Sròn Uamha fort from north, 31/3/1993. Photograph by the author.*

Sròn Albannach [731 494], in Kilcalmonell Parish, was described by the O.S. as 'the south end of a ridged hill', and interpreted 'Scottish Nose or Scotchman's Nose',[1456] a curiosity, but not unprecedented. There was a settlement there, 'Stronalbanach' on the 1801 Langlands map.

Strone [625 103], once a remote shepherd's cottage in Southend, is *An t-Sròn*, 'The nose', with a valley of the same name, **Gleann na Sròine**.[1457] Archibald and Agnes Todd were in Strone for well over half-a-century (see EILEIRG), and I believe the steading was last occupied in the 1960s. Certainly, when I was there with a tree-planting squad in 1968, it was disused, but we used it as a 'bothy', and one day I scratched all our names on the kitchen wall, with the message: 'Snowbound. 1st March 1968. Planting trees.'[1458]

Auchnastrone [875 565] at Claonaig is *Achadh na Sròine*, 'Field of the point', and was also a settlement. In 1803 it was recorded as 'Achenesroine', in C1851 as 'Auchnastron', with nine houses occupied there, and in C1891 as 'Auchnastrone', with only one house occupied, by a fisherman. On the farm of Drumnamucklach, near Killean, D. J. Macdonald recorded – his own spelling and interpretation – the field-name **Tigh na stroine**, 'Nose House'.[1459] **Sròn nan Cliabh**, 'Promontory of the Creels', is a ridge on Beachmenach farm, which Ian MacDonald (2011) understood to be the 'old boundary of Achapharic and Taychroman'. **Sròn a' Chonnaidh** [c. 854 652] is inland near the head of West Loch Tarbert. The feature has disappeared in coniferous forest and is obscure on O.S. maps. The Survey translated it as 'The Fuel Promontory',[1460] and I guess it was a spot where wood was collected or stacked.

Peter MacIntosh described **Sròin-na-h-eanachair** as a 'hill in Carradale ... in which, it is said, an old creature resides from generation to generation, who makes a great noise before the death of individuals of a certain clan'.[1461] Cuthbert Bede retailed the same yarn, which he claimed to have heard from 'the man at the wheel' during his steamer voyage to Campbeltown in 1859,[1462] but the words are clearly MacIntosh's, ineffectually disguised. Duncan Reid ponderously translated the name as 'the point or nose of the sagacious old person'.[1463] There is no mapped place-name resembling it, unless the O.S. **Sròn na Sean-Mhathaire** [c. 782 380], 'The Grandmother's Nose', relates to the same place.

For **Sròn Achadh a' Chipein Bhuidhe**, 885 595 is a very general location for a feature described by the O.S. as 'a prominent projection on grazing of Coalfin'. The O.S. interpretation, 'The point (nose) of the yellow tether stake field', was later questioned, somewhat irrationally, in a pencilled note in the name-book: 'The name is too long and the word Achadh is not essentially requisite.'[1464]

SRUTH is a stream. **Sruth na Maoile** is the Gaelic name for the North Channel, between Kintyre and the north of Ireland. It means 'The Mull Stream' and was well named, since mid-way into flood-tide something like a billion tons of water is on the move from the Atlantic into the northern Irish Sea through that channel; and back again, twice daily.[1465] With its tide-rips and counter-currents and eddies, Sruth na Maoile, and the coasts which compress its volume, is no place for dithering around in small boats, let alone the skin-covered curraghs of history. The disappearance of the Irish trader Breccán, with all his company and 50 vessels, into the whirlpool between Rathlin Island and the Irish mainland, is recorded in the Book of Ballymote.[1466] That whirlpool was named *Coire Bhreacáin* – 'Breccán's Cauldron' – after him, but its namesake, between the islands of Jura and Scarba, is now better known. From the mighty to the minuscule ... The feature named **An Struthlag** [799 325] on O.S. maps appears to mark a tidal reef north of Saddell, but it represents *sruthlag*, 'little stream', from the 'beautiful spring water' which issued from the shore below high water-mark; skiff fishermen could land there and replenish their water supplies.[1467] **Knockstruan**, one of the four parts into which the farm of Trodigal, Machrihanish, was formerly divided, represents *Cnoc an t-sruthain*, 'Hill of the brook'. It appears in C1841 as 'Knockantruan', between 'Knockanymore' [641 200] and 'Ballochaphrison [636 195], when occupied by James Kelly, 'farmer', and Malcolm Kelly, 'crofter'. **Sruthan ceann na tràighe** [642 207], which runs in front of the villas at Machrihanish, edging the golf course, is 'Brook at the end of the shore'.[1468]

STAC. Visualise a tooth, blunt or sharp, scale it up to 40 or 50 ft. high, stick it on or near the seashore, and you have a typical Kintyre *stac*. Macbain (p 344) has 'a precipice, a steep hill' as his definitions, but the Kintyre *stac* corresponds to Scottish stack, 'a columnar isolated rock'. The common origin, however, is Norse *stakkr*, a 'stack', as of hay.

Two unmapped South Kintyre place-names may have a Scots rather than a Gaelic origin. **The Stackie** [759 237] is a chunky tower of rock on the shore between Smerby and Peninver, which I heard referred to tautologically by fishermen as 'The Stackie Rock'. To the south is Stackie or Smerby Cove, a cave occupied by tinkers and vagrants into the 20th century, and latterly frequented by winkle-pickers and 'coasters'.[1469] **The Stacks** [597 174] are two rocks on the shore at Earadale Point, south of Machrihanish. They are visible with the naked eye from the A83, like two tiny teeth at the foot of the most distant headland. I climbed down to them and on to them in May 1982 and June 1983. On the first occasion, I photographed herring gull chicks hatching, and lay for nearly an hour on the northern stack, 'enjoying the marvellous heat of the sun and listening to the breaking seas ... '[1470]

Stac a' Chagair [680 406], north of Muasdale, is 'The Whispering Stack', which was said to 'whisper musical sounds into the listener's ear'.[1471] The suggestion is not as fanciful as might at first appear. A rock-face known as **The Singing Rock** [597 166], at the north end of the Inneans Bay, produces similar effects, probably by amplification of natural sounds, such as wind and waves.[1472] Adam MacPhail, Glenbarr, told me that when road improvements were made north of Muasdale, during his lifetime – he was born in 1907 – two of the stacs, including Stac a' Chagair, were spared the attention of the shot-blaster, 'because there's somethin sacred about them'.[1473]

61. STAC. The southernmost Stack at Earadale Point, 9/8/1981. Photograph by the author.

Stac a' Chrochaire [680 407], another Muasdale feature, is 'The Hangman's Stack.' All that D. J. Macdonald had to say of this was that it signified 'a summary method of administrating justice',[1474] while Cuthbert Bede, in more expansive mode, linked it with Dùn Dòmhnuill – see under DÙN – which was 'annually visited by "the great Macdonald" when he collected his rents'. From nearby Stac a' Chrochaire 'doubtless, those who were behind-hand with rent or civility, were suspended with very little ceremony'.[1475] **Stac an Fhamhair** [680 402], 'The Giant's Stack', again at Muasdale, is close to Dùn an Fhamhair, to which refer under DÙN for the tradition. Muasdale is without doubt the place to view stacs: from the village north, there are many of them, named and unnamed, visible from the road.

62. SUIDHE. Bellochantuy in a postcard published by Raphael Tuck & Sons, c. 1930. The church, post office and garage have since been demolished. Author's collection.

SUIDHE is 'seat' or 'sitting' and implies a resting-place. The best known Kintyre place-name containing this element is **Bellochantuy** – *Bealach an t-suidhe*, 'The pass of sitting' – for which see under BEALACH. **Suidhe nan Eun**, 'Sitting-place of the Birds', is a cairn with a large upright stone in the middle of it high on Beachmenach hill. Ian MacDonald's father kept ewes there, and Ian, up there in mornings in his youth, would occasionally see a Golden Eagle perched on the stone. **Cnoc an t-Suidhe** [883 584], 'Hill of the

Seat', was on the grazing of Coalfin farm, Skipness. About 350 yards south of its summit, Angus Graham noted a rock-face from which an unsuccessful attempt had been made to cut a millstone.[1476] The custom of funeral processions' resting at certain places on their way to burial-grounds and laying the foundation of memorial cairns, is referred to under CÀRN. I have found no Kintyre tradition of this, but there is a record from Islay relating to the place-name *Uisge-an-t-suidhe*, 'Water of the seat or resting-place'. Hector MacLean, Ballygrant, recalled that mourners – some of them with nine miles to travel – would sit beside the stream 'to take refreshment of bread, cheese, and whisky'.[1477] **Emillia's Seat** is shown on the Roy map just south of Saddell Bay. The woman named 'Amelia' is a mystery, but the name was certainly known in Kintyre in the 18th century and appears in the Killean and Kilchenzie parish registers as 'Melly' and 'Mellie', presumably representing a Gaelic form.[1478]

TARSUINN is 'transverse, across', from *tar*, 'across', and *sainn* of *ursainn*, which is glossed as 'a door-post'.[1479] *Tar*, of course, also appears in **Tarbert**, the village which is half-in and half-out of Kintyre. The name means 'isthmus', and is from *tairm-bert*, 'an over-bringing', with reference to the overland dragging of boats.[1480] **Cruach Tarsuinn** [874 614], which stands at 994 ft. north-west of Skipness, was interpreted 'Cross hill' by the O.S.[1481] The idea expressed in *tarsuinn* is perhaps better understood attached to a stream, as in **Allt Tarsuinn**, Bardaravine, which the O.S. interpreted as 'Oblique Burn, i.e. flowing from side to side'.[1482] The word *trasd* contains much the same idea, 'across', e.g. **Allt Trasda**, 'Transverse Stream', one in Killean and Kilchenzie [691 287] and one in Southend [610 128].

TEANGA is 'tongue' and describes a tongue-shaped portion of land. Regarding the best known of the Kintyre place-names, **Tangy** [674 277], D. J. Macdonald noted that 'The configuration of the land exactly resembles a tongue'.[1483] Tangy Estate was in the possession of a MacEachan family, which has been identified as an offshoot of the MacEachans of Kingairloch in Morvern, until the death of the 8th and last chief, Charles, who died unmarried in 1698.[1484] A rental of 1688 refers to 'Mc eachine of Tangzie'. The estate was acquired by Colonel Charles Campbell of Barbreck in the 18th century,[1485] and in 1870 James Macalister Hall purchased it for £45,500.[1486] With the retirement of Lachlan Clark in 1897 ended three generations' connection with Tangy, his father and grandfather having been farmers and millers there.[1487]

Teangachoisin [739 396] is differently spelt in every record of it I have seen. I have chosen the above spelling because the generic *teanga* is clear ... but read on. The spellings in the baptismal records of Saddell and Skipness are fairly consistent (only the fathers' names are given here): 1736 Gilbert MacIlchallum, 'Tengiechosen'; 1783 Donald McAlpin, 'Teangachoisin'; 1796 Hugh Mitchell, 'Tengachoisin'. The spelling is 'Tayahoisan' on the 1801 Langlands map and 'Tayinhoisan' on the *Glencreggan* map (1861). The name is preserved in **Teanchoisin Glen** [747 403], through which the parish boundary of Saddell and Killean passes. Ian MacDonald in 2011 recalled a tradition that three lairds could meet there and 'talk to each other on their own lands'. 'Teangachoisin' was still occupied – by farm worker Charles McMillan and family – when C1841 was taken. The meaning of the second element is uncertain, though Gillies ventured *an chòisin*, 'little cave', having made the generic *tigh*, 'house'.[1488] Ian A. Fraser suggests *Teanga a' chòsain*, 'Tongue of the nook', from *còsan*, a term which occurs in topographic names, with *oisinn*, 'corner', 'angle', also possible, but less likely.[1489] **Teanga Mhór** [776 318], near Saddell, is the 'Big Tongue'. **The Tongue** appears in English describing a 'sheep heft' in Balnabraid Glen; the steading of Balnabraid [753 158] was said to have stood at the lower end of the feature.[1490]

63. *TEINE. Dùn [a'] theine, as the name may be, from the east. Photograph by the author, 6/6/2012.*

TEINE is 'fire'. The main Kintyre feature having this element is **Beinn a' Theine** [601 073], which rises to 1263 ft. The O.S. spelling was adjusted in *The Place-Names of the Parish of Southend* (p 10) to *Beinn aithinne*, 'Firebrand hill'. Cameron Gillies considered the O.S. form a 'bad rendering' of *Beinn Theine*, 'the fire mountain'.[1491] The O.S. interpretation in 1866 was 'The firy (*sic*) mountain'.[1492]

There are at least two possibilities here. There may be a connection with the pagan Mayday Beltane festival, when fires were lit on hilltops. Of this 'superstition of the Druids', MacIntosh in 1857 remarked that it had not 'altogether departed from Kintyre'.[1493] Alternatively, on this commanding height on the Mull, in view of the Antrim coast, signal beacons may have been lit. In 1638, when the Earl of Antrim was threatening to invade Argyll, among the defensive proposals was 'a series of beacons ... to be established to flash out warnings if any invasion took place'.[1494]

Wallace Clark recounted that in April 1568, when Shane O'Neill attacked the MacDonnells of Antrim under Sorley Boy, 'James, Lord of the Isles, Sorley's elder brother, seeing from his castle on the north tip of Kintyre smoke signals for assistance from his castle on the south tip of Kintyre, took the first boat crew available and set off in his galley at the start of the ebb to come to Sorley's assistance'.[1495] The northern castle must have been Tarbert and the southern Dunaverty, but, with all respect, the signal at the latter must have been one hell of a conflagration to have been visible 40 miles away. If the emergency was indeed signalled from the south of Kintyre to the north, it seems likelier that more than one beacon would have been required and that these would have been lit on high ground.

It is clear from the Ordnance Survey name-books of the mid-1860s that there was a persistent tradition of beacons' being lit on coastal duns. **Dùn Mhic Choigil** [656 301] was one such,[1496] as was that at **Port a' Chaisteil**, for which see under CAISTEAL.

Local pronunciation suggests that the headland marked **Dùn na h-Òighe** [741 090], 'The Virgin's Hillock', on O.S. maps, might also have a connection with fire and would be better represented as *Dùn [a'] theine* or *Dùn aithinne*, meanings as above. The Admiralty spelling in the mid-19th century was 'Dunnighn Pt.' That headland is prominent and flat-topped, like a miniature Dunaverty, but there is no evidence of its ever having been fortified. Still, it has an appearance – a feeling, even, when one is on it – of historical significance, and, owing to its location on Macharioch, I formed the notion that it might have been a point for signalling across to Sanda.

In July 2000, I was on the headland with a trowel in my rucksack and decided to sound a distinctive pit on the summit. I inserted the trowel until it touched rock, then removed a small section of sandy turf, but there was no sign of burnt matter.[1497]

Allt a' Theine was recorded by the O.S. in 1866 and rather oddly interpreted as 'Fire Water'. It was described as a 'small stream about 12 or 13 chains in length', flowing into Conieglen Water south of Keprigan farm, and the informant was clearly Angus McEachran, Kilblaan.[1498] A long field on the farm of West Skeroblingarry, near Park Loch, was known as **Teine bheag**, 'Little fire',[1499] but, sadly, no explanation of the name is known.

TIGH is 'house'. **Tayinloan** is the best known of the Kintyre place-names containing this element, but see under LÒN. The name **Tigh-Amorirna** appears on a 1750 map of Kintyre in the British Museum. It has been interpreted as *Tigh mór-thighearna*, 'The house of the great lord', and linked with the chief of Clan Iain Mhóir's dwelling at Machrimore, which was destroyed by the Earl of Sussex in 1558.[1500] **Tigh nam Feadag**, 'Plover House', was on North Beachmore farm. Ian MacDonald recalled Golden Plover (*Pluvialis apricaria*) nesting on Beachmenach hill; but the Lapwing, or 'Peeweep' (*Vanellus vanellus*), was more common. **Tighnalenadh** [687 411] first appears in baptismal records in the late 18th century and was the popular name for North Crubasdale; in C1901, 'Tighnalena' was added in brackets beside 'North Crusbasdale Farm'. John Cameron suggested the derivations *Tigh an lèanna*, 'Ale house', or *Tigh nan lèanan*, 'House of the meadows'. The name in some of its forms might be confused with 'Tayinloan', e.g. in an obituary in 1922 of Catherine McDougall, widow of Lachlan D. Thomson, joiner in Barr, she was described as a daughter of John McDougall and Catherine McNiven, 'Taynalain Farm'.[1501] Ian MacDonald (2011) associated the farm with the McGeachy family which later established the ironmonger's shop in Union Street, Campbeltown. **Tigh na Craoibhe** [897 575], 'House of the Tree', at Skipness, was unoccupied by C1901.

The endings of both **Glenahanty** [630 143] and **Knockhanty** [641 200] in Campbeltown Parish were interpreted – but tentatively – by the K.A.S. place-names committee as *sean* + *tigh*, the first 'Glen of the old house' and the second 'Hillock of the old house', though *Cnoc an tighe*, 'Hill of the house', in the latter case, might serve just as well. The discussion, however, produced some odd suggestions. For Knockhanty, which is on record in 1481 as 'The Knokantie', Donald

McKinlay, by way of explanation, evoked 'the eternal roll and sound of the waves', which owes more to imagination than to etymology. For Glenahanty, Edward McCallum – his only appearance in the records – ventured 'The glen of the one house', which he explained as 'the only house which remained there after the epidemic of plague in Kintyre'. This may be assumed to refer to the plague of 1647, but the name goes back much further than that horrific event, with a record in 1481, 'Glenhawindee'. 'Siol Chuinn' in 1921: 'Much of the beauty of Glenahanty has been lost since I saw it first. Then the houses were thatch-covered and ferns grew out of the walls; now it is roofed with the less romantic, if more sanitary, corrugated iron.'[1502]

TÌR is 'land'. **Kintyre** itself, the subject of this book, is from Gaelic *Ceann tìre*, 'head of land' or 'end of land'. That there was another similar name, *Sáil-tíre*, 'Land's heel', is evident from the Norse *Saltiri, Salltiri* and, 'less correctly', *Satiri*.[1503]

The other main *tìr* place-name is **Tirfergus**, above Drumlemble. Actually, there are five names now: two farms, High [655 183] and Low [664 184], Glen, Hill and Burn. The name represents *Tìr Fhearghais*, 'Land of Fergus'. The identity of Fergus is unknown, which is perhaps not surprising because the name is surely medieval in origin. Captain White in 1873 was prepared to push the name back even further, citing a traditional connection with Fergus Mór mac Eirc, founder in the 5th century of the kingdom of Dalriada in Scotland,[1504] a notion he may have adopted from Peter MacIntosh.[1505] The first record of 'The two Tereferguse' appears in a charter of 1481, and in the following century the forms 'Terargus' (1502), 'Terargis' (1507), 'Teiragus' (1562) and 'Tiriearrois' (1596) appear.[1506]

Tirfergus was associated with the distinguished MacNeill (later Macneal) family, which emerged from obscurity in the person of Lachlan MacNeill Buidhe (c. 1611-95). He was married twice, had 15 children and at least 80 grandchildren, and acquired extensive lands in Kintyre: Tirfergus and Largiebaan in 1660 and Lossit, Knockhantie and Glenahantie in 1668.

A tradition explaining his wealth was recorded from the memory of Neil Fleming, gamekeeper at Lossit, in 1853, when he was about 55 years old. Neil had been brought up at Machrihanish with his maternal grandfather, Archibald MacMath, in whose house also lived an ancient man, one Torquil Macneal, known as 'Little Torquil' or 'The Prophet'. As a child, Neil often fell asleep on his grandfather's knee listening to him and Torquil talking over the history of the

Macneals. The story was told that Lachlan's father, Neil Buidhe, was sent to Ireland during 'the plague' which struck Kintyre in 1647. He was engaged to a MacKillop girl and, when he returned, found all her family dead and the girl herself very ill. She wouldn't allow him near her, for fear of infecting him, and told him to go back to Ireland and stay there until matters would improve, and then to return, and, if she had died, to look in the west corner of the house and he would find there 'what would be good to himself and those who might come after him'. She died, and when Neil came back he found a hoard of gold at a depth of three feet in that corner. This was the money that bought or feud Tirfergus. A. I. B. Stewart argues that if the story is transferred from Neil to his son Lachlan, 'there are several facts which make it more credible', but I shall let the dubious tale stand alone, and direct the interested reader to A. I. B.'s 'Lachlan McNeill Buidhe', *Kintyre Magazine* No. 19, p 18.

Lachlan's house appears to have stood near the present farm-steading of Low Tirfergus, but no description of it has survived. Three carved stones, however, survived its demolition and were incorporated in the masonry of an outbuilding at the steading. One of them is part of a commemorative panel and bears the initials of Lachlan MacNeill and the date August 1667. The two other relics are fragments of carved human heads.[1507] To the south of the steading there is an orchard, perhaps also connected with the MacNeill house, which produced fruit – apples, plums and cherries – until within the past quarter-century.[1508]

Teirdonald in Southend is 'lost'. The name goes back to 1481 when it was spelt 'Teredonyll', and recurs nine times, for the last time in 1605, as 'Teirdonald' and 'Turdonald'. The derivation *Tìr Dhòmhnuill*, 'Donald's land', has been proposed, and Archie McEachran suggested that it was 'probably an ancient name for half of Ballybrenan, the other half being Keremeanach'.[1509]

TOBAR is simply a well, and all wells had names in times when people had to fetch water for the house and often had to go out of their way for a drink when they needed one; so water was valued all the more for the efforts required in getting it. I was thinking just such thoughts on a day in early March 2012, when Murdo MacDonald and I stood at the piped spring at the south end of the Inneans Bay, sipping cool water from the very base of Cnoc Moy before starting homeward. That spring has no name, but the pipe was fixed in the ground by Neil Brown, a joiner in Campbeltown, and if he had been around a couple of centuries ago and scooped out a well there, I guess it might have ended up with the name 'Tobar Néill'. Was the water better-tasting than any other water I'd drank that year or the year before? I imagine it was, but can offer no more than that evaluation. Connoisseurship of plain water is more a notion of past times, and, when mixed in with sentiment, could be a potent draught.

Of **Tobar a' chath** [676 248], the well near the old parish church at Kilchenzie, also known as **Tobar an t-Sagairt**, 'The Priest's Well', D. J. Macdonald was told by James MacCallum, Muasdale, that when Peter Macmillan was dying, he 'wished to send for a drink of the water of this well. He believed that it would make him well again'. His son was David Macmillan,[1510] who farmed Low Clachaig, his birthplace, and who died in 1922 at the age of 83.[1511]

In 1921, 'Siol Chuinn' visited **Saint Catherine's Well** [643 115] in Glenadale. His companion was there for water to take to 'an old Glenbreckrie lady, one of the well-known McNeills of Amod, who, like David of old, wished to taste the waters of the well, where she had drunk as a child'. After a search, he and his companion found the well 'hidden in an alcove underlying a group of alders'.[1512] This was a holy well, as many wells formerly were, and when Frances Hood first visited it, in the 1970s, the well-bottom was covered with quartz pebbles and the adjacent bushes festooned with rags, a survival of the ancient pilgrims' practice of hanging up a rosary or a strip torn from their clothing. Coins were thrown into the well for luck, and Calum Bannatyne recalled that boys going to the school at Glenbreackerie would 'take days at raidin it'.[1513]

When Colonel Charles Mactaggart, who had a distinguished career in the Indian Medical Service, was visiting a hospital in India, the resident doctor, knowing that he was from Campbeltown, asked him if he had ever heard of 'Creag na h-Iolaire'. – 'Yes,' Mactaggart replied, 'I know the name well, but why do you ask me that?' – 'Oh, just because we have a lady patient in the hospital who is a native of Campbeltown, and while delirious she has continually kept on repeating the words, "Oh for a draught of "Creag na h-Iolaire."'' Her name was Mrs Dan Currie.[1514] The spring **Creag na h-Iolaire** – see under IOLAIRE – is not, of course, a *tobar* name, but its water was enjoyed by the population of nearby Dalintober, which leads on to that best-known of *tobar* place-names in Kintyre.

Dalintober is an anglicised form of Gaelic *Dail an Tobair*, 'The Well Field'. It could also be translated 'Spring Field', and, indeed, 'Springfield House' and 'Springfield Terrace', at the east end of High

Street, express that alternative. Dalintober came into existence as a planned village, created by John Campbell of Glensaddell, an estate which is commemorated in 'Saddell Street'. Campbell's plan was to offer a harbour where traders were exempt from payment of landing and shipping dues, and the proposal proved an attractive one. In 1766, merchants began buying up plots of land on which to build dwelling-houses and warehouses. This initiative, however, upset the magistrates of Campbeltown, who saw it as unfair competition which would reduce their harbour revenue. At that time, Dalintober lay outwith the burgh boundaries, in the old Parish of Kilchousland, but the village's special status ended in 1844, when the Council, after four years of litigation, established that goods landed or shipped at Dalintober were not exempt from dues.[1515]

Dalintober Quay, built about 1765, failed to fulfil commercial expectations, though cargoes of coal were brought in and potatoes and other local produce shipped out. It was, from the outset, a tidal harbour and unsuited to the accommodation of trading vessels. For the same reason, when a fishing community began to form in Dalintober in the early 19th century, the fleet of skiffs was moored offshore and the quay used mainly for landing crews, nets and fish. The Dalintober fishermen held themselves apart from their town counterparts. Indeed, there was great rivalry between the two sets of fishermen. Dalintober, until the mid-20th century, was largely self-sufficient as a community, with its own bakers, butchers, grocers, and publicans, and a separate burial-ground at Kilchousland. Until the reclamation of the 'Mussel Ebb' – which became Kinloch Green – towards the end of the 19th century, a ferry-boat ran from Dalintober Quay to Campbeltown Old Quay, to eliminate the long walk around the Lochend. Dalintober Quay was spoiled, both functionally and aesthetically, by its extension during the Second World War to serve air-sea rescue vessels. The extension was removed after the war, but an unsightly concrete ramp was left. By then, however, Dalintober had ceased to be an independent fishing community, and the few families which invested, post-war, in modern ring-netters, kept their boats with the Campbeltown fleet, and they themselves, in increasing numbers, migrated into town.

Tobar na foinneachan, near Port-an-dùin, on Glenacardoch shore, was described as 'gushing from the foot of a rock close to the sea'. Its meaning is 'Well of the warts', and it was believed to have 'healing properties which effectively removed these excrescences'. **Tobar Mhìcheil** [683 357], on Barrmains farm, is 'Michael's Well'. Neil MacDonald told D. J. Macdonald that 'a great many white stones were in this well', and Rev Macdonald himself noted close to it 'a heap of small white pebbles, doubtless the votive offerings of patients visiting the well'.[1516] **Tobar an Fhigheadair** [808 604], 'The Weaver's Well', is by the roadside south of Whitehouse. For **Camus an Tobair** see under CAMUS.

Tobar an Tighearna [872 684], 'The Lord's or Chief's Well', is to the south of Tarbert, beyond the Castle. It is named **Tobar an Fhoin** on O.S. maps and spoken of as **Jacob's Well**. When I asked George Campbell Hay in 1980 about this well, he recalled that there used to be 'a wee mug in a recess in the rock, for people tae have a drink',[1517] a common provision. (In South Kintyre around the mid-20th century, there was a vogue for leaving half of a coconut shell beside a well as a drinking dish, which led to the expression 'coconut wells', which mystified me until I discovered its origin.) Earlier, in 1948, Campbell Hay described the well in writing and remarked that emigrants from 'the hill-villages of Kilcalmonell' would pray there before setting out overseas, and that some would carry away a bottle of its water. 'By it, some say, the folk who had left the Church of Patronage worshipped at the time of the Disruption, until they had built their own church.' One of his later Gaelic poems, *Fàire (Aig Tobar an Tighearna)*, was set at the well.[1518]

64. *TOBAR. The author's daughters Amelia (L) and Sarah seated on the steps leading down to Crocknaheilan spring, Campbeltown, 9/3/1992. Photograph by the author.*

TOM in Kintyre could be 'bush',[1519] but meant something different in place-names, probably a knoll – 'hummock', as defined in *The Place-Names of the Parish of Campbeltown*.   It was also in the vocabulary of Kintyre fishermen for a herring shoal, its specific sense lost to the post-Gaelic-speaking generation. I had thought it might equate with English 'lump' (of herring), but the late Gilbert Clark in Islay suggested to me in 1977 that it meant a 'bunch' of herring, as in *tom fraoich*, 'heather bunch'. **Tomaig** [708 194, etc], on the outskirts of Campbeltown, was described in a lease of 1709, under 'Tumack', as 'of old a part and pendicle of Knockriochbeg'.[1520] The land was divided into five smallholdings for ex-soldiers after the death of the fifth and last laird of Knockrioch, Lorn MacNeill Stewart, in 1927. **Tomaig Glen** is to the west of Ben Gullion. *Tomach*, 'hummocky land', has been suggested.[1521] **Eilean Toman** [c. 627 210] – this spelling from an old estate map at Lossit House – is off Uisaed, Machrihanish, and is a bare rock in the sea on which no bush grows or could ever have grown. The derivation *Eilean tomain*, 'Hummock island', has been suggested.[1522] The rock appears on an Admiralty chart, surveyed in 1846, as 'Ilinaham Point'. See also under MACHAIR. There appear to be no other *tom* names in Kintyre, not even in lists of field-names and other minor features.

TÒN in place-names is 'backside', for which 'fundament' is a favoured euphemism in older dictionaries. There are few place-names containing *tòn* in Kintyre, of which **Tonrioch** is the main one, but see under RIABHACH. **Tonadippen**, at Carradale, equates with 'South Dippen' [801 366]. The 'Duncan McDougall Fisherman of Lonaduppin' (for Tonaduppin) in 1821,[1523] is recorded on his gravestone in Brackley as a fisherman in 'South Duppin'. The earliest record appears to be 'Ton Duppine' in 1751, and as 'Tonaduppin' it was recorded as uninhabited in C1901. The name may be interpreted as 'Backside of the twopennyland'. See also DAPHEIGHINN, of which 'Dippen' is an anglicised form.

TORC is from Old Celtic *torko-s*. In Early Irish, *torc* had the meanings 'wild boar' and 'lord'.[1524] The main meaning in Gaelic is 'hog' or 'boar',[1525] and the word's presence in Kintyre place-names is a huge one. **Beinn an Tuirc** [752 361], 'Hill of the Boar', preserves an Ossianic legend and is also, at 1491 ft., the highest hill in Kintyre. Before the O.S. established the true dimensions of Beinn an Tuirc in 1867, its height tended to be overestimated. In the *Second Statistical*

Account of Saddell and Skipness parish (p 437), 'Benintuirk' is given as 2170 ft. high, a figure repeated on the map published with *Glencreggan* in 1861. As Professor MacKinnon has remarked, 'Every Beinn-an-Tuirc or "Boar's Hill" in Scotland, from the Mull of Kintyre to Glenshee in the east of Perthshire – and they are many – is held to be the identical hill on which Brown Diarmad met his death'.[1526]

This is Peter MacIntosh's version of the legend of the boar, as published in his *History of Kintyre* (p 53): 'The tradition is that a very large boar haunted this mountain, and was very dangerous to persons going that way. King Fingal at that time being in Kintyre with his brave Fingalians, ordered one of his men called Diarmid, to kill the wild boar. Diarmid, who was a great hunter, obeyed, and killed it, which stirred up the envy of some of the men. It is said that Diarmid was only vulnerable in one part – the heel. Fingal with his men viewed the wild boar, and were astonished at its great length. Diarmid was ordered to measure it with his bare feet. He did so, beginning at the head, [and] the strong bristles pressed downwards yielded with him. Fingal, who through some jealousy wished Diarmid dead, ordered him to measure the beast against the grain, which Diarmid did; when the bristles pierced the vulnerable part of his heel, and he soon bled to death.'

This is a very attenuated version of a complex tale from the mythological Fenian Cycle, which survived in many versions, both written and oral, in Ireland and in Gaelic Scotland. MacIntosh's 'King Fingal' equates with the hero Fionn mac Cumhaill, who led the Fianna warrior-band, and whose 'jealousy', to which MacIntosh cryptically alludes, will be explained in terms of a 'love triangle'.

When Fionn's wife Maigneis dies, his men agree that he must have another wife to soothe his grief, and decide that the worthiest woman of all is Gráinne, daughter of High King Cormac mac Airt. Fionn, however, is older than Gráinne's father, a realisation which distresses her. At the wedding feast she falls in love with Diarmuid, one of Fionn's handsome young warriors. She asks him to run away with her, but he refuses at first out of loyalty to old Fionn, and only agrees when she threatens him with a *geas*, or supernatural enchantment. She has already drugged the rest of the wedding guests, who are deep in sleep, and the two slip away.

Fionn, angered by the double betrayal, pursues the lovers, but they evade his vengeance, and eventually Diarmuid's foster-father Aengus negotiates a reconciliation ... of sorts. When Fionn organises a boar hunt, Diarmid goes along, despite a prediction that he will meet his death; and, indeed, the beast wounds him mortally just as he delivers the death-blow. But Fionn can save Diarmuid – the power is literally in his own hands. All he need do is let Diarmuid drink from his hands; but twice he cups water from a well to take to Diarmuid, and twice he lets it trickle through his fingers before he reaches the dying warrior. Then his grandson Oscar intervenes with menace, and Fionn fetches water for a third time, but when he returns from the well Diarmuid is already dead.

The fierce Wild Boar (*Sus scrofa*), with the Red Deer – see EILEIRG, 'deer-trap' – was once the prime beast of the chase, and is still widely hunted in many parts of Europe. But it is a woodland animal, and when woodlands are felled, the Wild Boar is bereft of its natural habitat. The species is believed to have become extinct in the wild in England in the 13th century, though it was reintroduced from France in the 17th.[1527] In Kintyre, the Wild Boar would have existed for as long as the peninsula remained well-wooded. Its extinction cannot be dated, even to the century, but Gibson and Colville (1975) believed that it was 'unlikely to have existed much beyond the 10th century'. A return of the species to a Kintyre which is once more heavily wooded is not inconceivable. A Lochaber farmer claimed in 2012 that he was losing lambs to the depredations of boars, which are once again wild in Scotland through illegal liberation or escape from captivity.[1528]

A story of the last 'wild pig' (*muc fhiadhaidh*) in Kintyre was recorded in Gaelic around 1940 by Nils M. Holmer. The storyteller was John Campbell, Seaside Cottage, Torrisdale, and this is an edited version. There was a little girl between Cour and the west side of Kintyre and she went on an errand to get a loan of a comb. On her way home, while between the two houses – there was a croft up there at that time – she met a wild pig which ate her. Not a piece of the girl was found, only the comb she was carrying. Crofters, farmers and shepherds turned out, and they put an end to the pigs.[1529]

A few relics of the Wild Boar's past presence have been discovered in Kintyre, and more may yet emerge. Bones found in the Piper's Cave on Ben Gullion and examined by Professor James Ritchie in 1944 almost certainly belonged to a Wild Boar,[1530] and a boar's skull was uncovered during drainage work in the Laggan. According to Dugald Macintyre, the tusks were so large that the drainer 'at first mistook them for the horns of a goat'. A local blacksmith fixed one of the tusks to a handle of his bellows, but 'a scientist secured it later, at a price, and presented it to an Edinburgh Museum'.[1531] This is clearly the same discovery referred to by Gibson and Colville, who located it on Parkfergus farm and dated it to 'the turn of the [19th] century'. By their spare account, the skull was destroyed but 'one of the tusks ultimately found its way to the Royal Scottish Museum'.[1532] John MacDonald tells me (24/11/2012) that the pool in the Backs Water known to anglers as **The Boar's Hole** [675 208] took its name from the incoming ditch which yielded the skull. See also MUC, 'pig'.

TÒRR was defined by Watson as 'a rounded hill',[1533] but in general it is a 'mound' or a 'heap'. The word was a Gaelic survival in the Kintyre fishermen's terminology, denoting a vast amount of herring. Neither Campbeltown nor Killean and Kilchenzie parish appears to have any place-name examples, and Southend, with five, has more than the other two parishes combined. I'll begin with Southend. Three of these *tòrr* names are at the Mull. **Tòrr Mór** [599 077] is 'big', and big it is at 1358 ft. **Tòrr na Lice** [c. 589 076], a rather indeterminate feature, is far below it, close to the sea, and is 'of the flat stone' (see LEAC). **Tòrr Dubh** [626 077] is 'black', to the east, and shares latitude 077 with Tòrr Mór. The fourth, **Tòrr Fada** [653 094], is still further east, clear of the Mull, and is 'long'. **Garbh Thòrr** [630 120], 'Rough Hill', is more to the north.[1534] There are two more of *mòr*, neither of them close to the Mull hill in magnitude, **Tòrr Mór** [839 650] in Kilcalmonell Parish and the other [809 397] north of Carradale harbour, which lent its name to a housing scheme in the village and was translated 'Great top' in 1867 by the O.S., which rendered the last one, **Tòrr a' Ghobhainn** [777 364], 'The smith's height'.[1535]

TRÀIGH is a sandy strand or shore. There are eight known *tràigh* place-names in Kintyre, all of them in the southern half and all of them vanished from spoken use. **Tràigh Bàn** (*Tràigh Bhàn*) was the 'local Gaelic name for Machrihanish Bay' and represents 'White Strand', which is also the meaning of **Geal Tràigh** [624 198], but in reverse construction. It is the last stretch of shore at the south end of the Galdrans, before the rocky coast begins, and anyone with only a passing familiarity with that shore might wonder at the aptness of the name, but, of course, sand comes and goes seasonally. That name was taken from an old estate map at Lossit House. '**Traisanes**' is marked on Timothy Pont's Map of 1610 near the mouth of the Backs (or Machrihanish) Water, and is clearly another name for Tràigh Bàn. It represents *Tràigh Sanais* or *Tràigh Shanais*, 'Strand of Sanish', but for the specific see Machrihanish under MACHAIR. On quiet nights, one can sometimes hear the surf on Machrihanish Bay from Campbeltown. A Kilmarnock minister, Rev. David Landsborough, claimed in 1883 that at times the 'roar' could be heard 'in the harbour of Ayr, a distance of 42 miles'. Professor MacKinnon repeated the claim four years later,[1536] but I must admit to finding it hard to believe.

65. *TRÀIGH. The strand of Machrihanish Bay, looking north from the mouth of the Backs Water, 18/4/2012. Photograph by the author.*

The name **Tràigh Réidh** [759 249] was given to Latimer MacInnes by a Mrs McMillan in Peninver village in 1939. It means 'level strand' and applies to the shore extending north from the village to Lussa Burn.[1537] Horse-racing took place there; in the *Campbeltown Journal* of 14/7/1853, a report appeared on Peninver 'race course'. The races were apparently organised by William MacDonald of Ballyshear (see under MACHAIR), and the Campbeltown steamers would disembark at Peninver those passengers who wished to attend. The racing was ultimately discontinued 'as a result of a fatal accident to one of the competitors'.[1538] **Allt Tràigh Leacainn** [763 288], 'The stream of the shore below the hill-slope',[1539] runs into the sea at the north end of Kildonan Bay, a rocky irregular shore which seems an unlikely 'strand'. **Tràigh nam Paitean** [663 345] is 'Paitean Shore'. D. J. Macdonald records, in *Annals of the Church and Parish of Killean* (p 12), that in 1700 'it was resolved to build a meeting-house at Corputchachan', and that 'Trainapattain' was suggested, but 'judged too remote from Kilchenzie'. **Tobar na Tràighe** [666 333], 'Well of the Shore', below Corputechan steading, takes its name from that *tràigh*. On Barlea farm, there was simply **An tràigh**, 'The strand'.[1540] The generic appears quite frequently in Irish place-names, the best known example being Tralee, which is *Tráigh Lí*, 'Strand of the (river) Lí'.[1541] Ballantrae in Ayrshire represents *Baile an Tràigh*, 'Township at the strand'.

UACHDAR is 'top' or 'summit', whence *uachdarach*, 'upper', one of the terms used in the naming of farm divisions. **Bàrr Uachdarach** [684 372] is, therefore, 'High Barr' (see BÀRR), as opposed to 'Low Barr' (later **Skernish**). One of the early names of the Laggan farm now called **Strath** [682 198] was 'Stra Uachtrach', which is *uachdarach* again, but this appellation is slightly puzzling since both it and its neighbour, 'Stra Ichtrach' (*ìochdrach*, 'lower'), which is now **Bleachfield** [681 207],[1542] are on the flattest land imaginable; none the less, Strath's being higher upstream on the Backs Water than Bleachfield may have justified the 'upper' and 'lower' distinctions.[1543] The geometric-sounding **Octoran** represents Gaelic *uachdaran*, 'upper lands'. There were two so named, one in Campbeltown Parish and the other in Southend. The most significant of them appears in 16th century Exchequer Rolls variously spelt – in 1502 and 1507, for example, 'Ochtoraan' and 'Uchtirane' – and appears to have been an earlier name for **Knocknaha** [688 179] or, at least, to have been incorporated into that holding. In any case, the name has long been obsolete, as has the other, which Archie McEachran tentatively identified with a Learside holding (adjoining Glenmurrell) otherwise known as 'Clachavulline' or 'Cnoc a' mheala'.[1544]

UAIGH is a grave. The word resembles UAMH(A) and *uaimh*, 'cave', and Dwelly allows *uaigh* the secondary meaning, 'cave'.[1545] There are only two *uaigh* place-names in Kintyre, and both are effectively forgotten. **Uaigh an fhamhair**, 'The giant's grave', was on Beacharra farm, but see under FAMHAIR. **Uaigh-Mhic-Caoga** [811 448] is 'MacCaig's Grave'. The tradition behind this name was recorded by Peter MacIntosh in the 19th century. The 'plague' referred to was the bubonic plague which General David Leslie's Covenanting army brought with it to Kintyre in 1647. 'A man, who lived in Upper Carradale glen, took the plague, and being afraid he would not be buried, got some young men, who undertook the charitable duty of digging his grave; he walked after them, sat down, and looked at them until the grave was finished. He then took with him his sword, stretched himself in the grave, and immediately expired, the young men covering him with kindred earth. The spot in which he was buried is pointed out, being in a beautiful green over the mouth of a large cave at Suineadale, and for many years afterwards went under the name of "Uaigh Mhic-caoga", or the grave of Mac Caog. An old man, who was above ninety years of age when he died, and who was brought up near the above place, gave me this anecdote, and added, that Mac Caog was my grandfather's grandfather.'[1546] Many of Peter's stories are now incredible, but the above account appears to me to have about it – allowing for the distortions inherent in oral transmission over several generations – a curious air of authenticity. Sunadale Cave was later associated with Jenny MacCallum, *Cailleach na h-Uamh* ('Old Woman of the Cave'), who lived there in the mid-19th century and, despite her apparent destitution, accumulated a hoard of money.[1547]

UAMH(A) is a cave. Some Kintyre caves have the Gaelic generic and some, particularly in the south of the peninsula, where the Gaelic language waned quicker, don't. In the Scots of South Kintyre, cave is 'cove'.

Uamha Ròpa [595 156], to the north of Largiebaan caves, is 'Rope Cave', a name which I'd like to be able to explain but cannot. As a mere guess, it may be connected with an attempt to enter the cave using a rope, but it is a sea-cave and its inner end is probably accessible only by boat. Its later name was **The Scarts' Den**, from the shags which nest there (see SGARBH).

Sròn Uamha [612 058] is 'Cave Point' (but see SRÒN). It is the southernmost point of Kintyre, and a small, tidy Iron Age fort sits on top of it. The cave beneath, as Duncan Colville noted, 'is difficult of access and can only be approached and entered from the north-west'.[1548] Sandy McSporran, a keen climber, offered to investigate the cave for me, and did so on 18/8/2012. He described the route down as 'a scramble' and the cave itself as a 'desolate place', which, by its physical nature, was unlikely to have been inhabited, though I daresay outlaws may have found its isolation appealing in the past. His very approximate estimates of its dimensions were 40 ft. high and 70 ft. deep. Inside, the only sign of life was ferns of the species *Asplenium marinum*.[1549] Small stalactites and stalagmites were the other notable features of the interior. At the very back of the cave there was a water-filled hollow, which he supposed contained sea-water driven in by storms. The entire cave was wet and slimy and not a place to linger in. Having made notes and taken photographs, he climbed back up to the fort and rejoined his companion, Robert Judge.

66. UAMH. Looking out to sea and the north coast of Antrim from the cave on Sròn Uamha, 18/8/2012. Photograph by Sandy McSporran.

Uamh Bealach-a-Chaochain [674 387], south of Muasdale, was an habitable cave and was in use into the 20th century. Ian MacDonald in 2002 told me of two cave-dwellers, one a Townsley and the other a MacCorvie, who 'depended on passing travellers for food as both were unable to walk'. Betsy Townsley, mother of the celebrated Traveller tradition-bearer, Duncan Williamson (1928-2007), was born in that cave.[1550] The Rev Donald MacDonald, in the *Statistical Account* of 1843, remarked on the cave's 'spring of excellent water, without any visible outlet'. See Bealach a' Chaochain under BEALACH for interpretation. **An Uamh Fhliuch**, 'The Wet Cave', north of Muasdale, was used by tramps and vagrants. Farther north still, by the roadside at Beachmenach, is **An Uamh Ruadh** [688 429], 'The Red Cave', with the remains of a dun above it. Charles Reppke recorded **Uamh na Mheirleach**, 'The Thief's

Cave', between Waterfoot and Torrisdale Bay. For **Uamh nan Calman**, 'Cave of the Pigeons', see under CALMAN, and for **Uamh Bhàltair**, 'Walter's Cave', under RUBHA.

UCHD is 'breast', which, transferred to the landscape, gives 'side of a hill'. **Uchd-an-Tùir** [662 280], 'Hillside of the tower', is now a forgotten name. In 1816 John Blair was a weaver at 'Uchcanture being a pendicle of Killarue, Tangy'.[1551] For **Cailleach Uchd an Tùir** see under CAILLEACH. **An t-Uchd**, 'the breast of the hill', was the slope above Skipness village which, in the early 19th century, was occupied by 50 to 60 families, according to Angus Graham.[1552] In C1841 it is down as 'Uchd of Colphin', and in 1851 as simply 'Coalfine', with 30 families there. **Uchd na Cìob**, 'Breast of the Moor Grass', was a field on Rhonadale farm, Carradale, recorded by Charles Reppke in 1942.

UINNSEANN is the Ash (*Fraxinus excelsior*), one of the most valued of native trees. It grows high and well, its wood is splendid for making things and it burns hot and long, even unseasoned. John Smith in 1798 referred to one tree in Campbeltown which measured 'above 12 feet in circumference'.[1553] In 1810, Colonel Matthew MacAlister of Rosshill complained that two Ash trees had been cut on his farm of Killagruer and asked for a warrant to search 12 neighbouring farms, and for the constables to 'apprehend anyone found in possession of the wood'. He later claimed that Finlay McQuilkan in Killegruar had been found with 'two ash sticks and some green ash bark', and asked for him to be fined, and imprisoned until the fine was paid. McQuilkan denied any knowledge of the sticks, which had become 'handles for flails'.[1554]

Lergnahuinsan [733 506] is *Learg na h-Uinnsinn*, 'Slope of the Ash', an old township south of Ballochroy which generated many outlandish-looking spellings in its time: 1502 'Leyrgnahunsyn'; 1545 'Largenhwnschon'; 1627 'Leargnahunscheoun'; 1675 'Lergnahunsheon'; 1683 'Lergynahunsane'; 1736 'Lergnahinshon'. In the census of 1851 there were three occupied houses there, but in 1867 the O.S. described only 'ruins of grazing farm belonging to C. McDonald Morton Esq. of Largie'.[1555] **Allt an Uinnsinn** [913 597], 'Stream of the Ash', runs past Culindrach steading, Skipness. **Mrs Black's Tree** was an Ash that grew at the north end of Camus na Ban-tigheara until 'a fellow sawed it doon for knees for a punt'.[1556] The identity of Mrs Black is unknown but she was from Tarbert. John Weir said she was 'turned a bit mentally' after her man was lost at sea, and that she would walk out there to 'see if his boat was coming home',[1557] but most accounts had her selling illicit whisky to the skiff fishermen from a tidal rock below the tree.[1558]

ULAIDH. Buried treasure, to judge by its recurrence in folklore and place-names, was a preoccupation among our ancestors, akin, I suppose, to modern-day dreams of winning the Lottery. While travelling towards the Empty Quarter with Arab guides in 1946, Wilfred Thesiger observed that 'they are all obsessed by dreams of buried treasure'. Finding their preoccupation tedious, he chided them and was answered: 'It is all very well for you; you have plenty; but for us a few *riyals* may make all the difference between starving and not starving.'[1559]

Dugald Macintyre (father of the author Dugald) had a treasure story set at Innean Dùnain, north of the Mull. A shepherd, John Tait, while looking among rocks for sheep, came across a strange little shelter in which he found a lot of money. He thought his best plan would be to go to the farm and borrow a bag. When asked at the farm what he wanted with a bag, he answered truthfully that he had found money. As soon as the farmer heard this, he began scheming to get the money for himself, and when he came across the skin of a black cow with the head and feet still on it, an idea came to him. He set off after Tait, and when he saw him stop and begin filling the bag, he covered himself with the skin and jumped out, roaring in the deepest of voices: 'Leave that alone – it belongs to me!' Tait turned, and, thinking the fearsome sight was the Devil, let out a wild yell and fled.[1560]

Dreaming of treasure is a common motif in such tales. D. J. Macdonald heard of a man by the name of MacGill who had a dream of treasure, wrapped in a foal's skin, which the fugitive Robert Bruce had buried in Barr Glen on his way across Kintyre from Ugadale. The hiding-place was revealed in the dream, and MacGill directed a shepherd in a neighbouring farm to the spot. The shepherd found it all right, and ran back to the farm in a state of excitement to fetch a spade, but when he returned he couldn't find the place again, and the treasure lies there to this day.[1560] An incomprehensible lapse, but such is the stuff of folk tales!

Macdonald had another story from which it would again appear that treasure must always, even when found, remain elusive. A herd was tending his cattle at 'Glen a canagh', Muasdale, when the bull began to paw the ground and hook out the earth with his horns.

When the herd went to have a look at what was going on, he found that an urn full of coins had been uncovered. He ran to the house to fetch a spade to dig it out, but on returning to the place he couldn't find the treasure.[1562]

Mrs Higginson in Skipness recorded a story containing precise details as to where treasure might be found. If one lay on one's back on top of Cruach Oragaig and could see 'the tops of Larachmore houses and the low farm of Oragaig', one would be lying on top of the treasure. This interests me for a reason other than increasing my personal wealth. I have yet to identify where Làrachmòr is, so from that hill top would it be possible to spot it? But it's a ruin by now, so there will be no roofs!

Here is yet another story of treasure found and then lost by indecision. Lower on Cruach Oragaig, there was a chest-shaped stone called the 'Kist of the rocky hill'. Long ago, an Escart woman was returning from Clachan on a fine summer evening. The sun was shining and as she was crossing at the Kist she saw every tuft of heather covered with gold coins. She was so frightened by the sight that she ran to Oragaig for help and for bags to put the money in. She got some men to go back with her, but when they reached the place the gold had vanished. The men said that if she had had a piece of iron and had stuck it in the spot, the money would have remained.[1563]

At Àirigh Fhuar, north of Skipness, there were supposed to have been 'flat stones ... with figures cut on them'. A Morrison family there was presumed to have 'dug all about them' and uncovered treasure, after which they took a farm in the Largieside. 'They never told what they found or whether they found anything or not, but while they were at Airdh Fhaur they were very poor.' In 'the olden times', Mrs Higginson observed, 'there were no banks near and people used to put their money in iron pots and bury them where they knew they would be safe. These treasures were called in Gaelic Ullidh pronounced oolly'.[1564]

John Campbell, about whom I wrote a chapter in *Kintyre: The Hidden Past*,[1565] had a story about the sacking of Saddell Monastery. Some monks fled into Saddell Glen with the monastery valuables, which they were able to bury in a calf's skin before the raiders overtook and slaughtered them in the **Dead Man's Slap** on **Creag Thormaid** [776 326]. The Cistercian treasure has never, of course, been found.[1566]

Ballochnahuilly [638 206] has been interpreted as *Bealach na h-ulaidhe*, 'The pass of the tomb or treasure', and linked with

Cnocan Sìthein [644 206], a Neolithic burial cairn 'close at hand';[1567] but it hardly seems 'close at hand' to me. *Ulaidh* as 'tomb' is an Irish meaning; indeed Macbain, in his etymological dictionary (p 388), derives *ulaidh* from Early Irish *ulad*, 'stone tomb'. The name, whatever it originally meant, was attached to a farm which stood on the site of the Ugadale Arms Hotel, and some walls remained until the 'cottages' in connection with Machrihanish Dunes Golf Club were built. **Gort na h-Ulaidhe** [744 268], on the northern slope of Glen Lussa, is 'The enclosure of the tomb or treasure', an interpretation evincing the same caution, or perhaps preoccupation with antiquity.[1568] This is indeed a 'tomb' – the largest and most elaborate chambered cairn in Kintyre – but a tradition was recorded in 1866 of a 'large wadge of gold' removed from it or the adjacent cairn.[1569] D. J. Macdonald recorded **Gortean na h-ullaidh**, 'Treasure field', on Ballure farm, and **Cnocan an òir**, 'Gold hillock,' on Kilmaluag farm in the late 19th century.[1570]

ÙRUISG represents an interesting supernatural being, which is often described as a 'brownie'. That, indeed, was the O.S. interpretation,[1571] and the interpretation in *The Place-Names of the Parish of Southend* (p 15) for **Creag an Ùruisg**, 'The Brownie's Rock', of which there are two, not far from each other. One [634 100] is north-west of Keramenach steading, and the other [626 118] north-west of High Glenadale. Dwelly's primary definition, of a 'being supposed to haunt lonely and sequestered places',[1572] is perhaps the neatest summary, but John Gregorson Campbell's account of 'The Urisk', of which the following are the opening paragraphs, is compelling.

> The Urisk was a large lubberly supernatural, of solitary habits and harmless character, that haunted lonely and mountainous places. Some identify him with Brownie, but he differs from the fraternity of tutelary beings in having his dwelling not in the houses or haunts of men but in solitudes and remote localities. There were male and female urisks, and the race was said to be the offspring of unions between mortals and Fairies – that is, of the *leannan sìth*.
>
> The urisk was usually seen in the evening, big and grey (*mòr glas*), sitting on the top of a rock and peering at the intruders on its solitude. The wayfarer whose path led along the mountain-side whose shattered rocks are loosely sprinkled, or along some desert moor, and who hurried for the fast approaching

nightfall, saw the urisk sitting motionless on the top of a rock and gazing at him, or slowly moving out of his way. It spoke to some people, and is even said to have thrashed them, but usually it did not meddle with the passer-by. On the contrary, it at times gave a safe convoy to those who were belated.[1573]

Appendix

West Kintyre Field Names
Rev. D. J. Macdonald

'What is in a name?' Oftentimes more than meets the eye. The solution of the question 'What is a field name?' is now and then hard to find.

Were there any call to offer an apology for devoting less or more attention to this neglected branch of investigation, it might be sufficient to say that the subject is of topographical and philological interest. Nor does this exhaust all that might be said in support of its claims to consideration. Time was when every plot of ground had its distinctive name. Field names were scattered broadcast over the face of the land. Individuality was thus stamped on almost every acre. Local colour flashed from the name of hill and dale. True, the poet sings of 'the dell without a name'. But we protest against the assumption. It does not fit into the state of things which enquiry into the subject brings out. Sober fact and prosaic realism force the conviction upon us that had the poet been less concerned with the muse, and the lover less under the influence of the blind god, the dell had not come down to us nameless in Hogg's popular song.

It is difficult to determine what degree of antiquity belongs to field names. The documentary evidence available in the case of wider areas and more important localities is not at hand, at least not to anything like the same extent. Crop may have succeeded crop of field names. There may have passed over them changes comparable to those that have passed over personal ones in the course of the centuries. But there seems to be evidence to show that they do possess, at least in several instances, the quality of permanence.

The tendencies are, however, towards the gradual disappearance of Gaelic field names. Various causes contribute to this effect. Occasionally a knowledge of the field names of a farm vanishes with the outgoing tenant; particularly when the incoming one hails from a distance, and knows no other than the Saxon tongue. The native population is not bound to the soil as in former days. Large areas, formerly devoted to agricultural purposes, are not infrequently converted into grazing lands or deer forests. Human contact with the soil is not so close and intimate as it was in the past. Population is more migratory. The increased facilities for communication with the greater world beyond the mountains, and the modern economic conditions of life, render it inevitable. Hence the avenues by which local lore of all kinds descended are becoming, one after another, blocked. There is less demand for field nomenclature, and, in consequence, the supply is diminished.

Further, it must be admitted, however greatly it may be deplored, that in many parts of the Highlands, perhaps in all, the language peculiar to those parts is being gradually eliminated, and is undergoing a process of decay. With the language, the field names go out, and much else. Charters ... or Feus, Leases, the Post Office, the School, the Church, all combine to give publicity and permanence to the names of farms, villages, and townships. But field names have few or no guarantees of the same kind for their advertisement or preservation. They are of the most unobtrusive nature. They are born to blush unseen. They live in monastic seclusion. The circle of their acquaintance is of the most limited and of the humblest, confined to the farm tenant and a few ploughmen and herds. Field names are unknown to fame. It is rarely one of them leaps into notoriety, and when it does it is at the expense of cloven skulls or other tragic events. Field names never appear in the newspapers nor in the rent roll, nor in a list of births, marriages, and deaths. No one writes a field name at the top of a sheet of notepaper. No correspondent to the *Times* or to the *Scotsman* gives a field name for his address. Even our best maps ignore them. The Ordnance and the Geological Survey maps do no more than touch the fringe of the subject. The tourist comes and goes without giving them a thought, and so does the commercial traveller, and the insurance and sewing-machine agent. When the aeronaut lands on 'terra firma', no reporter, describing the exciting event, ever dreams of mentioning the name of the field on which the visitant from cloudland has made his descent. The collector for the schemes of the Church, or for the town hospital, may cross many a field on the round of benevolence, but little he or she recks of the name by which the spot over which they travel is known. The motorist has scarce time to realise the names of the counties through which he rushes, probably at illegal speed, on his dusty and perilous career. How much less can he concern himself with the names of the fields that seem to fly past, as he pursues his adventurous way? The marvel is that any field names have at all survived, so general is the neglect with which they have been treated.

Field names are to local, social, and industrial conditions of a bygone time, what fossils are to natural history. They contain vestiges of the past. They indicate changes that have come to pass in the circumstances of the land and its inhabitants. They may be compared to raised sea-beaches which mark the heights at which our coasts were washed by waves that have long since receded from, and ceased to beat on, our shores. They furnish us with verbal testimony that what is now meadow was once on a time marsh, that what is now arable was peat-moss, that what is now cleared was then wooded. We know a waterless 'Lochan Dughail', with a lake-dwelling too, and a treeless 'Beathach Mor'. 'Beinn an tuirc' and 'Lag na beisd' tell us of a time when the boar haunted the hill, and the wild-cat lurked in the bosky hollow. That methods of agriculture were employed which have been, in more recent time, discarded, and crops raised which are no longer cultivated, is borne out by the names 'Cul na feannag' and 'Cùl na lìn'. No one ever plants potatoes in lazy-beds, nowadays, in West Kintyre, or raises a crop of flax. We have 'Creagan na' meann', but no longer a flock of kids. The Ayrshire browses around the rocks on which the frisky creatures used to disport themselves.

But field names have a psychological, as well as other forms of interest. It has been often said that children are unconsciously poetical. So were the authors of field names. By means of them we can trace the play of fancy and imagination. They point to the exercise of powers of observation. We can gather how the eye and the ear were engaged. We can detect how the salient features of a place were singled out, and its appropriate appellation attached to it, and how the resemblances between things were recognised and named.

Field names may likewise be cited to give evidence about popular beliefs touching the supernatural, current in bygone times. We come on 'Leac an fhamhair', and we immediately infer that the existence of 'giants' in those days was accepted. 'Lub an eich chlaimhaich' and 'Loch an eich' point to reminiscences of the water-horse or kelpie.

The meaning of by far the greater number of the field names, included in the following lists, lies on the surface. The signification of a few is difficult to determine. Their form has become changed to an extent that makes them almost, if not altogether, unrecognisable, except to the expert etymologist. What, for example, is to be made of a field which sounds 'an dathan dubh'? Is the original form 'an damh-fhonn dubh' – The black ox-land? And what is 'Acha' da-chonachar' or 'Lamalum'? Some, again, are commonplace, prosaic, utilitarian in the extreme, as 'Cùl na h-ath' and 'Pairc nam ba'; others have the charm of poetic form and melodious sound. It will be admitted, we think, that 'Ruighe a' lìn' and 'Suidh' an eoin' and 'Leum na h-earb' are of this description. One or two are comical, for example 'An deile spàgach' – The splay-footed field.

All the field names in the ... lists lie within the united Parishes of Killean and Kilchenzie – a district of spacious extent, as the writer knows to his cost. Twenty-five farms contributed to supply them. They were taken down from the dictation of Archibald McCorquodale, Auchadaduie (deceased); Archibald Taylor, High Crubesdale (deceased); John Smith, Balergie (deceased); Neil MacPhater, Kilmory (deceased); Angus MacDougall, Beacharra; Mrs Taylor, High Crubesdale; John MacNeill, Glenbarr; Rev. D. Black, Kilmory, Arran (deceased); David Macmillan, Clachaig; David Macdonald, Muasdale; Duncan Darroch, Largie; Duncan MacConnel, Tangy; Alexander MacMillan, Glencardoch; and Rev. Wm. Robertson, M. A., Shapinsay.

From 'West Kintyre Field Names', *Transactions of the Gaelic Society of Inverness*, Vol. XXVII, 1908-11, pp. 31-34.

Abbreviated sources

A1 – Argyll: An Inventory of the Ancient Monuments. Volume 1, Kintyre, H.M.S.O. 1971.

AD – Records of Lord Advocate's Department, Scottish Record Office.

AF – Agriculture and Fisheries, Scottish Record Office.

AH – Argyllshire Herald, weekly newspaper (1854-1918).

AK – Annals of Killean, Rev D. J. Macdonald: see below.

AKK – Antiquities of Killean and Kilchenzie, Rev D. J. Macdonald, published in 1934 with *Annals of Killean*, but each paper separately page-numbered.

AS – Archaeological Sketches in Scotland, District of Kintyre, Captain T. P. White, Edinburgh 1873.

BHSSK – By Hill and Shore in South Kintyre, Angus Martin, Glasgow 2011.

C – Census, 1841-1901.

CA – Commons of Argyll, ed D. C. MacTavish, Lochgilphead 1935.

CC – Campbeltown Courier, weekly newspaper (1873-).

CJ – Campbeltown Journal, newspaper (1851-55).

CO – Argyll & Bute Council archive, Lochgilphead.

CP – Campbeltown Parish.

CPNS – The History of the Celtic Place-Names of Scotland, William J. Watson, 1926.

CSD – The Concise Scots Dictionary, Mairi Robinson, Aberdeen 1985.

GK – The Gaelic of Kintyre, Nils M. Holmer, Dublin 1962.

HK – History of Kintyre, Peter MacIntosh, Campbeltown 1857, but 1861 edition referred to.

HTL – Hearth Tax List, a record of hearths in Kintyre in February 1694. Scottish Record Office, E 69/3.

IGED – Illustrated Gaelic to English Dictionary, Edward Dwelly, Glasgow, 9th edition (1977).

IPN – Irish Place Names, D. & L. Flanagan, Dublin 2002.

JPA – Justices of the Peace in Argyll, Proceedings etc. of the JP Courts 1686-1825, F. Bigwood, 2001.

JWK – 'Jottings from West Kintyre', D. J. Macdonald, *TGSI* 1894-96, Volume 20.

KANHS – Kintyre Antiquarian and Natural History Society, earlier KAS (below).

KAS – Kintyre Antiquarian Society, founded in 1921 and from 1970 known as KANHS (above).

KB – Kintyre Birds: Notes, Quotes and Anecdotes, Angus Martin, Campbeltown 2008.

KCL – Kintyre Country Life, Angus Martin, Edinburgh 1987.

KF – Kintyre Families, Angus Martin, Campbeltown 2010.

KGR – Kilkerran Graveyard Revisited, Angus Martin, Glasgow & Campbeltown 2010.

KI – Kintyre Instructions: The 5th Duke of Argyll's Instructions to his Kintyre Chamberlain, 1785-1805, Eric R. Cregeen & Angus Martin, Glasgow 2011.

KKP – Killean and Kilchenzie Parish.

KL – Kintyre Leases, extracted by Duncan Colville from originals loaned to him by Duke of Argyll (1958), and made publicly available by Mr Rory Colville (1980).

KM – The Kintyre Magazine, Campbeltown, 1977-; issue number then page numbers.

KP – Kilcalmonell Parish.

KSC – Kintyre in the 17th Century, Andrew McKerral, Edinburgh 1948.

KTHP – Kintyre: The Hidden Past, Angus Martin, Edinburgh 1984.

LDA – Copy Depositions of the Witnesses adduced for John MacDonald of Largie against the Duke of Argyll, 31/1/1736, in Inveraray Castle archive, AGN 2727.

LKT – List of Kintyre Tenants, transcribed by A.I.B. Stewart from copy leases in a bound volume in possession of the Duke of Argyll.

MCEJ – MacNeill of Carskey: His Estate Journal, 1703-1743, ed F. Forbes MacKay, Edinburgh 1955.

MSK – Meanders in South Kintyre, James McNeill, Campbeltown 1997.

NK – North Kintyre: see OSNB.

OIPN – 'On Islay Place-Names', *P.S.A.S.* Vol. 16 (1881-2), Capt. F. W. L. Thomas.

OPR – Old Parish Registers.

OS – Ordnance Survey.

OSNB – Ordnance Survey Name-Book. Campbeltown Parish (CP), book no. 78; Kilcalmonell Parish (KP), no. 11 (also contains material from Kilberry Parish); Killean and Kilchenzie Parish (KKP), no. 13; North Kintyre (NK), no. 60 (containing additional material from Kilcalmonell and Saddell and Skipness parishes); Saddell and Skipness Parish (SSP), no. 25; Southend Parish (SP), no. 26; South Kintyre, no. 75 (containing additional material from Campbeltown and Southend parishes); West Loch Tarbert (WLT), no. 59 (contains some material from Kilcalmonell Parish). Consulted on microfilm in the library of the Royal Commission on the Ancient and Historical Monuments of Scotland, Edinburgh.

PEDGL – A Pronouncing and Etymological Dictionary of the Gaelic Language, M. Maclennan, Edinburgh 1925.

PNA – The Place-Names of Arran, Ian A. Fraser, Glasgow 1999.

PNAHP – 'The Place-Names of Argyll: An Historical Perspective', Ian A. Fraser, *TGSI* Vol. LIV, but page numbers cited here refer to reprint in booklet form, Inverness 1988.

PNARG – *The Place-Names of Argyll*, H. Cameron Gillies, London 1906.

PNHIS – *Place Names, Highlands & Islands of Scotland*, Alexander Macbain, Stirling 1922.

PNNI –*Place-Names of Northern Ireland*, Vol. 7, County Antrim II, 1997, Fiachra Mac Gabhann.

PNPC – *The Place-Names of the Parish of Campbeltown*, Duncan Colville (1943) and Angus Martin, Campbeltown 2009 (edition referred to).

PNPGC – *The Place Names of the Parish of Gigha and Cara*, Campbeltown 1945.

PNPNA – 'Place Names and Personal Names in Argyll', Professor Donald MacKinnon, *The Scotsman*, I-XVII, 9/11/1887-18/1/1888.

PNPS – *The Place-Names of the Parish of Southend*, Duncan Colville (1938) and Angus Martin, Campbeltown 2009 (edition referred to).

Sched – Schedules. These are the bound volumes which contain the research records for the above three booklets and are held in the KANHS archive, at present in Argyll and Bute Council archive, Lochgilphead.

PNRGLV– *Place-Names in the Rhinns of Galloway and Luce Valley*, John MacQueen, Stranraer 2002.

RA – *Records of Argyll*, ed. Lord Archibald Campbell, Edinburgh 1885.

RP – Register of Poor, Argyll and Bute Council archive.

SK – South Kintyre: see OSNB.

SOG – 'The Shadow of "Onomastic Graffiti"', D. Rixson, *The Journal of Scottish Names Studies* 4, 2010.

SP – Southend Parish.

SPN – *Scottish Place-Names*, W. F. H. Nicolaisen, London 1976.

SSP – Saddell and Skipness Parish.

TGSI – *Transactions of the Gaelic Society of Inverness*.

TKG – *An Historical and Genealogical Tour of Kilkerran Graveyard*, Angus Martin, Campbeltown 2006.

TRNF – *The Ring-Net Fishermen*, Angus Martin, Edinburgh 1981.

WHT – Work Horse Tax, 1797-98, being a tax of 2s on all work horses. Scottish Record Office, refs. E326 10/1 & 10/7, being identical records except in spellings.

WKFN – 'West Kintyre Field Names', D. J. Macdonald, *TGSI*, Vol. 27, 1908-11.

WLT – West Loch Tarbert area: see OSNB.

Key to years cited in text

1481 = *Origines Parochiales Scotiae*, p 31. Charter by King James III to John of Ila, Lord of the Isles.

1495 = *Ib.*, p 29. Charter by King James IV to Sir Dn. Forestare.

1496 = *Ib.*, p 31. Charter by James IV to Lachlan Makgilleone of Dowarde.

1498 = *Saddell Abbey*, J. Macmaster Campbell, pp. 18 & 20, charter to abbey.

1500 = *Origines Parochiales Scotiae*, p 25. Charters by King James IV to his servitor Adam Rede of Sterquhite.

1502 = Exchequer Rolls.

1507 = *Ib.*

1511 = *Origines Parochiales Scotiae*, p 30. Charter by Arch. Earl of Argyle to his son Archibald.

1545 = *Ib.* Charter by Queen Mary to James Makconnyl of Dunnyveyg and Glennys.

1549 = *Ib.*, p 30. Queen Mary confirmed Grant by deceased Arch. Campbell of Skypinche.

1556 = *Ib.*, p 24. Charter of James, Bishop of Argyll, to James, Duke of Chastellarault, Earl of Arran.

1564 = *Ib.*, p 25. Charter by John, Bishop of the Isles, to Colin, Earl of Argyll, and his Countess.

1576 = *Ib.* Charter by John, Bishop of the Isles, to Colin, Earl of Argyll, and his Countess, and from the Latin charter in the Tangy Mill Thirlage Case Record, House of Lords, 1832.

1584 = *Ib.*, Charter by Patrick, commendator of Whitherne, with the consent of the convent, to Archibald Campbell, Lord of the fief of Argyll.

1596 = Highland Papers, Court Held at Loch Kilkeran.

1605 = *Ib.*, Court Held at Loch Kilkeran.

1620 = *Argyll Sasines*, Vol 1, Herbert Campbell. Sasine No. 110, 113, 10 & 125.

1623 = *Ib.*, Vol 2, Herbert Campbell. Sasine No. 174.

1626 = *Ib.*, Vol 2, Sasine No. 198.

1627 = *Ib.*, Vol 2, Sasine No. 218 & 229.

1631 = *Ib.*, Vol 2, Sasine No. 387.

1634 = *Ib.*, Vol 2, Sasine No. 499 & 504.

1651 = *Ib.*, Vol 1, Sasine No. 341.

1654 = *Ib.*, Vol 2, Sasine No. 821.

1655 - *Ib.*, Vol 2, Sasine No. 883.

1658 = *Ib.*, Vol 1, Sasine No. 372.

1669 = *Ib.*, Vol 2, Sasines No. 1495, 1527 & 1529.

1675 = *Ib.*, Vol 1, Sasine No. 660.

1683 = 'Sheriff Court Tarbert, 1683', I. MacDonald & A.I.B. Stewart, in *KM*

No 26.

1685 = *Commons of Argyll*, ed. Duncan C. MacTavish, Lochgilphead 1935.

1688 Valuation Roll, United Shires of Argyle & Tarbert, 1688. Copied from the original roll (which is partly burnt) in the County Offices, Lochgilphead, 1924, probably by Duncan C. MacTavish.

1692 = *Commons of Argyll*, ed. Duncan C. MacTavish, Lochgilphead 1935.

1736 = Copy Depositions of the Witnesses adduced for John Macdonald of Largie against the Duke of Argyll, 31/1/1736. Inveraray Castle archive.

1738 = 'Decreet settling the Marches – Duke of Argyll against Macdonald of Largie', 22/2/1738.

1751 = Valued Rent Roll.

1827 = Alexander Macalister of Loup and Torrisdale against William Duke of Argyll, Tangy Mill thirlage dispute, heard in the House of Lords.

Sources and Notes

1. *Night Falls on Ardnamurchan: The Twilight of a Crofting Family*, 1984, pp. 185-86.
2. *PNHIS*, p 341.
3. *Collins Encyclopaedia of Scotland*, ed. J. & J. Keay, 1994, p 84.
4. *AH* 30/9/1876.
5. *KI*, p 140.
6. *AH* 23/12/1882.
7. *CC* 29/3/1913.
8. *Ib.*, 17/6 & 24/6/1922.
9. *AH* 10/12/1880.
10. *CC* 13/1/1923, copied from 'Highland Notes' in the *Glasgow Weekly Herald*.
11. *KTHP*, pp. 13-14; *CC* 9/4/1938, 'Scandinavian Expert Studying the Gaelic of Kintyre'; *A Short History of Largieside*, S.W.R.I., 1966, p 32.
12. *CC* obit. 18/2/1951.
13. *PNPS*, p 4.
14. *Ib.*
15. A. Graham, *Skipness*, 1993, pp. 57-58.
16. M. Slater, by e-mail, 25/4/2012.
17. John McCallum, by e-mail, 26/1/2012, & *CC* 28/10/1933.
18. *CC* 8/4/1922, 10/1/1931 & 27/6/1936.
19. *CC* 17/2/1945, & Elizabeth Marrison, by e-mail, 9/6/2012.
20. A. McEachran, letter to D. Colville, 31/10/1936.
21. *PNPS*, p 4.
22. Letter to N. Conley, 9/12/1956, in D. Colville's papers in KANHS archive.
23. Letter to D. Colville, 11/12/1956, *ib.*
24. Letter to N. Conley, 14/12/1956, *ib.*
25. *CC* 25/1/1921.
26. *KTHP*, p 17.
27. *AH* 20/10/1888.
28. *CC* 24/6/1922.
29. C. Reppke, by e-mail, 13/1/2012.
30. Agnes Stewart, by e-mail, 15/1/2012. 'Pursell' was Edward Pursell (1891-1964), headmaster, Gaelic poet, landscape painter and prize-winning horticulturalist. See *TKG*, pp 52-53.
31. *PNPC*, p. 22.
32. Recorded 15/2/1977.
33. *SPN*, p 141.
34. *PNRGLV*, p 74.
35. WKFN, pp. 35-40.
36. KL, p 7.

37. *PNPC*, p 9 & Sched.
38. Alexander Macalister of Loup and Torrisdale against William Duke of Argyll, Tangy Mill thirlage dispute, heard in the House of Lords; Auchalochy tenanted by Alexander Ballantine 'for upwards of 50 years back'; also OPR, KKP, baptisms.
39. KL, pp. 8 & 10, & OSNB, CP, p 43.
40. *PNPC*, p 5.
41. *PNA*, p 98.
42. Kintyre Charters Vol. 1, in D. Colville's place-names collection, KANHS archive.
43. *CC* 9/6/1900.
44. LKT.
45. PNPNA, XVI, 12/1/1888.
46. *PNPC*, p 10.
47. Letter to author, 24/7/2010.
48. *PNPS*, p 6.
49. *PNPC*, p 37.
50. OSNB, KKP, p 31, *CC* 26/1/1918, & WKFN, p 34.
51. PNPNA, XV, 12/1/1888.
52. *PNRGLV*, p 38.
53. *CSD*, p 609.
54. *PNRGLV*, p 38.
55. *SPN*, p 89, distribution map.
56. Murdo MacDonald, letter to author, 10/12/2010.
57. *PNPC*, pp. 25 & 35. For derivation of Meal Kist Glen refer to *KTHP*, p 166.
58. *PNARG*, p 25.
59. *PNPC*, pp. 8 & 9. Arinascavach was also, and erroneously, included in *PNPS*, in Sched of which the data will be found.
60. Letter to author, 31/5/2012.
61. OPR, KKP, & *CC* 16/7/1921.
62. OSNB, KP, p 22.
63. D. Colville notebook, KANHS archive.
64. *A1*, p 200.
65. Transcribed by D. Colville, but the author could not trace it in expected sources.
66. I. A. Fraser, letter to author, 18/8/2012.
67. *EDGL*, p 108.
68. *PNPC*, pp. 17 & 18 & Sched.
69. *RA*, p 377.
70. LDA.
71. *PNNI*, p 36.
72. *EDGL*, p 14.
73. Recorded 22/1/1977.
74. *The Commissary Court of Argyll*, F. Bigwood, 2001, p 385.

75. Register of Poor, SSP, CO6/7/34/5, entry numbers 177, 208, 209 & 223.
76. I. A. Fraser, letter to author, 4/7/2012.
77. *AKK*, p 8.
78. I. MacDonald, 'The Twa Brigs', *KM* No. 18, pp. 10-11, in which legal document is quoted in its entirety; A1, p 206, for architectural data; A. Munro, *The Story of Burns and Highland Mary*, 1896, p 34; *KF*, p 63.
79. *AH* 8/1/1898.
80. *PNPC*, p 7.
81. *KF*, pp. 21-22.
82. *PNPS*, p 7.
83. *RA*, p 377.
84. OSNB, WLT, p 66.
85. OSNB, SSP, p 86, & 'The Mammals of Kintyre', J. A. Gibson & D. Colville, *The Western Naturalist*, 1975, pp. 5-6.
86. *CC* 24/6/1882.
87. *PNARG*, p 23.
88. HTL, p 44.
89. *KF*, pp. 31-32.
90. By e-mail, 4/5/2012.
91. OSNB, CP, p 31.
92. *PNPC*, pp. 8 & 23, & Sched.
93. Personal communication, 3/7/2012.
94. Personal communication, 5/7/2012, & A. Martin, *Herring Fishermen of Kintyre and Ayrshire*, p 49, for checking the hauls by punt.
95. Recorded 23/2/1977.
96. *Ib.*
97. *PNA*, pp. 96 & 149.
98. OSNB, SSP, pp. 71, 70, & 65.
99. *A1*, p 157.
100. *KM* No. 5, p 17.
101. *CJ* 23/9/1852.
102. *KM* No. 55, p 26.
103. OSNB, SSP, p 32.
104. *PNPC*, p 40.
105. *AH* 5/3/1870.
106. WKFN, p 35.
107. G. Márkus, by e-mail, 26/7/2102.
108. LKT.
109. *PNHIS*, p 104.
110. *KM* No. 26, p 11, 'Sheriff Court Tarbert, 1683', & *PNPC*, p 8, & Sched.
111. E. MacDougall from Mrs B. Wilkie, by e-mail, 9/8/2012, & A. Martin, 'George Wyllie and his Kintyre Connections', *KM* No. 72, p 6.
112. *PNARG*, p 188.
113. *KCL*, pp. 27-28 & 37.

114. 19/1/1847, Duncan Colville's papers, KANHS archive.
115. *PNPS*, p 7.
116. *PNPC*, p 31 & Sched.
117. WKFN, p 36.
118. PNAHP, p 27.
119. *PNPC*, p 9.
120. G. Márkus, by e-mail, 26/7/2012.
121. *PNPC*, pp. 9 & 10.
122. *KI*, pp. 26-27.
123. *IPN*, pp. 20-26.
124. *HK*, p 83.
125. OIPN, p 244, quoted from Hector MacLean, Ballygrant.
126. *PNPC*, p 10.
127. *KF*, p 23.
128. *IPN*, p 177.
129. *PNPC*, p 10.
130. WKFN, p 40.
131. *CPNS*, p 182.
132. *The Shieling*, 1990, p 233.
133. *KCL*, p 81.
134. *The Shieling, op. cit.*
135. *KF*, p 58.
136. *Ib.*, p 10.
137. KL, p 25.
138. *MCEJ*, p 69.
139. *KF*, p 61.
140. *PNPS*, pp. 8-9, all information from Balmacvicar to Balimacmurchie, unless otherwise indicated.
141. *KTHP*, pp. 6-8, & *PNPC*, p 54.
142. *KTHP*, pp. 10-11.
143. *PNPC*, p 10 & Sched.
144. J. C. MacLeod, by e-mail, 4/5/2012.
145. *EDGL*, p 28.
146. *IGED*, p 64.
147. By e-mail, 26/7/2012.
148. 'The Light Coloured Slopes', *Scottish Wildlife*, No. 20, p 30.
149. 'Siol Chuinn', 'Beyond Cnoc Moy: A Few Days Wandering on the Moil Hills', *CC* 20/8/1921.
150. *BHSSK*, p 50.
151. *AH* 21/6/1884.
152. *PNPS*, pp. 30 & 18.
153. OSNB, SK, p 22.
154. *PNPC*, p 22 & Sched.
155. By e-mail, 7/4/2012.
156. By e-mail, 23/6/2012.

157. OSNB, KP, p 5.
158. *Tarbert in Picture and Story*, p 108.
159. Recorded 11/6/1976.
160. *KI*, p 16.
161. JWK, pp. 57-58.
162. By e-mail, 29/5/2012.
163. PNAHP, p 21.
164. *Glencreggan*, Vol. I, p 240.
165. OPR, KKP.
166. By e-mail, 26/7/2012.
167. OSNB, KKP, p 63.
168. *AH* 17/7 & 30/10/1869.
169. Macalister genealogical notes in above paragraphs from *CC* 24/12/1921, 'The Late Major Macalister of Glenbarr'.
170. JWK, p 65.
171. *AH* 29/7/1871.
172. *PNPC*, pp. 9 & 11 & Sched.
173. Letter to author, 31/5/2012.
174. *PNPC*, p 11.
175. *EDGL*, p 32, & *IPN*, p 28.
176. JWK, p 55.
177. KL, p 31.
178. OSNB, KKP, p 65.
179. I. A. Fraser, letter to author, 31/5/2012, *IGED*, p 161 & OSNB, KKP, p 40.
180. *Inhabitants of the Argyll Estate, 1779*, ed. E.R. Cregeen, 1963, p 118.
181. *KF*, p 34.
182. *AH* 31/3/1866.
183. *EDGL*, p 192.
184. *CSD*, p 226.
185. *KCL*, p 89.
186. C. Bede, *Glencreggan*, Vol. 2, p 228, & Michael Davis, 'The Victorian Largie Castle', *KM* No.40, pp. 20-23.
187. OSNB, KKP, p 18.
188. *HK*, p 68.
189. *AH* 12/2/1864, 'The Western Townships of Canada'.
190. *CC* 7/4/1917.
191. *PNPC*, p 10 & Sched.
192. *CPNS*, p 480.
193. *PNARG*, p xvi.
194. *IPN*, p 29.
195. *PNPS*, p 10.
196. C. Bede, *Glencreggan*, Vol. I, p 112.
197. *AS*, p 85.
198. P. Berresford Ellis, *Erin's Blood Royal*, 2002, p 196.

199. OSNB, NK, p 74.

200. *The Oxford Names Companion*, 2002, p 940.

201. In 1787, Florence, daughter of Hugh Milloy in 'Geugan', baptised on 11/12/1790: OPR, KKP.

202. *A1*, pp. 6 & 32-33.

203. OSNB, KKP, p 26.

204. *IGED*, p 79.

205. *A1*, p 10.

206. Mrs Finlay Clark, Glenbarr, recorded 3/3/1977.

207. Letter dated 6/4/1937 in papers of Duncan Colville in KANHS archive.

208. Argyll & Bute Council archive, DR4/9/96.

209. OPR, KP.

210. *KTHP*, pp. 3 & 59.

211. A. Martin, *Laggan Days*, 2008, p 10. See also 'Allt Beithe – The Desertion of a Settlement', by John Smith in *Kist* No. 36, pp. 20-24, 'Allt Beithe and Lagan Roaig', by A. K. Smith in *KM* No. 70, pp. 16-19, and 'A Walk to Allt Beithe', by A. Martin, *ib.*, pp. 20-21.

212. *PNPC*, p 5, & WKFN, p 40.

213. *EDGL*, p 37.

214. *CPNS*, p 480.

215. Recorded 23/2/1977.

216. *TRNF*, p 247.

217. OSNB, SP, p 75.

218. *PNPS*, p 10 & Sched.

219. *The Oxford Names Companion*, 2002, p 832, & *EDGL*, p 262.

220. *EDGL*, p 39.

221. JWK, p 65.

222. *PNPS*, p 10 & Sched.

223. WKFN, p 39.

224. Charter, *Origines Parochiales Scotiae*.

225. AD 14/54/216, precognition of Donald MacDonald, pp. 36-38.

226. *AH* 16/1/1875.

227. *PEDGL*, p 42.

228. *IGED*, p 106.

229. *SPN*, p 56.

230. *PNPC*, p 13, & Sched.

231. *Ib.*, p 13, & *PNA*, p 109.

232. *PNPS*, p 11.

233. By e-mail, 26/7/2012.

234. *PNPC*, p 12.

235. *Ib.*, p 13, & Sched.

236. OSNB, NK, p 121.

237. *EDGL*, p 45.

238. KL, p 87.

239. WHT, p 5.
240. OSNB, KKP, p 67.
241. OSNB, KP, p 42.
242. *PNPC*, p 10.
243. *PNPS*, pp. 11 & 26.
244. *Second Statistical Account*, SSP, 1843, p 438.
245. OPR, SSP.
246. Personal communication and photographs, 16/8/2012.
247. OSNB, KP, p 8.
248. A. Martin, *Laggan Days*, p 11.
249. 'Siol Chuinn', *CC* 20/8/1921.
250. *PNPS*, p 11 & Sched.
251. Letter to author, 31/5/2012.
252. OSNB, SSP, p 53.
253. WKFN, pp. 37 & 38.
254. OSNB, NK, pp. 55 & 54.
255. I. Henderson, by e-mail, 23/6/2012, & OSNB, SK, p 26, alternative spelling.
256. *PNARG*, xx.
257. *PNPC*, p 30.
258. OSNB, CP, p 98, *KSC*, p 18.
259. *AH* 20/5/1864.
260. C. Reppke, 1943, in D. Colville's papers.
261. *PNPC*, p 14.
262. *EDGL*, p 62.
263. *PNPS*, p 12.
264. *PNARG*, p 25.
265. *The Ancient Churches and Chapels of Kintyre*, Campbeltown 1934, p 67.
266. *A1*, p 156.
267. *EDGL*, p 63.
268. *KCL*, pp. 33-34.
269. D. J. Macdonald, Notebook 1897, p 25. Translation G. Márkus, by e-mail 5/9/2012.
270. OSNB, KKP, p 59.
271. OSNB, NK, p 48.
272. *EDGL*, p 65.
273. *PNPS*, p 26.
274. *KSC*, p 17.
275. D. Colville, 'A Survey of the Place Names of the Burgh of Campbeltown', *CC* 29/5/1937.
276. OSNB, KKP, p 83.
277. D. J. Macdonald, Notebook 1897, p 21.
278. WKFN, p 35.
279. OSNB, NK, p 70.

280. OSNB, WLT, p 69.

281. *PNPS*, p 12.

282. 'Place Names of the Landward Parish of Campbeltown', MS. 1922, KANHS archive.

283. *PNPC*, p 30 & Sched.

284. KL, pp. 153 & 35.

285. *PNARG*, p 29.

286. *PNPC*, p 30.

287. Adam McNaughton, 'Hamish Henderson in Kintyre', *KM* No. 62, p 3.

288. Agnes Stewart, by e-mail, 16/4/2012.

289. SOG, p 147.

290. WKFN, p 40.

291. *KB*, p 34.

292. *EDGL*, pp. 66, 67 & 97.

293. OSNB, NK, p 41.

294. WKFN, p 40.

295. *TRNF*, p 246.

296. Recorded 5/4/1976.

297. *TRNF*, pp. 104-5.

298. OSNB, NK, p 25.

299. *KCL*, p 65.

300. *PNPS*, p 19 & Sched.

301. *EDGL*, p 70.

302. Largely adapted from A. Martin in *KI*, p 150.

303. *PNPS*, p 23 & Sched.

304. Letter to author, 31/5/2012.

305. *PNPC*, pp. 38, 53 & 56.

306. *IGED*, p 169.

307. *PEDGL*, p 73.

308. PNAHP, p 20.

309. LDA.

310. *IDEG*, p 169.

311. 'Notes on the Standing Stones of Kintyre', *Proceedings of the Society of Antiquities of Scotland*, Vol. LXIV, 1929-30, pp. 302-3.

312. Recorded 23/2/1977.

313. WKFN, p 37, JWK, p 58.

314. *EDGL*, p 73.

315. OSNB, SSP, p 51.

316. *Proceedings of the Society of Antiquities of Scotland*, Vol. LXIV, p 310.

317. 'Sketches of Kintyre', *Transactions of the Gaelic Society of Glasgow*, Vol I, 1887-91, p 61.

318. I. A. Fraser, letter to author 27/6/2012.

319. *Ib.*, 18/4/2012.

320. *A1*, p 64.

321. D. Colville, *Proceedings of the Society of Antiquities of Scotland*, Vol. LXIV, p 306.
322. PNPNA, IV, 25/11/1887.
323. A. Martin, *Fish and Fisherfolk*, p 57.
324. *CC* 27/10/1960.
325. *MSK*, p 22.
326. A. Martin, *Fish and Fisherfolk*, pp. 52 & 53.
327. *PNPS*, p 12, and confirmed in OSNB, SP, p 77: 'A small rock out from the shore of Carskey, called in English, Winged Rock.'
328. *PNPS*, p 12 & Schedules.
329. *TRNF*, p 246.
330. *EDGL*, p 71.
331. *PNA*, p 155.
332. *PNPS*, p 6 & p 12 & Sched.
333. Uppsala 1938, p 174.
334. C. Reppke, list of Carradale place-names, in Duncan Colville's papers, KANHS archive.
335. Letter to Latimer McInnes, 29/4/1943, fn. *Ib.*
336. C. Bede, *Argyll's Highlands*, 1902, pp. 212-13.
337. WKFN, p 40.
338. OSNB, KP, p 65.
339. A. MacPhail, recorded 3/7/1977.
340. J. A. Gibson & D. Colville, *The Western Naturalist*, 1975, p 13.
341. N. S. Robins & D. E. Meek, *The Kingdom of MacBrayne*, 2006, p 157.
342. OSNB, KP, p 15.
343. *PNPC*, p 15.
344. *Book of Blaan*, 1965, p 20.
345. *PNPC*, p 15 & Sched.
346. WKFN, p 37.
347. *EDGL*, p 77.
348. 'The Tinkers', *A Companion to Scottish Culture*, ed. D. Daiches, 1981, p 377.
349. *CPNS*, p 122.
350. *KSC*, p 179.
351. OIPN, p 270.
352. *PNPS*, p 23 & Sched.
353. WHT, p 12.
354. *CC* 13/3/1920.
355. N. S. Newton, *Kintyre*, 1999, p 107, & *PNARG*, p 31.
356. *AH* 20/10/1888.
357. *CC* 3/1/1930.
358. *A1*, p 20.
359. Letter to author, 10/12/1982.
360. *A1*, p 155.
361. *Tarbert Past and Present*, pp. 95 & 133.

362. OSNB, SP, p 71, & *PNPC*, p 28.

363. OSNB, KP, p 17, under Cladh Bhrìde.

364. D. Mitchell, *Tarbert in Picture and Story*, p 111; T. H. Thomson, *The Ancient Churches and Chapels of Kintyre*, p 53; & *A1*, p 120.

365. OSNB, KP, p 23.

366. *A1*, p 120.

367. 1851, Archibald Brown, shepherd there.

368. D. H. Farmer, *The Oxford Dictionary of Saints*, 1987, p 85, & *CPNS*, p 277.

369. *PNPS*, p 23.

370. G. Márkus, by e-mail, 26/7/2012.

371. *KTHP*, p 210.

372. *CPNS*, pp. 188-89.

373. *PNARG*, p 180.

374. *HK*, p 140.

375. *KI*, p 116.

376. *CPNS*, pp. 187 & 279, & *PNPS*, p 23.

377. By e-mail, 26/7/2102.

378. *HK*, pp. 116 & 136.

379. *AS*, pp. 49-50.

380. *CC* 18/6/1921.

381. *AH* 24/3/1866, 'Southend Fifty Years Ago'; see also A. Martin, *TKG*, p 30.

382. *CC* 13/5/1916.

383. *CPNS*, p 303.

384. *PNPC*, p 29.

385. *KI*, pp. 94-96.

386. *PNPS*, p 23.

387. CC 2/8/1924, 'Antiquaries at Southend', letter to the editor.

388. D. H. Farmer, *The Oxford Dictionary of Saints*, p 120.

389. *PNPC*, p 29 & Sched.

390. *CPNS*, p 278.

391. *TKG*, p iv.

392. *A1*, p 160.

393. *Ib.*, pp. 145-46.

394. PNPNA, IX, 13/12/1887.

395. *CPNS*, p 302.

396. P. MacIntosh, *HK*, p 137.

397. *JPA*, p 52.

398. *A1*, p 147.

399. *CC* 12/7/1924.

400. *CPNS*, p 287.

401. This entry from Murdo MacDonald, by letter 28/6/2012.

402. *PNRGLV*, p 39.

403. *A1*, p 138.

404. *PNPC*, p 30, & D. H. Farmer, *The Oxford Dictionary of Saints*, p 3.
405. *A1*, p 139.
406. *AS*, p 129.
407. *AKK*, p 7.
408. *CPNS*, p 292.
409. *KF*, p 60.
410. Recorded 3/7/1977.
411. *AS*, p 186.
412. *A1*, p 102.
413. *Ib.*, p 139.
414. *AS*, p 140.
415. *KI*, p 119.
416. KL, p 133.
417. *AH* 14/3/1874.
418. KL, p 119.
419. *PNPC*, p 30.
420. *CPNS*, p 302.
421. G. Márkus, by e-mail, 23/8/2012.
422. *PNPC*, p 30 & Sched.
423. *AH* 14/3/1874.
424. KL, p 136.
425. *PNPC*, p 15.
426. *Ib.*, p 5.
427. *JPA*, p 46.
428. OSNB, SK, p 5.
429. *PNPC*, p 15.
430. *JPA*, p 134.
431. KL, p 61.
432. *AH* 26/9/1874.
433. *PNPC*, p 15 & Sched.
434. *TRNF*, p 247.
435. *PNPS*, p 13.
436. *EDGL*, p 85.
437. *PNI*, p 194.
438. LDA.
439. *EDGL*, p 85.
440. *Tarbert in Picture and Story*, p 116.
441. *HK*, p 68.
442. *Glencreggan*, Vol. 2, p 246.
443. *KF*, p 67, & Jean C. MacLeod, *KM* 71, pp. 2-7.
444. PNPNA, VIII, 8/12/1887.
445. WHT, p 13.
446. *A1*, p 110.
447. *HK*, p 147, & OSNB, KKP, p 60.
448. *A1*, p 110.

449. OSNB, NK, p 57.
450. *KSC*, p 162.
451. *KF*, p 8.
452. *PNPS*, pp. 6, 8 & 16 & Sched, & C1841.
453. OSNB, KP, p 39.
454. *AS*, p 186.
455. OSNB, SSP, p 16.
456. *EDGL*, p 87.
457. JWK, p 65.
458. J. Hill, 'Geology and Scenery of South Kintyre', *The Campbeltown Book*, p 19.
459. *PNPS*, p 13.
460. *PNARG*, pp. xvi-iii, & 'The Place Names of Kintyre', *CC* 23/6/1900.
461. OSNB, NK, p 20.
462. *PNPS*, p 14.
463. OSNB, SP, p 69.
464. I. A. Fraser, letter to author, 27/6/2012.
465. *AKK*, p 5.
466. *A1*, p 47.
467. *AKK*, p 5.
468. N. Thomson, recorded 15/7/1977.
469. OSNB, KKP, p 46.
470. *PNPS*, pp. 16 & 34.
471. *Ib.*, p 14.
472. OSNB, SP, p 13.
473. *PNPS*, p 16.
474. Letter to author, 31/5/2012.
475. OSNB, SP, p 97.
476. *AH* 19/3/1881.
477. KL, p 73.
478. *PNPS*, p 15 & Sched.
479. *PNARG*, p 25.
480. By e-mail, 26/7/2012.
481. OSNB, SP, p 6.
482. Letter to author, 31/5/2012.
483. *PNPS*, p 15 & Sched.
484. 'Row Coroloch' and 'Rudh-Corralach' are represented on Langlands maps: 'Rueacorilach' in 1793 (one building) and 'R. Corilachs' (two) in 1801, north of Corrylach on modern maps and close to the junction of Collusca and Bordadubh Waters, on the west side. 'Rudh', which presumably served to distinguish one steading from the other, suggests *rubha*, 'promontory'.
485. *PNA*, p 75.
486. *PNPC*, p 37, & *GK*, p 71.
487. *HK*, p 72.

488. CO 6/7/4/20.
489. *AH* 15/4/1871. In an article on Tait, 'A Vagrant of Kintyre', in *CC* 9/2/1912, the writer explains that Tait's pronunciation of 'Pharoah' was 'Fah-ro'.
490. Southend Census records, as stated; *CC* 5/4/1924; & memorial to Neil Campbell, 'farmer Corrylach', in Kilcolmkill.
491. C. Bannatyne, recorded 17/3/1977.
492. OSNB, KP, p 39.
493. *PNHIS*, p 352.
494. *PNARG*, p 14.
495. *CPNS*, p 506.
496. *PNA*, p 121.
497. *PNPC*, p 50.
498. C. Reppke, 1943.
499. OSNB, SSP, p 19.
500. *IGED*, p 267.
501. *TRNF*, p 140.
502. D. MacFarlane, 24/1 & 4/5/1975.
503. *PNPC*, p 18.
504. A. Martin, *KM* No. 35, p 16.
505. *JPA*, p 12.
506. KL, p 67.
507. *JPA*, p 107.
508. A. Martin, *Sixteen Walks in South Kintyre*, p 34.
509. *KTHP*, pp. 152-53.
510. *EDGL*, p 105, & *IGED*, p 268.
511. OSNB, NK, p 35.
512. *PNPC*, p 16.
513. OSNB, NK, p 29.
514. *PNPC*, p 19.
515. SOG, p 150.
516. *PNPC*, p 19.
517. *IPN*, p 65.
518. *PNPC*, p 19.
519. *Ib.* & Sched.
520. *Ib.*, p 8.
521. *CC* 3/6/1922.
522. *AS*, p 130.
523. *RA*, pp. 374-75.
524. *KF*, p 41.
525. D. Colville 'Notes on the Standing Stones of Kintyre', *Proceedings of the Society of Antiquities of Scotland*, Vol. LXIV, 1929-30, p 310, fn. 2.
526. *Kintyre*, 1999, p 107.
527. Letter to author, 18/4/2012.
528. *EDGL*, p 109.

529. *PNPS*, p 15, 'The Craft' (various), & *PNPC*, p 11, 'Barn Craft'.
530. James Hunter, *The Companion to Gaelic Scotland*, ed. D. S. Thomson, 1983, p 206.
531. Quoted in *KI*, p 197. I am indebted to Professor James Hunter for having identified the 'Mr Murdoch' in that report.
532. *AH* 1/8/1885.
533. OSNB, SSP, p 39, & *JPA*, p 60.
534. AD14 21/186.
535. OSNB, NK, p 47.
536. *CJ* 29/1/1852.
537. *EDGL*, p 49.
538. OSNB, NK, p 21.
539. *EDGL*, p 109.
540. By e-mail, 9/8/2012.
541. *KB*, pp. 15-16.
542. *CSD*, p 235.
543. *PNPS*, pp. 22 & 15.
544. OPR, KKP, & *KTHP*, p 35, based on AD14 56/199.
545. MS. in D. Colville's place-names collection, KANHS archive.
546. *KF*, p 38.
547. OSNB, NK, p 91.
548. *KF*, p 44.
549. WKFN, p 40.
550. OSNB, NK, pp. 40 & 43.
551. *Ib.*, p 8.
552. Recorded 14/5/1979.
553. *CC* 26/7/1879.
554. A. Martin, *Fish and Fisherfolk*, p 27.
555. *Ib.*, p 49.
556. *MSK*, p 21.
557. *AKK*, p 7.
558. D. Colville's place-names MSS., KANHS archive.
559. *CC* 20/11/1915.
560. OSNB, SSP, p 69; G. McKinlay, recorded 23/2/1977; *PNPC*, p 39.
561. *Ib.*, SSP, p 7 etc, & *TRNF*, p 246.
562. *Ib.*, SK, p 49.
563. *Ib.*, NK, p 41.
564. *CJ* 29/1/1852.
565. Higginson MS.
566. Recorded 24/1/1975.
567. *AH* 27/7/1872.
568. *A1*, p 69.
569. *AH* 17/7/1869, 21/1/1871 & 20/10/1883.
570. *Ib.* 6/4/1889 & RP CP 1254.
571. *CPNS*, p 144.

572. OSNB, SK, p 45.
573. 'Siol Chuinn', *CC* 20/8/1921.
574. Map in the office of C. & D. Mactaggart, solicitors, Campbeltown, and copy bound with Sched *PNPS*.
575. *IPN*, p 61.
576. *IGED*, p 307.
577. G. Márkus, by e-mail, 26/7/2012.
578. Letter to author, 31/5/2012.
579. Valuation Roll 1936/37.
580. *CC* 20/8/1921.
581. LKT.
582. *KI*, p 57.
583. *PNPS*, p 16 & Sched.
584. *Ib.*, p 16.
585. *Ib.*, p 16, WKFN, p 40, and L. MacInnes, from James McDougall, 1938.
586. WKFN, pp. 35-37.
587. WHT, p 6.
588. SOG, p 140.
589. *A1*, p 79.
590. *PNPS*, p 11.
591. *Ib.*, p 18 & Sched.
592. *PNHIS*, p 350.
593. *KM* No. 66, p 27.
594. OSNB, NK, p 51.
595. OSNB, SSP, p 65.
596. *CSD*, p 674.
597. *PNPC*, pp. 17 & 18.
598. *PNPS*, p 24 & Sched, & OSNB, SP, p 14.
599. OSNB, KP, pp. 13 & 14; note in Duncan Colville's place-names papers in KANHS archive; and Rob Reid, Achnacarnan, confirmation of location of Dippen, by e-mail 27/10/2012.
600. *PNPC*, p 20.
601. KL, p 108.
602. *KCL*, p 143.
603. *EDGL*, p 126.
604. G. Márkus, by e-mail, 26/7/2012.
605. *PNA*, p 104.
606. *TRNF*, p 63.
607. *PNPS*, pp. 38 & 10.
608. *EDGL*, p 132.
609. OSNB, NK, p 15.
610. WKFN, p 40.
611. *EDGL*, p 137.
612. WKFN, p 37.

613. *EDGL*, p 138.

614. *CSD*, p 153.

615. WKFN, pp. 37 & 39.

616. OSNB, NK, p 50.

617. *PNPC*, p 50.

618. *IPN*, p 70.

619. *PNPC*, p 23 & Sched, and KL, p 82.

620. *PNPS*, p 17.

621. *KCL*, pp. 139-40.

622. OSNB, NK, p 15.

623. *CPNS*, p 505.

624. *Argyllshire Herald and Campbeltown Monthly Review*, Nov 1851, quoted in *CC* 18/8/1923.

625. *AH* 29/7/1882.

626. *Ib.*, 9/3/1867.

627. A. Graham, *Skipness*, pp. 119-20.

628. *PNPC*, pp. 21-22 & Sched.

629. *Ib.*, p 22 & Sched.

630. *KF*, pp. 72 & 65, & KL, p 84A.

631. *PNPC*, p 21.

632. *PNRGLV*, p 43.

633. *PNPC*, pp. 21 & 51.

634. WKFN, p 37.

635. *Ib.*, p 38.

636. *IGED*, p 373.

637. *CPNS*, p 237.

638. A. Martin, 'Gordon Bottomley Was Here', *KM* No. 71, pp. 18-19, & A. MacVicar, 'Voices on Dunaverty', a review published in *CC* 13/5/1939.

639. *A1*, pp. 70-71.

640. *Ib.*, p 18.

641. JWK, pp. 56-57.

642. *A1*, p 81.

643. *AKK*, p 3.

644. *Ib.*, pp. 1-2.

645. *A1*, p 82.

646. *AKK*, p 2.

647. OSNB, SSP, p 20.

648. A. Graham, *Skipness*, pp. xvii, 118 & 125, & A. Martin, *KM* No. 43, p 24.

649. *CPNS*, p 24.

650. R. Black, 'The Horse People of Kintyre', *KM* No. 36, p 14.

651. *CPNS*, p 24.

652. *CC* 22/2/1913.

653. E. V. Lucas, *Reading, Writing, and Remembering*, 1932, p 82.

654. *CC* 22/2/1913.

655. *KF*, p 35.
656. *KCL*, pp. 62-63.
657. *CC* 29/11/1919, obit.
658. *KF*, pp. 34-35.
659. R. Black, 'The Horse People of Kintyre', *KM* No. 36, p 14.
660. *AKK*, p 5.
661. *GK*, p 122.
662. Translated by Kenneth D. MacDonald.
663. Personal communication, 2011.
664. Higginson MS.
665. A. MacPhail, recorded 4/3/1977.
666. *AKK*, p 5.
667. WKFN p 37.
668. Letter to D. Colville, 14/3/1954, in his place-names papers in KANHS archive.
669. OSNB, SSP, p 5.
670. Letter to author, 18/8/2012.
671. *LIDAPK*, p 173.
672. *PNPS*, pp. 31 & 18 & Sched.
673. *PNARG*, p 26.
674. By e-mail, 29/5/2012.
675. *AS*, p 111.
676. *CPNS*, p 272.
677. *AS*, p 111.
678. Notes on Rev. D. J. Macdonald's Paper on Place-names of Landward Parish of Campbeltown by Sheriff J. Macmaster Campbell, 1922, in D. Colville's place-names papers in KANHS archive.
679. *PNPC*, p 34.
680. *Evening News*, Edinburgh, 7/2/2012.
681. M. Peacock, by e-mail, 16/2/2012.
682. Recorded 22/1/1977.
683. Letter to D. Colville, 14/3/1954, in his place-names papers in KANHS archive.
684. J. Weir, 1975; H. MacFarlane, 1975; G. Campbell Hay, 1980.
685. *Tarbert in Picture and Story*, p 109.
686. OSNB, WLT, p 81.
687. *CC* 5/5/1923, letter to the editor.
688. Recorded 23/2/1977.
689. G. McKinlay, recorded 22/1/1977.
690. *PNPC*, p 23.
691. OSNB, SK, p 9.
692. *A1*, p 179, & *PNPC*, p 23.
693. *HK*, p 65.
694. KL, p 178.
695. *CPNS*, p 184.

696. G. Márkus, by e-mail, 26/7/2012.

697. *PNRGLV*, p 82.

698. *CPNS*, p 490.

699. OSNB, SK, p 48.

700. *AH* 20/5/1871.

701. *CC* 20/8/1921.

702. *GK*, p 4.

703. OSNB, SK, p 48.

704. *CPNS*, p 489.

705. A. McKerral, *Two Old Kintyre Lawsuits*, Campbeltown 1941, p 9.

706. *PNPS*, p 18 & Sched.

707. *LIDAPK*, p 42.

708. KL, pp. 21 & 91.

709. *CC* 1/4/1916.

710. *CPNS*, p 489.

711. J. A. Gibson & D. Colville, *The Western Naturalist*, 1975, p 17.

712. WKFN, p 40, last reference only.

713. JWK, p 65.

714. WHT, p 5.

715. *JPA*, p 115.

716. *AH* 15/8/1868.

717. WKFN, p 40.

718. *Ib.*, pp. 39 & 40.

719. *MSK*, p 38.

720. *EDGL*, p 162.

721. WKFN, p 38.

722. *AKK*, p 7.

723. *PNPC*, pp. 7 & 24 & Sched.

724. *PNPS*, p 32.

725. *BHSSK*, p 6.

726. *AH* 10/4/1863.

727. *PNPS*, p 19 & Sched, including Appendix.

728. *PNARG*, p 26.

729. *PNA*, p 126.

730. *Book of Blaan*, p 72.

731. *KB*, p 48.

732. *PNPC*, p 16.

733. *EDGL*, p 168, & *IGED*, p 422.

734. *PNPC*, p 44.

735. OSNB, SSP, p 44.

736. WKFN, p 37.

737. *IGED*, p 422.

738. *PNA*, pp. 21 & 22.

739. LKT.

740. *MCEJ*, pp. 110 & 114.

741. *A1*, p 197.
742. Letter to author, 30/5/2012.
743. WKFN, p 37.
744. *CSD*, p 197.
745. *EDGL*, p 171.
746. OSNB, KKP, p 29.
747. *Collected Poems and Songs of George Campbell Hay*, ed. Michel Byrne, 2000, Vol. 1, p 323.
748. *PNPC*, p 24.
749. Recorded 22/1/1977.
750. *TRNF*, p 105.
751. Letter to author, 28/12/1979.
752. A. Martin, *Laggan Days*, 2008, p 4.
753. *Second Statistical Account*, KKP, 1843, p 385.
754. *A1*, pp. 83-84.
755. WKFN, p 37.
756. *CPNS*, p 437.
757. *Scottish Place-Name Papers*, 2002, p 185.
758. *Gaelic Words and Expressions from South Uist and Eriskay*, Rev Fr. Allan McDonald, ed. J. L. Campbell, 1991, p 126.
759. D. Macintyre, *Wild Life of the Highlands*, 1936, pp. 255-56.
760. *KB*, p 51.
761. *CC* 17/12/1921, 'Argyll Vermin Club'.
762. *BHSSK*, p 260.
763. *CC* 23/6/1900 & *PNARG*, p 31.
764. Letter to author, 18/4/2012.
765. All OPR, KP.
766. *PNPC*, p 24.
767. OSNB, SK, p 62.
768. *PNPS*, p 34 & Sched.
769. *General View of the Agriculture of the County of Argyll*, p 17, fn.
770. *CC* 14/10/1916.
771. *Ib.*, 18/9/1915; N. Mitchison, 'The Haldanes in Kintyre', *KM* No. 5, pp. 25-27; *HK*, pp. 66-67.
772. *PNPC*, p 44.
773. WKFN, p 40.
774. OPR, SSP.
775. *AH* 28/12/1872.
776. Recorded 24/1/1975.
777. From 'Kintyre', *Wind on Loch Fyne*, 1948, p 2.
778. *PNPS*, p 23 & Sched.
779. *EDGL*, p 188.
780. *PNPGC*, p 17.
781. *AH* 19/12/1868 & 11/3/1871.
782. *PNPS*, p 22 & Sched, & KL, p 116.

783. HTL, p 43.
784. LKT.
785. *MCEJ*, p 60.
786. *LIDAPK*, p 15.
787. *KCL*, p 184.
788. KL, p 116.
789. WKFN, p 36.
790. *PNA*, p 94.
791. LDA.
792. *PNPS*, p 19.
793. *PNPC*, p 25.
794. JWK, p 65.
795. J. Hill, 'Geology and Scenery of South Kintyre', *The Campbeltown Book*, pp. 12 & 17.
796. *KB*, p 4.
797. *PNPC*, p 32.
798. *PNPS*, pp. 26 & 36.
799. A. Graham, *Skipness*, p 99.
800. OSNB, SSP, p 5.
801. *JPA*, p 63.
802. OPR, KKP.
803. *AH* 25/9/1857.
804. *Ib.*, 13/10/1888.
805. *IGED*, 481.
806. *PNPC*, p 25 & Sched.
807. *KTHP*, p 213, & *KF*, p 59.
808. *PNHIS*, p 48.
809. *EDGL*, p 195, & *IGED*, p 497.
810. OSNB, KP, p 9.
811. I. A. Fraser, letter to author, 18/4/2012.
812. *PNPC*, p 25.
813. LKT.
814. Duke of Argyll's Instructions to Factor in Kintyre, October 1758; transcripts in papers of E. R. Cregeen, & *JPA*, p 44.
815. A. McEachran, letter to D. Colville, 7/5/1937, in his place-names papers in KANHS archive, & *PNPS*, p 8.
816. LKT.
817. *IPN*, p 91.
818. *PNARG*, p xix.
819. OSNB, KKP, p 37.
820. I. MacDonald, 2011.
821. *CC* 3/4/1920.
822. *AH* 18/11/1871.
823. *PNPC*, pp. 22 & 32.
824. *Ib.*, p 6.

825. *IGED*, p 502.
826. *AH* 25/7/1874, notice of let, when described as capable of carrying 1500 sheep and 'a few cattle'.
827. *BHSSK*, p 233.
828. Mrs K. McNaughton, 31/12/1990 & 8/1/1995.
829. *PNPS*, p 20 & Sched.
830. LKT.
831. *CC* 23/8/1919.
832. *PNPC*, p 26.
833. *KTHP*, p 221, & *BHSSK*, p 91.
834. KL, p 107.
835. *AH* 21/12/1855.
836. LKT.
837. *CC* 9/4/1938, 'Scandinavian Expert Studying the Gaelic of Kintyre'.
838. *GK*, p 107.
839. Dr Jacob King, by e-mail, 25/7/2012.
840. *PNPC*, pp. 26 & 54.
841. OSNB, NK, p 24.
842. A. Martin, *Laggan Days*, pp. 5-6.
843. Information from Jim and Muriel Adam, Edinburgh, 8/2/2012
844. *AH* 13/1/1912.
845. Information from J. and M. Adam, 8/2/2012.
846. *PNPS*, p 7.
847. *CC* 21/5/1921, obit. L. MacNeill; 20/8/1921; 25/11/1922; KL, p 19; *KF*, p 53.
848. Jean C. MacLeod, *KM* No. 70, pp. 2-5.
849. HTL, p 49.
850. WHT, p 6.
851. OSNB, KKP, p 52.
852. Recorded 22/1/1977.
853. PNPNA, XII, 24/12/1887, & D. Mitchell, *Tarbert in Picture and Story*, p 20.
854. KL, pp. 31 & 83.
855. WKFN, p 39.
856. *KCL*, p 120.
857. OSNB, SK, p 50.
858. *KF*, p 70.
859. *HK*, pp. 112-13.
860. *PNPS*, p 21 & Sched. Fiachra Mac Gabhann (by e-mail 2/12/2012) explains that 'The Gobbins' is almost certainly from *An Gobán*, 'the little point (of land)' with an English plural -s, possibly (but not necessarily) reflecting a plural use in Irish (*Na Gobáin*).
861. *CC* 30/9/1933.
862. *EDGL*, p 200.
863. *KTHP*, pp. 156-58.

864. *JPA*, p 10.
865. *KM* No. 50, p 34.
866. J. A. Gibson & D. Colville, *The Western Naturalist*, 1975, p 19.
867. *KTHP*, p 158.
868. *GK*, p 135, translated by Kenneth D. MacDonald.
869. C. Bede, *Argyll's Highlands*, p 49.
870. OSNB, SP, p 40.
871. *KTHP*, p 171.
872. WKFN, pp. 37 & 33.
873. *IGED*, pp. 516 & 518.
874. *IPN*, p 93.
875. *EDGL*, pp. 189 & 202.
876. *PNARG*, p 16.
877. *PNPC*, p 26 & Sched.
878. *KI*, p 138.
879. WKFN, p 36.
880. *CC* 16/8/1924.
881. *BHSSK*, p 145.
882. WKFN, pp. 35-40.
883. G. Márkus, by e-mail, 26/7/2012.
884. Letter to author, 18/4/2012.
885. *KSC*, p 162.
886. OSNB, NK, p 75.
887. *JPA*, p 104.
888. *PNA*, p 82.
889. *PEDGL*, p 191.
890. *IGED*, p 525.
891. *IPN*, p 97.
892. A. Martin, *Laggan Days*, p 10.
893. *Paper Archipelagos*, 2011, p 16.
894. *Ib.*
895. Iain McAlister, personal communication, 16/8/2012.
896. Recorded 18/3/1976; see also *TRNF*, 101-2.
897. G. C. Hay, 14/5/1979.
898. *KM* No. 45, p 11.
899. HTL, p 45.
900. WHT, p 11.
901. *PNPS*, p 21.
902. A. Martin, *Memories of the Inans, Largybaan and Craigaig, 1980-85*, 2007, p 14.
903. *RA*, p 221.
904. *Ib.*, pp. 367-68.
905. OSNB, SK, p 20.
906. *IGED*, p 531.
907. OSNB, NK, p 22.

908. *AS*, p 49.

909. *PNPC*, p 11.

910. *CJ* 6/11/1851, 'Rambles in Kintyre'.

911. *EDGL*, p 213.

912. *CA*, p 53.

913. *PNA*, pp. 130-31.

914. Donall Mac Giolla Easbuig, quoted in *PNNI*, below.

915. *PNNI*, pp. 317-18.

916. *PNPC*, p 27.

917. *PNPS*, p 22, quoted in Appendix for Innean Beithe.

918. *PNNI*, p 318.

919. Dr D. W. Stewart, by e-mail, 20/1/2012.

920. *IGED*, p 40.

921. *Ib.*, p 39.

922. J. de Vere Lode, *Colonsay and Oronsay*, cited in letter, dated 2/5/1935, to D. Colville from 'J. R. C.', in D. C.'s loose papers, KANHS archive.

923. OSNB, SK, p 23.

924. WKFN, p 38.

925. Donald Armour, via his daughter Ina Semple, e-mail, 25/1/2012.

926. *PNPC*, pp. 8 & 53 & Sched.

927. A. Martin, *Sixteen Walks in South Kintyre*, 1994, p 38.

928. HTL, p 47.

929. *KCL*, p 72.

930. *LIDAPK*, p 40.

931. *PNPC*, p 27 & Sched.

932. A. Stewart, by e-mail, 9/1/2012.

933. OSNB, SK, p 27.

934. *CC* 12/9/1885, 'Account of Burial Places in Kintyre'.

935. *Exchequer Rolls* Vol. XII, Kintyre Rentals, p 325 *et seq.*; *KSC*, p 11, but McKerral excludes 'Innynkew Callache' from the list, naming only the other five; & *KF*, pp. 55-56.

936. LKT. Philip Watson, in his *Rathlin Nature & Folklore* (pp. 160-61), mentions a similarly-named place on Rathlin, Ínéan nabh Fear Liath, which translates as the 'Innean of the Nine Grey Men'. Nine men were said to have drowned in a shipwreck there, and the same number of grey-haired men were supposed to have been seen later walking up to the cliff-top. Watson looked at 12 coastal features named innean on Rathlin; a few are cove-shaped, but many are 'steep and quite narrow'.

937. *PNPS*, p 22.

938. *GK*, p 42.

939. Letter, 1/1/1940.

940. W. J. Watson, *Scottish Place-Names Papers*, 2002, p 76.

941. Letter to author, 31/5/2012.

942. KL, p 111.

943. *CC* 22/11/1924.

944. *KF*, p 29, & A. McEachran, KAS No. 347.

945. *PNPS*, p 15, & *KB*, p 16.

946. *Birds of Argyll*, 2007, p 132.

947. *A1*, p 66.

948. In D. Colville's papers, KANHS archive.

949. E. Lafferty, 19/5/2005.

950. *AH* 18/12/1875 & 30/1/1869.

951. *PNPC*, p 18.

952. Higginson MS.

953. *KB*, p 19.

954. *CC* 15/1/1876.

955. By e-mail, 26/7 & 23/8/2012.

956. KL, pp. 144, 146 & 148.

957. *CC* 19/12/1921.

958. *BHSSK*, p 211.

959. Letter, 13/2/1980.

960. H. MacFarlane, recorded 22/1/1977.

961. H. MacFarlane, 1975, and W. McDougall, 1980.

962. A. Graham, *Skipness*, p 120.

963. OIPN, p 253.

964. *Connemara: Listening to the Wind*, 2007 edition, pp. 93-94.

965. *PNPS*, pp. 39-40.

966. *KF*, p 73.

967. Letter to author, 18/4/2012.

968. *PNPS*, p 24.

969. *PNPC*, pp. 27 & 32.

970. *Ib.*, p 32.

971. *CC* 18/1/1913, obit Margaret Fullarton Beith, who was born at Lagnagarach c. 1815.

972. *PNPC*, p 32, & Sched.

973. I. A. Fraser, letter to author, 23/7/2012.

974. JWK, p 65.

975. SOG, p 150.

976. OSNB, KP, p 5.

977. *IGED*, p 610.

978. *Tarbert in Picture and Story*, pp. 11-12.

979. OPR, KKP.

980. *KM* No. 26, p 6.

981. *CC* 18/9/1915, 'Beyond the Allotted Span'.

982. OSNB, SSP, p 103.

983. *Ib.*, CP, p 33.

984. G. McSporran, 29/2/2012.

985. *CC* 7/8/1937.

986. *Ib.*, 30/9/1933, 'The Goings', & 26/10/1929. *AH* 27/7/1878 refers to

a projected channel swim by Frederick Cavill.

987. G. McSporran, 29/2/2012.
988. A. Graham, 8/3/2012.
989. *PNPC*, pp. 32 & 25.
990. *Ib.*, p 32, & Marco Sonzogni, 'All Black Joyce', *Times Literary Supplement*, 19/10/2012.
991. KL, p 149.
992. OPR, KKP.
993. KL, p 149.
994. Alexander Macalister of Loup and Torrisdale against William Duke of Argyll, Tangy Mill thirlage dispute, heard in House of Lords.
995. *AH* 25/6/1870.
996. *CC* 16/4/1927.
997. Argyll & Bute Council archive, DR 4/9/5.
998. *AH* 21/10/1876.
999. OSNB, NK, p 5.
1000. *Ib.*, p 22, & *PNPS*, p 25.
1001. WKFN, p 35.
1002. *EDGL*, p 225.
1003. *PNARG*, p 16.
1004. *PNHIS*, p 356.
1005. *IPN*, p 107.
1006. OSNB, NK, p 6.
1007. *PNPS*, p 25.
1008. OSNB, NK, p 24.
1009. WKFN, p 39.
1010. *CPNS*, p 200.
1011. *CC* 18/9/1915, 'Beyond the Alloted Span'.
1012. *AKK*, p 7.
1013. *GK*, p 70.
1014. *PNA*, p 87.
1015. *KF*, pp. 33-34.
1016. *AH* 26/9/1874.
1017. *CC* 24/9/1921, obit.
1018. *A1*, pp. 160-1.
1019. *GK*, p 159.
1020. I. MacDonald, *KM* No. 4, p 24.
1021. *PNPC*, pp. 16, 32 & 5.
1022. *PNPS*, p 26.
1023. WKFN, p 36.
1024. *CC* 31/12/1921.
1025. *PNARG*, p 21.
1026. *PNHIS*, p 352.
1027. *PNARG*, p 207.
1028. *PNHIS*, p 264, *PNPS*, p 24, & LKT.

1029. Argyll & Bute Council archive, DR 4/9/91.

1030. A. McEachran, letter to D. Colville, 7/5/1937, KANHS archive.

1031. *PNPS*, p 25.

1032. PNPNA, XVI, 12/1/1888.

1033. WKFN, p 37.

1034. *HK*, pp. 83-84.

1035. Higginson MS.

1036. *MCEJ*, pp. 82-83.

1037. *KCL*, pp. 125-27, & *KI*, pp. 121-24.

1038. Recorded 15/11/1980.

1039. Letter to author, 15/3/2012.

1040. Recorded 15/2/1977.

1041. WKFN, p 37.

1042. *PNPS*, pp. 13 & 14.

1043. OSNB, WLT, p 66.

1044. *CC* 7/6/1919.

1045. *BHSSK*, p 245.

1046. I. A. Fraser, letter to author, 21/12/2011.

1047. KL, p 152.

1048. *PNPC*, p 33 & Sched. 'Glecknahavil' was still marked on the O.S. 1-inch map of Kintyre, 1925 edition.

1049. Miss Isabella McCorkindale, personal communication, 3/7/2012.

1050. Mrs S. Buchanan Ross, personal communication, 3/7/2012.

1051. *KI*, p 130.

1052. *HK*, p 57.

1053. *KI*, p 181.

1054. D. S. Galbraith v McCrummen & others, quoted by D. Colville in *PNPC* Sched under 'Lochsanish'.

1055. *HK*, p 57.

1056. *Ib.*, pp. 14-15.

1057. *PNPC*, p 12.

1058. Map annotated by D. Colville, in KANHS archive, No. 225/228.

1059. *HK*, p 15.

1060. OSNB, CP, p 37.

1061. *HK*, pp. 57-58.

1062. D. Mitchell, *Tarbert in Picture and Story*, p 112, & *A1*, p 94.

1063. *Tarbert in Picture and Story*, p 94.

1064. D. Colville, annotation on KANHS map.

1065. *Tarbert in Picture and Story*, pp. 112-14.

1066. I. MacDonald, 'Three Lochs in North Kintyre', *KM* No. 33, p 24.

1067. *CC* 23/6/1900.

1068. OPR, KP, baptism.

1069. OSNB, NK, p 45.

1070. *Ib.*, KP, p 35.

1071. *PNARG*, pp. 31 & 203.

1072. *PNHIS*, p 354.
1073. I. MacDonald, 2011.
1074. OSNB, NK, p 72.
1075. Iain McAlister, 13/8/2012, from his father Jim McAlister.
1076. *AH* 10/3/1866.
1077. Murdo MacDonald, letter to author, 30/7/2012.
1078. *PNPC*, p 33.
1079. *Ib.*
1080. Letter to author, 2/3/1978.
1081. J. McCullasky, AF 37/22.
1082. WKFN, p 36.
1083. *PNPC*, p 25 & Sched.
1084. G. Márkus, by e-mail, 26/7/2012.
1085. *IGED*, p 598.
1086. C. Bede, *Glencreggan*, Vol. 2, p 228.
1087. *KCL*, p 113.
1088. *AH* 3/8/1867.
1089. WKFN p 38.
1090. OSNB, SSP, p 31.
1091. *PNPS*, p 26 & Sched.
1092. LKT.
1093. *A1*, p 80.
1094. *EDGL*, p 233.
1095. *IGED*, p 599.
1096. *IPN*, pp. 116-17.
1097. *PNHIS*, p 351.
1098. Dublin 1869-1913, vol ii, p 430.
1099. *PNNI*, p 158.
1100. *KI*, pp. 86 & 89.
1101. *PNPC*, p 34 & Sched.
1102. *PNRGLV*, p 38.
1103. *PNNI*, p 158.
1104. *EDGL*, p 233.
1105. *BHSSK*, pp. 248-49.
1106. *AKK*, p 14.
1107. *TKG*, p 28.
1108. *EDGL*, p 234.
1109. *KCL*, pp. 36, 52, & 162.
1110. *CJ* 11/11/1852.
1111. Recorded 22/1/1977.
1112. *KSC*, p 9.
1113. I. MacDonald, *KM* No. 33, p 24.
1114. OSNB, KKP, p 78.
1115. Recorded 22/1/1977.
1116. A. Martin, 'Fishing Boat Names of the Scottish West Coast', *Fishing*

Boats No. 18, pp. 20-21.

1117. *IGED*, pp. 609 & 610.

1118. *IPN*, p 117.

1119. OPR, KKP Baptismal Register, & Co 6/7/4/20

1120. *PNA*, p 136.

1121. *HK*, pp. 59 & 60.

1122. *PNARG*, p 17.

1123. *Collected Poems and Songs of George Campbell Hay*, ed. Michel Byrne, 2000, Vol. 1, p 261.

1124. *CPNS*, pp. 506-7.

1125. *PNPC*, p 34 & Sched.

1126. *MSK*, p 25.

1127. *PNPC*, p 34.

1128. *AH* 12/8/1911.

1129. Quoted in *CC* 13/12/1924, J. Macmaster Campbell, 'The Island and House of Sanda'. See also R. A. MacDonald, *The Kingdom of the Isles*, p 90.

1130. *AH* 4/5/1867.

1131. *KCL*, p 176.

1132. *CC* 24/1/1877.

1133. *PNPS*, p 26.

1134. *Ib.*

1135. *KI*, pp. 89-90.

1136. *PNPS*, pp. 9 (Ballyshear) & 26 (Macharioch), & Sched thereof. There are contradictory genealogical accounts of the MacDonalds of Ballyshear in local sources, but I have preferred the information of Rev D. J. Macdonald, *CC* 19/7/1924, letter to editor.

1137. *CC* 5/7/1924, 'Kintyre Antiquarian Society Outing at Southend'.

1138. *Ib.*, 19/7/1924, letter to the editor.

1139. *Ib*, 2/8/1924, letter to the editor.

1140. Jehanne Wake, *Princess Louise: Queen Victoria's Unconventional Daughter*, 1988, pp. 158-59.

1141. *IGED*, p 621.

1142. *PNPC*, p 20.

1143. J. A. Gibson & D. Colville, *The Western Naturalist*, 1975, p 9.

1144. KL, p 78.

1145. OSNB, CP, p 87.

1146. *PNA*, p 160.

1147. OSNB, SSP, pp. 32 & 85, & OSNB, NK, p 97.

1148. *Ib.*, SP, p 33.

1149. G. C. Hay, 15/11/1980.

1150. Stefan Bukzacki, *Fauna Britannica*, 2002, p 404.

1151. J. A. Gibson & D. Colville, *The Western Naturalist*, p 9.

1152. S. Bukzacki, *op. cit.*, p 403.

1153. *Connemara: Listening to the Wind*, Penguin Books 2007 edition, p

80.
1154. *PNPC*, p 36 & Sched.
1155. WHT, p 7.
1156. *TKG*, p 2.
1157. *CPNS*, p 506.
1158. OSNB, SK, p 21.
1159. *HK*, p 47.
1160. *IGED*, p 629.
1161. *EDGL*, p 242.
1162. *KI*, p 104.
1163. *AH* 11/7/1868.
1164. *MSK*, p 18.
1165. *CC* 8/2/1936.
1166. *AS*, p 130.
1167. PNAHP, p 33.
1168. *AS*, p 178.
1169. WKFN, p 36.
1170. KL, pp. 82 & 158.
1171. *MCEJ*, pp. 78 & 88, & *PNPS*, p 27, & Sched.
1172. *PNPC*, p 35.
1173. WHT, p 13.
1174. *PNPC*, pp. 35 & 36.
1175. *EDGL*, p 253.
1176. KL pp. 156 A & C.
1177. *AH* 9/3/1867, 'Southend 50 Years Ago'.
1178. OSNB, SP, p 15.
1179. *CC* 20/8/1921.
1180. OSNB, KKP, p 15.
1181. Ian MacDonald, letter to author, 2011.
1182. LDA.
1183. I. A. Fraser, letter to author, 18/4/2012.
1184. AD14 40/24.
1185. I. A. Fraser, letter to author, 18/4/2012.
1186. *EDGL*, p 254.
1187. *PNA*, p 160.
1188. WKFN, pp. 39 & 40.
1189. *CC* 16/6/1900.
1190. *PNPC*, p 43.
1191. *Ib.*, p 18.
1192. *Tarbert in Picture and Story*, p 4.
1193. *PNPC*, p 20.
1194. JWK, p 65.
1195. *CC* 23/6/1900, 'The Place Names of Kintyre'.
1196. LKT.
1197. *PNPC*, p 16.

1198. *PNPS*, p 27 & Sched.

1199. *EDGL*, p 255.

1200. *KCL*, pp. 123-24.

1201. OPR, KP.

1202. *PNPS*, p 17.

1203. *PNARG*, p 23.

1204. *PNPS*, p 29 & Sched.

1205. *PNNI*, pp. 248 & 323.

1206. WKFN, p 39.

1207. *BHSSK*, pp. 267-70.

1208. *Ib.*, pp. 268-269.

1209. *AH* 6/5/1865.

1210. *Ib.*, 27/5/1865.

1211. *KF*, p 36.

1212. *CC* 15/7/1911.

1213. *HK*, p 61.

1214. *PNPC*, p 8 & Sched.

1215. *LIDAPK*, p 69.

1216. WHT, p 11.

1217. *CJ* 1/9/1852, 'Southend', quoted in *KI*, p 16.

1218. Higginson MS.

1219. *PNA*, p 90.

1220. OPR, KKP.

1221. I. McAlister, personal communication, 23/1/2012.

1222. Dr M. Burgess, by e-mail, 28/7/2012.

1223. By e-mail, 7/8/2012.

1224. I. McAlister, by e-mail, 13/8/2012.

1225. *PNARG*, p xx.

1226. *IGED*, p 703.

1227. LDA.

1228. *IGED*, p 708.

1229. A. McDonald, *Gaelic Words and Expressions from South Uist and Eriskay*, 1991, p 191.

1230. W. Weyndling, *Ferry Tales of Argyll and the Isles*, 1996, pp. 96-98.

1231. *BHSSK*, p 103.

1232. *PNPC*, p 37.

1233. *BHSSK*, p 101.

1234. *PNPC*, pp. 37 & 55; *PNPS*, p 28; & *BHSSK*, p 101.

1235. By e-mail, 26/7/2012.

1236. *PEDGL*, p 254.

1237. *PNPC*, p 37.

1238. *KF*, p 14.

1239. Alexander Macalister of Loup and Torrisdale against William Duke of Argyll, Tangy Mill thirlage dispute, heard in House of Lords.

1240. WKFN, pp. 35-39.

1241. *KF*, p 40.
1242. *EDGL*, p 274.
1243. *KSC*, p 180.
1244. OSNB, CP, p 30.
1245. *PNARG*, p 30.
1246. *PNPC*, p 38 & Sched.
1247. OSNB, SP, p 70.
1248. *BHSSK*, p 84.
1249. *PNARG*, p 211.
1250. *PNPS*, p 28 & Sched; *PNPC*, p 38, & Sched for 'Pingina'.
1251. 1894, Vol. 2, p 217.
1252. *IGED*, p 727.
1253. *AH* 26/5/1883.
1254. *CC* 17/1/1933
1255. *AH* 3/10/1874.
1256. A. Stewart, by e-mail, 15/1 & 16/1/2012.
1257. OSNB, SP, p 10.
1258. *PNPS*, p 29.
1259. H. MacFarlane, 1977 & W. McDougall, 1979.
1260. A. Graham, *Skipness*, p 99.
1261. *PNPC*, p 38 & Sched.
1262. 1938, p. 201.
1263. *KTHP*, p 178.
1264. *KM* No. 54, p 19, & *PNPC*, pp. 42 & 28.
1265. KL, p 115.
1266. *JPA*, p 55.
1267. A. Stewart, by e-mail, 17/1 & 18/1/2012..
1268. AD14 21/186, p 41.
1269. OPR, SSP.
1270. A settlement, Port a' Chnoc, existed at Skipness in the 19th century, its name derived from nearby Cnoc Mór, 'Big Hill'.
1271. *TRNF*, p 249.
1272. RP, SSP, CO 6/7/34/5.
1273. OSNB, SSP, p 70.
1274. *PNPC*, p 39.
1275. A. Martin, 'The Mull of Kintyre Hand-line Fishery', *Northern Studies*, Vol. 20, 1983, p 62.
1276. OSNB, SP, p 76.
1277. A. Martin, *Fish and Fisherfolk*, pp. 59-61.
1278. *PNPS*, p 39.
1279. OSNB, SP, p 80.
1280. *JPA*, p 59.
1281. *PNPS*, p 29.
1282. OSNB, SP, p 77.
1283. *PNPS*, p 8.

1284. Letter to author, 15/7/2012.

1285. *CC* 4/11/1916 & *TRNF*, p 247.

1286. *EDGL*, p 283.

1287. OSNB, CP, p 6.

1288. N. Mitchison, 'The Haldanes in Kintyre', *KM* No. 5, pp. 25-27.

1289. LKT.

1290. *PNPS*, pp. 29-30.

1291. SOG, p 148.

1292. *AH* 30/3/1867, 'Southend Fifty Years Ago'.

1293. *JPA*, p 85

1294. *PNPC*, p 39.

1295. KL, p 168B.

1296. *JPA*, p 134.

1297. OSNB, SSP, p 89.

1298. *EDGL*, p 288.

1299. *Ib.*, p 752.

1300. *IGED*, p 756.

1301. *IPN*, p 136.

1302. PNPNA, XVI, 12/1/1888.

1303. *PNARG*, p xxi.

1304. By e-mail, 20/2/2012.

1305. *PNPC*, pp. 31 & 45.

1306. *EDGL*, p 243.

1307. *PNPC*, p 35.

1308. *KF*, p 76.

1309. *PNA*, p 142.

1310. H. MacFarlane, recorded 22/1/1977.

1311. Recorded 15/11/1980.

1312. Letter to author, 21/11/1979.

1313. *PNARG*, pp. xx-xxi.

1314. *PNNI*, p 145.

1315. *CC* 13/11/1915 & 27/11/1920.

1316. N. Thomson, recorded 15/7/1977.

1317. OSNB, NK, p 70, & OSNB SSP, p 49, latter two.

1318. *PNPS*, p 31.

1319. I. A. Fraser, letter to author, 31/5/2012.

1320. OSNB, KKP, p 5.

1321. JWK, p 65.

1322. *PNARG*, p 32.

1323. WHT, p 5.

1324. OSNB, KKP, p 9.

1325. Recorded 23/2/1977.

1326. *PNPC*, p 39.

1327. *Ib.*, p 40.

1328. *EDGL*, p 297.

1329. WKFN, pp. 35-40.
1330. *PNPS*, pp. 30 & 37.
1331. OSNB, SK, p 64, & *PNPS*, p 20.
1332. *AH* 27/4/1867.
1333. *KCL*, p 37.
1334. OSNB, CP, p 78.
1335. *PNPC*, p 17 & Sched.
1336. WKFN p 37.
1337. PNPNA, IX, 13/12/1887.
1338. *KTHP*, p. 103.
1339. *A1*, p 61.
1340. *Ib.*, pp. 116 & 164.
1341. *KTHP*, p 214.
1342. *AS*, p 130.
1343. *A Sense of Place*, ed. G. Cruikshank, 1988, p 4.
1344. *CC* 17/8/1961, Dugald Semple, 'Archbishop Found Peace Here', & *KF*, p 34.
1345. *PNPC*, p 39.
1346. *EDGL*, p 299.
1347. *IGED*, p 782.
1348. A. Martin, *Fish and Fisherfolk*, pp. 52-55.
1349. Recorded 6/8/1977, but see also *KCL*, p 169.
1350. *PNPC*, p 40.
1351. *Ib.*
1352. *IGED*, p 786.
1353. *PNPS*, p 31, *BHSSK*, pp. 72-73, & *CC* 26/7/1913.
1354. OSNB, NK, p 12.
1355. *Collected Poems and Songs of George Campbell Hay*, ed. Michel Byrne, 2000, Vol. 2, p 93.
1356. *CC* 16/4/1938.
1357. N. Mitchison, *Essays and Journalism, Vol. 2, Carradale,* ed. M. Burgess, 2009, pp. 140, 185-87, & 210.
1358. *PNPS*, p 37.
1359. *Tarbert in Picture and Story*, p 116, & *A1*, p 153.
1360. *EDGL*, p 306.
1361. *PNPS*, p 12.
1362. *PNPC*, p 15.
1363. *AH* 18/2/1871.
1364. *JPA*, p 39.
1365. *PNA*, p 93.
1366. *IPN*, pp. 141-42.
1367. Hugh Fife, *Warriors and Guardians*, 1994, p 90.
1368. OSNB, NK, p 44.
1369. *EDGL*, p 118.
1370. *CC* 23/6/1900.

1371. OSNB, SSP, p 83.
1372. G. McKinlay, recorded 23/2/1977.
1373. Moira Burgess, 'Naomi Writing Carradale', *KM* No. 61, pp. 3 & 4.
1374. *CSD*, p 584.
1375. *KB*, pp. 13-14.
1376. S. Bukzacki, *Fauna Britannica*, 2002, pp. 210-12.
1377. *PNPC*, p 40.
1378. Letter, 2/2/2012.
1379. *PEDGL*, p 290.
1380. JWK, p 59.
1381. N. Thomson, recorded 15/7/1977.
1382. *MSK*, p 18.
1383. *TKG*, pp. 1-2.
1384. *KTHP*, p 146, & J. McMillan, recorded 7/8/1977.
1385. OSNB, SSP, p 69.
1386. I. Henderson, by e-mail, 23/6/2012.
1387. G. C. Hay, 15/11/1980.
1388. *KSC*, p 13.
1389. *PNPC*, p 41.
1390. OSNB, CP, p 125.
1391. *PNPC*, p 41 & Sched; letter in D.C.'s papers, KANHS archive.
1392. Letter to author, 22/6/2012.
1393. *PNPC*, p 41.
1394. OSNB, SK, p 13.
1395. *TRNF*, p 252, & *PNPC*, p 21.
1396. *PNPS*, p 34.
1397. *Mactalla*, spring 1955, pp. 16-17, courtesy of Mr Murdo MacDonald.
1398. J. A. Gibson & D. Colville, *The Western Naturalist*, 1975, p 9.
1399. Quoted in Dugald Macintyre, *Highland Gamekeeper*, pp. 22-24.
1400. *GK*, p 133, translated by Dr D. W. Stewart, by e-mail, 13/2/2012.
1401. *CC* 21/1/1922. 'Roin' is given as a place-name in the last line, but 'Goin' seems more likely.
1402. J. A. Gibson & D. Colville, *op. cit.*, pp. 9-10.
1403. D. McCallum, recorded 31/3/1977 & 12/6/1977.
1404. Higginson MS.
1405. Recorded 15/7/1977.
1406. *IGED*, p 846.
1407. JWK, p 60.
1408. *AKK*, p 6.
1409. Recorded 7/3/1977.
1410. *AKK*, p 6, & JWK, p 61.
1411. *AKK*, pp. 5 & 6.
1412. *PNPC*, p 16 & Sched; *A1*, p 44.
1413. *PNPS*, p 31.
1414. M. Burgess, by e-mail, 24/2/2012.

1415. OPR, SSP, baptismal registers, the preceding four.

1416. *CC* 16/6/1900.

1417. *PNARG*, p 31.

1418. I. A. Fraser, letter to author, 18/4/2012.

1419. Glasgow 2008, pp. 183-98.

1420. OSNB, SK, p 20.

1421. *BHSSK*, pp. 233-34.

1422. By e-mail, 24/2/2012.

1423. *KCL*, p 157

1424. *PNPS*, p 32.

1425. *IGED*, p 852.

1426. *HK*, pp. 47 & 61.

1427. *Glencreggan*, Vol. 1, p 214.

1428. OSNB, SK, p 31.

1429. *PNPC*, p 42.

1430. *IGED*, p 852.

1431. PNPNA, IV, 25/11/1887.

1432. OSNB, SSP, p 4.

1433. *Ib.*, SK, p 26.

1434. *BHSSK*, p 256.

1435. Letter to the author, 21/12/2011.

1436. WKFN, pp. 36 & 39

1437. C. Reppke, 1943.

1438. *PNPC*, p 42.

1439. *PNPS*, pp. 32 & 34.

1440. Recorded 14/5/1979.

1441. *PNA*, p 162.

1442. OSNB, SP, p 24, e.g.

1443. Recorded 23/2/1977.

1444. *PNPC*, p 42.

1445. *PNPS*, p 32 & Sched; KL, pp. 55 & 176; *LIDAPK*, pp. 33-34; & *KI*, p 170.

1446. *IGED*, pp. 891-92.

1447. *CPNS*, p 428.

1448. *IPN*, p 143.

1449. *PNPC*, p 43.

1450. *HK*, p 98.

1451. OSNB, CP, p 51.

1452. *PNPC*, p 43 & Sched.

1453. *CC* 12/6/1920.

1454. David Mayo, by e-mail, 27/6/2012.

1455. *The Commissary Court of Argyll*, F. Bigwood, 2001, p 182.

1456. OSNB, NK, p 33.

1457. *PNPS*, p 33.

1458. *BHSSK*, pp. 266-67.

1459. WKFN, p 35.

1460. OSNB, NK, p 7.

1461. *HK*, p 22.

1462. *Glencreggan*, 1861, Vol. 1, p 42.

1463. 'Sketches of Kintyre', *Transactions of the Gaelic Society of Glasgow*
     Vol. I, 1887-91, p 63.

1464. OSNB, NK, p 32.

1465. W. Clark, 'Tides in the Waters of the Moyle', *KM* No. 43, p 9.

1466. *CPNS*, p 94.

1467. *TRNF*, p 104, & A. Martin, *Herring Fishermen of Kintyre and
     Ayrshire*, p 137.

1468. *PNPC*, pp. 31 & 42.

1469. *PNPC*, p 42, & *KTHP*, pp. 126 & 195.

1470. A. Martin, *Memories of the Inneans, Largybaan and Craigaig:
     1980-85*, 2007, p 22.

1471. *AKK*, p 3.

1472. *PNPC*, p 58.

1473. Recorded 3/7/1997.

1474. *AKK*, p 3.

1475. *Glencreggan*, Vol. 2, p 241.

1476. *Skipness*, p 21.

1477. OIPN, p 271, quoted by Capt. F. W. L. Thomas.

1478. *BHSSK*, pp. 74 & 76.

1479. *EDGL* pp. 361 & 390.

1480. *CPNS*, pp. 505-6.

1481. OSNB, NK, p 23.

1482. *Ib.*, WLT, p 79.

1483. JWK, p 65.

1484. *KF*, pp. 34-35.

1485. *KI*, p 102.

1486. *AH* 14/5/1870.

1487. *KF*, p 9.

1488. *PNARG*, p 31.

1489. Letter to author, 18/4/2012.

1490. *PNPC*, p 59.

1491. *CC* 12/5/1900.

1492. OSNB, SK, p 52.

1493. *HK*, p 21.

1494. D. Stevenson, *Alasdair MacColla and the Highland Problem in the
     17th century*, 1980, p 67.

1495. 'Tides in the Waters of the Moyle', *KM* No. 43, p 11.

1496. OSNB, KKP, p 77.

1497. *BHSSK*, p 141.

1498. OSNB, SP, p 43.

1499. *PNPC*, p 44.

1500. *PNPS*, p 33.
1501. *CC* 3/6/1922.
1502. *PNPC*, pp. 25 & 30 & Sched, & *CC* 20/8/1921.
1503. *CPNS*, p 92.
1504. *AS*, p 7.
1505. *HK*, p 61.
1506. *PNPC*, p 44 & Sched.
1507. *A1*, p 208.
1508. *PNPC*, p 37.
1509. *PNPS*, p 33 & Sched.
1510. D. J. Macdonald, MS. notebook of 1897, p 27.
1511. *KF*, p 50.
1512. *CC* 20/8/1921.
1513. *BHSSK*, p 193.
1514. D. Colville, 'A Survey of the Place Names of the Burgh of Campbeltown', *CC* 29/5/1937.
1515. *Ib.*, 1/5/1937.
1516. *AKK*, p 8, & MS. notebook 1897, p 16.
1517. Recorded 15/11/1980.
1518. *Collected Poems and Songs of George Campbell Hay*, ed. M. Byrne, 2000, Vol I, p 393, & Vol. II, p 240.
1519. *GK*, p 21.
1520. LKT.
1521. *PNPC*, p 44, & *KI*, p 142.
1522. *PNPC*, p 23.
1523. AD14 21/170, p 47.
1524. *PEDGL*, p 347.
1525. *IGED*, p 964.
1526. PNPNA, X, 21/12/1887.
1527. Stefan Bukzacki, *Fauna Britannica*, pp. 443-44.
1528. J. A. Gibson & D. Colville, *The Western Naturalist*, 1975, p 16, & *The Herald*, 8/9/2012, p 13.
1529. *GK*, p 135, translated by Dr D. W. Stewart, by e-mail, 13/2/2012.
1530. *CC* 6/5/1944.
1531. *BHSSK*, p 59.
1532. J. A. Gibson & D. Colville, *The Western Naturalist*, 1975, p 16.
1533. *CPNS*, p 145.
1534. *PNPS*, pp. 19 & 34.
1535. OSNB, SSP, p 60, & OSNB NK, p 98.
1536. *AH* 25/8/1883 & PNPNA, XVI, 12/1/1888.
1537. *PNPC*, p 45.
1538. *CC* 2/8/1924, letter to the editor, 'Antiquaries at Southend'.
1539. *PNPC*, p 7.
1540. WKFN, p 35.
1541. *IPN*, p 156.

1542. *PNPC*, p 43 & Sched.

1543. Pointed out by G. Márkus, by e-mail, 26/7/2012.

1544. *PNPC*, p 37 & Sched.

1545. *IDEG*, p 986.

1546. *HK*, p 81.

1547. *KTHP*, pp. 123-24.

1548. *PNPS*, pp. 34 & 32.

1549. Identified by Hartwig Schutz, 19/10/2012, by e-mail.

1550. *KF*, p 58.

1551. AD14 16/62, p 1.

1552. *Skipness*, pp. 52-53.

1553. *General View of the Agriculture of Argyll*, p 162.

1554. *JPA*, pp. 101 & 102.

1555. OSNB, NK, p 33.

1556. D. MacFarlane, recorded 24/1/1975.

1557. J. Weir, recorded 25/11/1975.

1558. *TRNF*, p 41.

1559. *Arabian Sands*, 1976 Penguin Books edition, p 96.

1560. *RA*, pp. 219-20.

1561. D. J. Macdonald, MS. notebook 1897.

1562. *Ib.*

1563. Higginson MS.

1564. *Ib.*

1565. 'John Campbell: Tradition-Bearer', pp. 72-81.

1566. Recorded 10/11/1980.

1567. *PNPC*, p 10.

1568. *Ib.* p 26.

1569. OSNB, SK, p 15.

1570. WKFN, p 38.

1571. In OSNB, SP, p. 33, & OSNB, SK, p 29, *ùruisg* is equated also with 'diviner'.

1572. *IGED*, p 1001.

1573. *The Gaelic Otherworlds*, ed. Ronald Black, 2008 edition, p 105.

Index of Kintyre Place-Names

This index generally does not contain place-names which are not explained or self-explanatory. Nor does it contain early or, except in rare cases, variant spellings; if a place-name has an anglicised form, generally that form only is indexed. Such names as 'Kintyre' and 'Campbeltown' which occur frequently but which have no substance attached to them are not fully indexed. Such constructions as 'A' Chruach' have been indexed according to the generic, as 'Chruach, A'. Finally, 'f' = field-name.

General Index

This is not a comprehensive index. Many passing references, particularly to named individuals, have not been incorporated.